Light on Tantra in Kashmir Shaivism

Abhinavagupta's Tantrāloka

Chapter Five

Revealed by His Holiness,

Swami Lakshmanjoo

WITH ORIGINAL AUDIO

Viresh Hughes, Editor

Lakshmanjoo Academy

Published by Lakshmanjoo Academy

First printing 2025

Printed in the United States of America

For information, address:
Lakshmanjoo Academy
www.lakshmanjooacademy.org

ISBN 978-1-947241-19-0 (hardcover)
ISBN 978-1-947241-18-3 (paperback)
ISBN 978-1-947241-20-6 (ebook)

This sacred text is dedicated to Swami Lakshmanjoo,
our beloved teacher and spiritual father
who has given us everything.
Glory be to Thee!

Table of Contents

Guide to Pronunciation	vi
Foreword	vii
Introduction	xi
Acknowledgements	xiii
Swami Lakshmanjoo	xvii

Tantrāloka
Fifth Chapter (Āhnika) – Āṇavopāya

Verse		Page
20-42	Buddhi Dhyānam - Intellectual Meditation	27
43-53	Prāṇa Tattva Samuccāra - Recitation of Breath	56
54-61	Daṇḍa Prayoga - Six States of Mantra Śakti	73
62-74	Cidātmatā Uccāra - Rise of God Consciousness	92
75-99	Paratattva Antaḥpraveśa - Entry in God Consciousness	130
100-111	Patha Lakṣaṇam - Recognizing the Path	165
112-127	The Threefold Liṅgas	185
128-130	Karaṇa Upāsana - Meditation on the Senses	205
131	Varṇatattvam - Meditation on Word	219

Appendix

1. Piṇḍanātha Mantra	268
2. Prāṇa Tattva Samuccāra from *Tantrāloka* 5.43-53	270
Bibliography	273
Index	275
Instructions to download audio	287

Topics according to Tantrāloka One index

In this first chapter on *āṇavopāya*, seven subjects will be discussed:

a) *Buddhi dhyānaṁ*, concentration with awareness, meditation with awareness, that is *buddhi dhyānam*. This is intellectual meditation, it is not a process of meditation, not routine-like. One process of meditation is intellectual meditation, when you meditate intellectually. When you meditate just like routine-like, it is not so fruitful. When you put subjective awareness in that, that is *buddhi dhyāna* (not with *mantra*).

b) *Prāṇa tattva samuccāra* is with *mantras*. *Prāṇatattva*, what is the essence of breath? The essence of breath is the center.

c) *Cidātmatā uccāra*, how the rise of God consciousness takes place.

d) *Paratattvāntaḥ praveśa*, how to get entry in the supreme state, the supreme essence.

e) *Patha lakṣaṇam*, the realistic characteristics of the spiritual path.

f) *Karaṇam*, what is the sevenfold *karaṇa upāsana*. *Karaṇaṁ* is pertaining to the organs, meditation pertaining to the organs. And it is *abhyāsam bodha*, this is intellectual meditation. It is not meditation just like a routine way. *Karaṇa upāsana* is the sevenfold ways, and you will get all these explained in many places in the *Tantrāloka*, not only at one place, because Abhinavagupta's theory is that the most subtle thing should not be discussed in one place. It should be discussed here and there so that the *sādhaka* (aspirant) won't find it easily unless he puts the force of awareness, then he will find it in the *Tantrāloka*, otherwise not. If you are so keen to know it, then you will find, you will search in the *Tantrāloka*.

g) *Varṇa tattvam*, what is the Word, the supreme Word.

Guide to Pronunciation

The following English words exemplify the pronunciation of selected Sanskrit vowels and consonants. The Romanized Sanskrit vowel or consonant is first listed and then an English word is given to aid you in its proper pronunciation.

a	as	a in ***A***merica.
ā	as	a in f***a***ther.
i	as	i in f***i***ll, l***i***ly.
ī	as	i in pol***i***ce.
u	as	u in f***u***ll.
ū	as	u in r***u***de.
ṛ	as	ri in mer***ri***ly.
ṛī	as	ri in ma***ri***ne.
e	as	e in pr***e***y.
ai	as	ai in ***ai***sle.
o	as	o in st***o***ne.
au	as	ou in h***ou***se.
ś	as	s in ***s***ure.
ṣ	as	sh in ***sh***un, bu***sh***.
s	as	s in ***s***aint, ***s***un.

Foreword

Let us briefly review the history of the Kashmir Series, which today comprises more than eighty-seven volumes, published from 1911–1925, by the Research Department of Jammu and Kashmir State. This project was initially sponsored by His Highness, Mahārāja Pratap Singh (1830-1885), and was continued by his nephew, Mahārāja Hari Singh Bahadur from 1926–1947. Fluent in both Sanskrit and the Persian language, Mahārāja Ranbir Singh had a great love for philosophy, and organized pundits and scribes to translate and transliterate various religious texts.

This work was continued during the ruling of Ranbir Singh's son and successor, Mahārāja Pratap Singh (1848-1925), who, like his father, exhibited great respect for all spiritual endeavors. Pratap Singh built numerous temples, refurbished those which stood dilapidated, and showed deep affection for saints and scholars of all traditions. On a small stretch of land adjacent to his palace, he organized the construction of a *kutiya* (cottage) where he accommodated a renown saint of the Kula System of Kashmir Shaivism, Swami Mana Kāk. The Mahārāja often paid his respects to the mysterious saint, and on the Swami's passing from this world, that same respect was transferred to the saint's chief disciple, Swami Rām. It so happened that Swami Rām was the family priest of one Kashmiri Pandit, Narayan Das Raina, who happened to be the father of Swami Lakshmanjoo.

Pundit Narayan Das was very industrious, and apart from being one of the first Kashmiri Pandits to learn the English language, he also organized the construction of the first houseboats for accommodating travelers to Kashmir. He had a close relationship with the Mahārāja, and was often called upon to render his services in numerous of ways.

History records that this was a time of a spiritual renaissance in Kashmir, but it is little known that it was Swami Rām who requested the Mahārāja to gather all of the important manuscripts of Shaiva Philosophy that had been scattered here and there during the 500 years of Mogul Rule (1320–1850). Naturally, the Mahārāja acceded to the Swami's request, and thus was initiated the Kashmir Series of Text and Studies (KSTS).

In 1906, Narayan Das and his wife, Arnimal, approached Swami Rām with the humble request that he bless them with a son. Swami

Rām handed Arnimal five almonds and said, "Take these, and not only will you have a son, but he will be a great saint in the tradition of Kashmir's Trika Shaivism. Ten months later, on the 9th of May, 1907, Swami Lakshmanjoo was born.

As Swamiji grew from childhood to adolescence, he exhibited clear signs of one who was destined for the spiritual path. Needless to say, by the time Swamiji was eighteen (1925), and ready to begin his formal study of the ancient teachings of Trika Shaivism, almost all of the major texts were available through the KSTS. Had this not been the case, it would have been an immense task to single-handedly collect all of the important Shaiva manuscripts for one's personal study. The Mahāraja's research program also procured a number of competent scholars, one of which Swamiji chose for his formal tuition in Sanskrit and Shaiva philosophy.

From the age of sixteen to eighteen, Swamiji studied Utpaladeva's *Śivastotrāvalī* and Abhinavagupta's *Bhagavad Gītā Saṁgraha* with his spiritual master, Swami Mahatab Kāk. At age nineteen, he was directed by his master to undertake a formal study of Sanskrit grammar along with an in-depth study of the important texts of Trika Shaivism. This he did with his *vidyā* teacher, Pandit Maheśvara Razdan. It was during this seven year period that Swamiji developed a profound respect for the teachings of Abhinavagupta. Later in life he would write, "Lord Shree-Kantha-Nath Shiva Himself appeared in Kashmir in the form of Abhinavagupta to enlighten all people. Madhurāja also asserts that Abhinavagupta was, in fact, the incarnation of Bhairava-Nath Shiva. In conclusion I would say that Abhinavagupta was the pride of Kashmir. He is even now the pride of Kashmir, as his works and teachings continue to deeply influence discerning people."

Abhinavagupta's *Tantrāloka* has been revered as the jewel of the Kashmir Series of Texts, and it is Swami Lakshmanjoo's oral commentary on chapter five of that work that we offer here. In his translation of this chapter, which forms volume IV of the Lakshmanjoo Academy *Tantrāloka* series, Swamiji used the Kashmir Series of Text and Studies, Number XXX, vol III (1921).

Swami Ram and Swami Lakshmanjoo with Swamiji's Parents

Introduction

In chapter two of the *Tantrāloka*, Abhinavagupta delineated the means (*upāya*) of *anupāya* (lit., no means) for the immediate recognition (*pratyabhijñā*) of God consciousness, and in chapters three and four, he detailed *śāmbhavopāya* (the means of Śiva) and *śāktopāya* (the means of Śiva's energy) for the realization of Universal God consciousness. From the fifth chapter onwards, Abhinavagupta directs our attention to the various practices associated with the so-called lowest *upāya*, *āṇavopāya*, the means pertaining to the individual (*aṇu*). Swamiji reminds us, however, "You should not think when you adopt the means of *āṇavopāya* you are adopting the inferior means. It is not inferior means, it is actually the real means, the real way."

While *śāmbhavopāya* and *śāktopāya* function within the internal realm of consciousness (in the spheres of will and knowledge respectively), *āṇavopaya*, also known as *kriyopāya* (the means pertaining to action), engages the external, active facets of consciousness in the field of the intellect (*buddhi*), breath (*prāṇa*), and the body (*deha*). In this fifth chapter, Abhinavagupta describes the highest practices within *āṇavopāya*, which are not far-removed from the preceding two supreme means of *śāmbhavopāya* and *śāktopāya*. Abhinavagupta's aim in this chapter is to elucidate how the loftiest practices of *śāmbhavopāya* and *śāktopāya* are to be integrated into the ostensibly inferior practices of *āṇavopāya*. Indeed, the descent of supreme awareness into the differentiated realm of action is the culmination of the advanced practices of *śāmbhavopāya* and *śāktopāya*. For most practitioners, however, *āṇavopāya* is the starting point of one's spiritual journey. Swamiji tells us:

"There must be awareness in your brain to hold that subjective consciousness. Once you have held this subjective consciousness, nothing else is to be done. You will then move to *śāktopāya*, and then to *śāmbhāvopāya*, and then to *anupāya*, and then reside in your own nature. It is why all my disciples undergo an extended period of practicing *abhyāsa* (meditation). *Hatāsh na hona chahiye* (Hindi: don't be discouraged). This is a journey, a long journey, but once it is held, it is held in a flash. It is not held successively–never! It will never come in your experience successively. When it is experienced, it is experienced in a flash or not at all. Just dive in, you are there."

The mastery of the less-advanced practices of *āṇavopāya* is indispensable in bolstering one's capacity not only to engage in the elevated practices of *śaktopāya* and *śāmbhavopāya*, but also in maintaining the highest state of undifferentiated awareness amidst the flux of the differentiated world of action (*vyutthāna*).

Let us dive in and read and listen to the revelatory words of Abhinavagupta through the voice of our beloved guide, Swami Lakshmanjoo.

Acknowledgments

First of all, I would like to thank our associate editors: John Hughes, George Barselaar, and Denise Hughes. They took the raw unedited audio transcript and transformed it into a polished document ready for publication. Being closely attuned to Swamiji's vision, they were able to lightly edit the manuscript without tarnishing the flow of the narrative. Recognizing that these revelations were meant to aid the student in gaining a deeper understanding of the philosophy and practices of Kashmir Shaivism, comprehensive footnotes and an appendix have been added. Lastly, I would like to thank Michael Van Winkle, our audio engineer who enhanced the original audio, George Barselaar for transcribing the audio, Claudia Dose, our creative director who was responsible for the creation of the overall design of this book, Nuno Ribeiro for formatting and typesetting the text, and Shanna Hughes for coordinating this project.

Swami Lakshmanjoo

Swami Lakshmanjoo

Swami Lakshmanjoo was born in Srinagar, Kashmir, on May 9, 1907. He was the most recent and the greatest of the long line of saints and masters of the Kashmir Shaiva tradition. From a young age, Swami Lakshmanjoo spent his life studying and practicing the teachings of this unique and sacred tradition. Having a complete intellectual and spiritual understanding of the philosophy and practice of Kashmir Shaivism, he was a true master in every respect.

Endowed with a photographic memory, learning was always easy for Swamiji. In addition to possessing a complete knowledge of Kashmir Shaivism, he had a vast knowledge of the traditional religious and philosophical schools and texts of India. Swamiji would freely draw upon other texts to clarify, expand, and substantiate his lectures. He could recall an entire text by simply remembering the first few words of a verse.

In time, his reputation as a learned philosopher and spiritual adept spread. Spiritual leaders and scholars journeyed from all over the world to receive his blessings and to ask questions about various aspects of Kashmir Shaiva philosophy. He gained renown as a humble devotee of Lord Shiva and as an accomplished master (*siddha*) of the non-dual tradition of Kashmir Shaivism.

Throughout his life, Swamiji taught his disciples and devotees the ways of devotion and awareness. He shunned fame and all forms of recognition. He knew Kashmir Shaivism was the most precious jewel and that, by God's grace, those who desired supreme knowledge would be attracted to its teachings. He taught freely, never asking anything in return, except that his students, young and old, should do their utmost to assimilate the teachings of his cherished tradition. His earnest wish was for Kashmir Shaivism to be preserved and made available to all humankind.

On the 27th of September, 1991, Swami Lakshmanjoo left his physical body and attained *mahāsamādhi*, the great liberation.

Swami Lakshmanjoo

Śrī Tantrāloka of Abhinavagupta

Chapter (Āhnika) Five – Āṇavopāya

Revealed by His holiness, Swami Lakshmanjoo
Ishwar Ashram, Srinagar,
Kashmir, 1974

LJA TA05A (00:00) start

SWAMIJI: The fifth *āhnika* is dealing with *āṇavopāya*. You already know that.

आणवेन विधिना परधाम प्रेप्सतामथ निरूप्यत एतत्॥ १ ॥

āṇavena vidhinā paradhāma prepsatāmatha nirūpyata etat //1//

For those aspirants who desire and wish to get entry in that supreme state of God consciousness through the *āṇava* way, through the *āṇava* means, the *āṇavopāya* means, for those this *āhnika* is explained.

LJA TA05A (00:38)

विकल्पस्यैव संस्कारे जाते निष्प्रतियोगिनि।
अभीष्टे वस्तुनि प्राप्तिर्निश्चिता भोगमोक्षयोः ॥ २ ॥

vikalpasyaiva saṁskāre jāte niṣpratiyogini /
abhīṣṭe vastuni prāptirniścitā bhogamokṣayoḥ //2//

Vikalpasyaiva saṁskāre jāte niṣpratiyogini, when the purification of impressions of *vikalpa*s (thoughts) have reached to that extent when further purification is not needed (that is *niṣpratiyogini*), *vikalpasyaiva saṁskāre niṣpratiyogini jāte*, when the *saṁskāra* (the purification) of *vikalpa*s (as is already explained in this fourth *āhnika*; *vikalpa saṁskāra* is the first subject there), when that *saṁskāra* gets its end, that is, when the purification of impressions is not further needed,…*

JOHN: "Purification" means in this sense? "Not further needed" means at what point?

SWAMIJI: For instance, you begin to be aware, you have to be aware on one thought, not the second thought. But the process of thoughts is always changing, you know already. According to our system and according to the Buddhist system, thoughts are changing.

JOHN: In flux, it is going on.

SWAMIJI: In flux, yes. But you have to stop that flux. You have to concentrate on one thought without interruption of another thought. It may be similar to that [one] thought, but you have to discard that thought. Just direct your mind towards one thought. That is *saṁskāra*, that is purification of that one thought. And when one thought is purified, then that thought doesn't need to go to other thoughts.

JOHN: So that your mind stays with that one thought all the time.

SWAMIJI: That one thought constantly.

…when that state comes and the purification of that impression is not needed,…

For instance, if you don't purify it in flux–you have to purify that thought in flux to remain established in one point–if you don't maintain awareness to purify it in one point, it will go astray, it will go astray at once. This is the way of these thoughts.

JOHN: So the way of purification is maintaining awareness.

SWAMIJI: When you maintain that one-pointedness in one thought, you have not to maintain it once and for all, you have to maintain it in a flux-movement.

JOHN: Because it comes again and again–this thought.

SWAMIJI: It comes again and again. And the time comes when this will be stand-still, that thought will be established only in one point. That is *niṣpratiyogini jāte*, when there is no *pratiyogi* (*pratiyogi*-thought does not rise).[1] Then what happens?

*…*abhīṣṭe vastuni prāptir niścitā bhoga mokṣayoḥ*, then you attain your desired object, that is, the state of God consciousness, the

1. *Pratiyogi*-thought: similar, opposite, or other thoughts.

realisation of God consciousness. It is *niścitā*, it is absolutely sure. *Bhoga mokṣayoḥ*, not for getting liberated from repeated births and deaths, but also for enjoyment of the world.

The way of liberation in Shaivism and the way of liberation in Vedānta differ from each other. The way of liberating yourself from repeated births and deaths according to the Vedānta theory, is *bas*, to discard each and every object of the world and each and every pleasure of the world, you have to discard it aside and sentence your mind towards God consciousness for good, then you will get complete liberation. This is Vedānta. But Shaivism does not agree [with] that. Shaivism says perfect liberation is that when you enjoy this whole world in its fullness and then become liberated. This is the real liberation. Real liberation is not like this (Swamiji covers himself with a blanket). Real liberation is like this, when you are expanded in the universe and get liberated. But this [demonstration] won't come in…this won't be recorded.

Now this purification of these impressions of thought are defined in two ways, this *saṁskāra* is defined in two ways. For some aspirants:

LJA TA05A (06:00)

विकल्पः कस्यचित्स्वात्मस्वातन्त्र्यादेव सुस्थिरः ।
उपायान्तरसापेक्ष्यवियोगेनैव जायते ॥ ३ ॥

vikalpaḥ kasyacitsvātma-svātantryādeva susthiraḥ /
upāyāntarasāpekṣya-viyogenaiva jāyate //3//

This *vikalpa* (thought) becomes well-established in one-pointedness to some aspirants by [their] own one-pointedness and by the internal force of awareness. When you maintain your internal force of awareness of one-pointedness, being one-pointed, then this *vikalpa saṁskāra* takes place in its fullness for some aspirants. But for some aspirants this does not happen, they have to adopt other means also, they have to adjust some other means also to make it established on one point–this *vikalpa*. Because *vikalpa* is the only way to achieve God consciousness, the state of God consciousness. Without *vikalpa*, you can't do, you can't…there is no journey without *vikalpa*.

JOHN: In *āṇavopāya.*
SWAMIJI: In *śāktopāya* also.
JOHN: Yes, but not in *śāmbhavopāya.*
SWAMIJI: There is also journey of awareness.
JOHN: But there is no *vikalpa.*
SWAMIJI: Not *vikalpa*, but there is awareness, one-pointed *vikalpa* is there.

Upāyāntara sāpekṣya viyogenaiva jāyate, and that one-pointedness of internal force comes into happening without adopting other means. By "other means" you must know, breathing exercise, *dhyāna*, *kāraṇa*, *upāsana* (all other *upāsana*), and recitation of mantras, and all others. Without adopting, without adjusting these things, only maintaining only awareness on that one-pointedness, and this purification of these impressions of thought become established in one point without adopting other means.

JOHN: What would be that point?
SWAMIJI: That is *śāktopāya.*
JOHN: That's *śāktopāya*
SWAMIJI: That is *śāktopāya.* And for other aspirants, *kasyacittu vikal-*...this is for *āṇavopāya.*
JOHN: The next one.
SWAMIJI: Next one:

LJA TA05A (08:30)

कस्यचित्तु विकल्पोऽसौ स्वात्मसंस्करणं प्रति।
उपायान्तरसापेक्षस्तत्रोक्तः पूर्वको विधिः ॥४॥

kasyacittu vikalpo'sau svātmasaṁskaraṇaṁ prati /
upāyāntarasāpekṣastatroktaḥ pūrvako vidhiḥ //4//

But for some inferior aspirants, this *vikalpa* becomes established in getting purification of its impression in one point, *upāyāntarasāpekṣa*, by adjusting, by adopting other means also side-by-side. You have to recite mantra, you have to adjust awareness on one-pointedness between two eyebrows or heart or throat or some other concentrating points. You have to do that adjustment–*tatrokta pūrvako vidhi*. These are the two ways of purification of mind, and in these two ways, the first way is already explained in the fourth *āhnika*. It means, the second way will be explained in this book. *Tatrokta pūrvako vidhi*, *arthāt aparo vakṣyate*.

LJA TA05A (09:44)

विकल्पो नाम चिन्मात्रस्वभावो यद्यपि स्थितः ।
तथापि निश्चयात्मासावणोः स्वातन्त्र्ययोजकः ॥५॥

vikalpo nāma cinmātra-svabhāvo yadyapi sthitaḥ /
tathāpi niścayātmāsāvaṇoḥ svātantryayojakaḥ //5//

Saṁskāra is *atiśaya*, *saṁskāra* is an adjustment, to add something more.

SCHOLAR: Intensification.

SWAMIJI: For instance, "This is a brush, this is a brush, this is a brush, this is a brush, this is a brush, this is a brush…this is a red brush."

SCHOLAR: *Tāratamya*.[2]

SWAMIJI: But "this red brush, this is a red brush," it must be avoided. "This is a brush, this is a brush" only must continue. The continuity of "this is a brush, this is a brush" must remain, not "this is a red brush," not "this is an oval-shaped brush," not "this brush has a handle." All these other adjustments should be avoided totally! This is what he means. So, other adjustments should be avoided. *Vikalpo nāma cinmātra svabhāvo yadyapi sthitaḥ*, although this *vikalpa*, this purification of this *vikalpa*, is already *cinmātra svabhāva*, is already one with God consciousness–in fact, this is one with God consciousness–but even then, *tathāpi niścayātmāsāu aṇoḥ svātantryayojakaḥ*, even then, this is differentiated perception by which it directs individuals towards its *svātantrya* of limited modes–limited modes! You know "mode"? Modes means, for instance, this is limited modes: "This is a

2. Gradation, distinction or difference.

brush, this is a brush, this is a brush," and you have to avoid "this is a red brush, this is a brush with a handle." All these adjustments of other thoughts, which are attached to this *vikalpa*, should be avoided totally, then one-pointedness will get its rise. Otherwise one-pointedness won't come in existence. The main purpose of *vikalpa saṁskāra* is one-pointedness, to achieve that one-pointedness, and that one-pointedness will come only in one thought without its [adjustment with] other thoughts. For instance, "you are Denise, you are Denise, you are Denise, you are Denise...you have got this nose," this [other] thought should be avoided. "You are beautiful," this thought should be avoided. "You are slim," this thought should be avoided. Only one thought should remain there, then this *saṁskāra* will get its reality. Then this *saṁskāra*, this purification of impressions are there.

JOHN: So the use of *vikalpa* here means...?

SWAMIJI: (Question ignored) *Pramādāttu praviṣṭasya vicāraṁ naiva kārayet* (laughs).[3]

SCHOLAR: *Mūḍhasyāpi*?

SWAMIJI: *Mūḍha-*?

SCHOLAR: *Adīkṣitasyāpi*?

SWAMIJI: *Adīkṣitasyāpi*, not *muḍhasya*. *Adīkṣitasyāpi praviṣṭasya, kathañcit praviṣṭasya vicāram naiva kārayet, tatra sāvadhānarūpeṇa bhavitavyam.*[4]

JOHN: This *vikalpa* you are using in the sense of differentiated thought, I mean, that's exactly what you...

SWAMIJI: Yes, differentiated thought must not leak there. They should not come, otherwise *śāktopāya* won't exist.

JOHN: But this *vikalpa*, as opposed to *nirvikalpa*, in a technical sense, means just "thought."

SWAMIJI: Just thought, one-pointedness of one thought, any thought! It does not mean only one thought that, "I am Bhairava," "I am Lord Śiva." Not only this thought.

JOHN: Whatever your master gives you.

SWAMIJI: Whatever your master has told you.

---

3. A verse quoted by Jayaratha in his commentary of *Tantrāloka* 28.9.

4. Swamiji is conversing in Sanskrit reiterating that it is imperative to be careful not to let other thoughts enter.

LJA TA05A (13:43)

निश्चयो बहुधा चैष तत्रोपायाश्च भेदिनः।
अणुशब्देन ते चोक्ता दूरान्तिकविभेदतः॥ ६॥

niścayo bahudhā caiṣa tatropāyāśca bhedinaḥ /
aṇuśabdena te coktā dūrāntikavibhedataḥ //6//

And this *niścaya*, this establishment of one-pointedness, comes in various ways here, in the next way of *saṁskāra* (purification). The first way of *saṁskāra* is already explained in the fourth *āhinka*. This next way of *saṁskāra*, in the field, in the world of the next way of *saṁskāra*s, the *niścaya*, this adjustment of *saṁskāra*, is variously adjusted in various ways. *Tatropāyāśca bhedinaḥ*, and there are means also, different means for different aspirants in *āṇavopāya*. *Aṇuśabdena te coktā*, and this is why all those means are called, are nominated as, *aṇu*, because *aṇu* means, that limited being, individual. These *upāya*s (these means) are meant for individual beings. *Dūrāntika vibhedataḥ*, some means are very near to the state of God consciousness, and some means are away, far away from the state of God consciousness.

LJA TA05A (15:12)

तत्र बुद्धौ तथा प्राणे देहे चापि प्रमातरि।
अपारमार्थिकेऽप्यस्मिन् परमार्थः प्रकाशते॥ ७॥

tatra buddhau tathā prāṇe dehe cāpi pramātari /
apāramārthike'pyasmin paramārthaḥ prakāśate //7//

Now, the objection here is that in *buddhi* (intellect), in *prāṇa* (breath), and in *deha* (body)...because only there are three places for adjusting this *saṁskāra*. The adjustment of *saṁskāra* is done in three places, three states: in *buddhi* (in the intellectual world), in the world of breathing (*prāṇa*), and in the world of the body (*deha*)–in the body, in the world of breathing, and in the world of intellect. (Verse repeated) But the objection is, how can that God consciousness, the realization of God consciousness, rise in these limited states of individual being? There are actually four states of the limited individual being. One state is *deha pramātṛ bhāva*, what is functioning in wakefulness, the state of wakefulness. And the other state of limited being is *puryaṣṭaka pramātṛ bhāva*, and it is that state when you get in the world of the dreaming state (that is another state of limited being).[5] The third state of limited being is *prāṇa pramātṛ bhāva*, when you get absorbed in the world of...

JOHN: Deep sleep.

SWAMIJI:...sound sleep. And the fourth is *śūnya pramātṛ bhāva*. *Śūnya pramātṛ bhāva* is when you get absorbed and lost for good. That is *śūnya*, voidness, nothing, you don't see anything there. But for functioning and practicing, only three states of individuality are supposed to function. These three individual states are functioning, not the fourth one. The fourth one is *śūnya pramātṛ bhāva*. In *śūnya pramātṛ bhāva*, there is neither rise nor fall. It is a standstill way of becoming absolutely [comatose] just like in chloroform. So there is no hope of rise or fall.

SCHOLAR: This is *bauddha samādhi*.

SWAMIJI: *Bauddha samādhi*, yes.[6]

JOHN: Is this different from *pralayākala pramātṛ bhāva*–this *śūnya*?

SWAMIJI: Absolutely it is *pralayākala*, one with *pralayākala*. There is no hope of rise in *pralayākala*.[7]

SCHOLAR: This is the state of realization of the Buddhists according to Abhinavagupta.

---

5. The *puryaṣṭaka* (lit., "city of eight") is comprised of *śabda*, *sparśa*, *rūpa*, *rasa* and *gandha* (i.e., the *tanmātras*), along with *mana* (mind), *ahaṁkāra* (ego) and *buddhi* (intellect). *Puryaṣṭaka* is the subtle body that stores the impressions of the limited soul, which are the cause of transmigration. "*Puryaṣṭaka* carries the impressions again and again, extracts impressions. Otherwise, if *puryaṣṭaka* is not existing, at the time of death you'll be united with God automatically without doing anything. *Puryaṣṭaka* is the trouble-maker." *Parātrīśikā Vivaraṇa* (LJA archive).

6. *Samādhi* (absorpotion) pertaining to the intellect (*buddhi*).

7. See *Kashmir Shaivism–The Secret Supreme*, "The Seven States of the Seven Perceivers" and "The Seven Processes of the Seven Perceivers", pp. 51-64.

JOHN: Buddhists and Vedāntins.

SWAMIJI: Buddhists and Vedāntins also.

SCHOLAR: Śabdabrahma Vedāntins.

SWAMIJI: Yes, Śabdabrahma Vedāntins.

SCHOLAR: So they don't realize this state of *vijñānākala pramātṛ bhāva*.

SWAMIJI: No, they can't.

JOHN: So that's why the master carries you through this *śūnya* because the disciple is just stuck there in that state.

SWAMIJI: The disciple is stuck there. *Tatra buddhau*...so he has taken in hand only three states of individuality for practice. The three states are: *deha pramātṛ bhāva*, *puryaṣṭaka pramātṛ bhāva*, and *prāṇa pramātṛ bhāva*.

SCHOLAR: So *puryaṣṭaka pramātṛ bhāva* is the five subtle objects of sense (*tanmātras*), mind, *buddhi* (intellect), and *ahaṁkāra* (ego).

SWAMIJI: Yes...*ahaṁkāra*–eight.

SCHOLAR: These being what are working in predominance in sleep.

SWAMIJI: In *puryaṣṭaka*, yes, in sleep.[8]

SCHOLAR: Taste, smell, etcetera.

SWAMIJI: Yes. *Śabda*, *sparśa*, *rūpa*, *rasa*, and *gandha*, and *manas*, *buddhi*, and *ahaṁkāra*.

JOHN: In deep sleep, what is...?

SWAMIJI: In deep sleep nothing exists, only impressions.

SCHOLAR: So the difference there between complete deep sleep (*apavedya suṣupti*[9]) and *apavedya pralayākala bhāva*[10] is that breath is operating in the *suṣupti* state.

SWAMIJI: Breath is operating in *suṣupti* whereas in *apavedya pralayākala* breath is not operating.

SCHOLAR: There is complete *nivṛtti* (suspension) of all functions.

SWAMIJI: (Statement ignored) So, some ignorant persons call it *samādhi* because there is no breathing also.

---

8. That is to say, during the state of dreaming, not in the state of sound sleep (*prāṇa pramātṛ bhāva*).

9. Viz., *prāṇa pramātṛ bhāva*.

10. Viz., *śūnya pramātṛ bhāva*.

SCHOLAR: How can they fall into that ignorance to such a complete dead end?

SWAMIJI: They remain in that *samādhi* for days together, and come out…

DENISE: The same.

SWAMIJI:…the same.

JOHN: They have the peace of deep sleep.

SWAMIJI: It is just like deep sleep without breath. But in deep sleep there is breathing, but whereas in this deep sleep there is breathing also rejected.

MARK D: Is that the kind of *samādhi hatha*-yogins go into when they sleep together for months together under the ground?

SWAMIJI: Yes, this is the same.

SCHOLAR: But when the Buddha attained *samādhi*, he experienced the voidness of all things.

SWAMIJI: Yes.

SCHOLAR: This is that state?

SWAMIJI: This is that state. So he came out from that *samādhi* and put before the public his experience that…

SCHOLAR: *Ānātmavāda* (The Doctrine of No Self).

SWAMIJI:…there is nothing, nothing is in the end.

SCHOLAR: There is no *ātma*, there is no Īśvara.

SWAMIJI: There is no Īśvara, there is only voidness, *nirvāṇa, kṛṣṇa-vartaneva.*[11]

SCHOLAR: [Buddha said], "And what is this *nirvāṇa*? I won't say, *bas*, I have nothing to say here." There was nothing to say?

SWAMIJI: (laughs) So, *yat kiñcit etat*, so Shaivism says: *yat kiñcit etat*, let it remain there.

tatra buddhau tathā prāṇe dehe cāpi pramātari /
apāramārthike'pyasmin paramārthaḥ prakāśate //7//
(verse repeated)

Although these three states of individuality in the intellectual world (*buddhi*), in the world of breath (*prāṇa*), and in the world of the physical

11. Just (*eva*) abiding (*vartana*) in darkness (*kṛṣṇa*).

body (*deha*), *apāramārthike'pyasmin*, although these three states are *apāramārthika*, these three states do not belong to the state of God consciousness, they are absolutely away from God consciousness, but still then, *paramārthaḥ prakāśate*, God consciousness can be practiced in these three states.

SCHOLAR: It can shine there.

SWAMIJI: It can shine there by the grace of your masters. Because… how? For that he relates the next *śloka*:

LJA TA05A (22:01)

यतः प्रकाशाच्चिन्मात्रात् प्राणाद्यव्यतिरेकवत्।

yataḥ prakāśāccinmātrāt prāṇādyavyatirekavat /8a

Because *prakāśāt cinmātrāt*, that supreme God consciousness which is filled with absolute consciousness, these three states are also residing in the same area, they are not away from that. From the Shaiva point of view, everything resides there, nothing is excluded there. You have already understood that.

JOHN: That was discussed in the first *āhnikā*.

SWAMIJI: Everything is included in that state of God consciousness. So, that state of God consciousness can be practiced in these limited states also. So, you should not worry, "How can we rise from the limited way to unlimited being?" Because these are all limited ways, limited ways of practice. For [example], breathing exercise, this is limited. How can this limited way of exercise make you rise to that unlimited being which is beyond everything? How can this body, which is the collection of organs, the collection of *prāṇa* (breath), all those things will carry you to that God consciousness? And how can contemplation, what you do between the two eyebrows, the heart, *kaṇṭha* (throat pit), *nabhi* (navel), any limited part of your body, how can this concentration carry you to that unlimited being, unlimited state of being? It is absolutely impossible. But as it is true that these limited states of body, intellect and breath are also residing in the same level of God consciousness, so there is possibility of rising.

LJA TA05A (24:11)

तस्यैव तु स्वतन्त्रत्वाद्द्विगुणं जडचिद्वपुः ॥ ८ ॥

tasyaiva tu svatantratvād-dviguṇaṁ jaḍacidvapuḥ //8//

And it is because of his independent free will (*svātantrya*)–free will of whom? Of Lord Śiva–that *dviguṇaṁ jaḍa cit vapuḥ*, he has created twofold individualities. In one class he has created that class with consciousness, and in another class he has created another class without consciousness. For instance, this bottle, it is without consciousness, but actually this is residing in that God consciousness. But it is his free independent will that it is without consciousness. And this [other] class is with consciousness. It is his free will that Shanna is filled with consciousness. *Tasyaiva tu svatantratvāt dviguṇaṁ jaḍa cit vapuḥ*. So, although this whole universe is filled with *jaḍa*...

SCHOLAR: Inertia, deadness.

SWAMIJI:...deadness, it is absolutely dull before that God consciousness, before the state of God consciousness it is dull, although there is a brain, there is an intellect, there is everything, there is all those cognitions, but still, from that point of view, from the point of that God consciousness, it is *jaḍa*, it is dull, it has no life,...

LJA TA05A (25:59)

उक्तं त्रैशिरसे चैतद्देव्यै चन्द्रार्धमौलिना।

uktaṁ traiśirase caitad-devyai candrārdhamaulinā /9a
(not recited)

...but it is said in the *Triśiro Bhairava Tantra* to Pārvatī by Lord Śiva Himself, the conclusion of this:

जीवः शक्तिः शिवस्यैव सर्वत्रैव स्थितापि सा ॥ ९ ॥
स्वरूपप्रत्यये रूढा ज्ञानस्योन्मीलनात्परा।

jīvaḥ śaktiḥ śivasyaiva sarvatraiva sthitāpi sā //9//
svarūpapratyaye rūḍhā jñānasyonmīlanātparā /

The energy of Lord Śiva has become…although this energy of Lord Śiva is established in each and every object of the world, in each and every dull and not dull, unconscious and conscious object of the world, although this energy of Lord Śiva is existing in the dull world and in the conscious world, *svarūpapratyaye rūḍhā jñānasyonmīlanātparā*, even then this energy is *svarūpa pratyaye rūḍhā*, She is bent upon finding out the truth of God consciousness in that sphere also. *Jñān-*…

JOHN: Is that the nature of this energy to…?

SWAMIJI: This is the nature of energy. And *svarūpa jñānasya unmīlanāt parā*, so this energy is supreme because it gives light to the real knowledge of God consciousness.

JOHN: So it gives light to the movement in *āṇavopāya*, is it?

SWAMIJI: *Āṇavopāya*, he had to explain it because *āṇavopāya* had no right to reach that state of God consciousness. It was so low, it was residing in [such] a low and individual state. How could it reach that point of God consciousness?

JOHN: So this energy naturally carries you to that.

SWAMIJI: Yes, because it is residing there, actually it is residing there. This breathing, this…not only the conscious world, the unconscious world also is residing there. It is why in the *Śivadṛṣṭi prakarana*, Somānanda has said:

tasmin athocyate sarvadikke śivatattve vyavasthite[12]

Now I will explain the reality of Lord Śiva, which is everywhere, which is existing everywhere: *tasmin jñāte athavā ajñāte*, if you know

---

12. *atha sthite sarvadikke śivatattve vyvasthite /*
tasmiñjñāte 'thavājñāte śivatvamanivāritam //
This verse, which does not appear in the text of the *Tantrāloka*, is from Somānanda's *Śivadṛṣṭi*, *āhnika* 7, *śloka* 1. Swamiji mentions this verse in various places throughout his teachings.

it, if you realize it, well and good; if you don't realize it, well and good, it is there. There is no worry to realize it, it is there.

JOHN: So the whole movement of the universe is then to that God consciousness…

SWAMIJI: Yes.

JOHN:…the movement of everything, the tendency of everything.

SWAMIJI: So, there is no worry that if you adopt the means of *āṇavopāya* you won't reach there. You will exactly reach there because *āṇavopāya* is also residing in the same surface of God consciousness.

SCHOLAR: So all that is necessary there is the grace of master.

SWAMIJI: Grace of master, yes.

SCHOLAR: Otherwise you can practice *āṇavopāya* for one million years…

SWAMIJI: You can practice *śāktopāya* for two hundred million years, still nothing will happen.

SCHOLAR: Without that *bhakti* (devotion).

SWAMIJI: Without that grace. Grace will be showered on you if you serve him wholeheartedly. Do you know how to serve him? The serving of your master is to adopt what he has told you to do.

LJA TA05A (29:32)

तस्य चिद्रूपतां सत्यां स्वातन्त्र्योल्लासकल्पनात्॥ १० ॥
पश्यञ्जडात्मताभागं तिरोधायाद्वयो भवेत्।

tasya cidrūpatāṁ satyāṁ svātantryollāsakalpanāt //10//
paśyañjaḍātmatābhāgaṁ tirodhāyādvayo bhavet /

Now, you have to adopt and travel from the individual way, in *āṇavopāya*. The individual way is, for instance, the way of the intellect (*buddhi*) is the individual way, the way of breath (*prāṇa*) is the individual way, and the way of perceptions in the body (*deha*) is the individual way. How you should travel on that individual way, he says that in this next *śloka*.

Tasya cidrūpatāṁ satyāṁ, where you must find out, in this individual way, where is the *cidrūpatā*, where is the *cidrūpatā*, where is the God consciousness, the touch of God consciousness, where that is existing. For instance, breathe in and breathe out, this is the individual way of breathing. You have to find out the touch of God consciousness–just to find out! And you will find out in the two ends. The state of God consciousness, the touch of God consciousness will be experienced in the ends of the two breaths. That you already know. *Tasya cidrūpatāṁ satyāṁ*, and that *cidrūpata* is already existing in each and every breath. *Svātantryollāsa kalpanāt*, and it is your *svātantrya ullāsa*; *svātantrya ullāsa*, you must breathe with force, with vigor, with devotion, with effort, and with great charm. If these things are not there, this devotion will become dull, this devotion becomes dull and nothing will happen. You may breathe in and out, in and out, in and out for centuries, for a hundred centuries, nothing will happen. But the only trick is there to maintain devotion while breathing–devotion, enthusiasm, eagerness and love for that. And there you should find out these two points of God consciousness (that is *cidrūpatā*). *Paśyan jaḍātmatābhāgaṁ tirodhāyā*, the *jaḍātmatābhāga*, the section of dullness, dullness of these should be avoided, should be ignored. What is dullness? Dullness is the breathing course. The course of breathing in is the course of dullness, the course of breathing out is the course of dullness. These two courses should be ignored totally, *advayo bhavet*, then you become one with God consciousness–in a moment (Swamiji snaps his fingers).

JOHN: The course of breathing in and out should be ignored.

SWAMIJI: Yes.

JOHN: Why?

SWAMIJI: Because it is *jaḍa* (unconscious)! [Breathing] in and out is *jaḍa*. *Ajaḍa* (conscious) is only that point, the junction.

SCHOLAR: So you mean that point of awareness between breaths pervades the whole span of breath,...

SWAMIJI: Yes.

SCHOLAR:...so there is no awareness of moving and coming and going in breath.

SWAMIJI: No, you have to move...

SCHOLAR: You have to move but no awareness must be dissolved.

SWAMIJI:...you have to move in and out but focus your mind towards that point while moving out, focus [your] mind towards that point while moving in. Which point? There are two points.

DEVOTEE: Beginning and end.

SWAMIJI: Beginning and end. And this whole sphere of the world of practice should be pervaded by these two points. For instance, give me your hand (Swamiji tickles the devotees hand). You see, this is *jaḍātmatā bhāga* (the unconscious aspect). What? This [tickling] is *jaḍatātmatā bhāga*, but the sensation you feel inside in your brain, that is *ajaḍa bhāga* (the conscious aspect). Remain there while doing this, while doing this remain there. Don't let you fall from that consciousness. That sensation inside, that is residing here, here. Understand? This is the trick.

DEVOTEE: You have to concentrate on that sensation, not this sensation.

SWAMIJI: Not this sensation, this is *jaḍa*. In the same way (Swamiji breathes in and out), this [breathing] is *jaḍa*, you have nothing to do [with that], just point out that center. Not only in the center, in the sphere of center. There are two spheres of centers. You have not [only] to point out the center in the two spheres of centers, but also in the course of breathing [in and out] you have to point out that. I have many-a-times told you the course of the 26th, January in Delhi.[13] You know where the President is seated there in that Janapatha[14], in the same way, you must focus your consciousness between those two ends during this course also, this dull course.[15]

LJA TA05A (35:09) end.
LJA TA05B (00:00) start.

---

13. India's Independence Day.

14. A public-owned house which serves as the residence of India's prime ministers.

15. "Just to make understood how you have to meditate: When a parade is going on, for instance, a parade of those girls from school, colleges, they parade there, the president is seated here on the side of the road on some chair, all those boys and girls are turning their faces towards the president [while] they walk. They walk and turn like this (Swamiji demonstrates). In the same way, you have to turn, you have to turn your observation towards the heart while moving outside." *Tantrāloka* 6.97a (LJA archive). See also *Śiva Sūtras* 3.36 for an explanation of "triple awareness."

You see:

buddhau prāṇe tathā dehe deśe yā jaḍatā sthitā /
tāṁ tirodhāya medhāvī saṁvidraśmimayo bhavet //[16]

This is a reference here.

In the intellectual body, in the body of *prāṇa–buddhau prāṇe*–and in the elementary body (*dehe*), and *deśe*–not only there–in external space, form,…*

SCHOLAR: *Standila, maṇḍalādi.*

SWAMIJI: Yes.

*…*yā jaḍatā sthitā*, this *jaḍatā* (dull course) is already there existing. *Tāṁ tirodhāya medhāvī*, the one who is a realized one, the one who is filled with awareness, he has to subside that *jaḍatā*, *tirodhāya*, and give rise to that consciousness, give rise to that conscious state in the beginning, in the end, and in the center.

SCHOLAR: But awareness is always growing in the extremities at first.

SWAMIJI: At first, and you have to develop awareness in such a way that this consciousness of that centering your mind pervades in each and every movement, in dull movement and in conscious movement also.

SCHOLAR: And then also in the progression of this *samādhi*, first in the point between waking and sleeping, and then with complete freedom moving from wake to sleep,…

SWAMIJI: Yes.

SCHOLAR:…and sleeping to waking, without loss of awareness.

SWAMIJI: It is why *krama mudrā* is also there.[17]

---

16. A quote of unstated origin from Jayaratha's commentary for verse 10.

17. "In the *Krama Sūtra*, it says that a yogi first enters *krama mudrā* in the introverted state. Then, owing to the intensity of *krama mudrā*, he emerges from the introverted state and enters into the outer, external cycle of consciousness. First, from outside, he goes inside, and then from inside he goes outside. This movement of going in and coming out and then again going in and coming out takes place by the force of the absorption (*samāveśa*) of *krama mudrā*, not by the effort of the yogi. Where the yogi travels from outside to inside and then from inside to outside, just to come to the understanding that outside and inside are not different aspects but one, that is *krama mudrā*. There is one more thing for you to

understand. The one who experiences this state of the absorption (*samāveśa*) of *krama mudrā* experiences this whole universe melting into nothingness in the great sky of God consciousness (*cidgagana*). Although he opens his eyes and perceives that everything is melting into that state, yet, when he strives to come out of that state, it becomes very difficult for him. As it is very difficult for us to enter into that state, in the same way it is very difficult for that yogi to come out of it. But why does he want to come out? He wants to come out for the fun of it, but he cannot come out. The intensity of God consciousness does not let him come out, yet he struggles to come out. Then for a moment he rises up, and after that, he again, filled with intoxication, rests inside. Then, again, he strives to come out. He continues trying to come out and he gets out briefly but then again he is united inside. This happens again and again and this called *krama mudrā*." *Self Realization in Kashmir Shaivism*, 5.114. "This is an automatic process. It does not come by functioning it, you can't function it…*Krama mudrā* is no *mudrā*, *krama mudrā* is automatic. [*Krama mudrā* is] just to observe that state of *samādhi* in [the external world] also. When it is not so clearly found outside, go again in *samādhi* and pull it out with that *samādhi* and see in the external world again. And again and again, again and again, you have to [experience] this way of *krama mudrā* until [you gain] entry in *jagadānanda*. When *jagadānanda* takes place, then everything is divine, no [more] *krama mudrā*." Swami Lakshmanjoo, *Light on Tantra in Kashmir Shaivism, Vol. 2* (Lakshmanjoo Academy 2021). "When you are established in the process of *krama mudrā*, then you experience that ecstasy in action. When you eat, you are in that bliss. When you talk, you are in that bliss. When you walk, you are in that bliss. Whatever you do, you remain in that Universal state. This is the state of *jīvanmukti*, liberated in life. This state is experienced, not by ordinary yogins, but only by great yogins. This is the real state of *cit kuṇḍalinī*. In the actual rise of *cit kuṇḍalinī*, you will only get a glimpse of it and then come out. The full rise of *cit kuṇḍalinī* takes place only by the grace of your master and by the grace of your own strength of awareness. The experience of establishing the full rise of *cit kuṇḍalinī* through the process of *krama mudrā* can take place in one day, one life, or one hundred lifetimes." *Kashmir Shaivism–The Secret Supreme*, 17.120. "The establishment of *krama mudrā* is called *jagadānanda*, which means 'universal bliss.' This is the seventh and last state of *turya*. In this state, the experience of the universal transcendental Being is never lost and the whole of the universe is experienced as one with your own transcendental I-consciousness." *Kashmir Shaivism–The Secret Supreme*, 16.114.

LJA TA05B (01:47)

तत्र स्वातन्त्र्यदृष्ट्या वा दर्पणे मुखबिम्बवत्॥ ११ ॥
विशुद्धं निजचैतन्यं निश्चिनोत्यतदात्मकम्।

tatra svātantryadṛṣṭyā vā darpaṇe mukhabimbavat //11//
viśuddhaṁ nijacaitanyaṁ niścinotyatadātmakam /

Tatra, there, he realizes himself absolutely separated from these three bodies; *niścinoti atadātamakam*, absolutely separated from these three bodies: absolutely separated from *prāṇa* (breath), absolutely separated from the intellect (*buddhi*), and absolutely separated from the physical body (*deha*) when he gets full entry in that God consciousness.

LJA TA05B (02:31)

बुद्धिप्राणादितो भिन्नं चैतन्यं निश्चितं बलात्॥ १२ ॥
सत्यतस्तदभिन्नं स्यात्तस्यान्योन्यविभेदतः।

buddhiprāṇādito bhinnaṁ caitanyaṁ niścitaṁ balāt //12//
satyatastadabhinnaṁ syāttasyānyonyavibhedataḥ /

By the force of ignorance (*balāt*; *bala* does not mean *ātma bala* there[18], *bala* is this force of ignorance), this is the pressure and force of ignorance that *buddhi prāṇādito bhinnaṁ caitanyaṁ niścitaṁ*, this is concluded that the state of the intellect, the state of breath, and the state of the physical body is absolutely separated from God consciousness. It is the force of ignorance, the force of ignorance has led you to this conclusion…which conclusion?

SCHOLAR: That these three are separate.

SWAMIJI: That these three are separated from God consciousness.

18. The force or strength of self.

SCHOLAR: But in the course of *āṇavopāya*, this winding up is emphasized.

SWAMIJI: Winding up is emphasized…

SCHOLAR: Though in *śāktopāya* this course of illusion is short.

SWAMIJI: (Scholars comment ignored) *Satyatas-*, *magar* (but) *tat abhinnam syāt tasyānyonyavibhedataḥ*, but that is *tat abhinnam*, in fact, in the true sense, that God consciousness is adjusted in each and every individual state of being–individual state of being: in *prāṇa* also, in the intellect also, and in the physical body also.

SCHOLAR: So this is in the meaning of *mantra vīrya*…

SWAMIJI: This is *mantra vīrya*, yes.

SCHOLAR:…that this is realized internally…

SWAMIJI: Yes, this is *mantra vīrya.*[19]

SCHOLAR:…and then moves into…

SWAMIJI: Yes.

SCHOLAR:…*saṁvit cakra.*

SWAMIJI:

LJA TA05B (04:09)

विश्वरूपाविभेदित्वं शुद्धत्वादेव जायते ॥ १३ ॥

viśvarūpāvibheditvaṁ śuddhatvādeva jāyate //13//

In fact, the collective individual form of all forms is held because it is perfect purity (*viśvarūpa avibheditvaṁ*; *avibheditvam*, the collective individual form, the collective form of individuality). The collective form is God consciousness. Separately, if you observe these three states separately, you are away from God consciousness. If you observe these three states collectively, then you are one with God consciousness even [in] these individual states, in different states, separated states also.

LJA TA05B (04:57)

19. The power of all mantras.

निष्ठितैकस्फुरन्मूर्तेर्मूर्त्यन्तरविरोधतः।

niṣṭhitaikasphuranmūrtermūrtyantaravirodhataḥ /14a

Because the limited establishment of three bodies…only three bodies are to be functioned, not the fourth one. Which one?

SCHOLAR: *Śūnya pramātṛ bhāva* (the state of voidness).

SWAMIJI: *Śūnya*, yes. Because the limited establishment of three bodies is existing when one formation out of these three is felt separate from the other two formations. This limitedness comes only when you see the intellectual body as separate from the physical body and the body of breath; and the body of breath as separate from the intellectual body and the physical body; and the physical body as separate from the intellectual body and the body of breath. When you collectively understand and observe what is the reality of that, that is God consciousness. So, there is possibility of rising to God consciousness by these limited ways. So *āṇavopāya* is no less than *śāktopāya* in that way. You should not think when you adopt the means of *āṇavopāya* you are adopting the inferior means. It is not inferior means, it is really the real means, the real way.

Next:

LJA TA05B (06:37)

अन्तः संविदि सत्सर्वं यद्यप्यपरथा धियि॥ १४॥
प्राणे देहेऽथवा कस्मात्सङ्क्रामेत्केन वा कथम्।
तथापि निर्विकल्पेऽस्मिन्विकल्पो नास्ति तं विना॥ १५॥
दृष्टेऽप्यदृष्टकल्पत्वं विकल्पेन तु निश्चयः।

antaḥ saṁvidi satsarvaṁ yadyapyaparathā dhiyi //14//
prāṇe dehe'thavā kasmātsaṅkrāmetkena vā katham /
tathāpi nirvikalpe'sminvikalpo nāsti taṁ vinā //15//
dṛṣṭe'pyadṛṣṭakalpatvaṁ vikalpena tu niścayaḥ /

Antaḥ saṁvidi satsarvaṁ yadyapi, although in internal God consciousness (*antaḥ saṁvidi*, in internal God consciousness), *sarvaṁ sat*, everything is existing in internal God consciousness, otherwise (*aparathā*, otherwise) *dhiyi prāṇe dehe kasmāt katham saṅkrāmet*, how can this God consciousness would be felt in these three limited bodies? It means that that God consciousness is existing in these three limited bodies, in these three limited states. *Tathāpi nirvikalpe'smin vikalpo nāsti*, even then, if it is *nirvikalpa*[20], the *nirvikalpa* state is already residing there, what is the use of practice? Why should we practice at all? It is only a waste of time. If the *nirvikalpa* state is already there in the body (*deha*), in the body of intellect (*buddhi*), and in the body of breath (*prāṇa*), that God consciousness is exactly residing there, if it is true, then what is the use of practice?

DENISE: To recognize it?

SWAMIJI: But it is recognized! It is already there, it is recognized, you can't live without that. *Tathāpi nirvikalpe'smin vikalpo nāsti*, even then, because in this *nirvikalpa* state of God consciousness, *vikalpo nāsti*, you don't find the taste of that, you don't find the effulgence, that pleasure, that joy, that joy of God consciousness is not there, so in order to find out that joy there, you have to practice, you have to do practice. *Taṁ vinā dṛṣṭe api adṛṣṭā kalpatvaṁ*, although it is there, it is just [like] *rathyāṁ gamane tṛṇa parṇādivat*,[21] when you walk on the road, you ride, you go in a motorcar or a chariot or anything, a cart, on the roadside there are leaves, there are blades of grass, you find them lying down on either side, right and left, but they leave no impression in your intellect, no *saṁskāra* (impression) of those things. In the same way, if God consciousness is existing there, they don't leave that impression. The impression [is felt] only when you are face-to-face observing that God consciousness, and that observing God consciousness face-to-face is done only in practice, is maintained only by practice. So practice is essential for this.

LJA TA05B (10:25)

20. The thought-less (*nirvikalpa*) state of God consciousness.

21. An example from the *Parātrīṁśikā Laghuvṛtti*.

बुद्धिप्राणशरीरेषु पारमेश्वर्यमञ्जसा ॥ १६ ॥
विकल्प्यं, शून्यरूपे न प्रमातरि विकल्पनम्।

buddhiprāṇaśarīreṣu pārameśvaryamañjasā //16//
vikalpyaṁ, śūnyarūpe na pramātari vikalpanam /

Now he explains: Why I have put practice for only three bodies, why not in the fourth body, the fourth body of *śūnya pramātā*? Why at the state of *śūnya pramātā*, in the state of *śūnya pramātā* (this voidness), why should we not practice if God consciousness is existing there? Actually God consciousness is there also. Why should we not practice God consciousness [there]? It is *śūnya pramātā*, it would be very easy that way because there is no *vikalpa* (thought), there is no *prāṇa* (there is no breath), there is nothing, there are no anxieties. It would be a very easy course to adopt the awareness of God consciousness in *śūnya*. For that he says this next *śloka*: *Buddhi prāṇa śarīreṣu pārameśvaryam añjasā vikalpyaṁ* (there should be a comma after "*vikalpyam*"). *Buddhi prāṇa śarīreṣu pārameśvaryam añjasā vikalpyaṁ*, the state of Parameśvara, the state of Lord Śiva, is *añjasā*, very easily, *vikalpyam*, understood and contemplated on in these three states–*buddhi*, *prāṇa*, and *śarīra* (in the intellectual state, in this state of breath, and in the state of body)–but *śūnya rūpe pramātari na vikalpanam*, in *śūnya rūpa pramātā* there is no thought, there is no awareness, so practice won't be adopted there. So we have discarded that kind of practice.

JOHN: Well, how does that state differ from *suṣupti*, the state of deep sleep?

SWAMIJI: Because there is breath, in *suṣupti* there is breath. In *śūnya pramātā* there is not breath also.

SCHOLAR: There is not voidness in *suṣupti*.

SWAMIJI: There is not voidness, but there is *saṁskāra*, there are some *saṁskāra*s (impressions). Now, there are three bodies, we have come to this conclusion that practice is done in three bodies, in the world of three bodies. One is the intellectual body, one is the body of breath, and the other is this physical body (elementary body). Do you mean that we have to concentrate on the intellect? Do you mean that we have to contemplate on breath? How it is done? For this he says:

LJA TA05B (13:15)

बुद्धिर्ध्यानमयी तत्र प्राण उच्चारणात्मकः ॥ १७ ॥

buddhirdhyānamayī tatra prāṇa uccāraṇātmakaḥ //17//

By *buddhi* (by intellect) you should mean *dhyānamayī* (contemplation, meditation, concentration). Concentration is done in the sphere of *buddhi*.

JOHN: *Dhyāna* means, technically?

SWAMIJI: *Dhyāna*.

JOHN: *Dhyāna* means, on/with form (with *mūrti*), contemplation with form?

SWAMIJI: Both, any contemplation with form or without form, that is *dhyāna*. If you concentrate between two breaths, that is also *dhyāna*. *Buddhir dhyānamayī tatra prāṇa uccāraṇātmaka*, and *prāṇa* (breath) is *uccāraṇa*. *Uccāraṇa*, what is *uccāraṇa*? Pronouncing.

DEVOTEE: Recitation.

SWAMIJI: Recitation.

JOHN: *Prāṇa* is *uccāra*?

SWAMIJI: *Prāṇa* is *uccāra*. *Prāṇa* means, *uccāra*! The practice of *prāṇa* means, *uccāra*.

JOHN: You mean, the recitation of mantra, etcetera.

SWAMIJI: And:

LJA TA05B (14:18)

उच्चारणं च प्राणाद्या व्यानान्ताः पञ्च वृत्तयः ।

uccāraṇaṁ ca prāṇādyā vyānāntāḥ pañca vṛttayaḥ /

Uccāraṇa is fivefold. Utterance is consumed in five operative states of breath. Utterance is consumed in the five operative states of breath, and those five operative states are: *prāṇa* (breathing in and out), *apāna* (this sucking in and throwing out by the rectum–the breath, this is power, that is *apāna*), and *samāna* is the equilibrium of all these systems,…*

JOHN: Which systems?

SWAMIJI: For instance, if blood is there, blood is sucked from you (because I have to induce blood on some particular patient, I am a doctor, I take from a syringe your blood and you lose that blood), but the *samāna prāṇa*, this is the worry of *samāna prāṇa* to maintain that blood at once in the body! In fifteen minutes, that blood will be maintained in your body. This is the function of *samāna*. For instance, there is too much of mucus in your body. This is the worry of *samāna* to keep it in equilibrium.

JOHN: But how does this function in utterance or *uccāra*–this *samāna*, this equilibrium?

SWAMIJI: It will be explained in the sixth *āhnika*. In the sixth *āhnika* it will be explained–the practice of *prāṇa*, the practice of *apāna*, the practice of *samāna*, *udāna*, and *vyāna*.

*…and *udāna*, *udāna* is just the worry of that breath which makes you digest everything in the body, and *vyāna* is to…

DEVOTEE: Reject.

SWAMIJI: Not reject.

SCHOLAR: Pervade.

SWAMIJI:…*vyāna* is [to] pervade life in each and every vein of your body–it is *vyāna*, this is the function of *vyāna*. So, these take place in the world of breath.

LJA TA05B (17:00)

आद्या तु प्राणनाभिख्यापरोच्चारात्मिका भवेत्॥ १८॥

ādyā tu prāṇanābhikhyāparoccārātmikā bhavet //18//
(not recited)

And in this breath, in the world of breath, we have classified this in two ways, two sections–the world of breath. One is *prāṇana* and the other is *prāṇa*. *Prāṇana* is, that is one breath which is *prāṇa*, it is all-pervading in the physical body. For that you have no practice.

And the other is *uccāraṇa*: *prāṇa*, *apāna*, *samāna*, *udāna*, and *vyāna* is the next. The first is *prāṇana*. *Yena dehasya sthabdhatā na bhavati*. For instance, this [hand] is flexible. This is flexible. How is it flexible? This is the functioning of that *prāṇa*, *prāṇana*, the sixth breath. This is all-pervading. For this you have not to practice, you have nothing to do. This is excluded in practice. Only these five states of breath are included in practice.

JOHN: So this *prāṇana* is like life-force.

SWAMIJI: It is life, it is just like life, flexible. Because that stiffness comes when you die–[*prāṇana*] does not exist.[22]

LJA TA05B (18:38)

शरीरस्याक्षविषयैतत्पिण्डत्वेन संस्थितिः ।

śarīrasyākṣaviṣayaitatpiṇḍatvena saṁsthitiḥ /

Now, the practice of the physical body is called the subjective state of *deha pramātā* in the collection of organs and its objects. *Śarīrasya akṣa viṣayai*, when organs are there and objects of organs are there, when they are adjusted collectively, then this is the practice of *śarīra* (body). For instance, you eat, you drink–there you have to practice (it is *āṇavopāya*). When you are chewing food and there is some technique, some trick given to you by your master, how to take food, how to sip water, how to drink wine, how to do everything according to this body, this is done in the field of *śarīra*.

LJA TA05B (19:53)

तत्र ध्यानमयं तावदनुत्तरमिहोच्यते ॥ १९ ॥

tatra dhyānamayaṁ tāvadanuttaramihocyate //19//

---

22. "*Prāṇana vṛtti* is that kind of state of breath which is not moving, without movement, breath without movement (i.e., without inhale and exhale)." *Tantrāloka* 6.8 (LJA archives).

First, we will connect our subject in *dhyāna*, we'll say supreme *dhyāna*, supreme concentration on formation. First is *buddhi dhyāna*, supreme excellent unsurpassed meditation is first, the first subject. The second subject is *prāṇa tattva samuccāra*, the automatic reciting of breath, recitation of breath. *Cidatmatā uccāra* is the third subject; *cidatmatā uccāra*, the *uccāra* of God consciousness. *Para tattvāntaḥ praveśa*, the entry in the supreme element of God consciousness. *Pathalakṣaṇam*, and recognizing the path. *Karaṇam*, and the way of *karaṇa upāsana*, the organic way of meditation. And *varṇa tattvaṁ*, the meditation on Word. *Bas*, these are the subjects to be explained in this *āṇavopāya*, the fifth *āhnika*. I think you have read that in its *anujjodeśa* (index).

SCHOLAR: In the first book.

SWAMIJI: In the first book. *Tatra dhyānamayaṁ tāvad-anuttaramihocyate*, unsurpassed meditation will be explained first in this *āhnika*.

LJA TA05B (21:42)

Buddhi Dhyānam
Intellectual Meditation

यः प्रकाशः स्वतन्त्रोऽयं चित्स्वभावो हृदि स्थितः।
सर्वतत्त्वमयः प्रोक्तमेतच्च त्रिशिरोमते॥ २०॥

yaḥ prakāśaḥ svatantro'yaṁ citsvabhāvo hṛdi sthitaḥ /
sarvatattvamayaḥ proktametacca triśiromate //20//

This is explained in the *Triśirobhairava Āgama* that that *prakāśa* is *svatantraḥ*, all-round independent with the light of His consciousness. And it is *cit svabhāva*, its nature is consciousness, and it is situated in the heart, and the heart is the center of all elements, thirty-six elements. The heart is not this [physical] heart. The heart is the center of all the thirty-six elements, and it is the independent light of consciousness, and this is said in the *Triśirobhairava Tantra*.

For instance, there are flowers, in the springtime all these trees and plants get blossomed with flowers, but these flowers don't bear fruit unless they are crossed, they get cross-pollination from other flowers. For instance, there is one blooming flower here and [another one] next [to it] on the other branch of the tree, and either this wind will carry this pollen from that flower to this flower and this flower will bear fruit, [or] if this is not done, it won't bear fruit. It is carried, this male pollen in female pollen is carried by wind or by bees to [another] flower. But this is not the case in the flower of a banana tree. A banana tree is independent, absolutely independent.

Have you understood which point I was explaining?

SCHOLAR: Yes, *kadalī*.

SWAMIJI: Banana tree. And this is only the banana flower in this universe which tallies with the state of God consciousness. And that God consciousness is also like a banana flower because it is independent, absolutely independent. It does not need the carrying [of] male pollen there in female pollen. And banana fruit, it is self-sufficient, it does not need carrier-bees or this wind. So it is *svatantra* (independent) exactly like the state of God consciousness. The state of God consciousness also, you find in the state of God consciousness in that universal center of heart that both things are simultaneously working there without any other help of any other agency, outward agency, as you find in other flowers of trees.

And now he reads that *Triśirobhairava Tantra*:

LJA TA05B (25:24)

कदलीसम्पुटाकारं सबाह्याभ्यन्तरान्तरम् ।
ईक्षते हृदयान्तःस्थं तत् पुष्पमिव तत्त्ववित् ॥ २१ ॥

kadalīsampuṭākāraṁ sabāhyābhyantarāntaram /
īkṣate hṛdayāntaḥstaṁ tatpuṣpamiva tattvavit //21//

Kadalī sampuṭā kāraṁ, this is just exactly like a bunch of flowery casket of bananas. Those flowery caskets of bananas are situated one in another. One is created from the upper portion, and the lower portion also creates another bunch of flowers, and they are interconnected with each other, and you get [pollination]. This pollen is automatically...

the upper portion flower is of that male and the lower portion of that flower is of that female, and the pollen of the upper portion is automatically thrown in the pollen of the lower flower, because they are interconnected like is. That is *kadalī sampuṭa, sampuṭa kāraṁ*, just like a casket of banana flowers. And *sabāhyābhyantarāntaram*, it is, from outside you feel…for instance, the banana flower, it is not just like a lotus flower. In a lotus flower, if you tear all those leaves of flowers, you won't get the pollen. The pollen is found only in the center of that lotus, but it is not the case in the banana flower. A banana flower, if you take off one leaf, you will see pollen there. If you take another leaf, there is another pollen. In each and every leaf of that banana flower, you get pollen. Pollen is seen after each and every leaf of a banana flower. And the lower portion of that banana flower become, produce those banana fruits afterwards. And the flower of the upper portion vanishes by-and-by and they bear banana fruit from downwards. This is the case in banana [flowers]. It is a unique case. It is just like the case of Lord Śiva. So he has given the example of banana flowers. And *sabāhyābhyantarāntaram*, the *tattvavit*, the realized and elevated soul, *tattvavit īkṣate*, experiences that state of God consciousness in the innermost center of those banana flowers. Because the first pollen he puts aside, the second pollen he puts aside, he takes off all these leaves and comes to that innermost center where he gets the real pollen, and that pollen is just like the state of God consciousness. *Īkṣate*, he experiences that *svarūpa*, *hṛdayāntaḥstham*, in his universal heart, just like that flower, banana flower.

SCHOLAR: There is no *sthāna dhyāna* here.

SWAMIJI: Huh?

SCHOLAR: There is no reference to *sthāna* here at all–this *hṛdi* in *hṛdayāntaḥstaṁ*. Nothing here.

SWAMIJI: It is not *sthāna*.[23]

SCHOLAR: It is not gross *dhyāna*.

SWAMIJI: It is not gross, it is *anuttaram, anuttaram*.[24]

---

23. As Swamiji will explain onwards, "*Sthāna kalpanā* is putting awareness of some point, e.g., the throat, *bhrukuṭi* (between the eyebrows), or heart, or something, which will be explained in the sixth *āhnika*."

24. Unsurpassed (*anuttaram*) meditation (*dhyāna*).

SCHOLAR: But not *śāktopāya*, this is *āṇavopāya*.

SWAMIJI: It is *āṇavopāya* touching *śāktopāya* and *śāmbhavopāya* also.

LJA TA05B (29:20)

सोमसूर्याग्निसङ्घट्टं तत्र ध्यायेदनन्यधीः।

somasūryāgnisaṅghaṭṭaṁ tatra dhyāyedananyadhīḥ /22a[25]

Tatra, in the center of the heart of consciousness–it is not the gross heart–in the center of the heart of consciousness (*tatra*), *ananyadhīḥ*, the yogi whose mind is filled with absolute awareness, *ananyadhīḥ*, without any other outward thoughts, *dhyāyet*, he experiences there at that point when his awareness is one-pointed, established in one-pointedness, he feels *soma sūrya agni saṅghaṭṭaṁ*, that *prāṇa*, *apāna*, and *samāna* have become diluted in one state. There is no breathing in and out and there is not that center. There is no inhaling course, there is no exhaling course, and there is no centralizing course. All these three courses vanish altogether in that center of God consciousness.

SCHOLAR: So, you have said *prāṇa*, *apāna*, and *udāna*[26] because this is, at this stage here, these first two verses are still operating in *āṇavopāya*.

SWAMIJI: It is *āṇavopāya*.

SCHOLAR: If this was *śāktopāya*, it would be *prameya* (objective), *pramāṇa* (cognitive), and *pramātṛ* (subjective)–these *soma-sūrya-agni tritaya* (triad).

SWAMIJI: That also he will travel at once, automatically.

SCHOLAR: But this point here we are talking of that point that emerges in (indaudible).

SWAMIJI: *Āṇavopāya*. It is in *āṇavopāya*, yes.

---

25. See also *Swamiji's Interview 1*, CD 530, 53:06 (LJA archive).

26. Swamiji said "*samāna*," not "*udāna*," but in the following two verses he adds *udāna* in this sequence where the breaths are merged in one, saying that, "In my point of view, *samāna* and *udāna* are one."

LJA TA05B (30:54)

तद्ध्यानारणिसङ्क्षोभान्महाभैरवहव्यभुक् ॥ २२ ॥
हृदयाख्ये महाकुण्डे जाज्वलन् स्फीततां व्रजेत् ।

taddhyānāraṇisaṅkṣobhānmahābhairavahavyabhuk //22//
hṛdayākhye mahākuṇḍe jājvalan sphītatāṁ vrajet /

That meditation, when [it] takes the shape of the agitation of fire-producing woods, two fire-producing woods (you know, *āraṇi, araṇi* are those woods, they produce fire by friction, they produce fire), and this *dhyāna* becomes just like the fire-producing woods, *tat dhyāna āraṇi saṅkṣobhāt*, by the agitation of those fire-producing woods of *dhyāna* (of meditation)–it is not actually woods; he has given similarity to *dhyāna* with these fire-producing woods–then what comes forth? *Mahā bhairava havyabhuk*, this supreme and great *havyabhuk*, fire of God consciousness, *jājvalan*, shines in *mahā kuṇḍe*, in the [great] *kuṇḍa. Kuṇḍa* means the pot in which fire is produced–*agni kuṇḍa, havan kuṇḍa. Kuṇḍa* is that portion on which we produce the fire of a *havan*. And that *kuṇḍa* has become the heart, the universal heart is the *kuṇḍa* there. and in that universal heart, universal center, *jājvalan*, that supreme fire of God consciousness is enlightened, and *sphītatāṁ vrajet*, it becomes absolutely…[it] takes its vivid form, vivid form of God consciousness, and his God consciousness is quite clear. He finds the truth of God consciousness shining there in his heart, in his heart of consciousness.

Na vrajet na viśet…no, this is [verse 26 of the] *Vijñāna Bhairava*:

LJA TA05B (33:10)

na vrajenna viśecchaktirmarudrūpā vikāsite /
nirvikalpatayā madhye tayā bhairavarūpadhṛt //[27]

---

27. Swamiji recites "*bhairavarūpadhṛt*" in place of the published "*bhairavarūpatā*."

When the energy of *prāṇa* neither goes in or out, then by that one-pointedness, the central path of *suṣumnā*, *marut rūpā śaktir na vrajet*, this *prāṇa* neither goes in nor goes out, when *nirvikalpatayā*, by one-pointedness, *nirvikalpatayā vikāsite madhye*, when by one-pointedness this *suṣumnā* gets enlightened,...*

DEVOTEE: *Suṣumnā* means?

SWAMIJI: The central path, the central path of God consciousness.

*...*tayā bhairava rūpadhṛt*, by that way, you become the holder of Bhairava, the holder of the formation of Bhairava.[28]

LJA TA05B (34:08)

तस्य शक्तिमतः स्फीतशक्तेर्भैरवतेजसः ॥ २३ ॥
मातृमानप्रमेयाख्यं धामाभेदेन भावयेत्।

tasya śaktimataḥ sphīta-śakterbhairavatejasaḥ //23//
mātṛmānaprameyākhyaṁ dhāmābhedena bhāvayet /

Not only he feels the union of *prāṇa*, *apāna*, and *samāna* or *udāna*, but when *śaktimataḥ*, that Śiva whose energies have become vividly visible (*sphīta śakter*), *bhairava tejasaḥ*, with the light of Bhairava, then *mātṛ-māna-prameyākhyaṁ dhāmābhedena bhāvayet*, he gets entry in *śāktopāya. Pramātā* (subjective), *pramāṇa* (cognitive), and *prameya* (objective), these three lights, *abhedena bhāvayet*, he sees that these three lights are also dissolved in one–God consciousness. This is the way he gets entry in *śāktopāya* at the very moment, just after another second.

---

28. "*Madhye nirvikalpatayā*, when you establish one-pointedness in the central path, central vein (*suṣumnā*; *madhye* means, in *suṣumnā*, in the central vein), when you maintain one-pointedness in that central vein (*nirvikalpatyā*), then what happens? *Śakti*, *marut-rūpā śakti*, this energy of breath neither goes out nor enters in (*na vrajet na viśet*) because *madhye vikāsite*, this central vein is *vikāsite*, already shined, it is already bloomed, and by this process, *bhairava-rūpatā bhavati*, one becomes one with Bhairava." *Vijñāna Bhairava* (LJA archive), 26.

LJA TA05B (35:19)

वह्न्यर्कसोमशक्तीनां तदेव त्रितयं भवेत्॥ २४॥

vahnyarkasomaśaktīnāṁ tadeva tritayaṁ bhavet //24//

These three limited states of being are called the energies of fire, sun, and moon. *Vahni arka soma śaktīnāṁ tadeva tritayaṁ bhavet*, because *vahni* (fire) is *pramātṛ* (subjective), *arka* (sun) is *pramāṇa* (cognition), and *soma* (moon) is *prameya* (objective), and these three lights also, these three lights of these *prakāśa*s (lights) also are dissolved in one *prakāśa*, one *prakāśa* of God consciousness. Then in the next step, he gets entry in *śāmbhavopāya* at the same time.

LJA TA05B (36:03)

परा परापरा चेयमपरा च सदोदिता।

parā parāparā ceyamaparā ca sadoditā /25a

And these also take the formation of *parā*, *parāparā*, and *aparā śakti* (supreme energy, and medium energy, and inferior energy of God consciousness). So, *prāṇa*, *apāna*, and *samāna* are transformed first in *pramātṛ*, *pramāṇa*, and *prameya*, and then…

SCHOLAR: *Prāṇa*, *apāna*, *udāna*?

SWAMIJI: *Samāna* or *udāna*, they are one. From my point of view, they are one.

SCHOLAR: *Nimīlana-unmīlana*.

SWAMIJI: Yes. And they get transformed in the shape or *pramātṛ bhāva*, *pramāṇa bhāva*, and *prameya bhāva*, and those three states get transformation in *parā*, *parāparā*, and *aparā*, hence *śāmbhavopāya* is there, the trance of *śāmbhavopāya* shines.

SCHOLAR: So here we are in *śakti cakra* and we are dealing with *pramāṇa*, *prameya*, and *pramātṛ*.

SWAMIJI: Yes.

SCHOLAR: And then here we are moving into *śāmbhava avasthā*.

SWAMIJI: *Śāmbhava avasthā*, yes.[29]

LJA TA05B (37:06)

सृष्टिसंस्थितिसंहारैस्तासां प्रत्येकतस्त्रिधा ॥ २५ ॥

sṛṣṭisaṁsthitisaṁhāraistāsāṁ pratyekatastridhā //25//

Then, after the *śāmbhava* state, when he gets entry in the *śāmbhava* state, then these three states come in the field of the external world also, in *sṛṣṭi*, *sthiti*, and *saṁhāra* (in creation, protection, and *saṁhāra*), and he handles *śāktopāya*, *śāktopāya* in the external world. From *śāmbhavopāya* he handles *śāktopāya* in the external world. In *śāktopāya*, he sees that he is the creator, he is the protector, and he is the destroyer. No other energy is doing that except…

SCHOLAR: *Ahaṁ parāmarśa*.

SWAMIJI: Yes. And:

LJA TA05B (37:52)

चतुर्थं चानवच्छिन्नं रूपमासामकल्पितम् ।

caturthaṁ cānavacchinnaṁ rūpamāsāmakalpitam /26a

And the yogi finds the fourth state of *anākhya bhāva* in each and every action of creation, protection, and destruction. In creation, protection, and destruction, he sees, while creating he runs to *anākṣa*, while protecting he runs to *anākṣa bhāva* (the state of *anākṣa*), and while destroying he runs to the *anākhya* state. So the *anākhya* state shines in each and every action to such a yogi.

JOHN: So everything carries him to that…

SWAMIJI: Yes, *anākhya*.

29. *Śāmbhava avasthā* is the state of *śāmbhavopāya*.

SCHOLAR: So this is completely transparent *unmīlana* in all his movements.

SWAMIJI: Yes, it is *unmīlana*, yes.[30]

LJA TA05B (38:37)

एवं द्वादश ता देव्यः सूर्यबिम्बवदास्थिताः ॥ २६ ॥
एकैकमासां वह्न्यर्कसोमतच्छान्तिभासनम् ।

evaṁ dvādaśa tā devyaḥ sūryabimbavadāsthitāḥ //26//
ekaikamāsāṁ vahnyarkasomatacchāntibhāsanam /

So these *parā*, *parāparā*, and *aparā* energies of Lord Śiva are found established in twelve states just like the twelve discs of the sun, the twelve rounds of the sun. The discs: five organs of action, five organs of cognition, and mind, and *buddhi* (intellect). These are twelve discs, because the organic world is said to be the world of suns. There are twelve suns. S-u-n, not s-o-n. Because *ekaikamāsāṁ vahni-arka-soma-tat-śānti-bhāsanam*, in these three states (*parā*, *parāparā*, and *aparā*) you find, he finds, the yogi finds that there is fire (*vahni*), there is *arka* (sun), there is *soma* (moon), and there is *anākhya*–in each! In *parā* you find four, in *parāparā* he finds four states, and in *aparā* also he finds four states. So four into three make twelve states

30. "*Anākhya* is found when that *saṁhṛti* (dissolution) is over and the *sṛṣṭi* (creation) of the other object has not begun yet. There is *anākhya*. That is *anākhya*." TĀ 4.145. "You have to find that real transcendental state of nothingness in each and every act. It is why it is called *anākhya cakra*. It is more than *turya*." TĀ 4.142-143. "*Unmīlana samādhi* is experienced in *turyātīta* and *nimīlana samādhi* is experienced in *turya*. This is the difference between *turya* and *turyātīta*. *Nimīlana samādhi* means, absorption of universal consciousness, when universal consciousness is absorbed in your nature. That is *turya*. When universal consciousness is expanded everywhere, that is *turyātīta* (viz., *unmīlana*)." Swami Lakshmanjoo, *Tantrāloka* 10:288 (LJA archive). "The state of *cidānanda* is *turya* and *jagadānanda* is *turyātīta*." *Tantrāloka* 10.278 (LJA archive).

of God consciousness, which twelve states of God consciousness are explained in the previous *āhnika* in *śāktopāya* in Dvādaśa Kālī (the Twelve Kālīs). *Etadānuttaraṁ*...huh?

SCHOLAR: So it's not that he experiences twelve separate states, it's that for him *tattvam dvādaśāyate*.

SWAMIJI: *Dvādaśāyate*, yes.

SCHOLAR: Twelve, one hundred and forty-four, one hundred and forty-four times twelve infinitely.

SWAMIJI: Yes, it is an infinite *cakra*. *Etadānuttaraṁ cakraṁ hṛdayāt*...he will explain it now:

LJA TA05B (40:35)

एतदानुत्तरं चक्रं हृदयाच्चक्षुरादिभिः ॥२७॥
व्योमभिर्निःसरत्येव तत्तद्विषयगोचरे।

etadānuttaraṁ cakraṁ hṛdayāccakṣurādibhiḥ //27//
vyomabhirniḥsaratyeva tattadviṣayagocare /

This is *anuttara cakra*. *Anuttara cakra* is the supreme wheel of God consciousness. The supreme wheel of God consciousness is not situated in the supreme state of God consciousness only. It is situated in each and every act of the world–this supreme state of God consciousness. So, whatever he does, whatever this yogi does in the external world or in internal God consciousness, he is residing in *anuttara cakra*. It is *anuttara cakra* he is residing in. This whole universe becomes *anuttara cakra* for him, because this whole universe is the explanation of *anuttara cakra*, this is the commentary of *anuttara cakra*. And it is proceeding, it flows out *hṛdayāt cakṣur ādibhiḥ vyomabhiḥ niḥsaratyeva*, it goes out, it goes out always from this universal center of heart to the objective centers, *tat tat viṣaya gocare*, through the passages of organic *śakti*s, organic energies. From *cakṣu* (eyes), that *anuttara cakra* flows out from the heart to its object of form. And from the skin it flows out through the skin to the object of that *sparśa* (touch). And through the tongue it flows out to taste. And this whole flowing out in the external world is *anuttara cakra* for him. It is no less than *anuttara cakra*. And it flows out, it does not get entry afterwards, because entry and exit become one for him. There is no entry afterwards, there is no question of entering.

SCHOLAR: Yes, the pure state of *visarga*.

SWAMIJI: He has not to enter. He has *entered* in God consciousness when he has entered in the external world with this *anuttara cakra*.

JOHN: The question of practice becomes absurd for him.

SWAMIJI: Yes. No, there is no practice.

LJA TA05B (43:26)

seyaṁ kriyātmikā śaktiḥ śivasya paśuvartinī /
bandhayitrī svamārgasthā jñātā siddhyupapādikā // [31]

That active energy of the Lord [which] sentences him towards limitations, when he sentences him towards limitations, is said [to be] the energy that binds, binding energy. When this same energy is recognized fully in its real way, then this energy of action carries him to God consciousness forever, for good.[32] So there is nothing to be done. It is why he has said:

---

31. *Spanda Kārikā* 3.16 referenced in Jayaratha's commentary.

32. "This is the active energy of God consciousness that plays, that functions in this world, in this cycle of the worldly cycle and the spiritual cycle, both. In the worldly cycle it works, and in the spiritual cycle also it works. And in the spiritual cycle it works just to make Śiva transform into the individual *paśu bhāva*, just into the state of a beast, becoming a beast. He wants that Śiva should become a beast. The energies of God try to make Śiva as a beast by their own power. This is *śakti*, this is the powerful active energy of Lord Śiva. *Bandhayitrī*, so it gives bondage to that person, to that Śiva, [but] *svamārgasthā*, when you are fully attentive, when you are fully attentive and you don't listen to those energies, [when] you turn a deaf ear to those energies [that tell you], "No, do this meditation this way, this way it will work, this way it will work" (this is a friendly distraction, this also you should not allow, go on with your own point), and when you are *svamārgasthā*, you are attentive to one point only, don't listen, keep a deaf ear to all those outside activities of the energies, *jñātā siddhyupapādikā*, then you will rise in God consciousness, there is no fear." Swami Lakshmanjoo, *The Mystery of Vibrationless-Vibration in Kashmir Shaivism* (Lakshmanjoo Academy 2016).

LJA TA05B (44:19)

yena yena nibadhyante jantavo raudrakarmaṇā /
sopāyena tu tenaiva mucyante bhavabandhanāt // [33]

By which savage forbidden acts ignorant individuals get entangled, by these very acts some fortunate ones get liberated from repeated births and deaths–by these very actions. *Yena yena nibadhyante*, *yena yena raudra karmaṇā*, *jantavo nibadhyante*, by which savage forbidden acts, *jantavaḥ*, these ignorant people, *nibadhyante*, are entangled in the wheel of repeated births and deaths, by these very actions, some fortunate persons, *sopāyena tu tenaiva mucyante bhavabandhanāt*, they get freedom from the repeated births and deaths–by these very actions!

LJA TA05B (45:12)

तच्चक्रभाभिस्तत्रार्थे सृष्टिस्थितिलयक्रमात् ॥ २८ ॥
सोमसूर्याग्निभासात्म रूपं समवतिष्ठते ।

taccakrabhābhistatrārthe sṛṣṭisthitilayakramāt //28//
somasūryāgnibhāsātma rūpaṁ samavatiṣṭhate /

Not only in the organic field, in the objective also he finds the same proceeding act, the same process. The same process shines for him in the objective field also, not only in the organic world. The organic world is that of the organs. The objective world is in each and every object of the world.

SCHOLAR: *Viṣayam ucyate.*

SWAMIJI: That is *viṣaya.*

SCHOLAR: *Tat tat viṣayam ucyate.*[34]

SWAMIJI: Yes. (Verse repeated) In this objective field also, that yogi finds that he is the creator of this objective world, he is the protector of

33. *Hevajra Tantra* II.2.50 referenced in Jayaratha's commentary.

34. Anything (*tat tat*) apprehended (*ucyate*) by the sensual organs (*viṣaya*).

the objective world, and he is the destroyer, and he is the concealer of the objective world, and he is the revealer of the objective world. *Sṛṣṭi*, *sthiti*, *saṁhāra*, *pidhāna* and *anugraha*, he does all these five acts in this objective world.

Evaṁ śabdādiviṣaye...it is not only in *rūpa*, it is not only in maintaining awareness in *rūpa*, in formations. In *śabda* (sound) also, while talking also he gets entry in that God consciousness, and through these five aspects of five acts: *sṛṣṭi*, *sthiti*, *saṁhāra*, *pidhāna* and *anugraha* (creation, protection, destruction, concealing and revealing).

JOHN: This is the most difficult way, no? Through this...

SWAMIJI: This is most difficult for him. This is most difficult, not for him, for us it is difficult–not for such a man who has entered to this extreme state of God consciousness.

LJA TA05B (47:22)

एवं शब्दादिविषये श्रोत्रादिव्योमवर्त्मना ॥ २९ ॥

evaṁ śabdādiviṣaye śrotrādivyomavartmanā //29//

In these objective worlds of *śabdas* (sounds), by the path of *śrotra ādi vyomavartmanā*, by the path of this air...

चक्रेणानेन पतता तादात्म्यं परिभावयेत्।

cakreṇānena patatā tādātmyaṁ paribhāvayet /30a

...he finds the oneness of God consciousness in words also. "This case of specks," when he hears this sound, "This is the case of specks," by this sound also he gets entry in that God consciousness, by hearing this sound also he gets entry in God consciousness. He has not to force his organic world to enter in God consciousness through this object. No. It is automatic. It becomes automatic for him to get entry in God consciousness by hearing a word, by just touching some other person, *bas*, just smelling–[by] *śabda*, *sparśa*, *rūpa*, *rasa* and *gandha*.

SCHOLAR: But this also to the whole *puryaṣṭaka*? Also to *mana*, *buddhi* and *ahaṁkāra* as well. Any sensation in his internal organs also.

SWAMIJI: Yes, any sensation, yes.

JOHN: So everything carries this man to God consciousness, there's nothing that doesn't carry him.

SWAMIJI: Yes, because of these five acts, five great acts of God: *sṛṣṭi*, *sthiti*, *saṁhāra*, *pidhāna* and *anugraha*.

SCHOLAR: But he has hidden in this passage the *vāha krama*.[35]

SWAMIJI: Yes, it is hidden.

LJA TA05B (48:58)

अनेन क्रमयोगेन यत्र यत्र पतत्यदः ॥ ३० ॥
चक्रं सर्वात्मकं तत्तत्सार्वभौममहीशवत्।

anena kramayogena yatra yatra patatyadaḥ //30//
cakraṁ sarvātmakaṁ tattatsārvabhaumamahīśavat /
(not recited or translated)

इत्थं विश्वाध्वपटलमयत्नेनैव लीयते ॥ ३१ ॥
भैरवीयमहाचक्रे संवित्तिपरिवारिते।

itthaṁ viśvādhvapaṭalamayatnenaiva līyate //31//
bhairavīyamahācakre saṁvittiparivārite /

By this way of meditation, by this way of automatic meditation, the multitude of the whole universe of differentiations, *ayatnenaiva līyate*, effortlessly melts away in *bhairavīya mahā cakre*, in the supreme great wheel of God consciousness, who is surrounded by *saṁvitti*, who is surrounded by the multitude of all organs and all objects.

35. The manner or process (*krama*) by which the senses carry (*vāha*) the yogi to the state of God consciousness.

SCHOLAR: All knowers and all objects.

SWAMIJI: All knowers, yes. *Bas.* To which point he has reached, this is supreme *dhyāna.*

LJA TA05B (49:49)

Discussion:

This is the explaining way of Abhinavagupta. He wants to explain the best thing first, and then makes him (the *sadhāka*) move down by-and-by.

SCHOLAR: So in this way he doesn't follow *Mālinīvijaya.*

SWAMIJI: No (affirmative).

SCHOLAR: He goes the opposite way to *Mālinīvijaya Tantra.*

SWAMIJI: Yes. Because his theory of understanding is that you should put the first-class way first, and if it is fortunately grasped by your disciple, well and good. If it is not grasped, then you toss him down, a little down, and teach him some inferior way. And when he does not grasp that also, then you toss him down [further]. Because he says: *acintyo hi śaktipāta krama*, the way of *śaktipāta*, *anugraha* (grace), is *acintya*, you can't understand the way of Lord Śiva. There may be *śaktipāta* in that soul, [so] why to produce the inferior way first? So you must produce the first-class way first. He may hold it and then he will shine just like the midday sun.

DEVOTEE: These are his own experiences–Abhinavagupta's?

SWAMIJI: Huh?

DEVOTEE: He was himself a yogi–Abhinavagupta?

SWAMIJI: Yes, yes, he was.

SCHOLAR: He was Bhairava!

SWAMIJI: (laughs) He was more than a yogi, more than Lord Śiva.

SCHOLAR: He says at the end: "*Śiva niśāmaya.*"[36]

JOHN: In this *buddhi dhyāna*, this is meditation with awareness. And in the introduction, in the first *āhnika*, you just differentiated…

SWAMIJI: *Śiva niśamaya. Kya gupśa "niśamaya"*?

DEVOTEE: Huh?

---

36. *Tantrāloka* 37.85.

SWAMIJI: "*Śiva niśamaya*! O Lord Śiva, just understand my teaching, understand my teaching."

DEVOTEE: So he is His guru?

SWAMIJI: Huh?

DEVOTEE: Is he His guru?

SWAMIJI: So he has become the master of Lord Śiva.

SCHOLAR: *Pratarūpa carācara.*

SWAMIJI: Yes. "Because it is the explanation of Your own nature..."

SCHOLAR: Who else will understand?

SWAMIJI: "...nobody will understand except You–this explanation of mine." *Śiva ko-...pukarta*, in the end of this book.

SCHOLAR: So this *buddhi dhyānaṁ*, this *anuttara dhyānaṁ*, which he has introduced here, is hidden in *prāṇa uccāra...*

SWAMIJI: Yes.

SCHOLAR:...as its heart.

SWAMIJI: Yes.

JOHN: This *buddhi dhyāna* you said differs from *dhyāna* without awareness. In the first *āhnika*, you said this is intellectual meditation, you said, and then you clarified that by saying it's meditation with awareness.

SWAMIJI: Yes.

JOHN: And then you said that of meditation without awareness has some fruit. What is meditation without awareness? Just *japa*, just repeating mantras or something?

SWAMIJI: Yes.

JOHN: It is mechanical-like, mechanical going on.

SWAMIJI: Yes, it is just routine-like then. That routine-like *dhyāna* is no use.

SCHOLAR: Like in these *paddhati*s (rituals) and priests reciting.

SWAMIJI: Yes. Like this (Swamiji breathes in and out). There must be awareness! You must find out the point. You may do it for centuries with no result. There must be awareness in your brain to hold that subjective consciousness. Once you have held this subjective consciousness, nothing is to be done. Then you will move to *śāktopāya*, and then to *śāmbhavopāya*, and then to *anupāya*, and then reside in your own nature. It is why all my disciples take a long period of this process of doing *abhyāsa* (meditation). *Hatāsh na hona chahiye* (don't be discouraged). This is also the way, this is the way you have to tread. This is a journey, a long journey. But once it is held, it is held in a flash.

It is not held successively–never! It will never come in your experience successively. When it is experienced, it is experienced in a flash, or not at all. Just dive in, *bas*, you are there.

SCHOLAR: So when people talk of continuity, it's not that state.

SWAMIJI: Huh?

SCHOLAR: When people talk of *samādhi* in continuity, they are speaking of some lower state of consciousness.

SWAMIJI: Yes. That is only the inferior way of *dhyāna*, not *samādhi* even. *Samādhi* does not last for more than twenty minutes in all.

SCHOLAR: Otherwise you are finished.

SWAMIJI: Yes, after twenty minutes your body…

SCHOLAR: *Katham*.

SWAMIJI:…*katham* (finished), you are dead. The body cannot tolerate that flavor of that God consciousness for more than twenty minutes. Only twenty minutes is the limit. Once you get entry in God consciousness for twenty minutes in continuation, think that your body is dead, you are no more existing in this universe, you have become one with that God consciousness.

JOHN: But what about that person in *anupāya*? He's in that God consciousness in continuity always.

SWAMIJI: Huh?

JOHN: That person existing in *anupāya*, he's in that God consciousness in continuity always. In *anupāya*…

SWAMIJI: *Anupāya*, yes.

JOHN: So why doesn't he leave his body? He stays with that God consciousness, he never loses that God consciousness.

SWAMIJI: Who?

JOHN: This person in *anupāya*.

SWAMIJI: No, he also has to leave his physical frame. If there is some defect in him, in his brain, [e.g., the desire] to teach others, then he has not become one with that God consciousness exactly.

SCHOLAR: Even though he was residing in *anupāya*. Even though he experiences that touch without means.

SWAMIJI: Yes. Because this sense of thinking that, "I have to teach others, I want to uplift others," means that there is sensation in his brain that somebody is ignorant: "Somebody is ignorant, I am not ignorant; I am realized and somebody is not realized." So there is a difference. When you get real entry in that God consciousness, you find that everybody is realized, that there is nothing to be done in this universe, so you leave this physical frame at once. From his point of view, everybody is realized.

DEVOTEE: No differentiated consciousness.

SWAMIJI: If this differentiated consciousness is living there, then there is that limitation, and that limitation makes you live in the body after your realization also.

JOHN: So a man in *anupāya* can also experience *samādhi* then also? He also can have…?

SWAMIJI: Yes, he can help. He can help if he is not well-established in that *samādhi*.

SCHOLAR: So Swamiji, when a master is enlightened, and after his physical death, how can he go on initiating and guiding his disciples?

SWAMIJI: Huh?

SCHOLAR: If the master, the Shaivite master can initiate and guide his disciples after his physical death, how can that be the case?

SWAMIJI: Just at the point of leaving the body. Have you gone through the Pratyabhijñā Darśana (The Doctrine of Recognition)?

SCHOLAR: Yes.

SWAMIJI: You will see there Abhinavagupta has related "*kathañcidāsādya*" in the very first explanation of that book. *Kathañcidāsādya*, this first *sūtra* of Utpaladeva, he commentates [upon] that, and in that commentary he has said: *Kathañcidāsādya janasyāpyupakāramicchan*, I have found the reality, I have experienced the reality of God consciousness and I want to uplift, enlighten others also at the same moment! *Anyathā katham āsādanatāratamyaprāptau paropadeśaḥ śakyakriyā*, because after two or three hours he will be no more existing in his body. So it is the question of those three hours of gap in which he can help [others].[37]

LJA TA05B (59:35) end
LJA TA05C (00:00) start

37. Abhinavagupta wrote two commentaries on Utpaladeva's *Īśvara Pratyabhijñā Kārikā*.

The conclusion of this *dhyāna* is that you have to fix your mind on that innermost center of the heart, universal heart, and then when it vibrates–it does not vibrate only inside, it vibrates outside also–and when it begins to vibrate outside, then you travel from *āṇavopāya* to *śāktopāya* to *śāmbhavopāya* and so on. This is the process of this supreme meditation.

JOHN: Vibration means?

SWAMIJI: Vibration of that bliss, because really the state of bliss is not stable.

JOHN: Smooth.

SWAMIJI: It is not stable.

SCHOLAR: *Śānta.*

SWAMIJI: It is not *śānta* (appeased). It is always *udita* (rising). It is filled with vibrations. Just like...it is why it is nominated as *spanda* also. Because *samādhi* explained in our Shaivism is not one-pointed. It is universal-pointed! It vibrates in each and every part and parcel of the world. This is the real *samādhi*. And he has to travel, the *sādhaka* who has great capacity of doing this *dhyāna*, he has to travel from the innermost center of the heart to the universal heart by-and-by. So he travels from the innermost center to the external universal center. And from the innermost center to the external universal center he has to travel from *āṇavopāya* to *śāktopāya*, and from *śāktopāya* to *śāmbhavopāya*. And when *śāmbhavopāya* ends there, this is the real way of destroying and discarding away all these differentiated perceptions of the universe, no *bheda* (duality) remains afterwards, no difference between individual and universal being exists.

So he has already said that, effortlessly by this process, *viśvādhvapaṭalam ayatnenaiva līyate* (verse 31), this multitude of the whole universe of differentiated perceptions effortlessly melts away in that supreme *cakra*, in that supreme great *cakra* of consciousness. Because it is really called...it is not *saṁvit udaya*, it is not the rise of consciousness, it is the rise of *saṁvit cakra*, the multitude of *saṁvit* (consciousness). It is why omnipresence and all-pervading-ness shine there. He can observe, Lord Śiva can observe each and every act of the world, inside and outside. Not one-by-one, not in a successive way, but simultaneously he observes everything what is happening in this world.

SCHOLAR: *Akramakrama kriyā.*[38]

SWAMIJI: Yes. And then, when this differentiated perception of the universe melts away, then the next *śloka* he begins to explain the second process. *Tataḥ saṁskāramātreṇa*…this is the *śloka* we have to read.

LJA TA05C (04:14)

ततः संस्कारमात्रेण विश्वस्यापि परिक्षये ॥ ३२ ॥
स्वात्मोच्छलत्तया भ्राम्यच्चक्रं सञ्चिन्तयेन्महत्।

tataḥ saṁskāramātreṇa viśvasyapi parikṣaye //32//
svātmocchalattayā bhrāmyaccakraṁ sañcintayenmahat /

When these differentiated universal perceptions are over, then only traces of those differentiated perceptions remain still vibrating, vibrating from inside. He feels, the *sādhaka* (aspirant) feels that there are some vibrations of differentiated perceptions, not living differentiated perceptions, only vibrations remain there. And those vibrations also are to be destroyed. So long, up to this point also, it is an internal process, it is not an external process. The external automatic process, it is an automatic process, you have not to function it. It functions by itself. *Tataḥ saṁskāra mātreṇa*, when those traces also are destroyed (traces of the differentiated universe, universal perceptions), *svātma ucchalattayā bhrāmyat cakraṁ sañcintayet*, then it is obviously, it can be understood, that there are no vibrations now left because all differentiated perceptions are over along with their traces. Then there is nothing what is vibrating. But vibration is still there moving, *svātma ucchalattayā*, the vibrations from the Self of God consciousness is vibrating still! It is vibrating still from inside to inside. It is only filled with vibrations. Vibrations…you know what vibrates there? Vibrates there the bliss, what you feel in sexual intercourse, and that bliss you can multiply…

"Multiply" is correct?

JOHN: Aha, multiply.

38. The mere appearance of successive action.

SWAMIJI:...multiply with billions and millions times to strengthen that blissful state. And that blissful state vibrates inside. That is *svātma ucchalattayā bhrāmyat cakraṁ sañcintayet mahat*. Then he must observe and understand that that *cakra* is vibrating in his own nature and directed to his own nature. That is the vibrating point of that God consciousness. And this is a great *cakra*. This is called a great *cakra* where there are no traces of differentiated perceptions found there. Only this vibrating force vibrates from inside. And that vibration makes the *sādhaka* filled with that joy of bliss, that sexual bliss. It is universal sexual bliss.

LJA TA05C (07:30)

ततस्तद्दाह्यविलयात् तत्संस्कारपरिक्षयात्॥ ३३ ॥
प्रशाम्यद्भावयेच्चक्रं ततः शान्तं ततः शमम्।

tatastaddāhyavilayāt tatsaṁskāraparikṣayāt //33//
praśāmyadbhāvayeccakraṁ tataḥ śāntaṁ tataḥ śamam /

Then *tat dāhya avilayāt*, when that *dāhya* (*dāhya* means, that which is to be destroyed),...

What is to be destroyed there? Those differentiated perceptions.

...those differentiated perceptions were to be destroyed and those have been destroyed, and *tat saṁskāra parikṣayāt*, and traces of those differentiated perceptions are also over, then one should find out there *praśāmyat bhāvayet cakraṁ*, this *cakra*, what is vibrating from inside, inside the state of God consciousness, it is *praśāmyat* (*praśāmyat* means, it is peaceful), it is peacefully vibrating. *Tataḥ śāntam tataḥ śamam*, then it happens, there are two states: one is *śānta*, one is *śama*. *Śānta* means, vibrating from inside to outside. *Śama* means, vibrating in inside and resting in inside. Vibrating from inside to outside is *śānta cakra*, and vibrating inside and resting inside is *śama cakra*. These two *cakra*s are found there filled with vibrations. So it seems it will go out again, this will vibrate in the whole universe again. That *svarūpa*, that sexual universal bliss, will vibrate again outside in the universe. It is automatic. And this vibration takes place by itself. You have to observe, the *sādhaka* has to observe there what is going on.

LJA TA05C (09:29)

अनेन ध्यानयोगेन विश्वं चक्रे विलीयते ॥ ३४ ॥
तत्संविदि ततः संविद्विलीनार्थैव भासते ।

anena dhyānayogena viśvaṁ cakre vilīyate //34//
tatsaṁvidi tataḥ saṁvidvilīnārthaiva bhāsate /

By this process, by this way of *dhyāna*, by this way of supreme *dhyāna* as it is explained in *āṇavopāya*, the first *dhyāna*, this whole universe, in conclusion, rests in that *cakra*, in that vibrating force of God consciousness. *Tat saṁvidi*, and that vibrating force of consciousness rests in its own nature–*tat saṁvidi*. So, *tataḥ saṁvit vilīnārthaiva bhāsate*, so this vibrating consciousness shines there just to dissolve and destroy–not destroy–dissolve or digest these whole universal vibrations. These whole universal vibrations are digested in that. He feels that the whole universal force is there. It can be created at any moment he likes. This is the state of real God consciousness.

Because:

LJA TA05C (10:51)

चित्स्वाभाव्यात् ततो भूयः सृष्टिर्यच्चिन्महेश्वरी ॥ ३५ ॥

citsvābhāvyāt tato bhūyaḥ sṛṣṭiryaccinmaheśvarī //35//

Cit, this is the nature of that God consciousness that *bhūyaḥ sṛṣṭiryat-*, that it vibrates again outside in the universe. When it is completely filled with that *saṁvit cakra*, the vibrating wheel of God consciousness, when it is...

SCHOLAR: In *śama* state.

SWAMIJI:...in *śama* state, then it goes again *udita*, it rises. Because this is the nature of God to rest inside and outside. But this process is automatic. This will be united with that *krama mudrā*, you know.[39]

---

39. "And then, by the will and knowledge and action of Parabhairava, it is taken again in the objective field and created in the universe. So, take rest in that supreme God consciousness, take it out in universe, and take it in God consciousness again, and then take it out for good in the universal state. This is the state of *bhukti* (enjoyment) and *mukti* (liberation), this is the state of *krama mudrā* [as] related, explained in our Shaivism. You have not to take this activity of the universe in God consciousness. You have to take it in first, and take it out also. And after taking it out, you have to take it again in, and then take it out, and then you see that outside flow is one with that God consciousness, universal God consciousness. It becomes one–divine! You become filled with divinity of God consciousness. He has touched the state of *krama mudrā* here, from *nimīlinā* to *unmīlinā*, from *unmīlinā* to *nimīlinā*, from *nimīlinā* to *unmīlinā* again." *Parātrīmśikā Laghvṛtti* (LJA archive) "*Unmilina samādhi* is experienced in *turyātīta*, and *nimilina samādhi* is experienced in *turya*; this is the difference between *turya* and *turyātīta*. In *turya* you are in *nimilina samādhi*. *Nimilina samādhi* means, absorption of universal consciousness; when universal consciousness is absorbed in your nature, that is *turya*. When universal consciousness is expanded everywhere, that is *turyātīta*. This is the difference between *nimilina* and *unmilina*. And that is *jagadānanda*; *unmilina* is *jagadānanda*, *nimilina* is *cidānanda*–this is the difference. This is the connecting rod, *krama mudrā* is the connecting rod, avenue. You can't get contact from *turya* to *turyātīta* unless *krama mudrā* is in-between. *Krama mudrā* will carry you there." *Tantrāloka* 10.287-288 (LJA archive) "All of the states of *turya* from *nijānanda* to *cidānanda* comprise the various phases of *nimīlana samādhi*. *Nimīlana samādhi* is internal subjective *samādhi*. In your moving through these six states of *turya*, this *samādhi* becomes ever more firm. With the occurrence of *krama mudrā*, *nimīlana samādhi* is transformed into *unmīlana samādhi*, which then becomes predominant. This is that state of extroverted *samādhi*, where you experience the state of *samādhi* at the same time you are experiencing the objective world. And when *unmīlana samādhi* becomes fixed and permanent, this is the state of *jagadānanda*." *Kashmir Shaivism–Secret Supreme*, "The Seven States of Turya." "And this movement of going in and out and vice versa takes the position by the force of *samāveśa* (trance), not by the effort of the yogi. [Moving from] outside and inside is just to get this understanding that outside and inside are not different aspects, just only one. The one who experiences this state of *samāveśa*, that yogi experiences that this whole universe melts into nothingness in that great ether (great void) of God consciousness. Then when he

LJA TA05C (11:43)

एवं प्रतिक्षणं विश्वं स्वसंविदि विलापयन्।
विसृजंश्च ततो भूयः शश्वद्भैरवतां व्रजेत्॥ ३६ ॥

evaṁ pratikṣaṇaṁ viśvaṁ svasaṁvidi vilāpayan /
viśṛjaṁśca tato bhūyaḥ śaśvadbhairavatāṁ vrajet //36//

In this way (*evaṁ*, in this way), *pratikṣaṇaṁ*, in each and every moment, in one second it vibrates inside, the next second it vibrates outside, the third second it vibrates again inside, the fourth second it vibrates again outside, in the same way, it vibrates in and out constantly in continuity. And this vibration is automatic. It is meant for vibrating this whole universe in one point.

JOHN: In one point means?

SWAMIJI: One point means…

---

strives to come out from that state, it is very difficult for him to come out. It is very difficult for us to go in and, in the same way, for that yogi, it is very difficult to come out." *Kuṇḍalinī Vijñāna Rahasyam* (LJA archive) "After *krama mudrā* is over, it has functioned properly and you are established in *krama mudrā*, then you have to put *udyoga*, the rise of *udyoga* (effort). By will you can get up from your *āsana* and try to step onwards for going outside in the compound, or taking meals, etcetera. You have to put that will, forced will. If you don't put that forced will, that *jagadānanda* will vanish." *Tantrāloka* 5.63 (LJA archive) "When you are established in the process of *krama mudrā*, then you experience that ecstasy in action. When you eat, you are in that bliss. When you talk, you are in that bliss. When you walk, you are in that bliss. Whatever you do, you remain in that Universal state. This is the state of *jīvanmukti*, liberated in life. This state is experienced, not by ordinary yogins, but only by great yogins. This is the real state of *cit kuṇḍalinī*. In the actual rise of *cit kuṇḍalinī*, you will only get a glimpse of it and then come out. The full rise of *cit kuṇḍalinī* takes place only by the grace of your master and by the grace of your own strength of awareness. The experience of establishing the full rise of *cit kuṇḍalinī* through the process of *krama mudrā* can take place in one day, one life, or one hundred lifetimes." *Kashmir Shaivism–The Secret Supreme* 17.120.

JOHN: In your own nature?

SWAMIJI:...your own nature, God consciousness, he feels only God consciousness everywhere in this movement also. *Evaṁ pratikṣaṇaṁ viśvaṁ svasaṁvidi vilāpayan, viśṛjaṁśca*, when these universal differentiated perceptions are dissolved, digested in one's own vibrating consciousness, and then are again created from that vibrating consciousness, what happens then? *Tato bhūyaḥ śaśvat bhairavatāṁ vrajet*, then he becomes established in the state of complete Bhairava. He becomes Bhairava then. There is no difference between Lord Śiva and that *sādhaka*.

Now he concludes how he vibrates in this whole universe:

LJA TA05C (13:26)

एवं त्रिशूलात् प्रभृति चतुष्पञ्चारकक्रमात्।
पञ्चाशदरपर्यन्तं चक्रं योगी विभावयेत्॥ ३७॥
चतुष्षष्टिशतारं वा सहस्रारमथापि वा।
असङ्ख्यारसहस्रं वा चक्रं ध्यायेदनन्यधीः॥ ३८॥

evaṁ triśūlāt prabhṛti catuṣpañcārakakramāt /
pañcāśadaraparyantaṁ cakraṁ yogī vibhāvayet //37//
catuṣṣaṣṭiśatāraṁ vā sahasrāramathāpi vā /
asaṅkhyārasahasraṁ vā cakraṁ dhyāyedananyadhīḥ //38//

So here, the *sādhaka* must remain at the top of awareness. That awareness should not be interfered by any other foreign movement. He has to remain absolutely aware. This way, *triśūlāt prabhṛti*, from *triśūla cakra* (*triśūla cakra* means, *pramātṛ cakra*, *pramāṇa cakra* and *prameya cakra*), he must find out, he must vibrate first in *pramātṛ cakra*, *pramāṇa cakra* and *prameya cakra*, he must infuse this vibrating God consciousness.

You know what is the formation of vibrating God consciousness? I have told you just now. It is absolutely multiplied with millions and billions times that sexual bliss. And that sexual bliss must be infused

–I have no words to [express this]–infused in these three *bhāva*s, in these three states (subjective state, cognitive state and objective state).

Then *catuṣ pañcāraka kramāt*–not only in that–then in fourfold *cakra* also: in wakefulness, in dreaming state, in dreamless state, and in *turya* also he must vibrate this state. And *pañcāraka kramāt*, fivefold *krama* is in fivefold actions–*sṛṣṭi*, *sthiti*, *saṁhāra*, *pidhāna* and *anugraha* (creation, protection, destruction, concealing and revealing)–in these five states also he must vibrate this very state of God consciousness. And *pañcāśat araparyantam*–not only in that–he must infuse this vibration of God consciousness in all the letters, all these…

SCHOLAR: *Mātṛkā cakra.*

SWAMIJI: *Mātṛkā cakra. Pañca śat araparyantam cakram yogī vibhāvayet*–not only in that–*catuḥ ṣaṣṭi śatāram vā*, then he must vibrate this in each and every energy of God consciousness. For instance, there are eight energies, eight energies are [multiplied by] eight energies each. Eight into eight means *catuḥ ṣaṣṭi*.

JOHN: Sixty-four.

SWAMIJI: Sixty-four. In those sixty-four energies he must infuse this vibrating force. Not only in sixty-four, *śatāraṁ vā*, in *śatāra*, in the hundredfold *cakra*. The hundredfold *cakra* is all those *pati pramātā cakra*s. There are one hundred *rudra*s. In *rudra*s also he must infuse that vibrating force of God consciousness. So, he will include the whole universe in his own nature. He has to include, he has to include this whole universe in his own vibrating Self. Unless it is included, he is not exactly Lord Śiva. So he has to become Lord Śiva. *Sahasrāram athāpi vā*, and he has to infuse this vibrating force in the thousand petal state of *brahmarandhra*. In *brahmarandhra* also he must vibrate this God consciousness, this vibrating force of God consciousness. Not only in that, *asaṅkhyāra sahasraṁ vā cakraṁ dhyāyet ananyadhīḥ*, he must infuse this–in conclusion–he must infuse this vibrating force in the whole universe (*asaṅkhyāra sahasraṁ vā*, where there is no number).

SCHOLAR: So, Jayaratha's interpretation of this section is at fault since he says: *na kevalam etadeva cakraṁ yoginā dhyeyaṁ yāvaccakrāntarāṇyapi*. He takes these as different processes of *dhyāna* from…

SWAMIJI: He has not exactly understood as understood by Abhinavagupta himself (laughs).

SCHOLAR: By your master. So, this *dhyāyet* here has taken to…

SWAMIJI: *Dhyāyet*, he was experienced. *Dhyāyet* means, experienced, he must experience this. *Dhyāyet* does not mean he has to meditate on that.

SCHOLAR: But Jayaratha has taken that to mean separate *buddhi dhyānam*.

SWAMIJI: As *dhyāyet*, yes.

SCHOLAR: So he says, "*ananyadhīḥ*[40]..."

SWAMIJI: Because it was *buddhi dhyāna* quoted by Abhinavagupta, so he has misunderstood it that it is exactly *buddhi dhyāna*, but it is not *buddhi dhyāna*.

SCHOLAR: Even though he says "*ananyadhī*" just to mislead.

SWAMIJI: Yes. But why to vibrate this universal God consciousness in this whole universe? Not only in this world, in one hundred and eighteen worlds he has to vibrate it and he has to *see* that "I am everywhere." So he observes everything, nothing is hidden to him, nothing is secret to him. He witnesses each and every act of the world. This is the position of Lord Śiva. You can't escape from his witnessing. He witnesses each and every act what you do.

LJA TA05C (19:14)

संविन्नाथस्य महतो देवस्योल्लासिसंविदः ।
नैवास्ति काचित्कलना विश्वशक्तेर्महेशितुः ॥ ३९ ॥

saṁvinnāthasya mahato devasyollāsisaṁvidaḥ /
naivāsti kācitkalanā viśvaśaktermaheśituḥ //39//

Saṁvit nātha, the Lord who is the Lord of consciousness, *mahato devasya*, who is the great Lord, great *devatā*, *ullāsi saṁvidaḥ*, whose consciousness is always vibrating (*ullāsi saṁvidaḥ*, it is *ṣaṣṭī*, the possessive case), *naivāsti kācit kalanā*, there is no limit to him because he has got universal energies, he is the possessor of universal energies and he is the master of the universe.

It is also said in the *Śrī Maṅgala Śāstra*, *Maṅgala Tantra*:

40. Without any other outward thoughts.

LJA TA05C (20:02)

शक्तयोऽस्य जगत् कृत्स्नं शक्तिमांस्तु महेश्वरः।
इति माङ्गलशास्त्रे तु श्रीश्रीकण्ठो न्यरूपयत्॥ ४० ॥

śaktayo'sya jagat kṛtsnaṁ śaktimāṁstu maheśvaraḥ /
iti māṅgalaśāstre tu śrī śrīkaṇṭho nyarūpayat //40//
(not recited in full)

His energies are this whole universe, this whole universe made of one hundred and eighteen worlds are his energies, and the possessor is he. He is the possessor of all these energies. This is quoted in the *Maṅgala Śāstre* by Lord Śiva himself.

LJA TA05C (20:30)

इत्येतत् प्रथमोपायरूपं ध्यानं न्यरूपयत्।
श्रीशम्भुनाथो मे तुष्टस्तस्मै श्रीसुमतिप्रभुः ॥ ४१ ॥

ityetat prathomopāyarūpaṁ dhyānaṁ nyarūpayat /
śrīśaṁbhunātho me tuṣṭastasmai śrīsumatiprabhuḥ //41//

This way, this supreme great meditation was revealed to me by my master when my master was completely pleased with me. He was *tuṣṭa*,…

SCHOLAR: Satisfied, entirely satisfied.

SWAMIJI:…entirely satisfied, entirely pleased with me, when my master was fully satisfied with me. His name was Śambhunātha. And Śambhunātha also learned this way of meditation from his master whose name was Sumatinātha. And Sumatinātha was also satisfied when he revealed this way of meditation to my master.

LJA TA05C (21:27)

अनयैव दिशान्यानि ध्यानान्यपि समाश्रयेत्।
अनुत्तरोपायधुरां यान्यायान्ति क्रमं विना॥४२॥

anayaiva diśānyāni dhyānānyapi samāśrayet /
anuttaropāyadhurāṁ yānyāyānti kramaṁ vinā //42//

In this way, in this way of process, this *sādhaka* must observe that other meditations, other inferior meditations are also sentenced–in this way he must meditate–that other meditation centers, other meditation processes, should be centered in this very meditation in the end. Because unless they are centered in this kind of meditation, all those other meditations are useless. So other meditations also, if he does breathing exercise, if he does meditation, if he does one-pointedness, if he does *cakita mudrā*[41], whatever he does, he must sentence all those processes to this point in the end. *Anuttara upāya dhurāṁ yāni āyānti kramaṁ vinā*, and those other meditations also, the processes of other meditations also are, in the end, they get entry in this kind of meditation. And this was explained to me by my master when he was absolutely satisfied, entirely satisfied with me. And to him also it was revealed by his master when he was satisfied with him.

JOHN: So this is the supreme meditation in *āṇavopāya*–this?

SWAMIJI: And this supreme meditation carries you…you know where?

JOHN: Quickly to *śāmbhavopāya*…

SWAMIJI: Not only *śāmbhavopāya*…

JOHN: To *anupāya*.

SWAMIJI:…to *anupāya*!

JOHN: Through *krama mudrā*.

SWAMIJI: Yes. The 43rd *śloka*:

---

41. "*Cakita mudrā* is the pose of astonishment. Actually this is Bhairavī *mudrā*. Because you do not breathe in and out. This is Bhairavī *mudrā*. Your eyes are wide open. Your mouth is open. You don't breathe." *Vijñāna Bhairava* (From a discussion on *Dhāraṇā* 54).

LJA TA05C (23:21)

Prāṇa Tattva Samuccāra
The Recitation of Breath

अथ प्राणस्य या वृत्तिः प्राणनाद्या निरूपिता।
तदुपायतया ब्रूमोऽनुत्तरप्रविकासनम्॥ ४३॥

atha prāṇasya yā vṛttiḥ prāṇanādyā nirūpitā /
tadupāyatayā brūmo'nuttarapravikāsanam //43//

Now, the *vṛtti* of *prāṇa*, the operating process of *prāṇa*, which is not only *prāṇa*, *prāṇanādyā nirūpitā*, which has to move to the extent of *prāṇana*, the state of *prāṇana*. *Prāṇa* must travel in such a way that it resides and is sentenced and resides in the state of *prāṇana*.[42]

SCHOLAR: *Prāṇanādyā*: *prāṇana*, *apānana*, etcetera?

SWAMIJI: *Ādyāḥ*. *Ādyāḥ padena*: *apānana*, *samānana*, *udānana* and *vyānana*.[43] It is not explained by Jayaratha in his commentary, so I had to explain it myself. He could not understand the reality of Abhinavagupta.

Tat upāyatayā brūmaḥ, that we will explain in putting forth the application of this process, *anuttara pravikāsanam*, so that the supreme God consciousness is exposed, supreme God consciousness takes place.

SCHOLAR: The way that that takes place through the function of *prāṇa*, *prāṇa vṛtti*.

SWAMIJI: *Prāṇa*, *prāṇa uccāra*.

---

42. "*Prāṇana vṛtti* is that kind of state of breath which is not moving, without movement, breath without movement. [It is] *sāmānya spanda*, not *viśeṣa spanda*. Life, it is only life." *Tantrāloka* 6.6 (LJA archive)

43. As Swamiji will explain onwards in verse 49, "*Prāṇa vṛtti* travels to *prāṇana vṛtti*, *apāna vṛtti* travels to *apānana vṛtti*, *samāna vṛtti* travels to *samānana vṛtti*, *udāna vṛtti* travels to *udānana vṛtti*, and *vyāna vṛtti* has to travel to *vyānana vṛtti*."

LJA TA05C (25:02)

निजानन्दे प्रमात्रंशमात्रे हृदि पुरा स्थितः।
शून्यतामात्रविश्रान्तेर्निरानन्दं विभावयेत्॥ ४४॥

nijānande pramātraṁśamātre hṛdi purā sthitaḥ /
śūnyatāmātraviśrānternirānandaṁ vibhāvayet //44//

Now, at this present stage, we are not in any state of *ānanda* (bliss) here, and it is nominated as *nijānanda*. It is *nijānanda*. When you are *nijānanda*, centered in your own subjective consciousness with full awareness…for instance, you breathe in and out, in and out, in and out very slowly with great awareness, you have to breathe in, breathe out and concentrate on the junction. Breathing in and breathing out is the state residing in the objective world and the cognitive world.

SCHOLAR: *Sūrya-soma.*

SWAMIJI: *Sūrya-soma.*[44] But you have not to go to that extent. You have to concentrate on the junction. Between the two breaths there is a junction, an automatic junction, and that junction is called *pramātraṁśa mātra*, there is subjective consciousness residing there.

SCHOLAR: This is in both junctions, *dvādaśānte* and in *hṛdaye*?

SWAMIJI: Both, *dvādaśānte* and *hṛdaye*, outside and inside also. These two junctions are the seats of *pramātṛ* (subjectivity), when you are aware on that junction with each and every breath. That is *pramātraṁśa mātre*. And that awareness should be functioned in your heart. That is the real heart. The heart is not only the center of the [physical] heart. There are three centers for the heart. One center is exactly the heart, this second center is the throat (*kaṇṭha*), and the third center is between the two eyebrows. These are the three centers for the heart where you have to concentrate on *pramātṛ bhāva*, subjective consciousness, and that subjective consciousness should take place between the two breaths.

---

44. Sun (*sūrya*) and moon (*soma*), viz., cognition and objectivity respectively.

Hṛdi purā sthitā, first you have to do that. *Purā*, at first the yogi has to do [that], just to put awareness on that junction. This is the state of *nijānanda*. *Nijānanda* is experienced by each and every being, realized or not realized–everybody experiences this state.

SCHOLAR: But yogis with awareness.

SWAMIJI: Yogis remain aware on this state, but everybody, they have to move further on the other states, to the other states. And what comes next? The next state is when he concentrates and he centers his awareness on that junction (that is, *pramātṛ bhāva*) in each and every breath, time comes–if he does it in continuity–time comes [when] his consciousness of awareness is melted in voidness and the breath becomes subtle and subtle and subtler, subtle and subtler by-and-by, and the time comes [when] he gets just giddiness. He gets giddiness, just forgets and is deprived of that awareness for one second, and again sits. Everybody has experienced this, I think. The yogi who practices this must know this, that he…but if his awareness continues for sometime, then it happens, otherwise it won't happen at all–this giddiness. And this, it is called *laya* (absorption). And this giddiness takes place only for one moment, one moment and he is aware again, again with his own practice, and he functions this breathing in and out with awareness again and again. But sometime, when this practice gets strength, it is stimulated in the continuity of awareness, by-and-by, by-and-by, by-and-by, and this voidness, this giddiness, this…

DENISE: Blacking out?

SWAMIJI: Yes. This blacking out takes place in continuity; just for two breaths, twice he breathes in and out, again, again, again, again, again, again. What happens next? *Śūnyata mātra viśrānter*, *nirānandaṁ vibhāvayet*, and he, *bas*, resides in that voidness. This is the state which is called *nirānanda*, this is the state which is called *prāṇana vṛtti*.

SCHOLAR: *Prāṇodaye*?

SWAMIJI: No.

SCHOLAR: This goes to the next *adhikāra* (state).

SWAMIJI: This is the next, the next *ānanda*.

LJA TA05C (31:10)

nijānande pramātraṁśamātre hṛdi purā sthitaḥ /
śūnyatāmātraviśrānternirānandaṁ vibhāvayet //44//
(verse repeated)

This is the first state of *nirānanda*.

SCHOLAR: So he starts from *nijānanda* to move to *nirānanda*.

SWAMIJI: *Nijānanda* is no state.

SCHOLAR: No state. It is the beginning point.

SWAMIJI: This is the beginning point where you have to begin; the beginning point of putting awareness on that subjective consciousness, *pramātṛ bhāva*. *Nirānanda* is a state. The first state is *nirānanda–laya*.

JOHN: That giddiness.

SWAMIJI: You go inside, inside, inside, inside, you just…but this is not the point to be maintained. You have to rise from that. And the rising point he begins in the next *śloka*.

LJA TA05C (32:01)

प्राणोदये प्रमेये तु परानन्दं विभावयेत्।
तत्रानन्तप्रमेयांशपूरणापाननिर्वृतः ॥४५॥
परानन्दगतस्तिष्ठेदपानशशिशोभितः।

prāṇodaye prameye tu parānandaṁ vibhāvayet /
tatrānantaprameyāṁśapūraṇāpānanirvṛtaḥ //45//
parānandagatastiṣṭhedapānaśaśiśobhitaḥ /

These, one *śloka* and a half is next (verse repeated). *Prāṇodaye*, when this *prāṇana–prāṇodaye* means, *prāṇana–prāṇana* takes place, that is the state of *spanda*, *spandana*.

SCHOLAR: In *śūnyatā*.

SWAMIJI: No, it is just after when *śūnyatā* (voidness) is in its fullness, when *śūnyatā* has appeared in its fullness…

SCHOLAR: Unbroken.

SWAMIJI:…not in negation of awareness–when *śūnyatā* is produced with awareness.

SCHOLAR: So first this is experienced as falling from the practice, then it becomes awareness in continuity in voidness.

SWAMIJI: Yes. And that awareness resides, when awareness resides there…where?

DEVOTEES: In voidness.

SWAMIJI: In voidness, then what happens? *Prāṇodaye*, *prāṇana* takes place, the rise of *prāṇana* takes place. He enters in another world, he enters in another world that is *prāṇana*. And that world is of *apānana vṛtti*, that world is of *apānana vṛtti*.

Just close your eyes tightly, just close your eyes tightly–tightly!–squeeze it, and you will find some sound from inside, you'll hear that sound from inside. Don't you hear? Or close your ear openings tightly, and you will hear that sound from inside.

DENISE: Internal sound.

SWAMIJI: It is that kind of sound. It is that kind of sound of that sexual intercourse–that sound is there. In sexual intercourse also that sound is there. Which sound? Of *apānana*. That is the sound of *apānana* that gives you joy, that gives you happiness, entire bliss.

SCHOLAR: So, *prāṇana* takes place in *śūnyatā*.

SWAMIJI: *Prāṇana* takes place in *śūnyatā*, yes.

SCHOLAR: And *prāṇana* there is defined as continuity of awareness in *śūnyatā*.

SWAMIJI: Yes.

SCHOLAR: And then from that comes the internal state of *apāna*.

SWAMIJI: *Apāna*, *apāna*, *apāna*. And *apānana vṛtti*, when *apānana prameya* [takes place]–that is *prameya* (objectivity); *prameye* means, *apāna vṛtti*–there you find that is *parānanda*, that is supreme *ānanda*. That is the next state of yoga that is called *parānanda*. *Parānanda bhāva* is the absolute state of happiness, because you feel that you have drowned in that sound, in that sound of bliss. That is the sound of bliss! That is *apānana vṛtti*. There you must know that this is the state of *parānanda*.

LJA TA05C (35:36)

And *tatra*, in that *parānanda*, *ananta prameyāṁśa pūraṇāpāna nirvṛtaḥ*; *ananta prameyāṁśa*, it is not only the objective world, the whole body of the objective world and the whole body of the cognitive world and the organic world is gathered, gathered from all-round, from all sides. You feel gathering of all objectivity and cognitivity in one point. You gather everything in that *apānana vṛtti*. This is the state of *parānanda*. In *apānana vṛtti* you feel that everything is gathered, breath is gathered, breathing in and out it is gathered in one point.

DENISE: Within yourself?

SWAMIJI: Yes, within yourself. You feel that it is gathered and it is balled in one point, not only breath, but all these differentiated perceptions. All differentiated perceptions of the organic field and all differentiated perceptions of the objective field, those are also gathered and balled in one point. He feels that it is balled. And it takes place on the right side, the right side here, just below the *tālu* (palate). It is why he says, *tatra ananta prameyāṁśa pūraṇa apāna nirvṛtaḥ. Ananta prameyāṁśa*–it is not only that–it is, he sees that this whole universe has fallen down, this whole universe is shattered to pieces; this whole world, all mountains have fallen down on him, in that *apānana vṛtti, tatra ananta prameyāṁśa pūraṇa* (*pūraṇa* means, gathering), *apāna nirvṛtaḥ*, by the squeezing functioned by *apāna, apāna vṛtti. Apāna* you know? That internal, that joyful sound. It is like that. It is not like that, it is just [that] you have enjoyed these sexual intercourses, [so] you can calculate that way. *Parānanda gatastiṣṭhet*, you must remain, you must establish your consciousness in that *parānanda bhāva, apāna śaśiśobhitaḥ*, which is glorified by *apānana vṛtti.*

SCHOLAR: No fear here.

SWAMIJI: What?

SCHOLAR: It means you must establish yourself whatever happens there in that state.

SWAMIJI: Yes.

SCHOLAR: A whole mountain falls on you...

SWAMIJI: If you feel that you are absolutely really surely dying, your physical frame is gone–you'll feel that–you must *tiṣṭhet*, you must establish yourself there. You must not be afraid of that.

SCHOLAR: There must be force of awareness and faith there at that point.

SWAMIJI: Yes.

SCHOLAR: Complete faith.

SWAMIJI: Because your master has told you...

DENISE: Don't be afraid.

SWAMIJI:...don't be afraid that...*bas*, this is finished, *apāna vṛtti* is finished. Now *samāna vṛtti*:

LJA TA05C (39:16)

ततोऽनन्तस्फुरन्मेयसङ्घट्टैकान्तनिर्वृतः ॥ ४६ ॥
समानभूमिमागत्य ब्रह्मानन्दमयो भवेत्।

tato'nantasphuranmeyasaṅghaṭṭaikāntanirvṛtaḥ //46//
samānabhūmimāgatya brahmānandamayo bhavet /

This is now the third state of *ānanda. Ananta sphurat meya saṅghaṭṭaikān-*, then those fearful forms, fearful, those…

SCHOLAR: Apparitions.

SWAMIJI:…apparitions and fearful impressions that take place in your awareness there in *apāna vṛtti*, they are gone, they subside when you remain there; when you establish your awareness in *apāna vṛtti*, then they are subsided by-and-by. Then what happens next? *Tato ananta sphurat meya saṅghaṭṭa ekānta nirvṛtaḥ*, then you find that everything is balled, everything is completely balled inside peacefully here. There is no breath, there is no breathing in and out, that is finished. *Ananta sphurat meya* (*meya* means, *prāṇāpāna*), *prāṇāpāna* and all that objective world and cognitive world, all that is balled inside in one-pointedness without fear. That fear is…

SCHOLAR: Dissolved.

SWAMIJI: Huh?

SCHOLAR: Dissolved by faith.

SWAMIJI: Yes. *Ananta sphurat meya saṅghaṭṭa*, it takes *saṅghaṭṭa*. *Saṅghaṭṭa* means, gathering.

SCHOLAR: Fusion into one point.

SWAMIJI: One point. *Ekānta nirvṛtaḥ*, he is absolutely *nirvṛta*, he is absolutely filled with the state of joy, with the state of bliss. *Samāna bhūmim āgatya*, that is the *samānana vṛtti*, that is the *samānana vṛtti*…

SCHOLAR: It's not *samāna*, [it's] *samānan*.

SWAMIJI: *Samānan. Samānabhūmi* (*bhūmi* means, *samānana vṛtti*), when you reach that *vṛtti* (state), *brahmānanda mayo bhavet*, this is the state of *brahmānanda*. So this is the third state. *Brahmānanda mayo bhavet*, till then, up to this.

LJA TA05C (41:36)

ततोऽपि मानमेयौघकलनाग्रासतत्परः ॥४७॥
उदानवह्नौ विश्रान्तो महानन्दं विभावयेत्।

tato'pi mānameyaughakalanāgrāsatatparaḥ //47//
udānavahnau viśrānto mahānandaṁ vibhāvayet /

Then what happens next to this yogi? *Tato'pi māna meya ogha kalanā*, the *kalanā*, the functioning of *māna* (cognition) and *meya* (objectivity), the functioning of *prāṇa* and *apāna*, the breathing process which is already balled in one point, *māna meya ogha kalanā grāsa tatparaḥ*, *grāsa tatparaḥ* means, [the yogi is] bent upon dissolving that, bent upon destroying that, destroying these movements of in and out–it is not destroying the movements of in and out only–along with the [objective] perceptions and cognitive perceptions also, and those hideous forms, they are over, there is no fear now, no fear appears to him then. *Kalanā grāsa tatparaḥ*, *udāna vahnau viśrānta*, then *udāna vahnau* takes place, that is *udānana vṛtti*. *Udāna vahni*, the fire of *udāna* (*udāna*, this fourth *vṛtti*), in that fourth *vṛtti*, *udānana* takes place. *Udānana* takes place where the yogi finds this ball is melted in sound, in that sound, in that sound of bliss. *Shsssssssssssssssssssssss sssssssssssh*, this is the sound that is produced there. *Shssssssssssssss ssssssssssssssssssssssh*, a very long sound, and it is melted, this ball is melted inside–finished. There is no breath, there is no breathing process–finished. *Udāna vahnau*, *viśrānta*, when he is established in that *udāna vahni*, *mahānandaṁ vibhāvayet*, this is the state of *mahānanda* there. *Mahānanda*…

SCHOLAR: [Jayaratha says], "*vibhāvayet*" *lakṣayedityartha-lakṣayet.*
SWAMIJI: *Vibhāvayet lakṣayet*. This commentary he has done…
SCHOLAR: He has no knowledge of…
SWAMIJI: No, he had not knowledge of this.

LJA TA05C (44:04)

तत्र विश्रान्तिमभ्येत्य शाम्यत्यस्मिन्महार्चिषि ॥ ४८ ॥

tatra viśrāntimabhyetya śāmyatyasminmahārciṣi //48//

When *tatra viśrāntim abhyetya*, when you are fully established in that state, when it gets entry, entry with sound, with this sound–that sound is not only the *shsssssssssssssssssssh* sound, that is *with* that bliss, with sexual joy, sexual joy appears there with that sound–*tatra viśrāntim abhyetya śāmyatyasmin mahārciṣi*, when you are established, when you are fully established there, when you have settled your awareness fully there, *śāmyatyasmin mahārciṣi*, then, in that supreme *teja* (supreme light), he gets dissolved, he gets melted, he melts for good!

LJA TA05C (45:19)

निरुपाधिर्महाव्याप्तिर्व्यानाख्योपाधिवर्जिता ।
तदा खलु चिदानन्दो यो जडानुपबृंहितः ॥ ४९ ॥

nirupādhirmahāvyāptirvyānākhyopādhivarjitā /
tadā khalu cidānando yo jaḍānupabṛṁhitaḥ //49//

Then there is the next, the fifth state of *ānanda*. That is through *vyāna vṛtti* to *vyānana vṛtti*.

Prāṇa vṛtti travels to *prāṇana vṛtti*, *apāna vṛtti* travels to *apānana vṛtti*, *samāna vṛtti* travels to *samānana vṛtti*, *udāna vṛtti* travels to *udānana vṛtti*, and *vyāna vṛtti* has to travel to *vyānana vṛtti*. My dear sir, this is not the thing to be written down. This is to be digested in your own consciousness.

SCHOLAR: I am not writing anything.

SWAMIJI: Huh?

SCHOLAR: I'm not writing.

SWAMIJI: Yes (laughs). *Nirupādhir mahā vyāpti*, and that is the supreme great pervasion, pervasion of that consciousness, *nirupādhir*, which is *nirupādhiḥ* (*nirupādhiḥ*, without any other foreign attributions, there is no foreign attributions). You know foreign attributions?

SCHOLAR: Yes, yes, *upādhi*.

SWAMIJI: No foreign...

SCHOLAR: Element.

SWAMIJI:...adjustments. You can't adjust it.

SCHOLAR: It is *svātantra*.

SWAMIJI: It is as it is. It is at it is, you can't add it.

Once when I was in Ramana Maharishi's ashram, [a disciple] told me that he has experienced this *cidānanda*: "Oh, I have...this whole skull is filled with pain, here pain, here pain, in arms, in legs, in..." (laughs) I thought it was only in imagination and nothing else. He (a real yogi) is filled with joy! Where is the question of pain there? There is no pain.

Nirupādhiḥ, it is without adjustments, there is nothing to be adjusted. No foreign matter will be adjusted there. It is unadjustable.

JOHN: It is just full of bliss, *bas*.

SWAMIJI: *Bas*, bliss, that is all.

JOHN: Nothing else.

DENISE: Why did he call it pain?

SWAMIJI: Because he had not experienced it properly.

DENISE: And had no understanding of it.

SWAMIJI: And it is *mahā vyāpti*, the great pervasion. The great pervasion is that pervasion where you pervade this whole universe. You don't pervade this whole universe only, also the negation of this whole universe you pervade. Not only the existence of universe is pervaded, but also the negation of the universe is also pervaded there.

JOHN: So this state is moving into *śāmbhavopāya* then, when you pervade the whole universe.

SWAMIJI: It is not an *upāya*, it is *vṛtti*, it is the state. These are the states, these are not the *upāya*s.

JOHN: No means there.

SWAMIJI: No, it is (indaudible).

SCHOLAR: This is the means, but it has nothing to do with division into means.

SWAMIJI: No division into means. It is just rise, rise from *prāṇa vṛtti* to *vyānana vṛtti*, *vyānana* state.

SCHOLAR: *Cidānanda* state.

SWAMIJI: *Nirupādhir mahāvyāptir vyānākhyā*. *Vyānākhyā*, it is nominated as *vyāna*. *Vyāna* is that which pervades. *Upādhi varjitā*, it is *upādhi varjitā*, without *upādhi*, without any adjustments. *Tadā khalu cidānanda*, then takes place *cidānanda*, the state of *cidānanda*, *yo jaḍa anupa bṛṁhitaḥ*, that *cidānanda* where there is no way, where there is no room for any *jaḍa*.[45]

LJA TA05C (49:29)

नह्यत्र संस्थितिः कापि विभक्ता जडरूपिणः।

nahyatra saṁsthitiḥ kāpi vibhaktā jaḍarūpiṇaḥ /50a

Jaḍa rūpiṇaḥ vibhakta saṁsthitiḥ na asti, there is no possibility of *jaḍa rūpa* (inert form). *Jaḍa rūpa* is not excluded, *jaḍa rūpatā* is not excluded there. On the contrary, *jaḍa rūpatā* also is included there. You can't say this is *cidānanda* and this is not *cidānanda*. When the state of *cidānanda* takes place,…

DEVOTEE: Nothing is excluded.

SWAMIJI:…nothing is excluded there. *Nahyatra saṁsthitiḥ kāpi vibhaktā jaḍa rūpiṇaḥ*. Not *jaḍa rūpa* (*jaḍa rūpa* means, contrary to this *cidānanda*), nothing remains outside *cidānanda*. *Cidānanda* has included everything–included!

DEVOTEE: All-embracing.

SWAMIJI: All-embracing. It has included everything in its being.[46] Now the sixth state of *ānanda* he explains:

LJA TA05C (50:50)

45. Inertness, objectivity.

46. "*Nijānanda* is in *āṇavopāya*, *nirānanda* is *āṇavopāya*, *parānanda* is *āṇavopāya*, [*brahmānanda* is *āṇavopāya*, *mahānanda* is *āṇavopāya*], up to *cidānanda*. *Cidānanda* is not *āṇavopāya*. *Cidānanda* is in *śāktopāya*." *Swamiji Interviews* (LJA archive).

यत्र कोऽपि व्यवच्छेदो नास्ति यद्विश्वतः स्फुरत् ॥ ५० ॥
यदनाहतसंवित्ति परमामृतबृंहितम् ।
यत्रास्ति भावनादीनां न मुख्या कापि सङ्गतिः ॥ ५१ ॥
तदेव जगदानन्दमस्मभ्यं शम्भुरूचिवान् ।

yatra ko'pi vyavacchedo nāsti yadviśvataḥ sphurat //50//
yadanāhatasaṁvitti paramāmṛtabṛṁhitam /
yatrāsti bhāvanādīnāṁ na mukhyā kāpi saṅgatiḥ //51//
tadeva jagadānandamasmabhyaṁ śambhurūcivān /

Yatra ko'pi vyavacchedo nāsti, where there is no *vyavaccheda*, excluding process, where there is no exclusion.

"Exclusion" is correct?

SCHOLAR: Yes.

SWAMIJI: You have not to exclude anything! *Yat viśvataḥ*, on the contrary, *yat viśvataḥ sphurat*, that which shines in universal states, in the whole cosmos (*yat viśvataḥ sphurat*), and *yat anāhata saṁvitti paramāmṛta bṛṁhitam*, and at the same time which is strengthened and which is nourished by that supreme nectar of God consciousness, that supreme nectar of God consciousness which is filled with the *anāhata saṁvitti*, with that knowledge which is beyond knowledge.

SCHOLAR: *Sadoditam.*

SWAMIJI: *Sadoditam* (ever-risen). With that knowledge, unknown knowledge.

SCHOLAR: It is not an effect, it is not *āhata*.

SWAMIJI: It is not *āhata*.[47] And in addition, *yatrāsti bhāvanādīnāṁ na mukhyā kāpi saṅgatiḥ*, and where there is no *saṅgatiḥ*, there is no entry, there is no acceptance of *samādhi*, of remaining in *samādhi* or remaining in awareness and so on (*yatrāsti bhāvanādīnāṁ na mukhyā kāpi saṅgatiḥ*). *Tadeva jagadānandam*, that is *jagadānanda*, that is the

47. Lit., struck.

state of *jagadānanda*. I don't tell you that this is the state of *jagadānanda*. This state of *jagadānanda* was explained to me by my great master, Śambhunātha. It is from Śambhunātha that I have learnt this state. *Bas*.

SCHOLAR: Jai Guru Dev.

Discussion:

JOHN: Where does that state of yawning take place?

SWAMIJI: Huh?

JOHN: In that lecture on seven states of *ānanda* before…

SWAMIJI: *Vyāna*, *vyāna*?

JOHN: That yawning, where you think you are dying and you feel…

SWAMIJI: But those are *upāya*s (the means), yawning are *upāya*s. These are states. These are states. These are states to…

DEVOTEE: These are actually to be experienced.

SWAMIJI: These are experience.

JOHN: One time you gave a lecture on these seven states of *ānanda* and you said at one point, after breath circles, there is this experiencing of yawning.

SWAMIJI: Yes, yes, yes, yes.

JOHN: That yawning takes place in which *upāna*, in which breath?

SWAMIJI: When this is balled…

JOHN: Balled.

SWAMIJI: Yes, when everything is balled, his mouth opens a bit automatically, automatically he, *aaaaahhh*.

SCHOLAR: Like he is choking.

DENISE: Like he is dying.

SWAMIJI: Because he is dying, because his physical body is dying.

DEVOTEE: But he has to maintain awareness in that.

SWAMIJI: Yes. You see, when you treat with electricity some insane man…

DENISE: Give him a shock.

SWAMIJI:…do you know–give him a shock–what happens to him? He dies, he actually dies, that patient actually dies. *Tamisha pos kasan* (Kashmiri), everything, all the symptoms of death appear to him. In the same way, it is dying, it is leaving this physical body aside and entering in that spiritual atmosphere. So this was the lesson of today. Very nice.

DEVOTEE: Thank you. Wonderful lesson.

LJA TA05C (55:01) end
LJA TA05D (00:00) start

SWAMIJI: So this secret of *prāṇa tattva samuccāra* is not, you should not think that it is a theory. It is not only *upadeśa* (teaching).

तत्र विश्रान्तिराधेया हृदयोच्चारयोगतः ॥५२॥

tatra viśrāntirādheyā hṛdayoccārayogataḥ //52//

You have to achieve rest in that, establishment. You have to become established in that state, *hṛdayoccārayogataḥ*, by the adoption of *hṛdayoccāra*. This *prāṇa tattva samuccāra* is to begin from *hṛdaya uccāra*, you have to establish your awareness in that heart.

JOHN: In one of those three hearts.

SWAMIJI: One of those three hearts, in the heart of these centers, these six centers of *ānanda*: *prāṇana*, *samānana*, *udānana*…

SCHOLAR: *Prāṇana*, *apānana*, *samānana*, *udānana* and *vyānana*.

SWAMIJI:…*vyānana*, *apānana*, yes. And it is not only *hṛdaya*, it is *hṛdayādi uccāra yogataḥ*. That is, you have to see the creation, protection, destruction, concealing, revealing and *anākhya*. In the first *ānanda* state, it is the creation of that God consciousness–creation, this is the state of creation, creating God consciousness. Then protecting of God consciousness is in the next [*ānanda*]. Creation of God consciousness is in the state of *nirānanda*, and protecting God consciousness is in the state of *parānanda*.

SCHOLAR: Protecting.

SWAMIJI: Protecting. And destroying God consciousness–it is not destroying God consciousness–destroying differentiated God consciousness is the next *ānanda*. Which is next *ānanda*?

SCHOLAR: *Brahmānanda*.

SWAMIJI: *Brahmānanda*. And concealing God consciousness is…

SCHOLAR: *Cidānanda*.

SWAMIJI: No. It is *mahānanda*.

SCHOLAR: *Mahānanda*.

SWAMIJI: And revealing God consciousness is *cidānanda*. And *jagadānanda* is *anākhya*, where God consciousness is not felt, it is your nature, it becomes your nature. So, when you are practicing, when you are breathing as I told you yesterday, breathing in and out with awareness in the center and you get entries, repeated entries in that voidness when you fall down, when you neglect, when you are disconnected, your awareness is disconnected repeatedly, there is an automatic disconnection of your awareness,…*

DEVOTEE: Giddiness.

SWAMIJI: It is not giddiness. Disconnection of awareness. It is why you do like this.

DENISE: You black out.

SWAMIJI: Yes. This is only disconnection of that awareness. Awareness is disconnected.

*…this is *sṛṣṭi*, this is the state of creation of that state, the first *ānanda* (*nirānanda*). And the next *ānanda*, when awareness is maintained, then it does not, you don't get disconnected. When awareness is not disconnected, in place of disconnection you get entry in that God consciousness. That is that state when that state is revealed when you are aware between sleeping and waking. That is the point. There you are aware when your awareness is maintained, it is not disconnected. Once it is disconnected, then you get dizziness. When you don't let it disconnect, then you get entry in that. That is *parānanda*. And when you get entry in that *parānanda*, that is protection, that is *sthiti*, that is the *sthiti* of this state. The next state [is] when you gather all those things, gather subjective, objective, cognitive, all these perceptions are repeatedly gathered and kept in one ball. That is the next state.

DEVOTEE: *Mahānanda*.

SWAMIJI: That is *brahmānanda*. *Samāna bhūmim āgatya brahmānanda mayo bhavet* (verse 46). This is *brahmānanda*, this is the next state, and this is destruction, this is *saṁhṛti* (*saṁhāra*, destruction), because everything is destroyed and kept in one ball.

DEVOTEE: Concealed.

SWAMIJI: It is not concealed. Concealed is something else. Concealed will take place next.

DEVOTEE: Destruction of differentiatedness.

SWAMIJI:…differentiated perceptions, thoughts, objectivities, everything. And this is destruction (*saṁhṛti*). And next takes place when this ball melts and rushes inside, rushes inside with that peculiar sound I pointed out yesterday. That is concealed.

SCHOLAR: *Mahānanda.*

SWAMIJI: That is *mahānanda*. That is concealing, because everything is concealed, kept inside. That ball melts and enters, rushes in that central vein. That is *mahānanda*. And then, when from the rectum it riseth again to the *sahasrāra cakra*, that is *cidānanda*. And [when] this *cidānanda* expands inside and outside, that is *jagadānanda*, that is *anākhya*, that is *anākhya cakra*.

SCHOLAR: *Anugraha anākhya.*

SWAMIJI: *Anugraha* (revealing) and *anākhya*.

JOHN: This expanding inside and outside is functioning of *krama mudrā* in this?

SWAMIJI: *Krama mudrā* is in *anākhya*.

JOHN: In *anākhya*.

SWAMIJI: In *anākhya*.

SCHOLAR: It is a bridge between *anugraha* state and *anākhya* state.

SWAMIJI: Yes.

LJA TA05D (07:30)

या तत्र सम्यग्विश्रान्तिः सानुत्तरमयी स्थितिः।

yā tatra samyagviśrāntiḥ sānuttaramayī sthitiḥ /

And when you are well-established in that state, in that supreme state, the last sixth state of *jagadānanda*, *sa anuttaramāyi sthiti*, that is called "establishment in that supreme God consciousness," that is perfect establishment in that supreme God consciousness.

JOHN: Can I ask one question before we go on?

SWAMIJI: Yes.

JOHN: In this first state where your awareness is broken by void (*śūnyatā*), this differs from having your awareness broken by thoughts or all kinds of other interruptions, or sleep.

SWAMIJI: Huh?

JOHN: I mean, in meditation you can have your awareness broken by thoughts also. Say you have your awareness of breath and some thought comes, that takes you away from awareness of breath, but that is another kind of losing awareness than this kind.

SWAMIJI: No, that is not recognized. That meditation is not recognized in the first state also. That is below that first state. When there are thoughts rising in your mind, that is not meditation at all.

DENISE: That's thinking.

SWAMIJI: That is thinking. You are nowhere then.

SCHOLAR: "This is my breath, this is in, this is out."

SWAMIJI: Yes. This must not happen at all. You have to leave that aside. It is no state. It is not *nijānanda*. *Nijānanda* is when your awareness is functioning in continuation on that point without any other foreign thought, but it is automatic that it is broken, it is broken by that voidness, because then your consciousness wants to get entry, the next entry. But as that entering in that, the strength of entering in that consciousness is less in your awareness, so you get disconn-...you get your...

SCHOLAR: Disconnected.

DENISE: Awareness breaks.

SWAMIJI: This breaks. There is no question of other thoughts. Other thoughts must not come at all. When other thoughts are also leaking there, then it is no state, then it is no stage at all.

DENISE: But it is not sleep, is it?

SWAMIJI: It is not sleep.

DENISE: Because it happens suddenly.

SWAMIJI: Yes, because he wants to get entry in that next state.

DENISE: But he doesn't have the capacity to have that.

SWAMIJI: He doesn't have the capacity, so his awareness is disconnected.

JOHN: So this is movement from *sakala* to *pralayākala*, this is this moving into this void.

SWAMIJI: No, it is moving...this is *pralayākala*, this is *pralayākala* –this.

JOHN: This falling into this...

SCHOLAR: *Śūnya* (void) state.

SWAMIJI: And it is moving from *pralayākala* to *vijñānākala.*

JOHN: And *vijñānākala* is when you don't lose awareness.

SWAMIJI: No, *vijñānākala* [is] when you get entry.

SCHOLAR: When you maintain awareness in *śūnyatā.*

SWAMIJI: What?

SCHOLAR: When you maintain awareness in that *śūnyatā*, then you have the *prāṇana* state.

SWAMIJI: In that gap, yes, we have got then the *apāna* state–*apānana*.

SCHOLAR: *Apānana*.

JOHN: That is *vijñānākala*.

SWAMIJI: This is *vijñānākala*, yes.

LJA TA05D (10:51)

Daṇḍa Prayoga
Six States of Mantra Śakti

इत्येतद्धृदयाद्येकस्वभावेऽपि स्वधामनि ॥ ५३ ॥
षट्प्राणोच्चारजं रूपमथ व्याप्त्या तदुच्यते ।

ityetaddhṛdayādyekasvabhāve'pi svadhāmani //53//
ṣaṭprāṇoccārajaṁ rūpamatha vyāptyā taducyate /

So, this way, *hṛdayādyeka svabhāve'pi svadhāmani. Svadhāmani* means, the center, the own center of this *vṛtti* (state), *vṛtti* and *śakti*, the real center which is *hṛdayādyeka svabhāve*, which is only heart, the heart of consciousness. In that heart of consciousness, we have already explained *ṣaṭ prāṇa uccārajaṁ rūpam*, the formation of sixfold *prāṇa uccāra*, sixfold *prāṇana uccāra. Prāṇana uccāra* is these six states of *ānanda. Atha vyāptyā taducyate*, now we will explain these six-fold states in *mantra vyāpti* (pervading in *mantra krama*). Mantras are also there. And there is only one mantra, and that mantra is *parābīja* (*parābīja* means, supreme mantra). Just like in Vedānta you find '*oṁ*' is the supreme mantra, and in Shaivism you find '*sauḥ*' is the supreme mantra. *Sauḥ*, this mantra is formed by three sections: *sa* is the first section, *au* is the second section, and *visarga* (*aḥ*) is the third section–*sauḥ*. *Sauḥ* is the mantra.

Now, he will pervade this way of six states in these mantras in the next *śloka*s:

LJA TA05D (12:57)

प्राणदण्डप्रयोगेन पूर्वापरसमीकृतेः ॥५४॥
चतुष्किकाम्बुजालम्बिलम्बिकासौधमाश्रयेत्।
त्रिशूलभूमिं क्रान्त्वातो नाडित्रितयसङ्गताम्॥५५॥
इच्छाज्ञानक्रियाशक्तिसमत्वे प्रविशेत् सुधीः।

prāṇadaṇḍaprayogena pūrvāparasamīkṛteḥ //54//
catuṣkikāmbujālambilambikāsaudhamāśrayet /
triśūlabhūmiṁ krāntvāto nāḍitritayasaṅgatām //55//
icchājñānakriyāśaktisamatve praviśet sudhīḥ /

The *sudhīḥ* (yogi) who has mastery on that awareness, who is master of that awareness, whose awareness is never disconnected, awareness of one-pointedness in continuity, to him, *prāṇa daṇda prayogena*, when he establishes the way of *prāṇa vṛtti* in *daṇḍa prayoga*,...*

Daṇḍa prayoga means, for instance, you breathe in and out, you breathe in and out, in and out, in and out. This is not *daṇḍa prayoga. Daṇḍa prayoga* is that way of movement of this breath, inside and outside, that it will move only in one point. You must not feel that these are two movements, [that] inside is one movement and outside is another movement. It must go in one line! It will go in one line only when this center, this junction of these two breaths is caught in awareness, is caught in the clutches of awareness. So, in that junction only it moves. When this *prāṇa* and *apāna*, this inside and outside breath moves in the junction, only in the junction, that it becomes only one line, this kind of movement of breath is called *daṇḍa prayoga*. This is the real thing we have to maintain. Inside moving and outside moving of breath, just like what you do in '*so'ham*', or this *cakrodaya*[48], or all

48. '*So'ham*' is internally reciting '*saḥ*' with the exhale and '*ham*' with the inhale. *Cakrodaya* is to be done in *padmāsana* (lotus pose), with a fully erect spine, and with sound. "When you take breath [in], you have to lengthen it, and when you

these things, they are very inferior to this. In fact, we have to study and observe that there must be only the junction, the junction only, there must be the kingdom of the junction in this movement, in these two movements. When the kingdom of the junction shines in these two movements, then you find there is only one breath, there is only one vibrating breath. It doesn't matter if it goes in or comes out, it must take the formation of one breath. That kind of *abhyāsa* is called *daṇḍa prayogạ*. This *daṇḍa prayoga*, if you do for only half an hour, you'll get entry in the next state of *ānanda*–just after half an hour. The question is maintaining awareness, awareness in continuity!

SCHOLAR: For one half an hour.

SWAMIJI: Yes, after half an hour you will get entry in God consciousness. It is decided by our masters, and they have experienced it.

*...*prāṇa daṇḍa prayogena*, when *daṇḍa prayoga* takes place of breath (*daṇḍa prayogạ* means, make it just like a stick),...*

SCHOLAR: Like a snake when you hit it.

SWAMIJI: Yes. *Yathā daṇḍāhataḥ sarpo daṇḍākāraḥ prajāyate*[49], when by striking with a stick on the body of a snake, the snake becomes just like a stick, he stands just like a stick. *Sā tathaiva vibuddhyeta guruṇā pratibodhitā*, this must be the position of breath by the grace of masters.

SCHOLAR: So this *daṇḍa prayoga* is misunderstood in the Śākta system. There it is some trick which is done with muscles and concentration.

SWAMIJI: No, it is not there.

SCHOLAR: That is a completely inferior process. What does that lead to?

SWAMIJI: It is automatic.

SCHOLAR: That is simply an exercise in imagination.

SWAMIJI: Yes, it is only imagination. And you get that *kuṇḍalinī vijñāna* and all those. Those are all imaginations.

---

take it out, you have to lengthen it; give it more span of space so that it moves very slowly in and out. And you have to adjust some mantras (e.g., *so'ham*) also with that." *Swamiji Interviews* 1978 (LJA archive).

49. Jayaratha references *Haṭharatnāvalī* Ch.II.37-42 in his commentary.

*...by that *daṇḍa prayoga*, *pūrvāparā samīkṛteḥ* (*pūrvāparā samīkṛteḥ* means, you don't find difference between inhale and exhale), inhaling and exhaling you don't find any difference, you feel there is only one vibrating movement–that is divine! And by that one vibrating movement, there are some advanced yogis who, after two or three vibrating movements, get entry in that God consciousness. They are such advanced [yogis]. Just they breathe in and out two or three times and get entry. *Pūrvāparā sāmīkṛteḥ*; *pūrva aparā* means, previous and latter, that is, breathing in and breathing out, *samīkṛteḥ*, they become one. You don't get differentiated perception in them, they become one just like a *daṇḍa* (stick).

SCHOLAR: Breath has not yet stopped.

SWAMIJI: Breath has not yet stopped. But there is only vibrating awareness, in one-pointed vibrating awareness. There is no...other thoughts have no courage to interfere there. It is just like the vibrating force of a lion, a tiger–nobody is allowed to interfere there. So there is no question of thoughts and all other things there. They will never leak there.

LJA TA05D (19:47)

Catuṣkikāmbujālambilambikāsaudhamāśrayet. Then what happens next? *Catuṣkikā*; *catuṣkikā*, just between the two eyebrows, between the center of two eyebrows and this throat pit,...*

(Swamiji demonstrates) This is called armpit. This is called throat pit–this.

SCHOLAR: *Kaṇṭhakūpa*.

SWAMIJI: *Kaṇṭhakūpa*. This is called *kaṇṭhakūpa*. From this and this (Swamiji demonstrates), between these two, just near the *tālu*. *Tālu* is "guttural"?

SCHOLAR: It's called the palate.

SWAMIJI: Palate, palate. And there...actually there are four ways, four openings. In these four openings, two openings are blocked already in ordinary life of a human being–there are only two openings (two openings: breathing in and out).

*...and there, by this *daṇḍa prayoga*, four openings take place–*catuṣkikā*. So, it is nominated as *catuṣkikā*, *chowk*, where there are four ways. *Catuṣkikā* means, *chowk* (*caura* in Hindi).

DENISE: North, south, east and west–just like a cross.

DEVOTEE: Crossroads.

SWAMIJI: Yes, crossroads, junction of a crossroad is there–cross openings. And those ordinary cross openings are blocked instead of the other two openings which were blocked already. Those are opened and the previous two openings are blocked. That is *catuṣkikā*, and there, at that state, it is just like *ambuja* (*ambuja* means, lotus), a lotus-shaped place there. *Ālambi lambikā*, this is *lambikā*, it is called *lambikā sthāna–catuṣpata*, four ways, a crossroad. And that *saudham āśrayet*, you must get mastery and establishment on that *saudha*, on those openings, two divine openings. When those two divine openings are there in one opening, all those thoughts, all those perceptions, all those last previous thoughts and all those things are balled there at one opening, at the first opening. And the next opening, it is melted inside as it is already explained. That *saudham*, that is *saudham* (*saudham* means, the place of nectar), that is the place of nectar. And this place of nectar is enjoyed, is experienced by other yogis by *khecarī mudrā*. They cut this connection of this front of this tongue and attach the tip of the tongue on that palate and they get the imagination that they are tasting that nectar. But that nectar is false nectar.

DENISE: They really do that?

SWAMIJI: Yes, yes. There are some yogis who do that.

SCHOLAR: *Haṭha* yogis.

SWAMIJI: *Haṭha* yogis. But that nectar is false, only from imagination. This is real nectar what takes place there when that ball is melted in that. And then, when the ball is melted there, you get the functioning of this breath that this breath along with all these thoughts and all perceptions gets entry in a rush, rushes inside in *madhyanāḍī* making this sound, *Shssssssssssssssss*, which I have already told you yesterday. And then, when it reaches at the point of rectum, when that force reaches at the point of rectum, it gives force to *kuṇḍalinī*, that "serpent power" which you call, and that serpent power, it is not "serpent" exactly, it is just God consciousness, the power of God consciousness–it rises from that rectum.[50]

---

50. "There is a center called *tālu* in Sanskrit which is located in the roof of the mouth at the soft palate. In Saivism, this center is known as *lambikā-sthāna*, the

place of *lambikā*. The state of *lambikā* cannot be established by any physical means because it is very subtle. There are four passages in *lambikā*. These two breaths, when they take the position of descending, arrive at the *lambikā* that is the passage from the right side. From the left side there is another *lambikā*. The *lambikā* that exists on the left side is presently active in us while the *lambikā* that exists on the right side is blocked. At the moment when the incoming and the outgoing breath collect and take the position of flowing down, the breath stops. There is no breathing in and out. The ordinary course of breathing ceases and you feel a choking sensation. Then the *lambikā* on the right side opens and the breath enters through that opening and rushes down. When the breath gains entry through the *lambikā*, it produces a sound which is like that internal sound produced when you close the ears by pressing your fingers on them. It is a continuous sound like the sound of the ocean. A sound like this is produced when the two breaths gain entry into the central channel through the *lambikā* and travel to the *mūlādhāra cakra* where they rest. At that point, the *mūlādhāra cakra* is penetrated. At the *mūlādhāra cakra*, there is a wheel (the Sanskrit word *cakra* means "wheel"). When the *mūlādhāra cakra* is penetrated, the yogi experiences the wheel (*cakra*) beginning to move with great force and sound. It moves in a clockwise direction. This is the state experienced by yogis at the first moment this occurs. Here the breath no longer exists. It has taken the form of *kuṇḍalinī*. Now *kuṇḍalinī* advances from the *mūlādhāra cakra* and rises to penetrate the *cakra* residing at the navel, known as the *nābhi cakra*. At this *cakra*, there also exists a wheel, and after being penetrated, this *cakra* also begins to move rapidly and make sound. At that time, the yogi does not feel that the *nābhi cakra* alone is moving; he feels that the *nābhi cakra* and the *mūlādhāra cakra* are both moving, just like wheels in a factory. Both *cakra*s are moving and both are producing a sound. The yogi hears this sound and this sound produces joy. All this I am relating from my own experience. Now from the *nābhi cakra*, this breath travels in the form of *kuṇḍalinī* up to the heart and penetrates the *cakra* residing there. This *cakra* is known as the heart (*hṛt*) *cakra*. After being penetrated, this *cakra* of the heart also begins to move rapidly and becomes filled with sound. The yogi feels this. Here also, the yogi not only experiences the movement of the heart *cakra*, he experiences the movement of *nābhi cakra* and *mūlādhāra cakra* as well. He experiences and feels the movements of all three *cakra*s. In this way successively, breath in the form of *kuṇḍalinī* continues to rise and penetrates the *cakra* of the throat (*kaṇṭha*) and the *cakra* of *bhrūmadhya* found between the two eyebrows. With this penetration, both of these *cakra*s begin to move rapidly along with sound.

LJA TA05D (24:58)

Triśūlabhūmiṁ krāntvā, this is *triśūla bhūmi*, this is the state of *triśūla bīja*. *Icchā śakti* and *jñāna śakti* and *kriyā śakti* are functioning there. *Icchā śakti* of God, *jñāna śakti* of God, and the *kriyā śakti* of God are functioning, these three energies are functioning from that rectum to *sahasrāra*, to *brahmarandhra*, simultaneously. So this state of God consciousness from the rectum to *sahasrāra* is called *triśūla bhūmi*. So, from the point of balling all those outward vibrations to its entry to the rectum, when it rushes to the rectum, it is the state of *sa*. The yogi must know that this is the state of *sa*, this is represented by the letter *sa* in the *sauḥ bīja*. And from the rectum, when it riseth up to the *sahasrāra cakra*, this is the representation of *triśūla bīja* (*au-kāra*). *Triśūla bhūmiṁ krāntvā*, when you have held the state of *triśūla bhūmi*, the state of *triśūla* (*triśūla bīja* means *au-kāra*: *icchā śakti*, *jñāna śakti* and *kriyā śakti*), *nāḍi tritaya saṅgatām*, then *nāḍi tritaya saṅgatām triśūla bhūmim* (this is the adjective), the qualification of *triśūla bhūmiṁ* is *nāḍi tritaya saṅgatām*, where *prāṇa*, *apāna*, and *samāna* (*prāṇa*, *apāna*, and the junction) are nowhere to be found differentiatedly, they have melted for good, they have become one with that consciousness.

SCHOLAR: There is no *pramāṇa* and *prameya* functioning separately.

This is what the yogi experiences. In this way, the yogi, in this state of manifestation of *prāṇa-kuṇḍalinī*, experiences the movement of all these *cakra*s, right from *mūlādhāra cakra* up to *bhrūmadhya cakra* simultaneously just like a great machine. From that very moment, the yogi experiences the appearance of the eight yogic powers (*aṇimā*, etcetera). Those yogis who are unfortunate experience the state of *prāṇa-kuṇḍalinī* in a second way. Their experience of the rise of *prāṇa-kuṇḍalinī* is the same as that experienced by great yogis up to and including the experience of *lambikā* and the traveling from *lambikā* to the *mūlādhāra cakra*. At that point, it is expected that from *mūlādhāra cakra*, *prāṇa-kuṇḍalinī* will rise, piercing the *cakra*s beginning with the *cakra* of the navel, then the *cakra* of the heart and so forth until it reaches and pierces *bhrūhmadhya*." *Self-Realization in Kashmir Shaivism*, "The Secret Knowledge of Kuṇḍalinī", pp 107-109.

SWAMIJI: There is no *prameya* (objective), *pramāṇa* (cognitive), or *pramatṛ bhāva* (subjective state). Then, *icchā jñāna kriyā śaktis-amatve*, then you should get entry in that triple energy of God consciousness where triple energy has melted in oneness. That is *visarga* (*aḥ*). That is *visarga*, and that is the state of *anākhya* in the end. And that is *visarga* in *para bīja–sa*, *au*, and *visarga* (*aḥ*). So these you have to adjust with this state. *Sa* will take place when this breath gets entry in the central vein up to the rectum.

JOHN: When breath is sipped down, when breath is sipped.

SWAMIJI: Sipped. This is the functioning of *sa*. And from there the rise of that power to *sahasrāra cakra*...yes, you were telling?

JOHN: So *au* is that *mūladhara cakra* to *sahasrāra cakra*.

SWAMIJI:...to *sahasrāra cakra*, it is *au*. And when *nāḍi tritaya saṅgatām*, and when you breathe, again you breathe in and out, [when] you breathe in and out, it is not breathing, you don't breathe from your own accord, you breathe out naturally. It is breathing out and just gulping, breathing out and gulping. It is not just like gulping also. It is just...it does not stop. You breathe out and there is no breathing at all, there is no breathing at all after breathing out. Once you breathe out, you don't breathe in. Instead of breathing in, it is there. There is no breathing in and out, that is finished. Only out and *bas*, stop, out and stop, out and stop.

JOHN: So out functions when your eyes open, is it? The out-breath functions in *krama mudrā* when your...

SWAMIJI: Yes, it is real *krama mudrā*.

JOHN:...when your eyes open.

SWAMIJI: Yes. No, they open automatically...

SCHOLAR: All senses are open.

SWAMIJI: All senses, not only eyes–all senses.

JOHN: And then coming in again, there's no breathing in.

SWAMIJI: No, there is no breathing in.

JOHN: You're just again just in.

SWAMIJI: Yes.

JOHN: Because you never left in.

SWAMIJI: Yes. That is *visarga*, that is the state of *visarga*. That *visarga*, the state of *visarga*, you must get entry in that in the end.

DENISE: And you remain in that forever?

SWAMIJI: You can't remain in that forever. It is automatic!

JOHN: This is establishing that state of this *jagadānanda.*

SWAMIJI: This is establishing *jagadānanda* in and out. *Bas*, now he will give an example. He had explained how *daṇḍa prayoga* of *prāṇa* takes place, *daṇḍa prayoga* just in one flash, in order to get entry in *ūrdhva kuṇḍalinī* state. For that he explains what one should do.

LJA TA05D (30:12)

एकां विकासिनीं भूयस्त्वसङ्कोचां विकस्वराम्॥ ५६ ॥
श्रयेद्भ्रूबिन्दुनादान्तशक्तिसोपानमालिकाम्।

ekāṁ vikāsinīṁ bhūyastvasaṅkocāṁ vikasvarām //56//
śrayedbhrūbindunādāntaśaktisopānamālikām /

This yogi must hold (must hold, *śrayet*), must hold the garland of successive energies right from *bhrūbindu* to *samāna*. This is a garland of energies, these are eight steps, eight successive states of energies. The first state is…of course, there are three more states, which are not explained here, that is, *a-kāra*, *u-kāra* and *ma-kāra*. Because, as this is residing in the state of *vaikharī*[51], so it has no place in the spiritual world, this *a-kāra*, *u-kāra* and *ma-kāra*.

JOHN: *Oṁ*.

SWAMIJI: *Oṁ* (a-u-m). Afterwards, when you get entry in further steps of that real God consciousness, they are eight states. One is *bindu*, that is *bhrūbindu*, this is the first energy–*bhrūbindu*. Next is *ardhacandra*, the next state of energy is *ardhacandra*. The third state of energy is *nirodhi*, the fourth is *nāda*, the fifth is *nādānta*, the sixth is *śakti*, the seventh is *vyāpinī*, and the eighth is *samāna*. So you have to cross all these stages of these energies. These are successive energies. This garland of successive energies one should hold by-and-by. Of course, this is a garland because this is only one energy. If we go deep in analyzing these eight energies, these energies, one feels that this is only one energy traveling from *bhrūbindu* to *samāna*. In fact, it is *ekāṁ*; *ekāṁ*, it is only

51. The gross level of speech (*vāc*).

one energy. So this garland of energy one should hold in such a way that it is *vikāsinīṁ*. At the first step, it is *vikāsinīṁ* (*vikāsinīṁ* means, blooming by-and-by, it has not fully bloomed). It is blooming *vikāsana śīlām*, blooming by-and-by. And *asaṅkocaṁ*, and it is *bhūyastva saṅkocaṁ*, and it becomes, by-and-by, successively it becomes, the limitation…

SCHOLAR: Less contracted.

SWAMIJI:…less contracted. At the first state, there is some limitation. The next state, there is less limitation. So, this state of limitation is also removed by-and-by. And finally it becomes *vikasvarām*, completely bloomed. And this kind of garland of energies a yogi has to hold by-and-by so that he travels from *bhrūbindu* to *samāna*, and in the end from *samāna* he will get entry in *unmanā*, which is the state of *ūrdhva kuṇḍalinī pada*. And when he enters in the state of *ūrdhva kuṇḍalinī pada*, for that he explains in the next *śloka*:

LJA TA05D (34:07)

तत्रोर्ध्वकुण्डलीभूमौ स्पन्दनोदरसुन्दरः ॥५७॥
विसर्गस्तत्र विश्राम्येन्मत्स्योदरदशाजुषि।

tatrordhvakuṇḍalībhūmau spandanodarasundaraḥ //57//
visargastatra viśrāmyenmatsyodaradaśājuṣi /

There, in the state of *ūrdhva kuṇḍalinī*, in the *ūrdhva kuṇḍalinī* state, *tatra ūrdhva kuṇḍalinī bhūmau*, a yogi has to find that there is *visarga*, there is creative discharge. In *ūrdhva kuṇḍalinī pada*, there is creative discharge, that discharge which is always creating something, which bears fruit in each and every step. It is always fruitful discharge. This discharge does not fail.

SCHOLAR: It is *sadodita* (ever-risen).

SWAMIJI: *Sadodita*-discharge. There a yogi finds that there is creative discharge in the *ūrdhva kuṇḍalinī* state, and that discharge is *spandanodarasundaraḥ*, *spandana udara sundaraḥ*, there is, it is beautified by *spandana*, by unlimited throb. That throbbing is never limited, that throbbing never ends. This kind of *visarga* he finds there–unlimited state of throbbing.

You know "throb"?

Tatra viśrāmya, there a yogi has to rest. At that state, a yogi has to rest, which is just like the state of *matsyodara daśājuṣi*, it is just like the state of *matsyodara* (*matsya* means, fish, the belly of a fish), just like the belly of a fish. The belly of fish is always in movement, it is never [still].

JOHN: Quivering.

SWAMIJI: Quivering, yes. Just like that, this is the state just like that. And there you have to rest, there you have to reside. Just to explain it clearly, he gives an example.

SCHOLAR: So this is given as injunctions using the optative, but in fact this is describing a spontaneous rise of experience.

SWAMIJI: This is spontaneous, this is not a junction.

SCHOLAR: So he says "*śrayet*",…

SWAMIJI: *Śrayet.*

SCHOLAR:…"*viśrāmyet*", etcetera.

SWAMIJI: Yes.

SCHOLAR: This is not *vidhi.*

SWAMIJI: This is not *vidhi* (injunction). It happens. *Śrayet* (must hold) means, *śrayati* (to hold).

SCHOLAR: It is a universal statement.

SWAMIJI: It is a universal statement.

LJA TA05D (37:03)

रासभी वडवा यद्वत्स्वधामानन्दमन्दिरम्॥५८॥
विकाससङ्कोचमयं प्रविश्य हृदि हृष्यति।

rāsabhī vaḍavā yadvatsvadhāmānandamandiram //58//
vikāsasaṅkocamayaṁ praviśya hṛdi hṛṣyati /

Just like at the time of [passing] urine [by a] female ass or a female horse (*vaḍavā* means, female horse; *rāsabhī* means, female ass), *yad-vat svadhāmānanda mandiram*, her place of the organ from which she passes urine, at the time when she passes urine, and after she has finished passing urine, and afterwards they have observed, all masters and I have also observed once in a female ass, that organ moves rapidly, [it] automatically expands and contracts, expands and contracts without functioning. That female ass does not function it. It happens, it is automatic, an automatic function, contraction and expansion, contraction and expansion for...I have observed it at least for five minutes, this contraction and expansion takes place in her organ. And *vikāsa saṅkocamayaṁ*, this is *vikāsa* and *saṅkoca* (*vikāsa* means, expansion; *saṅkoca* means, contraction). This way, *praviśya hṛdi hṛṣyati*, she gets satisfaction afterwards and that is the end of this function of passing urine. But in the ordinary course in human beings, it is not like that. Human beings, you have to function it just to remove all the remaining store of urine; you have to function it with contraction and expansion, you have to do it.

JOHN: Yourself.

SWAMIJI: But here, in this case, in this female ass and in a female horse, it works automatic. In the same way, this is the state of *ūrdhva kuṇḍalinī pada* where this kind of function takes place automatically. *Tad vat*...this was an example.

LJA TA05D (39:43)

तद्वन्मुहुर्लीनसृष्टभावव्रातसुनिर्भराम् ॥ ५९ ॥
श्रयेद्विकाससङ्कोचरूढभैरवयामलाम् ।

tadvanmuhurlīnasṛṣṭabhāvavrātasunirbharām //59//
śrayedvikāsasaṅkocarūḍhabhairavayāmalām /

Tadvat, in the same way, *muhur*, over and over again (*muhur*, over and over again), *līna sṛṣṭa*, *līna*, when he finds, a yogi finds that this whole universe along with the objective world and the cognitive world and the subjective world also (*parimita pramātṛ bhāva*, along with *parimita pramātṛ bhāva* and the world of *pramāṇa* and the world of *prameya*), all this world, *muhur*, over and over again, *līna*, gets dissolved in his own Self, in his own Self of God consciousness, and then *sṛṣṭa*, gets expanded again,...*

And it is over and over again, it is not only once, twice, thrice, four times–it is over and over again. He finds this kind of functioning automatically taking place over and over again in continuation. This is the automatic process in order to unite this objective world in the world of God consciousness so that there is no difference between God consciousness and this objective world. The objective world is united with the state of God consciousness. This is what a yogi feels there

*...this is the state of *ūrdhva kuṇḍalinī pada*, and this state is called *krama mudrā* also. This is *krama mudrā*. It is *krama*, it is successive, but it is *mudrā*, it is automatic. *Tadvat muhuḥ līna sṛṣṭa bhāva vrāta sunirbharām*; *bhāva vrāta sunirbharām*, this whole masses of this objective world along with its cognitive world and subjective world, *śrayet*, he possesses, a yogi possesses, *vikāsa saṅkoca rūḍha bhairava yāmalam*, the copulation of Bhairava and Bhairavī, which is established in this expansion and contraction.

JOHN: So this is that copulation where the objectivity has entered into subjectivity, and subjectivity has entered into objectivity.

SWAMIJI: Yes. No, not only objectivity–objectivity, cognitivity and subjectivity. Limited subjectivity is also united in that unlimited subjective universal consciousness.

SCHOLAR: So this *bhairavayāmala* is really Trika there.

SWAMIJI: Yes. *Bhairavayāmala* means, *eka śeṣa samāsa*.

SCHOLAR: Bhairava and Bhairavī.

SWAMIJI: *Bhairavasya bhairavyāśca yāmalam*, this is the copulation of Bhairava and Bhairavī. Bhairava means internal state of God consciousness, Bhairavī means external state of universal consciousness. External state of universal consciousness is united in the internal state of God consciousness so that there remains no difference between God consciousness and universal consciousness–they become one. That is the end of this process.

JOHN: And that takes some time. That *krama mudrā* may function one time in that yogi, or a number of days or weeks or years or...?

SWAMIJI: No, it functions only for five minutes and he comes out in *vyutthāna* (external world) afterwards. It is not one course, it is not a one time course. *Krama mudrā* is the course for your whole life. This functioning takes place only for a few minutes, one or two minutes, and then he is out in *vyutthāna*. And then he has to begin again in practicing with awareness and getting inside that state of God consciousness, and then *krama mudrā* will take place again for one or two minutes in the same way, in the same way and he experiences it. This is what I have experienced. I don't know what others have experienced. They may have experienced for more time, but I am thrown out at once. Just after two minutes I am thrown out.

DEVOTEE: Can you conceive it can be more or less permanent after long practice?

SWAMIJI: Yes, it is my imagination that…yes.

DEVOTEE: It can be conceived that it can.

SWAMIJI: Yes.

JOHN: But the state that gives rise to, *jagadānanda*, that's a permanent state.

SWAMIJI: Yes, this is…when *jagadānanda* is achieved then, then it is permanent.

JOHN: Is that *anupāya*? Is that *jagadānanda anupāya* where…?

SWAMIJI: There is no *upāya*, there is no *upāya*, because *upāya*s end there. In *krama mudrā*, all *upāya*s end. There is nothing to be done, it happens, it is automatic from above. This is a process-less process.

SCHOLAR: A misunderstanding has emerged here. This time-span involved in entering into *krama mudrā*, its shortness is not to do with its imperfection, but its very nature. You said before that its naturally in the state of *visarga*…

SWAMIJI: It is natural.

SCHOLAR:…as soon as you enter into that, you must come out, there is no…it is the nature of God.

SWAMIJI: You have to come out because you have to see whether this universe is one with that God consciousness.

SCHOLAR: This is not Vedāntic state where you go in for two hours, three hours, five hours.

SWAMIJI: No, no, no (affirmative).

SCHOLAR: That is *pralayākala bhāva*.

SWAMIJI: No, the last limit of time of *samādhi*, span of time of *samādhi*, is only twenty-four minutes. After twenty-four minutes, if you reside in *samādhi* for [more than] twenty-four minutes, then you have to throw this physical frame at once. This physical frame won't tolerate that bliss.

SCHOLAR: So don't practice too much.

DEVOTEES: (laughter)

SWAMIJI: (laughs)

LJA TA05D (46:04)

एकीकृतमहामूलशूलवैसर्गिके हृदि ॥ ६० ॥
परस्मिन्नेति विश्रान्तिं सर्वापूरणयोगतः ।

ekīkṛtamahāmūlaśūlavaisargike hṛdi //60//
parasminneti viśrāntiṁ sarvāpūraṇayogataḥ /

Now he puts the conclusion of this process, this automatic process. This is not a process to be functioned, this is an automatic process.

After that, *ekīkṛta mahāmūla śūla vaisargike hṛdi parasminneti viśrāntiṁ sarvā pūraṇa yogataḥ. Mahāmūla*, *śūla* and *vaisargika*; *mahāmūla*, *śūla* and *vaisargika*, these are three states of God consciousness. *Mahāmūla* is the state of…*mahāmūla* means, *māya*, the original cause; the original cause is *mahāmūla*, that is *māyā*. That is *mahāmūla*. And *śūla* is the triple state of three energies, triple state of God's energies: *icchā śakti*, *jñāna śakti* and *kriyā śakti*. This is the state of *śūla*. *Vaisargike* is *visarga*, the state of *visarga* where there is internal *visarga* and external flow, out-flow and in-flow. And these three states (*mahāmūla* means all these elements up to *māyā*),…

SCHOLAR: As one, *piṇḍīkūta*.

SWAMIJI:…*ekīkrta*, a yogi feels that they are only consumed in one state, and that one state is *sa*, that one state is *sa*, the letter *sa*, and *sa* has consumed all these elements right from this earth up to *māyā*. From earth to *māyā*, all these states are consumed in one point, and that is *sa*.

SCHOLAR: So this is third *brahma*, the state of third *brahma*.

SWAMIJI: Yes, this is the third *brahma*.

oṁ tat sat iti nideśo brahmaṇastrividhaḥ smṛtaḥ //[52]

This is the third *brahma*. *Śūla*, the next state is *śūla*. *Śūla* is this *icchā śakti*, *jñāna śakti* and *kriyā śakti* (the energy of will, energy of knowledge, and the energy of action). These three energies are

52. *Bhagavad Gītā*, 17.23

consumed in one point, and that is *au*, that is the letter *au*. He feels that these energies are not differentiatedly perceived–to this yogi. The yogi feels that these three energies of will, knowledge and action are consumed in one point, and that one point is called *au-kāra*. And from the grammatical point of view, this *au-kāra* is called *śūlabīja* and *triśūla bīja* because there are three arrows: one arrow of *icchā*, one arrow of *jñāna*, and one arrow of *kriyā*.

SCHOLAR: Why is it that in *sauḥ mantroddhāra* that we have this *au-kāra* representing three energies, whereas in *pañca piṇḍanātha* we have *e-kāra* representing three energies?

SWAMIJI: Yes, because this *sauḥ* is the creative.

SCHOLAR: So here energy is at its fullest extent.

SWAMIJI: It is the creative state of God consciousness, and that is the destructive state of God consciousness. *Piṇḍanātha* is the destructive state–not actually destructive, it does not destroy the state of God consciousness–it is only the destructive way of his being.

SCHOLAR: But this movement here from *mahāmūla* into *triśūla* is also *nimīlinā krama*, isn't it here as he is describing it?

SWAMIJI: No, it is not *nimīlana krama*. It is *unmīlana*.

SCHOLAR: But *unmīlana krama* is not functioning there through *krama mudrā* at the end there in *vaisargika pada*?

SWAMIJI: That is *unmīlana*, exactly *unmīlana*, and this is *krama mudrā*. And in that *krama mudrā*, the state of *krama mudrā*, these three states, that is, from earth to *māyā* (this class of elements), and *śūla*, from Śuddhavidyā to Sadāśiva (this class of elements), and Śakti and Śiva (and this third class of elements), are found in one point, and that point is *sa* for the first, *au* for the second class, and *visarga* (two *bindu*s ':'), *visarga* for the third class, Śiva and Śakti. And this triple way of states, *parasmin hṛdi viśrāntim eti*, resides in the supreme heart of God consciousness, because *sarvā pūraṇa yogataḥ*, nothing is excluded there; *sarvā pūraṇa yogataḥ*, everything is included there, nothing is excluded, nothing is kept outside this. *Ekīkṛtamahāmūla-śūlavaisargike hṛdi, parasmin hṛdi, viśrāntiṁ eti*, a yogi resides *sarvāpūraṇa yogataḥ*, because he includes everything in his own nature–when it is included. And in that *piṇḍanātha*, he excludes, it is *saṁhāra hṛdayam*, he winds up, it is the process of winding, and this is the process of expanding outside. Unless you expand in the external universe, you have not reached the top of the state of universal God consciousness.

LJA TA05D (52:35)

अत्र तत्पूर्णवृत्त्यैव विश्वावेशमयं स्थितम्॥ ६१ ॥
प्रकाशस्यात्मविश्रान्तावहमित्येव दृश्यताम्।

atra tatpūrṇavṛttyaiva viśvāveśamayaṁ sthitam //61//
prakāśasyātmaviśrāntāvahamityeva dṛśyatām /

This is the real state of *ahaṁ*, and *piṇḍanātha* is the real state of *ma-ha-a* (*piṇḍanātha*) because it is destructive, when you wind up.

SCHOLAR: Bhairava *hṛdayam*.

SWAMIJI: *A* is *anuttara*, *a* is supreme, *ha* is the connecting-rod (*śakti*), *ma* is the individuality. You travel from the supreme through this connecting-rod energy to the individual surface where you find that universal God consciousness. In *piṇḍanātha*, you have to do it…

JOHN: In the opposite way.

SWAMIJI:…in the opposite way. You have to carry this individuality, the being of individuality, through this connecting-rod to Śiva. So it is a winding process. This process is indicated by this *piṇḍanātha*: *r-kṣ-kh-e-ṁ*. And this process is…and that *piṇḍanātha* is called *ma-ha-a* in *ahaṁ*. And this is real *ahaṁ*, this *sauḥ* is the state of real *ahaṁ*.

Atra, in this state of *sauḥ bīja*, *pūrṇa vṛttyaiva*, in fullness, *viśvāveśamayam*, *ahaṁ*, *ahaṁ dṛśyatām*, is experienced, *ahaṁ* is felt, *ahaṁ* is experienced by yogis, that *ahaṁ*, *viśvāveśamayam*, where the whole universe gets entry in that state. The whole universe gets entry in that supreme *ahaṁ*. And that *ahaṁ* is experienced by yogis in this state of God consciousness because *prakāśasya ātma viśrāntau*, *prakāśya* (*prakāśa* means, the reality of God consciousness), *ātma viśrāntau*, gets absorbed in his own nature of individuality–individuality. *Prakāśasya ātma viśrāntāu*; *prakāśasya iyam svarūpe viśrāntau*, when *prakāśa* travels from the innermost center to the external state of his consciousness, that is *ahaṁ*.

Bas, here ends our lesson. We have finished *prāṇa tattva samuccāra*. Now, in this connection he has to explain *cidātma uccāra*. *Cidātma uccāra* is another subject to be explained. When shall we explain it?

DENISE: Tomorrow?

SWAMIJI: (laughs) Not tomorrow. Thursday.

LJA TA05D (55:30) end.
LJA TA05E (00:00) start.

From *apāna vṛtti* you have to travel to the *apānana* state, from *samāna vṛtti* you have to travel to the *samānana* state, and from *udāna vṛtti* you have to travel to the *udānana* state, and from *vyāna vṛtti* to *vyānana vṛtti*, and where the *vyānana* state is observed, there you find the rise of *cidānanda*, and from there you have to go out to *jagadānanda*. This is *prāṇa tattva samuccāra*. Now, after you get entry in the *jagadānanda* state, what happens? Because *jagadānanda* is just consuming in and expanding, exposing outside. This is the state of *jagadānanda*, which is as you find in this *krama mudrā*. But *krama mudrā* is functioning only…it is only functioning, it is not in act. It is not in act. It is only while you are sitting in *samādhi* and going out and entering inside again simultaneously, continually. This is the state of *jagadānanda*. When you achieve, when this *jagadānanda* is well-established, then you have to find out *jagadānanda* in the very action of the outward world. And for that he will lead you to *cidātma uccāra*, that is *cidātma uccāra*.

SCHOLAR: This is the fruit of *prāṇa tattva samuccāra*.

SWAMIJI: Yes. *Samuccāra* will go to both–*prāṇa tattva samuccāra*, *cidātma uccāra*.

SCHOLAR: But this is the fruit of *prāṇa tattva samuccāra*.

SWAMIJI: Free?

SCHOLAR: Fruit, fruit.

SWAMIJI: Fruit, yes, fruit (*phala*). Because *anuttaraṁ śāntaṁ paraṁ brahmaivāsti*. This is commentary, we have to read the commentary. Without commentary you can't understand. *Anuttaraṁ śāntaṁ paraṁ brahmaivāsti*, in fact, when you go in, in that *krama mudrā*, in *jagadānanda*, when you are established in *jagadānanda*, you find inside–what do you find inside?–inside you find *anuttaraṁ śāntaṁ paraṁ brahmaiva*, peaceful *paraṁ brahma*, without any differentiated perception. In the next step, you find differentiated perception, movement in the world of differentiated perception–this is the next step.

SCHOLAR: Rising from above to below.

SWAMIJI: Rising from above, yes, this is a rise. You have to rise from above to below. This is also rise. *Iti tatra ko nāmā* (comm.), and this rise is not…this is not a rise for good. You have to extract it again inside to see, to observe the state of *śānta* (appeased) *brahma*. And the next moment you have to observe the state of *udita* (rising) *brahma* in the external world. In the next state, you have to find again the state of *śānta brahma* and then *udita brahma, śānta brahma, udita brahma,* simultaneously without any break.

SCHOLAR: So this is *krama mudrā.*

SWAMIJI: This is the state of *krama mudrā.* And this *krama mudrā* is not to be functioned, it is automatic, it takes place...

JOHN: In *samādhi*?

SWAMIJI: It is in *samādhi,* yes, it is the real *samādhi.* This is the real *samādhi* when you get entry in *jagadānanda.*

JOHN: But now this could be walking and going or coming?

SWAMIJI: No, no, walking, going is not...it is only in *samādhi.*

DEVOTEE: Not in actual active action.

SWAMIJI: No, he just perceives outside and gets entry again inside.

SCHOLAR: But establishment of *jagadānanda* is maintaining that *śāntoditā* state even in the movement of the senses.

SWAMIJI: For that he has to explain *cidātma uccāra. Cidātma uccāra* is the next subject...

SCHOLAR: This is the point of that...

SWAMIJI: Yes. This is the...

SCHOLAR: Where you proceed beyond Vedānta.

SWAMIJI:...where you proceed, yes. When *tatra ko nāmāyam ahaṁ parāmarśa yasyāpi viśrānti dhāmatā syāt* (comm.)? So *ahaṁ parāmarśa* is there.[53] Why you have to move out again and again? *Ityāśaṅkāṁ śamayituṁ*, for that, to subside this doubt, *prāṇa tattva samuccāra ānantaryeṇa anujoddeśoddiṣṭaṁ cidātmanoccāramavatārayati* (comm.), now he takes the explanation in hand of *cidātma uccāra. Cidātma uccāra* is to be done, *cidātma uccāra* in the very activity of the world–in eating, in drinking, in hearing, in smelling, in touching. In touching also, you must feel that, the rise of *cidātma*, the rise of God consciousness. God consciousness must be held while eating, while doing, while talking.

SCHOLAR: *Sarvas avasthās.*

SWAMIJI: *Sarvas avasthās.*[54] That is *cidātma uccāra.* For that he has to explain *cidātma uccāra.*

---

53. *Aham parāmarśa* (Self-awareness) is there.

54. In all (*sarva*) states (*avasthā*).

LJA TA05E (05:27)

Cidātma Uccāra
Rise of God Consciousness

अनुत्तरविमर्शे प्राग्व्यापारादिविवर्जिते ॥ ६२ ॥
चिद्विमर्शपराहङ्कृत् प्रथमोल्लासिनी स्फुरेत् ।

anuttaravimarśe prāgvyāpārādivivarjite //62//
cidvimarśaparāhaṅkṛt prathamollāsinī sphuret /

Prāk, in the very beginning, in the very beginning of that *jagadānanda*, the rise of *jagadānanda*, when *jagadānanda* takes place, first a *sādhaka* feels the entire bliss of God consciousness in his own nature for one second. The next second he feels he is thrown out in external *vyutthāna* (external world) just to realize God consciousness outside also. But *prāk*, in the previous state of *jagadānanda*, *anuttara vimarśe*, that *vimarśa* (awareness) of *anuttara* is *vyāpārādi vivarjite*, there is no *vyāpāra*, there is no differentiated activity, it is only residing in one's own consciousness without any break. This is *śānta paraṁ brahma*. *Cit vimarśa parā*, this is *cit vimarśa parā*, bent upon *cit vimarśa*, bent upon realizing one's own consciousness of God (*cit vimarśa parā*). This *ahaṁkṛt*, this *ahaṁ parāmarśa* is *prathama ullāsinī*, it takes place first. First, this kind of situation of *jagadānanda* takes place.

Prāk means, *pūrvakoṭau*, in the first step. There are two steps: *pūrva koṭi* and *aparā koṭi*. *Pūrva koṭi* is for transcendental bliss, *aparā koṭi* is for universal bliss.

SCHOLAR: So this first state is in *nimīlana*, not in…?

SWAMIJI: No, these two states are simultaneously working in *jagadānanda*. You have already understood that.

SCHOLAR: But the two points are that of *śānta* and *udita*.

SWAMIJI: But these two points, one is *śānta*, the next is *udita*: one is the transcendental state of God consciousness, and the next is the universal state of God consciousness. After realizing the universal state of God consciousness, you have to go back again in the transcendental state of God consciousness. From that, you have to get outside in the universal state of God consciousness, and in continuation.

SCHOLAR: Until *sāmarasyam* (oneness) is achieved.

SWAMIJI: This is the process, this is the simultaneous functioning of *jagadānanda*. And in this *jagadānanda*, he has taken, he wants to explain these two parts, two stages–the first stage and the second stage. The first stage is that *ahaṁkṛt*, that stage of *ahaṁ parāmarśa*, which is *cit vimarśa parā*, bent upon finding out the *cit vimarśa*, transcendental state of God consciousness. The next is the state of universal God consciousness. This *prathama ullāsinī daśā* takes place first–*prathama ullāsinī*. The first state takes place first in the state of *jagadānanda*, the rise of *jagadānanda*.

LJA TA05E (08:50)

तत उद्योगसक्तेन स द्वादशकलात्मना ॥ ६३ ॥
सूर्येणाभासयेद्भावं पूरयेदथ चर्चयेत्।

tata udyogasaktena sa dvādaśakalātmanā //63//
sūryeṇābhāsayedbhāvaṁ pūrayedatha carcayet /
(not recited)

Tata udyogasaktena, then you have to put *icchā* (will) there. Then *sa dvādaśakalātmanā*, when *dvādaśakalā*, he gets entry in *dvādaśakalā*, he gets entry in *pramāṇa bhāva* (*pramāṇa bhāva* means, in the field of organs)…

SCHOLAR: *Karaṇeśvarī.*

SWAMIJI: In the field of organs. When he begins to perceive objects with his eyes, with nose, with skin, with tongue, with everything, that is *dvādaśakalā*; that is *dvādaśakalā*, the states of twelvefold states. The twelvefold states are the states of *pramāṇa daśā*, the states of *pramāṇa bhāva*: five organs of actions, five organs of cognition, and *mana* (mind) and *buddhi* (intellect), and in the world of the *vācaka* world, in the *vācaka* world from *a* to *visarga* (*aḥ*), these twelve states.[55]

SCHOLAR: *Śānta varjam.*

SWAMIJI: *Śānta varjam*, yes, *śānta varjam* without those eunuch…

JOHN: Without those eunuch letters.

SCHOLAR: *Ṛ-ṝ-li-lī.*

SWAMIJI:…eunuch letters, four letters, *ṛ-ṝ-li-lī.*

DEVOTEE: Neuter, *hai na* (isn't it)?

SWAMIJI: Neuter. Neuter *ke bagar* (without). Neuter is excluded in Shaivism, because those who are established in this neuter state of Śiva, they are not authorized in Shaivism. They are unauthorized.

SCHOLAR: This is this kingdom of Īśvara Sahib. There was that man you explained.

SWAMIJI: Yes, Īśvara Sahib, yes. He was always inside, for thirty-five years he was in silence.

DEVOTEE: Who?

SWAMIJI: One master in our *maṭhikā* (tradition), in our *guru krama* (succession of masters). His name was Īśvara Sahib.

So, in the first state, *nistaraṅgajaladhiprakṣye* (comm.), there is no wave, there are no tides of going outside. *Anuttarātmani vimarśe*, it is only transcendental *vimarśa* (awareness) of Self. *Parasmin prakāśe prathamamullasanaśīlā*, this is the first state of God consciousness that rises first in the field of *jagadānanda. Ata eva vyatiriktavimṛśyābhāvāt cidvimarśaparā*, it is why he has said it is *cit vimarśa parā*, it is bent

55. "The word *vācya* means 'that which is observed, spoken, told.' So *vācyādhva* is the path of that which is observed, seen, realized. It is called *vācyādhva* because it is seen, it is observed, it is created, it is felt. It is the objective cycle of this creation. Now, we must turn to its observer, the creator of this *adhvan*. The creator of the threefold path of the universe known as *vācyādhva* is called *vācakādhva*. The meaning of the word *vācaka* is 'that which observes, sees, and creates.' And so that path which observes, sees, and creates is called *vācakādhva*. And, like *vācyādhva*, *vācakādhva* is also composed of three paths: gross (*sthūla*), subtle (*sūkṣma*), and subtlest (*para*). Gross (*sthūla*) *vācakādhva* is called *padādhva* and consists of sentences; sentences are said to be gross. Subtle (*sukṣma*) *vācakādhva* is called *mantrādhva* and consists of words, because words are known to be more subtle than sentences. Subtler than *mantrādhva*, the world of words, is the path of letters, called *varṇādhva*." *The Secret Supreme*, "The Six Fold Path of the Universe (*ṣaḍadhvan*)", pg. 12-13.

upon finding out God consciousness within, without any wavering movements of the external world.

Do you understand my English (laughs)?

DEVOTEE: Yes, Sir.

SWAMIJI: *Acha* (okay). *Yenāsya sarvatraiva svātantryamudiyāt, svasvātantryamāhātmyādeva hi anuttaraprakāśātmā parameśvaraḥ svaṁ svarūpaṁ gopayitvā pramāṇādidaśā madhiśayānaḥ pṛthag-bhāvajātamābhāsayet* (comm.), then he comes down in the external world, in universal consciousness. And then, when universal consciousness also takes place, now you have to observe *udyoga*, you have to put *udyoga* (effort). Without *udyoga*, you cannot travel in the active world, the active world of actions. For instance, you are outside in *jagadānanda*, you are perceiving the state of *jagadānanda* inside and outside in the state of *krama mudrā*. After *krama mudrā* is over, [after] it has functioned properly and you are established in *krama mudrā*, then you have to put *udyoga*, the rise of *udyoga* (will). By will you can get up from your *āsana* (seat) and try to step onwards for going outside in the compound or taking meals or...you have to put that will, forced will. If you don't put that forced will, that *jagadānanda* won't...it will vanish.

SCHOLAR: But this *udyoga* rises spontaneously as the fruit of *jagadānanda*.

SWAMIJI: This is the fruit of *jagadānanda*, but you have to put *udyoga* also.

SCHOLAR: But the ability to put that is a spontaneous capacity.

SWAMIJI: Yes, you must have ability. As long as there is no ability, you have to again get in the functioning of *jagadānanda* again.

SCHOLAR: Because this is the absolute strength to be able to...

SWAMIJI: This is the absolute strength–*cidātma uccāra. Cidātma uccāra* must take place in each and every act of this world, external world. For instance, you take food, while taking food you must find this state of *jagadānanda*, while chewing food you must feel that state. If you don't feel that state, leave that aside, leave food-taking aside, keep it away and go back to the *jagadānanda* state again. So you have to put *udyoga* first.

LJA TA05E (14:18)

Tata udyogasaktena sa dvādaśakalātmanā sūryeṇa (verse 63), then you have to travel from *pramātṛ bhāva* to *pramāṇa bhāva*. From *pramātṛ bhāva*, from the state of subjective consciousness, you have to travel to cognitive consciousness, consciousness of five senses–you have to travel there. That is *dvādaśakalā*, that is *sūrya*, because *sūryaṁ pramāṇam ityahuḥ soma meyam pracakṣate* (comm.), *pramātṛ rūpa to agni hai* (*pramātṛ* is fire), *sūrya pramāṇkar hata hai*…*sūrya* (the sun) is *pramāṇa* (cognition), *soma* (moon) is *prameya* (objective), and *agni* (fire) is *pramātṛ* (subjective). Because I was accustomed to explain to him in Hindi, so (laughs)…

DENISE: It came out in Hindi.

SWAMIJI: Yes. *Sūryeṇa ābhāsayed bhāvaṁ*, so, this *bhāva* (state), whatever *bhāva* it is, it may be smelling, it may be touching, it may be tasting, it may be perceiving through eyes (*rūpa*)–*śabda*, *sparśa*, *rūpa*, *rasa* and *gandha*, any *bhāva*–and that *bhāva*, *sūryeṇa ābhāsayet*, by this *sūrya*, by the way of this cognitive field, he has to *ābhāsayet*, he has to create this, he has to create this…for instance, I look at you, I have created you, and then I get the taste of you. That [taste] is *pūraṇa* (satisfying), that is *sthiti* (preservation). And *carcayet*, then I have to wind up your state in my own God consciousness–that is *carcayet*. *Ābhāsayet*, *pūrayet*, *carcayet*, so those three state takes place simultaneously there.

SCHOLAR: *Sṛjyet sthāpayet…?*

SWAMIJI: *Sṛjyet sthāpayet saṁharet. Sṛjyet* (you should create), you should protect (*sthāpayet*), and you should wind up, you should take it in (*saṁharet*).

DEVOTEE: Absorb back.

SWAMIJI: Absorb back.

SCHOLAR: In *viśrānti*.

SWAMIJI: *Tato ahaṁ parāmarśa sphuraṇāddhetoḥ* (comm.), because this is the way of *ahaṁ parāmarśa* (Self-awareness) that has to travel from inside to the outside world. *Sa paraḥ prakāśāḥ*, and the traveling is done by *para prakāśa*, supreme *prakāśa*, supreme *prakāśa* of God consciousness. God consciousness has to travel outside. It is not individual consciousness which is traveling. If individual consciousness is traveling, that is incorrect traveling. So you should wind up that traveling, you should stop that traveling, you should go inside the same state of *jagadānanda*. You should try to find out that *jagadānanda* again because it means that *jagadānanda* is not well-established. When *jagadānanda* is well-established, then you can travel in the outside world also with it.

JOHN: So that *udyoga* means that you take that *jagadānanda*…

SWAMIJI: Outside.

JOHN:…and get up and do things, you don't lose that.

SWAMIJI: Yes. You must not be away from that *jagadānanda* in the very action. If you are away, then you have to wind up that.

JOHN: So the skill in that is getting up and being able to carry that with you without losing it.

SWAMIJI: Yes, without losing it.

SCHOLAR: So *jagadānanda* here is not the ultimate state for a Shaiva *sādhaka*.

SWAMIJI: Where?

SCHOLAR: Since he must apply *udyoga* and take it into the field of the senses as well.

SWAMIJI: Into the field of senses, yes.

SCHOLAR: Previously I had understood that *jagadānanda* was the complete state of *unmīlana*.

SWAMIJI: No, it will be complete only when it will get entry in *cidātma uccāra*, in the very action of worldly activities.

DEVOTEE: It is the perfection of *jagadānanda*.

SWAMIJI: This is the perfection of *jagadānanda*.

DEVOTEE: The culmination.

SWAMIJI: Yes.

LJA TA05E (18:10)

Saṅkucitapramātṛbhūmikāvabhāsanapurassaram (comm.), and you have to travel from *saṅkucita bhāva* with *asaṅkucita bhāva*, you have to travel in darkness with light. It is not traveling in light. The permanent light you find only in the first state of *jagadānanda*, in *krama mudrā*, and when it is established, then you have to take that light in your hand and travel in darkness! That is darkness outside, the external world. So in darkness you have to hold light. So this is tough work for a *sādhaka*. If it is not done properly, if you are not successful in doing this, you have to again wind up in your own previous state [because] *cidātma uccāra* is incorrect *cidātma uccāra*. *Cidātma uccāra* must be correctly functioned.

JOHN: So *krama mudrā* helps that...

SWAMIJI: Yes, *krama mudrā* helps.

JOHN:...it helps you prepare for that.

SWAMIJI: Because you get more capacity, more strength in residing in *krama mudrā*; more strength and more capacity, more ability in going out *with* it, with this light. Because you have to go out in darkness, and in darkness you have to catch, you have to carry the light of inside.

SCHOLAR: So in *krama mudrā*, you experience illumination of the cognitive field, but you are inactive.

SWAMIJI: You are inactive, inactive.

SCHOLAR: It is *asphuṭa* (non-vivid) *unmīlanam.*

SWAMIJI: Yes. *Unmīlane-nimīlanam, nimīlane-unmīlanam, asphuṭa rupatāya* (not vivid) in *krama mudrā*. But in this *cidātma uccāra*, it is perfect *unmīlana*.

SCHOLAR: *Sphuṭatāma* (absolutely vivid).

SWAMIJI: Yes, then you are complete, you achieve the completion of Bhairava *bhāva*. So, *ekaikam bhāvam* (comm.), you have to find out *ekaikam bhāvam*. I touch only the commentary here and there. *Ekaikam bhāvam*: for instance, there is food, on the table food is placed for you to take, you have to take it, and you have to see that while taking your food, are you in that *krama mudrā*. While chewing it, while tasting it, while chewing it, or everything, you must see that you are in *krama mudrā*. If you are not in *krama mudrā*, it is a sin to take food! Food is not meant for those who cannot take food in *krama mudrā*. "*Yatra yeśāṁ mokṣaprādhānyam taireva viṣayāsevyāḥ*" are the words of Abhinavagupta.[56]

SCHOLAR: Only those who...

SWAMIJI: Only those are authorized to take food who have the ability to find out the state of God consciousness while doing that. Those who have not the ability, they should starve, they should starve and leave this body. They have no right to live in this world.

DEVOTEE: Too harsh.

SWAMIJI: Huh? (laughs)

DENISE: Then we wouldn't have any more lectures (laughs).

SWAMIJI: (laughs)

56. Abhinavagupta's commentary of *Bhagavad Gītā* 3.11.

DENISE: We'd all be dead.

JOHN: So this is the state of oneness.

SWAMIJI: This is the state of oneness, yes.

JOHN: So then, in this state, you told me one time that there was the state of a yogi where if he is driving a car, he is God, the car is God, and the road is also God–he experiences himself as the road also.

SWAMIJI: But he must experience…yes, this is that, this is that, this is that state.[57]

JOHN: So he experiences himself as food, he experiences himself as the table that he is eating on, everything.

SWAMIJI: Because that taste is there, the taste of that complete God consciousness is felt in each and every movement.

JOHN: So in this state when it's completely complete, then the whole world ceases to be darkness and becomes light, is it?

SWAMIJI: Yes, it is filled with light! Because there is no darkness, darkness cannot…the basis of darkness is light, darkness cannot shine without light. Because when you say, "This is darkness," it means it is…

DEVOTEE: Negation of light.

SCHOLAR: *Nabhakusuma* (a sky-flower).

SWAMIJI: No.

DENISE: Absence of light.

SWAMIJI: No, it is not absence of light. You are seeing, you are observing darkness; when you are observing darkness, it is light, it is not darkness at all.

DEVOTEE: It is light, a form of light, yes.

SCHOLAR: *Prakāśamaprakāśayet.*

SWAMIJI: So, when *carcayet*, when the state of *carcana*…*carcana* means, when you take this [food] and when you have filled your stomach, filled your stomach with that meal. It is why he has put "*carcayet*"; in place of "*saṁharet*" (destruction), he has put "*carcayet*" (pursue, study). He has to find out God consciousness there.

SCHOLAR: *Carcayet* has the sense of *carvayet. Saṁhāret.*

SWAMIJI: *Carcayet* is just to find out–*viveka.*

SCHOLAR: *Sāraṁ uddharet.*

SWAMIJI: *Sāraṁ uddharet* (extract the essence).

---

57. See also *Bhagavad Gītā* 4.24.

DEVOTEE: *Svātmasātkāryeṇa–saṁharet*?

SWAMIJI: *Svātmasātkāryeṇa antarbhāvaṁ nayet. Svātmasātkāryeṇa antarbhāvaṁ nayet*, not *saṁharet*, it is not destroyed, it is just to get inside your own God consciousness. That is the state of *pramiti bhāva* in *pramātṛ bhāva*. First you have to take the state of *prameya bhāva* (objectivity), then from *prameya bhāva* you have to travel to *pramāṇa bhāva* (cognition), then from *pramāṇa bhāva* you have to travel to *pramātṛ bhāva* (subjectivity-cum-objectivity), and from *pramātṛ bhāva* you have to travel to *pramiti bhāva* (pure subjectivity). And when *pramiti bhāva* is [held], there again the functioning of *krama mudrā* will take place vividly, and then you can do some other act. This is the state of the beginning, the beginning of *cidātma uccāra*. When *cidātma uccāra* is complete, then there is no need to travel back to *krama mudrā*. It is just to see whether this *cidātma uccāra* is functioning properly or incorrectly. When *cidātma uccāra* is not functioning properly, then you have to move back to the *jagadānanda* state, the previous *jagadānanda* state.

SCHOLAR: In *krama mudrā*.

SWAMIJI: In *krama mudrā*. And after you are residing in *krama mudrā*, you have to go out again to see and to perceive if *cidātma uccāra* is functioning properly. If *cidātma uccāra* is functioning properly and you are established in *cidātma uccāra*, then there is no need to get entry in *jagadānanda* at all. Then you are absolutely residing in *jagadānanda* completely.

JOHN: So this *pramiti bhāva*, it exists in the state of *jagadānanda* only?

SWAMIJI: Yes, *pramiti bhāva* is just when you taste it, taste one hand-full of rice, and you get entry in that. That is *pramiti bhāva*.

JOHN: So it doesn't exist before *jagadānanda–pramiti bhāva*.

SWAMIJI: No, no. *Bas*, we will do this much. Now the 64th [verse] is to take place on Saturday.

LJA TA05E (25:44)

Discussion:

SCHOLAR: Swami Rām used to enter *samādhi* through taking snuff. You told me that.

SWAMIJI: Yes (laughs). Everything!

SCHOLAR: But you said it was his habit after lunch to take some snuff.

SWAMIJI: Yes, it was his habit, but that habit ended in that *jagadānanda* in the end. Then it was not a habit, it was only the functioning in *jagadānanda* in him.

DEVOTEE: Who was this, Swamiji?

SWAMIJI: My grand-master, Swami Rām.

JOHN: So this *jagadānanda* in its fullness…

SWAMIJI: He used to [take] snuff after [eating].

DEVOTEE: Cigarette.

SWAMIJI: Not a cigarette. He smoked, he smoked that hubble-bubble (hooka), but smoked in a peculiar way. He smoked just like this (Swamiji demonstrates), not in this flickering position. Then his mouth remained for hours together like that. They were heroes, heroes in Shaivite scholars. And that Īśvara Sahib was unauthorized.

SCHOLAR: *Anādhikārī…*

SWAMIJI: *Anādhikārī* (unauthorized). In our Shaivism, there are previous masters also, six previous masters authorized and six previous masters unauthorized. Unauthorized masters are those who have carried their consciousness inside this transcendental God consciousness, and authorized were those who had carried this consciousness in the very active world–those were authorized.

JOHN: This state of *jagadānanda*, is this the state of *anupāya*? Completion, the state of…?

SWAMIJI: It is not an *upāya* (a means). *Upāya* ends there. All functioning of *upāya*s are ended there.

JOHN: But you said *anupāya* is also not an *upāya*. In real sense, *anupāya* is no *upāya*.

SWAMIJI: It is no *upāya*, but it is in the beginning of that *jagadānanda*.

JOHN: In the beginning.

SWAMIJI: But when *jagadānanda* is there, there are no *upāya*s, the question of the rise of *upāya*s does not arise.

JOHN: In the first book, when you explained *anupāya*, you explained there are two kinds of negatives: a partial-negative and a complete-negative. And you said that in the beginning of *anupāya*, there was a partial-negative like when a woman has no stomach in some sense, so she…there is some kind of…

SWAMIJI: There is some kind of *upāya*. And that some kind of *upāya* vanishes also in the state of *jagadānanda*.

JOHN: And then when it vanishes, then you have that complete negation. That would be the real state of *anupāya*, that highest. That's what I am wondering.

SWAMIJI: Yes.

JOHN: Is that…? In other words, this is the highest state.

SWAMIJI: This is the highest state–after *anupāya*.

SCHOLAR: But when you take resort of some sensation when you come from *jagadānanda* to perform *cidātma uccāra*, there is some element of means there. Is this not *prasaja-pratiṣedha* here? It is not *vyudāsa*.

SWAMIJI: No, it is not *vyudāsa*.[58]

SCHOLAR: Some trace of *upāya* is still existing there to go, you were saying, to find *krama mudrā* in that state.

SWAMIJI: No, *upāya*, it is an automatic function, you have not to function. It is only, the functioning is of *udyoga*, you have to take a firm will that, "I will go out with this God consciousness."

SCHOLAR: But that taking of a firm will, is that not spontaneous?

SWAMIJI: "I will walk *with* this God consciousness, I will talk and I will fight with each other *with* God consciousness." And you have to make this a firm will. It is not an easy job (laughs).

JOHN: So this *udyoga*, isn't this a touch of *upāya* there?

SWAMIJI: What?

JOHN: Isn't this a touch of *anupāya* in *udyoga* in that first sense of partial-negation where you have to take will, some means?

SWAMIJI: Yes, some, slight.

JOHN: Slight.

SWAMIJI: Slight, slight trace of *anupāya*.

SCHOLAR: There is no limitation in that, that desire, so it must be spontaneously rising from the nature of the Self. Is that correct?

SWAMIJI: Yes. It is spontaneous, yes, it is correct.

SCHOLAR: It is not like saying, "Oh, I must study the *Tantrāloka*" or "I must come and see Swamiji today."

SWAMIJI: No, no. This is not this way a course. This is a spontaneous course. These things are found only in the *Tantrāloka*, not in

---

58. Viz., *paryudāsa pratiṣedha*. See *Tantrāloka* 2.2.

other schools of Kashmir Shaivism.

SCHOLAR: Schools of…?

SWAMIJI: Kashmir Shaivism, other schools.

SCHOLAR: Other schools aside from Kashmir Shaivism?

SWAMIJI: No, I mean the Krama System. This is only found in this Kaula system–Kaula, Kaula. The Kaula system is more than the Kula system.

JOHN: What is that initiation in *anupāya* that you spoke about that takes you to that state in one second? You said some…

SWAMIJI: This is only slight, that slight initiation is that when you are seated before your master who is residing in the *anupāya*-state, but you realize that he is in the *anupāya*-state. This is the only initiation.

JOHN: And that just carries you in one moment.

SWAMIJI: And this carries you and this "poison" of that bliss is transformed in your brain at once.

DEVOTEE: Once more, please (inaudible).

SWAMIJI: No, it was not our subject.

DEVOTEE: No, I know, but whatever it is, yes.

SWAMIJI: It was the *bhujaṅgavat garalasaṁkrāmaḥ*: he has to sit, the *anupāya sādhaka* who is extremely to the top-most state of the *upāya*s, who has reached that top-most state, he has not to do anything, he has not to do any *sādhanā* (practice), just sit before a realized master and just understand that, "My master is in the trance of ultimate God consciousness," and that realizing will carry you to that God consciousness. This disciple also will become just like the master. *Dīpaḥ dīpamevoditam*, just like one candle lights another candle in the same manner, in the same glamour. I don't know if "glamour" is correct. "Glamour"? "Splendor."

DEVOTEE: Splendor.

SWAMIJI: Splendor. So there is no difference between the master and disciple there, he is as good as the master.

JOHN: So this is that seeing a master as Śiva and disciple as Sadāśiva. In those different stages moving from where the master is the *ṛṣi* (seer) and…

SWAMIJI: That is *sambandha*. This is the contact of the guru and the *śiṣya*, master and disciple.

JOHN: And the supreme contact is what you were just speaking about, is it?

SWAMIJI: Yes.

JOHN: Where you see your master, you really realize your master as Lord Śiva, and then you are also carried to that.

SWAMIJI: Yes, when you are in the Sadāśiva state. When you reside in the Sadāśiva state, then you are carried to the Śiva state, then you will be carried.

JOHN: And that is real contact.

SCHOLAR: So that is why in the…

SWAMIJI: That is *para sambandha*. [Then] *parāparā sambandha*, *avāntara sambandha*, *antarāla sambandha*, and *divya sambandha*, and *adivya sambandha*. This you have read in the first *āhnika*.[59]

SCHOLAR: So this contemplation of the master as Paramaśiva-*bhaṭṭāraka* (Lord) is the essence of the Kaula system there.

SWAMIJI: Yes.

SCHOLAR: The whole course of contemplation is the contemplation of *guru-maṇḍalam*.

SWAMIJI: Yes. *Bas*?

LJA TA05E (33:48)

In the previous two *ślokas*, it is explained that in the conduct of this *cidātma uccāra*, you have to conduct this *cidātma uccāra* from the *jagadānanda* state, where in the *jagadānanda* state everything is in a peaceful movement; although it is in and out, but it is in a peaceful state. And it is *vyāpārādi vivarjite*, there is no *vyāpāra* (activity), there is no that kind of *vyāpāra* in coming out and doing worldly activities. It is only the functioning inside and outside while sitting. This is the state of *jagadānanda*.

SCHOLAR: Through *krama mudrā*.

SWAMIJI: Through *krama mudrā*, yes. And then you have to put *udyoga* (effort) to come down from *para pramātṛ bhāva* in the world of cognition (*pramāṇa daśa*).

SCHOLAR: *Dvādaśakalātmanā udyogena*.

SWAMIJI: So it is *dvādaśakalā*. *Dvādaśakalā* means twelvefold: five organs of knowledge and five organs of action, mind and intellect.

---

59. The contacts between master and disciple.

These twelve things are functioning in *pramāṇa bhāva*, in the cognitive world. And in the objective world, twelve are not functioning; in the objective world, sixteen things are functioning. There is no functioning of intellect there in the objective world. In the objective world, the intellect does not function, only mind functions with five senses of action, five senses of knowledge, and five these *śabda*, *sparśa*, *rūpa*, *rasa* and *gandha* (the five *tanmātras*). Five *tanmātras*, five senses of knowledge, and five senses of action function there, along with mind. Not intellect, intellect is not there.

JOHN: Why not intellect? Because it is the judging faculty?

SWAMIJI: Judging is only done in *pramāṇa daśā*, judging is not done in *prameya daśā* (in the objective world), but mind is there.

SCHOLAR: How does mind operate there? Could you distinguish for us between…?

SWAMIJI: Because without mind…because you feel, you feel that taste.

SCHOLAR: But there's no objective decision that, "This is known by me." That's *pramāṇa daśā.*

SWAMIJI: That is *pramāṇa daśā.* No, when you travel to *prameya daśā*, there is no intellect, there is only *bhoga*, just to enjoy–enjoyment and mind.

SCHOLAR: So there is the impression in *mana* (mind) only.

SWAMIJI: Yes.

SCHOLAR: So this is the sixteen *vikāras* (changes).

SWAMIJI: Yes. So these two are already explained in previous two *ślokas*. Now, he goes down in *prameya daśā*, in the objective world *with* that vibrating God consciousness, because vibrating God consciousness is not to be neglected there also.

LJA TA05E (37:13)

अथेन्दुः षोडशकलो विसर्गग्रासमन्थरः ॥ ६४ ॥

सञ्जीवन्यमृतं बोधवह्नौ विसृजति स्फुरन्।

इच्छाज्ञानक्रियाशक्तिसूक्ष्मरन्ध्रस्त्रुगग्रगम्॥ ६५ ॥

तदेवममृतं दिव्यं संविद्देवीषु तर्पकम्।

athenduḥ ṣoḍaśakalo visargagrāsamantharaḥ //64//
sañjīvanyamṛtaṁ bodhavahnau visṛjati sphuran /
icchājñānakriyāśaktisūkṣmarandhrasrugagragam //65//
tadevamamṛtaṁ divyaṁ saṁviddevīṣu tarpakam /

Atha, after getting entry in that *pramiti bhāva,...**

Because in *sūrya daśā* (cognitive state), he had to get entry in *sṛṣṭi* (creation) first in *prameya bhāva* (objectivity), then *sthiti* (protection) in *pramāṇa bhāva* (cognition), and then *saṁhṛti* (destruction) in *pramiti bhāva* (pure subjectivity). There is no *pramātṛ bhāva* (limited subjectivity). *Pramātṛ bhāva* will remain only in the field of ignorance because *pramātṛ daśā* is that state where there is impression of objectivity also there adjusted in the subjective consciousness. When in subjective consciousness there is no touch of [objective] impression, that is *pramiti bhāva*–that is *pramiti bhāva.* So you have to rise to *pramiti bhāva* in that state of twelvefold cognitive world.[60]

SCHOLAR: So, when he is in the state of *pramāṇa,...*

SWAMIJI: Yes.

SCHOLAR:...*dvādaśakalātmanā udyoga saktena, sūryeṇa* (verse 63), that is creation, preservation, and destruction in *pramāṇa daśā* only. Now we are moving here into the sphere of...

SWAMIJI: Yes, that *pramāṇa daśā* is exactly *pramiti daśā.*

SCHOLAR: When it is in its fullness, when it is established.

SWAMIJI: Yes, *carcayet*, yes.

SCHOLAR: And now we are moving here into the expansion of (inaudible) *ānākhya cakra.*

SWAMIJI: External world, yes.

JOHN: So *pramātṛ* only exists in ignorance, it is only limited ego–in *pramātṛ.*

SWAMIJI: *Pramiti* is that state of *pramātṛ* where there is no impression of objectivity.

SCHOLAR: *Pramātṛ anākhyadaśa.*

SWAMIJI: *Pramātṛ anākhyadaśa. Pramātur anākhyadaśa.*

---

60. Viz., the twelve Kālīs as revealed in the fourth *āhnika* of the *Tantrāloka.*

*...*athendu ṣoḍaśakalā*, then he has to travel to sixteenfold *vikāsa*, sixteenfold expansion of the external universal field. It is not that sixteenfold external universal field which is perceived by ordinary people, in ordinary individuals. It is something else.

SCHOLAR: *Bhāsācakra.*

SWAMIJI: It is *anākhya cakra.*

SCHOLAR: It is *bhāsā cakram.*

SWAMIJI: It is *bhāsā* (light). *Ṣoḍaśakalā*, and that *ṣoḍaśakalā induḥ* (*induḥ* means, objective world) is *visarga grāsa mantharaḥ*; *visarga grāsa mantharaḥ*, by the intake of *visarga*, strong intaking of *visarga*–intake. It is not out-take.

SCHOLAR: *Mantharaḥ*?

SWAMIJI: *Mantharaḥ, visrabdha*, strong.

SCHOLAR: *Dṛḍha*, established.

SWAMIJI: Yes. And then *sañjīvanī amṛtam, sañjīvanī amṛtam* is created.[61] *Sañjīvanī amṛtam* means, that nectar which is beyond this objective world, which is in the background of the objective world. That is *sañjīvanī*, that is the seventeenth *kalā*. That is the seventeenth *kalā* found in the background of sixteen *kalā*s. [Behind] all sixteen *kalā*s, you find that seventeenth state, the seventeenth state where there is no impression of objectivity, the impression of objectivity does not remain. He finds in the objective world the state of above-objectivity.

JOHN: Permeating that, he sees, it's like, it shines through.

SWAMIJI: Yes.

DENISE: The transcendental state?

SWAMIJI: Yes, it is transcendental state. And that *amṛta, visṛjati bodha vahnau*, is created, not in the state of *para pramātṛ bhāva*, it is created in *mita pramātṛ bhāva.*

SCHOLAR: *Miti pramātṛ bhāva.*

SWAMIJI: *Mita pramātṛ bhāva* (limited subjectivity). Because he is coming down in individuality, in the surface of ignorance. In the surface of ignorance, in the surface of darkness, he has to observe the highest light, highest light of transcendental God consciousness.

JOHN: Is this seventeenth *kalā.*

---

61. Sañjīvanī is a mythical plant believed to cure all ailments. In the *Rāmāyaṇa*, Hanuman went searching for this plant to cure Rāmā's ailing brother, Lakṣmaṇa.

SWAMIJI: This is the seventeenth *kalā*.

SCHOLAR: So he is rising here?

SWAMIJI: It is rise.

SCHOLAR: *Anuttara vimarśe prāg vyāpāradivarjite*, he is rising from above to below here through these next verses.

SWAMIJI: Yes, it is rise from above to below. This is also a rise, this is the highest rise.

SCHOLAR: This is the real rise.

SWAMIJI: This is the real rise.

SCHOLAR: Others are only a springboard.

SWAMIJI: When you once rise to the objective world, up to the extent of objectivity, then there is no question of falling down again in this universal field of ignorance. The question does not arise of that. You will never fall!

LJA TA05E (42:05)

Icchājñānakriyāśakti-sūkṣmarandhrasrugagragam (verse 65), and that *bodha agni* (that *bodha agni* means, *mita pramātṛ daśā*, individual subjective consciousness), it is just like fire, it is just like fire there; individual subjective consciousness takes the part of fire there, *agni*, *mahān agni*. And in that *agni* you have to put this *amṛta* (this nectar), which has risen from sixteen movements to the seventeenth, which has risen from sixteen movements to the seventeenth.

JOHN: These sixteen movements are these sixteen: five organs of cognition, action, *tanmātra*s and *manas*.

SWAMIJI: Yes, and mind. From there…

SCHOLAR: Can you explain *visarga* there in *visarga grāsa mantharaḥ*?

SWAMIJI: *Visarga* is intake. You have to extract that *visarga* from above to make it travel in below so that it rises there also.

SCHOLAR: *Visarga grāsa*.

SWAMIJI: *Visarga grāsa* is there intake. *Grāsa* is not destroying *visarga*, *grāsa* is the intake of *visarga*. You have to carry that *visarga* from above to below.

SCHOLAR: That's *saptadaśī kalā*.

SWAMIJI: That is *saptadaśī kalā* (the seventeenth *kalā*). *Icchā jñāna kriyā śakti sūkṣma randhra sruk agragam*, so this *sañjīvanī kalā*, this state of the sixteenth–no, I have no word for it–sixteenth *saṁvit*...

JOHN: These sixteenfold...?

DEVOTEE: What is the text?

SWAMIJI: *Sañjīvanī*, this is *sañjīvanī*. *Sañjīvanī* means, *saptadaśī kalā*, the seventeenth *kalā*, seventeenth position...

SCHOLAR: Phase of consciousness.

SWAMIJI:...phase of objective world.

JOHN: Phase of consciousness.

SWAMIJI: Yes.

SCHOLAR: *Saṁvit kalā*.

SWAMIJI: And that is offered in the fire of *mita pramātṛ daśā*. That is offered in the fire of *mita pramātṛ daśā* by that ladle, by the sacrificial ladle. Ladle means, that spoon.

SCHOLAR: *Sruka*.

SWAMIJI: *Sruka*.

JOHN: What is the spoon here?

SWAMIJI: Spoon is *icchā*, *jñāna* and *kriyā*. *Icchā śakti* is the spoon, *jñāna śakti* is the spoon, and *kriyā śakti* is the spoon.

SCHOLAR: *Au*, *trisūla*.

SWAMIJI: *Trisūla* (trident). And *sūkṣma randhra sruk agragam*, and you have to take the *āhūti*, you have to take the *āhūti*, this offering, offering to be offered in the fire of *mita pramātṛ bhāva*, by this ladle, by the sacrificial ladle, you have to take that *āhūti*–you have not to *put* that *āhūti*–you have to take that *āhūti*, *sūkṣma randhra sruk agragam*, you have to take that *āhūti* from each and every first start of cognitive movement.

SCHOLAR: *Acha*.

SWAMIJI: For instance, you perceive form through eyes. You have to see, you have to put that sacrificial ladle in the very start of that perception, in the very start of perception which is *nirvikalpa*, *nirvikalpa jñāna daśā*. From there you have to carry this sensation of *rūpa* (form). You have not to carry the sensation of *rūpa* like this. You have to carry it from above.

SCHOLAR: *Mantrabhūmyām*.

SWAMIJI: *Mantrabhūmyā*.[62]

JOHN: Then it permeates all the rest of perception, is it?

62. From the supreme principle, God consciousness.

SWAMIJI: Yes. That is *sūkṣma randhra sruk agragam*, you have to put that on the top of that ladle, sacrificial ladle. And that sacrificial ladle is will, knowledge and action. *Tadevam amṛtaṁ divyam saṁvid devīsu tarpakam*–then what happens next?–*tadevam amṛtam divyam*, that *alaukik divyam*, the unique transcendental nectar which has been flown out from *sañjīvanī kalā* in the field of the objective world, that *divyam amṛtam* is *saṁvit devīṣu tarpakam*, then your eyes are set in absolute peace, your nose is set in absolute peace, everything, all your organs, all these sixteen organs of yours get entry in that absolute peace.

LJA TA05E (47:12)

tāstṛptāḥ svātmanā pūrṇaṁ hṛdayaikāntaśāyinam /
cidvyoma bhairavadevamabhedenādhiśrayate //
(*Tantrāloka* 3.264)

SCHOLAR: *Haṭhapāka krama* (abrupt process).

SWAMIJI: Yes. When there is no curiosity of eating, you have eaten food, you have…

DENISE: Smelled.

SWAMIJI:…smelled the perfume, you have heard the beautiful songs, you have touched beautiful things, and by this sensation, *tarpaṇa* (satisfaction) takes place of *saṁvid devī.*

SCHOLAR: In *cidātma uccāra.* So this is the real *cidātma uccāra.*

SWAMIJI: This is the real *cidātma uccāra.* That is *tarpakam.* So they will carry you and you will be established in God consciousness eternally! There is no fear of coming out from that. This is the *cidātma uccāra.* So *cidātma uccāra* is absolutely the vibrating flow carried from transcendental God consciousness to universal God consciousness. This is *cidātma uccāra.*

JOHN: And that happens by taking that seventeenth *kalā*, that transcendental God consciousness, before perception…

SWAMIJI: Yes, seventeenth *kalā*, in each and every act of world; in each and every act of the world, nothing will be done. When it is done, what happens next?

LJA TA05E (48:41)

विसर्गामृतमेतावद् बोधाख्ये हुतभोजिनि ॥ ६६ ॥
विसृष्टं चेद्भवेत्सर्वं हुतं षोढाध्वमण्डलम्।

visargāmṛtametāvad bodhākhye hutabhojini //66//
visṛṣṭaṁ cedbhavetsarvaṁ hutaṁ ṣoḍhādhvamaṇḍalam /

Not only he, the *sādhaka*, is satisfied with this tasting of this supreme nectar of universal God consciousness, *visargāmṛtam*, this *visarga amṛta,…**

This *visarga amṛta* means, that nectar which is carried from above to below just to give it a rise, a rise in below. If you don't rise in below, you will never rise, you will never rise, you will fall again and again. If you only rise to the above states, there is the apprehension of falling again and again in this objective world. When you rise *in* the objective world, there is no question of falling again.

SCHOLAR: *Nirañjana.*

SWAMIJI: Because he has already fallen in rise, so there is no question of falling again. You see, when you want to protect your house, property, everything, you must ask the thief to protect it. You must depute a thief to protect it, so nothing will be lost, nothing will be stolen. If you ask a saint to protect it, thieves will steal it. But if you will ask a thief himself to take care of that property, who has the courage to steal it? It is there, it is protected. So, the chief thief is the external world, and if you maintain God consciousness in the external world, nothing will be lost, never it will be lost.

*…*visarga amṛtam etāvat*, this *visarga amṛta*, this nectar of intaking in the out-take, *visarga amṛtam*, this nectar of intaking in the out-take,…

Is it correct?

SCHOLAR: Yes, it makes sense.

SWAMIJI:…and when *bodhākhye hutabhojini*, when it is *visṛṣṭam* (offered) in the individual limited state of subjectivity, in the fire of limited ego, *sarvaṁ ṣoḍhādhva maṇḍalam* (indaudible), then you must know that this whole universe has become gold. This whole universe has got, has taken entry in that supreme universal God consciousness. Nothing is excluded.

SCHOLAR: *Rasāyanavedavat.*

SWAMIJI: Yes. *Sarvabhāvamaya-*...this reference also:

LJA TA05E (51:45)

sarvabhāvamayabhāvamaṇḍalaṁ viśvaśaktimayaśaktibarhiṣi /
juhato mama samo'sti ko'paroviśvamedhamayayañayājinaḥ //
(verse from commentary for verse 66)

I think this *śloka* is composed by Abhinavagupta himself somewhere.

Sarva bhāva maya bhāva maṇḍalaṁ, this objective world, which is filled with universal objectivity (*sarva bhāva maya bhāva maṇḍalaṁ*, this objective world which is filled with universal objectivity–this), and *viśvaśakti*, and this objective world which is filled with universal objectivity, is *juhato*, is offered by me (*mama*; *mama juhataḥ*, I offer this, this universal objectivity, this objective world filled with universal objectivity), I offer that in the fire of *viśva śakti mayi śakti barhiṣi*, in the fire of supreme energy (*śakti barhiṣi*; *barhiṣi* means, fire).

SCHOLAR: *Barhiṣi* is?

SWAMIJI: *Barhiṣi* is "fire" there, not "grass."

SCHOLAR: Not this grass they put down.

SWAMIJI: No. Barhiṣi is fire. It means grass also, but not...

SCHOLAR: This is *upalakṣaṇam* (metaphor).

SWAMIJI: Not *upalakṣaṇam*, it is meant, *barhiṣi* has this meaning also. *Barhiṣi* means fire also, not only grass, not *kuśā* grass only. *Barhiṣi* means fire, fire of universal energy which is *viśvaśaktimaya*, which is filled with universal energies. This universal energy, the fire in the universal energy, in the fire of universal energy which is filled with universal energies, all universal energies, I offer this universal objectivity in the fire of that universal energy. *Mama samo asti ko aparaḥ*, so there is no parallel to me in this world in adopting *viśvamedha yajña*.

One is *naramedha yajña*, when you offer in that fire the body of a human being–that is called *naramedha yajña*. And in that fire, when you offer that *aśva* (a horse), it is called *aśvamedha yajña*. When you offer *paśu* (a beast) in that *havan*, it is called *paśumedha yajña*. When you offer this whole universe, it is called *viśvamedha yajña*.

And I am that person who adopts this *viśvamedha yajña*. And to me, there is no comparison to me then afterwards, nobody can compare with me. I am the only unique *viśvamedha yajña yāji*.

LJA TA05E (54:47)

यतोऽनुत्तरनाथस्य विसर्गः कुलनायिका।
तत्क्षोभः कादिहान्तं तत्प्रसरस्तत्त्वपद्धतिः ॥६७॥

yato'nuttaranāthasya visargaḥ kulanāyikā /
tatkṣobhaḥ kādihāntaṁ tatprasarastattvapaddhatiḥ //67//

But now he puts this *śloka* because there is possibility of this doubt: If *viśvamedha yajña* is adopted by this great elevated yogi, how this whole universe is offered? He has offered only *his* universe. You see, everybody has got his own universe attached to him. You have got your own universe attached to you. You offer that in the fire of God consciousness and you are [performing] *viśvamedha yajña* according to your point of view. But this whole universe won't get burnt, it is still there. But he says to that:

yato'nuttaranāthasya visargaḥ kulanāyikā /
tatkṣobhaḥ kādihāntaṁ tat-prasarastattvapaddhatiḥ //67//
(verse repeated)

Because as *anuttara nāthasya*, the supreme *anuttara nātha*, the supreme master of the universe (that is, Lord Śiva) and his energy is *kulanāyikā*, leader of this whole universe (the leader of, the adopter of the whole universe is his energy), and that energy is *visarga* (*aḥ*), vibrating creative force, vibrating creative force is his energy, vibration of his Self is his formation, is the formation of the Lord, the vibration of his Self, the vibrating creative force is his energy, as it is like that, then *tatkṣobhaḥ*, when this vibrating creative force is agitated by him, agitated towards the external world, *tatkṣobhaḥ*, that agitation is *kādihāntaṁ prasaraḥ*, that is the creation from *ka* to *aparā visarga* (*ha*), *ka* to *ha*, and that is *tattva paddhatiḥ*, that is the creation of thirty-six elements, that is the creation of five *kalā*s, and that is the creation of one hundred and eighteen worlds, so if that is offered in that...

SCHOLAR: Fire of individuality.

SWAMIJI:...that fire of individual subjective consciousness with that spoon, with that ladle, then this whole universe is finished; *arthāt*, this whole universe is in-taken in that supreme God consciousness.

LJA TA05E (57:40)

anuttaraṁ paraṁ dhāma tadevākulamucyate /
visargastasya nāthasya kaulikī śaktirucyate //
(*Tantrāloka* 3.143, quoted in the commentary)

The supreme *anuttara* (supreme state) is *akula* (*akula dhāma*), and his creative energy, his creative energy is called *kaulikī*-energy. He is himself *akula* and his creative energy is *kaulikī*-energy. *Pṛthivyādīni tattvāni puruṣāntani*...next, there:

LJA TA05E (58:16)

pṛthivyādīni tattvāni puruṣāntāni pañcasu /
kramāt kādiṣu vargeṣu makārenteṣu suvrate //
(*Parātriṁśikā Vivaraṇa*, verse 7, quoted in the commentary)

Suvrate[63], O Pārvatī, right from *pṛthvī* (earth), right from the *pṛthvī* element to the *puruṣāntāni*, to the element of *puruṣa* (these are twenty-five elements; from *pṛthvī* to *puruṣa tattva*, these are twenty-five elements), in these twenty-five elements, *kramāt*, in succession, successively, *kādiṣu vargeṣu makārānteṣu*, they are found from *ka* to *ma-kāra*, from *ka* to *ma*. *Ka* is the indicator of *pṛthvī*, and when *ma* is the indicator of *puruṣa*. *Ma* is the representative of *puruṣa*, *ka* is the representative of the element *pṛthvī*.

SCHOLAR: Earth, materiality.

63. Lit., O virtuous wife.

SWAMIJI: From *ka* to *ma*. *Ka-kha-ga-gha-ṇa*, *ca-cha-ja-jha-ña*, *ṭa-ṭha-ḍha-ḍa-ṇa…kucuṭutupu*. From grammarians point of view, *ku-cu-ṭu-tu-pu*.

LJA TA05E (59:33)

vāyvagnisalilendrāṇāṁ dhāraṇānāṁ catuṣṭayam
(*Parātriṁśikā*, verse 7, quoted in the commentary)

Then there are four *dhāraṇa*s, four maintaining energies, those energies which maintain the individual consciousness in a human being. Individual consciousness is maintained by these four energies, that is *ṣaṭ kañcuka*, that is the six coverings.

SCHOLAR: This is the end of Western philosophy here.

SWAMIJI: Huh?

SCHOLAR: This is where Western philosophy ends.

SWAMIJI: Yes. *Vāyvagni*…this is *Parātriṁśikā*, this is reference of *Parātriṁśikā*. *Vāyu*, *agni*, *salila*, *indrāṇāṁ*. *Vāyu* means *ya*, *agni* means *ra*, *salilam* means *la*, and *indrā bīja* means *va*. *Ya-ra-la-va*, these *antaḥsthānāṁ catuṣṭayam*. These are four *dhāraṇa*s, the maintaining energy of individuality in man.[64]

tadūrdhvaṁ śādivikhyātaṁ purastādbrahmapañcakam //
amūlā tatkramājjñeyā kṣāntā sṛṣṭirudāhṛtā /
(*Parātriṁśikā*, verse 7, quoted in the commentary, not recited in full)

---

64. "In [Śaiva] Tantras, they are nominated as *dhāraṇā*. These five elements, *kalā*, *vidyā*, *ragā*, *kāla*, *niyati* with *māyā* are called *dhāraṇā* because they give life to individual being, individual being lives in these five elements. Without these five elements, there was no life to individual being, there was only the sphere of Lord Śiva. If these five elements would not be there, there was no question of individual being to exist. Individual being lives only on the basis of these five elements. So they are nominated as *dhāraṇā*. *Dhāraṇā* means that which gives you life to exist. Pāṇini says it is *antaḥstha* (internal), because it is found inside the individual being, and we say that it is not *antaḥstha*, it is *dhāraṇā* because it gives life to individual being. Individual being is created, individual being is glorified, by these five elements." Swami Lakshmanjoo, trans., Kṣemarāja's *Śiva Sūtra Vimarśinī* (LJA archive).

Above that is *brahmapañcaka*, the five *brahmans*.

LJA TA05E (1:00:46) end.
LJA TA05F (00:00) start.

Śuddhavidyā, Īśvara, Sadāśiva and Śakti, these are five elevated elements of God, in the end, above.

JOHN: Śiva is not there?

SWAMIJI: Śiva is all-pervading, all-pervading power.

JOHN: Then why do they say five elements when there is...?

SWAMIJI: Śuddhavidyā, Īśvara, Sadāśiva...

JOHN: Śakti.

SWAMIJI:...and...

JOHN:...*vijñānākala*?

SWAMIJI: No, *vijñānākala*, no *vijñānākala*. Śuddhavidyā, Īśvara, Sadāśiva, Śakti, and Anāśritaśiva. Anāśritaśiva will go.[65]

JOHN: Why do they say four *dhāraṇā* before when there are six, six of these, six states?

SWAMIJI: Six are in-taken in four from the intellectual point of view. Actually these are not six, these are four.

JOHN: Which two are lost?

SWAMIJI: They are not lost, they are in-taken in these.

SCHOLAR: Embraced by those.

JOHN: Which ones are embraced? Which ones are the real four?

SWAMIJI: *Kalā* will be in-taken in *kāla*, and *niyati*...not *niyati*. *Kalākālaniyativaśat*, *rāga* and *niyati*, *rāga* and *niyati* will been in-taken in one point–*rāga* and *niyati*.

JOHN: *Rāga* and *niyati* and *kāla* and *kalā*.

SWAMIJI: "I love Denise, there is no doubt about it, I love Denise," this is *niyati*. "I love beautiful things, I love beautiful things," this is *rāga*–"I love beautiful things."

SCHOLAR: Because *niyati* is specific attachment.

---

65. "Anāśritaśiva is the first element (*kṣa*), Śakti is the second element (*ha*), third element is Sadāśiva (*sa*), fourth element is Īśvara (*ṣa*) and fifth element is Śuddhavidyā (*śa*)." *Parātrīśikā Vivaraṇa* (LJA archive).

SWAMIJI: *Niyati* is specific. Only "this," "this," it is *niyati*. *Rāga* is general.

JOHN: How about *kāla* and *kalā*?

SCHOLAR: So the specific is embraced in the general.

SWAMIJI: Yes. And *kalā* and *kāla* are also like this.

JOHN: And time, one is time, so all these individual creativities are subsumed in the fact that you are bound by time.

SWAMIJI: I have to study with Dr. Basu, then at 9 I have to study with John, and afterwards I have to go to Srinagar (actually I have to go to Srinagar if it is so), and I have to take food, this is *kalā* (limited action), this is *kalā*, and *kāla* (time) has also in-taken this, *kāla* has also passed.

SCHOLAR: That is *kāla*.

SWAMIJI: That is *kāla*. *Kāla* and *kalā* are in-taken in one point.

SCHOLAR: *Kalāyatiti kāla*.

SWAMIJI: *Rāga* and *niyati*, not *vidyā* and…*rāga* and *niyati*. *Rāga* is attachment, general attachment; *niyati* is specific attachment. So there are only four *dhāraṇas*: *ya*, *ra*, *la* and *va*. *Tadūrdhvaṁ śādi vikhyātaṁ*, above that is *śādi*, beginning from *śa*, ending in *ha*; *śa-ṣa-sa-ha* and *kṣa* (ending in *kṣa*). That is *brahmapañcakam*, five states of *brahmans*. *Amūlā tatkramājjñeyā kṣāntā sṛṣṭirudāhṛtā*, it is why *kṣa* is called Anāśritaśiva there, because the *kṣa*-state has no positive masculine energy.

SCHOLAR: It is like the love of two women.

SWAMIJI: Love of two women, yes. So it is Anāśritaśiva. It is Śiva, but no good, no use.[66]

66. Anāśritaśiva is represented by the neuter vowels, *ṛ-rī-li-lī*. "Anāśritaśiva is that state of Śiva who does not understand, who does not recognize the differentiated world. Śiva is that Śiva who recognizes this differentiated world, he recognizes [the world] as one with his own nature. But Anāśritaśiva does not recognize this world as one with his own nature, he is afraid of this differentiated world, so he has discarded this differentiated world in the state of Anāśritaśiva." *Parātrīśikā Vivaraṇa* (LJA archive) "It is blissful, absolutely blissful, because this is the rise of spiritual sex, but within, without any contact…*Kṣobha antarasya asadbhāvāt*, because there is not an other thing that would be agitated. Because a virgin girl won't recognize the agitation from a male. A virgin girl will never allow a male to [agitate her] by his sexual desire. In the same way, this state of Anāśritaśiva is not *kṣobhāntarasya asadbhāvāt*,

SCHOLAR: *Grasāgrasa.*

SWAMIJI: It is just [like when] a woman marries another woman. *Amūlā tatkramājjñeyā kṣāntā sṛṣṭirudāhṛtā*, that *sṛṣṭi* (creation) is *amūlā*, begining from *a*. It is beginning from *a*, you must know that it is beginning from *a*, and *kṣāntā*, and ending in *kṣa*.

LJA TA05F (04:07)

Nanu yadi nāmānuttaranāthasya visargaḥ kaulikī śaktiḥ (comm.), if this *visarga*, this creative force of that supreme Lord Śiva is *kaulikī śakti*, energy of *kaulikī*, then is it pointed [out] in *mātṛkā cakra*? Is it pointed [out] in the world of *mātṛkā*, that is, in the world of these letters?

JOHN: You mean, "indicated."

SWAMIJI: Is it indicated there? He says it is indicated there.

अंअ इति कुलेश्वर्या सहितो हि कुलेशिता।

aṁa iti kuleśvaryā sahito hi kuleśitā /68a

Aṁ-aḥ is the indicator of these two. *Aṁ* first, *aḥ* next. *Aṁ* is the indicator of Lord Śiva, *aḥ* is the indicator of that creative energy, creative energy of *kaulikī śakti*. *Aṁ aḥ iti*; *iti*, that means, *a*, *aṁ* and *aḥ iti*, means, *kuleśvaryā sahitā kuleśitā*, *kuleśvara* with *kuleśvarī*.

JOHN: Would you say [that again]? *A-aṁ-aḥ*, three letters here, three?

SCHOLAR: No, two: *aṁ* and *aḥ*.

SWAMIJI: No, *aṁ* and *aḥ*.

SWAMIJI: There is *visarga*, there is *visarga*, [but] *visarga* (*ḥ*) is omitted [from "*aṁaḥ*"] from Pāṇini's point of view. *Aṁ-aḥ*, because there is *aśa-pratyāhāra*, the letter *i* [in] "*iti*."[67] *Aṁ-aḥ-iti*. *Aiuṅ ṛlik eoṅ*, *aiuṅ*, *a-i*, *aiuṅ–aiuṅ ṛlik*.

---

there is no other agency which would agitate this." Swami Lakshmanjoo, *Tantrāloka* Volume 2, Lakshmanjoo Academy (2021), 139.

67. From Pāṇini's *Aṣṭādhyāyī* 8.3.17.

LJA TA05F (05:54)

Nanu śaktimataḥ khalu śaktirananyā (comm.), now an objection is there, one objection, one point which is doubtful there: *śaktimataḥ khalu śaktirananyā*, this is the absolute truth in our Shaivism that *śakti*, energy, is inseparable, it is not separated from Lord Śiva, from *śaktimān*, the energy-holder, the possessor of energy. *Śaktimataḥ śakteśca viśleṣo nāsti* (comm.), they are not separated, [so] why these are called two, why these are separated in two letters, *aṁ* and *aḥ*? Why, there aught to be only one word just like *aḥ*, because in *aḥ* (:) one point was Śiva's point and the next point was of *śakti*. It would be better than creating these two letters. But he says:

परो विसर्गविश्लेषस्तन्मयं विश्वमुच्यते ॥ ६८ ॥

paro visargaviśleṣastanmayaṁ viśvamucyate //68b//

The next movement of Lord Śiva, the next creative movement of Lord Śiva…the first creative in-take creative movement, the first is in-take creative movement, the next is out-take creative movement.

I use words of my own (laughs). I don't know if they are correct or incorrect, but you can understand, just to make you understand.

The next *parā* (*parā* means, next movement, next creative movement), the next out-take creative movement is *visarga viśleṣa. Visarga viśleṣa* is out-taking that creative energy in the universal state–*visarga viśleṣa. Tanmayaṁ viśvaṁ ucyate*, and, in fact, this universe is based on that next creative movement. It is not based on *aṁ*. *Aṁ* is also a creative movement, but the creative movement of God consciousness, not Universal consciousness. So there are two points of Lord Śiva: one is creative in his own nature, one is creative in the external field of his glory.

JOHN: So universal God consciousness begins at *māyā tattva*?

SWAMIJI: There is no question of *māyā tattva. Māyā tattva* is not born here because it is *cidātma uccāra*. [In] *cidātma uccāra*, there is no question of *māyā tattva* or all these phases.

JOHN: But you said that you take that internal transcendental God consciousness into the universal God consciousness, so that expansion...

SWAMIJI: There is no *māyā tattva.*

JOHN: There is no...

SWAMIJI: *Māyā tattva* will remain only when there is absence of consciousness. When there is absence of consciousness in the universe and when there is absence of consciousness in the transcendental state, that is *māyā tattva.*

JOHN: So existing in transcendental God consciousness is existing at the level of Śiva *tattva*?

SWAMIJI: Yes, Śiva *tattva.*

JOHN: In *nimīlana.*

SWAMIJI: Yes.

JOHN: And so all expansion from that point outward is all universal God consciousness from Sadāśiva to Śuddhavidyā to...all.

SWAMIJI: Yes, it is all universal, yes.

DEVOTEE: *Tanmayaṁ viśvam*, "*tat*" (that) means?

SWAMIJI: *Para viśleṣa mayaṁ. Para visarga viśleṣa mayaṁ.* Because:

LJA TA05F (09:40)

śaktiśca śaktimāṁśceti padārthdvayamucyate /
śaktayo'sya jagat kṛtsnaṁ śaktimāṁstu maheśvaraḥ //
(verse from the *Sarvamaṅgalā Śāstra*, quoted in the commentary, not recited in full)

There are only two elements found in this universe, found in one hundred and eighteen worlds: *śakti* and *śaktimān. Śakti* is the expansion of the universe, and its holder, its possessor, is Śiva, that is all, *bas*. That is the next lesson pertaining to the same subject, *cidātma uccāra.*

JOHN: So this seventeenth *kalā*, which is this state of *pramiti bhāva* ...is it the state of *pramiti bhāva*–the seventeenth *kalā*?

SWAMIJI: Yes.

JOHN: That's brought into the objective world of sixteen states of objectivity.

SWAMIJI: Yes, it is infused outside.

JOHN: It's made to permeate them.

SWAMIJI: It is infused outside.

JOHN: So what you do is, what they are saying is, you hold that *pramiti bhāva* which you have…

SWAMIJI: Nothing is excluded, nothing is to be excluded. If you exclude even one point, then you are no more, then you are no more complete.

DEVOTEE: Except intellect.

SWAMIJI: But intellect…

JOHN: Is already permeated in *pramāṇa bhāva*.

SWAMIJI: Intellect is already there.

DEVOTEE: But in sixteen, you said intellect is not working.

SWAMIJI: Intellect is not working, it is automatic.

DEVOTEE: It is automatic, yes.

SCHOLAR: Can you summarize the sequence from…?

SWAMIJI: Of *cidātma uccāra*?

SCHOLAR: Yes.

SWAMIJI: *Cidātma uccāra* will be summarized after completing *cidātma uccāra* on that very day, the next day, the next lesson. It will be summarized.

LJA TA05F (11:14)

This was the subject on *cidātma uccāra*–it will be finished today–the vibrating movement of God consciousness, when God consciousness vibrates in the external world.

वित्प्राणगुणदेहान्तर्बहिर्द्रव्यमयीमिमाम्।
अर्चयेज्जुहुयाद्ध्यायेदित्थं सञ्जीवनीं कलाम्॥ ६९॥

vitprāṇaguṇadehāntarbahirdravyamayīmimām /
arcayejjuhuyāddhyāyeditthaṁ sañjīvanīṁ kalām //69//

Ittham, in this way, when there is *paro visarga viśleṣas tanmayam ucya-*…the first vibrating movement of consciousness, and then the next vibrating movement of consciousness takes place (that is *visarga*).

In this way (*ittham*, in this way), *sañjīvanī kalām*, the state of that *sañjīvanīṁ kalā*, the seventeenth *kalā*,…*

The state of seventeenth *kalā* means, *pramātṛ kalā* (subjectivity) without the adjustment of *prameya bhāva* (objectivity) there. When *prameya bhāva* is adjusted in *pramātṛ kalā*, that is the sixteenth *kalā*. When *prameya* is not adjusted, it is digested in that, it is the seventeenth *kalā*.

*…that is *sañjīvanī kalā*, the life-giving state of God consciousness, which is *vit* ("*vit*" will go to *sañjīvanī kalā*; *kathaṁ bhūtāṁ sañjīvanīṁ kalāṁ vit*, that is *vit*, the supreme state of consciousness), and that supreme state of consciousness, which is *sañjīvanī kalā*, which has vibrated in *prāṇa pramātṛ bhāva* first, *guṇa*, in *puryaṣṭaka pramātṛ bhāva*, *deha*, in *deha pramātṛ bhāva* (in sound-sleep, in the dreaming state, and in wakefulness[68]), *vit-prāṇa-guṇa deha-antar*, it is internal, internal movement of *sañjīvanī kalā*, and there is an external movement also found of *sañjīvanī kalā*, and that *sañjīvanī kalā* is *bahir dravya*,…*

Bahir dravya are those threefold *dravyas* (substances) you know: *madya*, *māṁsa* and *maithuna*. *Madya* means liquor, and meat (*māṁsa*), and sex (*maithuna*).

*…*bahir dravya mayīm*, in these three also, that *sañjīvanī kalā* exists externally, and that *sañjīvanī kalā* is to be worshipped (*arcayet*), is to be offered [with] whatever you get from your organs of senses, and *dhyāyet*, and is to be meditated on–*arcayet*, *juhuyāt*, *dhyāyet*.

Alright? We should not expose it more, but he (Abhinavagupta) exposes again. What should I do?

LJA TA05F (14:33)

आनन्दनाडीयुगलस्पन्दनावहितौ स्थितः ।
एनां विसर्गनिःष्यन्दसौधभूमिं प्रपद्यते ॥ ७० ॥

ānandanāḍīyugalaspandanāvahitau sthitaḥ /
enāṁ visarganiḥṣyandasaudhabhūmiṁ prapadyate //70//

---

68. *Prāṇa* (breath) is sound sleep, *puryaṣṭaka* (mind, intellect, ego, and the five *tanmātras*) is the dreaming state, and *deha* (body) is wakefulness.

Why he has gone to this extent that this *sañjīvanī kalā* is to be worshipped in *dravya*s also, in these threefold substances, threefold exciting substances? These are exciting substances. This excitement does not mean it [only] excites you for giving excitement in your senses–no. It will excite the internal force of God consciousness. It must excite that also. If that excitement does not take place while doing this kind of adoption of these three substances, it is the wrong method then, it will end in the wrong way, there is no fruit in that. So, while doing these three, while moving in these three substances, the rise of God consciousness should take place simultaneously, side-by-side, then it is okay.

(Verse repeated) *Ānanda nāḍī yugala*, *yugala* means twofold *ānanda nāḍī*, the veins producing excitement of joy, and those are *varāṅga lakṣaṇam*. *Upastha* and *yoni*, the name of these male [and female sexual] organs is meant only in the individuality of worldly life, but the spiritual name for these two, the spiritual name, when these function in a spiritual way, then they are nominated as *varāṅga*, *varāṇga lakṣaṇam*. Because they are united both, they are called *varāṅga*.

SCHOLAR: The superior limb of the body.

SWAMIJI: Superior limbs of your body, the super-most limbs of your body producing that excitement to the extent of God consciousness.

JOHN: Highest excitement.

SWAMIJI: There is no higher excitement than this. So *ānanda nāḍī yugala*, when these two are joined and they get a throb with each other (*spandana*, throbbing sensation), and when one is *avahitau sthitau*, when one absolutely establishes his awareness on that point, at that very moment,...*

JOHN: At that moment of those organs? At the point of those organs?

SWAMIJI: At the point of that...what is that called?

SCHOLAR: Orgasm.

SWAMIJI: Orgasm. And then what happens?

*...*enaṁ visarga niḥṣyanda saudha bhūmiṁ prapadyate*, then he is sentenced to the state where the *saudha bhūmi*, where the collection of nectar of creative flow exists, the nectar of God consciousness. It is not only there you have to find God consciousness, not only in the sexual way of the senses.

JOHN: Sexual act.

SWAMIJI: Sexual act. For that he explains the next verse:

LJA TA05F (18:31)

शाक्ते क्षोभे कुलावेशे सर्वनाड्यग्रगोचरे।
व्याप्तौ सर्वात्मसङ्कोचे हृदयं प्रविशेत्सुधीः ॥७१॥

śākte kṣobhe kulāveśe sarvanāḍyagragocare /
vyāptau sarvātmasaṅkoce hṛdayaṁ praviśetsudhīḥ //71//

This supreme *sādhaka* (aspirant) with that God consciousness (*sudhīḥ*),…*

"*Sudhīḥ*" means?

SCHOLAR: Whose awareness is perfected?

SWAMIJI: Perfected.

*…he has to enter in his heart, in his heart of God consciousness (in his *hṛdayaṁ praviśet*), not only in *śākte kṣobhe*, not only when the other partner is agitated, not only in the contact of male and female, [but in] *kulāveśa* also. *Śākte kṣobhe* is when you are agitated with each other.

JOHN: In sexual act.

SWAMIJI: In sexual act. *Kulāveśe* is when you are not agitated at all, but you are agitated within your self only, without your second, better-half or worst-half. "Worst-half" means man, "better-half" is woman. That is what I have heard.

DEVOTEES: (laughter)

SWAMIJI: *Kulāveśe*; *kulāveśe* is when you are away from each other, *kulāveśe*, but you get entry in that *kulā*, in the substance of that sexual excitement by memory.

JOHN: By memory.

SWAMIJI: By memory. That is *kulāveśe*, when you get entry in that memory. It is not just ordinary memory. It is that kind of memory which carries you to the orgasm without…

JOHN: So you have orgasm without a partner.

SWAMIJI:…without a partner. This is *kulāveśe*. There also you have to get entry in that supreme heart of God consciousness. This is Shaivism. *Sarvanāḍyagragocare*, and *sarva nāḍyagra gocare* is another path, another way to get entry in the state of God consciousness. *Sarva nāḍyagra gocare*, when there is…each and every limb of your body, on the tip of each and every limb of your body (that is *sarva nāḍī agra gocare*), for instance, the tip of the nose, armpits, and the throat-pit, all these things, these, these (Swamiji demonstrates)…

SCHOLAR: All places where, in fact, you have sensitivity, ticklishness.

SWAMIJI: Sensitivity, where you have more sensitivity.

JOHN: Ticklish.

SWAMIJI: Yes. By tickling that, you have to tickle that. "Tickle," you know?

DEVOTEE: Yes, yes.

SCHOLAR: *Kuhakam.*

SWAMIJI: *Kuhanā prayoga.*[69] That is *sarva nāḍī agra gocare.* When you do that kind of act, you will get entry–if you are aware–you will get entry in the state of God consciousness.

JOHN: Through *sparśa* (touch).

SWAMIJI: Yes, by that tickling. And *vyāptau*, *vyāptau* is another way. *Vyāptau* means when you pervade the whole universe, that, "I am the whole universe, one hundred and eighteen worlds, I am pervading in all the one hundred and eighteen worlds. I am Bhairava myself! I have penetrated, I am penetrating each and every blade of the universe, each and every point of universe." That is *vyāptau.* That is *vikāsa samādhi*, it is called, it is nominated, the technical name for this is *vikāsa* (expansive) *samādhi. Sarvātma saṅkoce*, when you get shrunk, when you collect all your senses from external objects and get entry in your internal Self of God consciousness (that is *sarvātma saṅkoce*), at that time also, *hṛdayaṁ praviśet*, you have to get entry in the universal heart of God consciousness.

JOHN: But you would automatically…

SWAMIJI: It is not only sex.

JOHN: But in *sarvātma saṅkoca*, you are already going…

SWAMIJI: These are the ways. Any way it seems clear to you, you can adopt that way.

JOHN: Is this *sarvātma saṅkoca…*

SWAMIJI: *Sarvātma saṅkoca.*

JOHN:…is this the time of fear?

---

69. The application (*prayoga*) of an interested performance of religious austerities (*kuhana*). See *Vijñāna Bhairava*, verse 66.

SWAMIJI: No, contraction. No, just contract everything from external objects.

SCHOLAR: Through practice.

SWAMIJI: Huh?

SCHOLAR: In practice, contraction.

SWAMIJI: It is practice, it is practice, it is not fear. Just contract everything from the external state to the internal state. Just like (Swamiji demonstrates), squeeze yourself from the external world. That is *sarvātma saṅkoca*. That is also a way. He has put all these ways because some yogis are *brahmacārins* (celibate). For them, *sarvātma saṅkoca* will do, *vyāpta* will do, and these two will do. And those who are householders, they are already with wives, with everything, they have that in hand, everything, so *śakte kṣobhe*, *kulāveśe*, *sarvanāḍyagragocare* will go to them. These three ways are meant for householders, and the other two are meant for *brahmacārins*. *Vyāptau*, those also, householders also can do.

LJA TA05F (24:05)

śākte kṣobhe kulāveśe sarvanāḍyagragocare /
vyāptau sarvātmasaṅkoce hṛdayaṁ praviśetsudhīḥ //71//
(verse repeated)

So this *hṛdaya* (heart), the center of universal God consciousness, is not excluded anywhere. You have to find it everywhere.

JOHN: This one is…

SWAMIJI: He has given the reference…

JOHN:…the tickling.

SWAMIJI:…tickling, yes.

JOHN: Is that [for] householders?

SWAMIJI: Yes. Who will tickle you? (laughs)

DEVOTEES: (laughter)

SWAMIJI: Tickling must be done from the opposite sex. Tickling must not be done…[if a] man will tickle you, you won't get that kind of excitement.

JOHN: So this is sexual excitement that comes from this tickling.

SWAMIJI: Yes, yes, yes, these three. (laughing) I told you to vacate all ladies. You didn't. What could I do? And he has put all these references, some of the *Vijñāna Bhairava*, and some of these…

JOHN: Could we read these, or no?

SWAMIJI: Some day, some other day. We will read them today. No, it is not worthwhile. *Acha* (okay), now he puts this objection: When there are so many ways to get entry in God consciousness, why you are stressing on this sexual act only more? What is the purpose of this sexual…? What is the greatness in that sexual act that you are stressing more this…?

What will you do? What will you say?

DENISE: Putting more stress on this.

SCHOLAR: Emphasizing this sexual aspect.

SWAMIJI: Putting more, emphasizing this sexual aspect. For that he says, explains in the next *śloka*, 72nd:

LJA TA05F (25:59)

सोमसूर्यकलाजालपरस्परनिघर्षतः ।
अग्नीषोमात्मके धाम्नि विसर्गानन्द उन्मिषेत् ॥ ७२ ॥

somasūryakalājālaparasparanigharṣataḥ /
agnīṣomātmake dhāmni visargānanda unmiṣet //72//

Soma sūrya kalā jāla paraspara nigharṣataḥ, *soma kalā*, *sūrya kalā*, these two *kalās*,…*

Soma kalā means, of the moon, substances, those *kalās*, the states of the moon. And the states of the sun (*sūrya kalā*). The states of the moon are all found in a woman. The states of the sun are all found in a man.

*…and this *kalājāla*, when these sixteen states and twelve states, *paraspara nigharṣataḥ*, get *saṅghaṭṭitaḥ* (fused)–where?–*agnīṣomātmake dhāmni*, in the place where *agni* (fire) and *soma* (moon) is found (*agni* and *soma*, that is, [where] *rakta* (blood) and *raitasa* (semen) is found, the *rakta* of a woman, *raitasa* of a man–that is *agnīṣomātmake dhāmni*), in that state, *visargānanda unmiṣet*, the *ānanda*, the supreme bliss of God consciousness gets rise very easily. And you have to put stress, so we are putting stress on this point only, more. There you have to do *sādhanā*. Where?

JOHN: In the sexual act.

SWAMIJI: No, in other acts. For instance, in *sarva nāḍyagragocare* also, in *vyāpti*, in *sarvātma saṅkoca*, you have to put strength of awareness. But here, awareness is already established.

JOHN: In the sexual act.

SWAMIJI: In the sexual act.

JOHN: For everybody. For everybody?

SWAMIJI: For everybody, but they are not aware of that, they don't know that, that they are fully aware. For instance, when you are embraced with your woman, with your wife, automatically your eyes are closed, your nose does not understand other smell, your eyes do not understand other forms, your, this organ…

JOHN: Ear.

SWAMIJI:…ear does not understand other sound, [except] only of that sex.

JOHN: You are completely one-pointed.

SWAMIJI: So this is automatic, automatic one-pointedness takes place there. So, in *visarga ānanda*, *visarga ānanda* takes place automatically there, and soon.

JOHN: So when you have that orgasm, at the moment of orgasm, at that point…

SWAMIJI: Before that also, before that also…

JOHN: That whole flow even…

SWAMIJI: Yes.

JOHN:…which we discussed in this third *āhnika*.

SWAMIJI: Yes.

LJA TA05F (28:55)

अलं रहस्यकथया गुप्तमेतत्स्वभावतः ।
योगिनीहृदयं तत्र विश्रान्तः स्यात्कृती बुधः ॥ ७३ ॥

alaṁ rahasyakathayā guptametatsvabhāvataḥ /
yoginīhṛdayaṁ tatra viśrāntaḥ syātkṛtī budhaḥ //73//
(not recited)

Alaṁ rahasyakathayā, let us stop this exposition of this secret state of God consciousness (*alaṁ rahasyakathayā*). *Guptametat svabhāvataḥ*, it is, although we expose it, it is still a secret! It will remain still a secret, nobody will know.

JOHN: Really understand, nobody will really understand.

SWAMIJI: Yes (laughs). *Yoginī hṛdayaṁ*, this is the heart of *yoginīs*. *Tatra viśrāntaḥ*, when in the heart of *yoginī hṛdaya*, in the *yoginīs*, *budhaḥ*, that who is fully aware gets established in that heart of *yoginī*, *kṛtī budhaḥ*, *kṛtī syāt*, he gets all his desired objects, desired things, whatever he desires are complete for him.

JOHN: So this *yoginī* is a female partner. *Yoginī* in this?

SWAMIJI: No. *Yoginī hṛdaya*, this is the heart of *yoginī*. The heart of *yoginī* is the union of these two organs in one point. That is *yoginī hṛdaya*. *Yoginī hṛdaya* is not a separated *hṛdaya*. Understand?

JOHN: *Haan* (yes).

SWAMIJI: *Alaṁ rahasya kathayā guptametat svabhāvataḥ* (laughs), this is already a secret, it will remain a secret, and it has remained a secret so far. This *yoginī hṛdaya* is that *yoginī hṛdaya*, this heart of *yoginī* where a fully aware, a fully elevated yogi, once established, once established, is *kṛtī*, becomes *kṛtī*. *Kṛtī* means, that person who has done what was to be done, who has completed what was to be completed. He has done everything.

SCHOLAR: He has scored.

SWAMIJI: And when he has done everything, then:

LJA TA05F (30:57)

हानादानतिरस्कारवृत्तौ रूढिमुपागतः।

hānādānatiraskāravṛttau rūḍhimupāgataḥ /

When he is established fully in that state of God consciousness where nothing is to be left, nothing is to be included, nothing is to be excluded, *hānādānatiraskāra vṛttau*, he achieves that state of God consciousness where nothing is to be ejected, nothing is to be obtained; nothing is to be left, nothing is to be...?

JOHN: Kept.

SWAMIJI: Kept.

अभेदवृत्तितः पश्येद्विश्वं चितिचमत्कृतेः ॥ ७४ ॥

abhedavṛttitaḥ paśyedviśvaṁ citicamatkṛteḥ //74//
(not recited)

Abhedavṛttitaḥ paśyet, then he experiences this whole universe, it is established in one point, and that point is the *camatkāra* of *cit*, the *camatkāra* of God consciousness. So this *camatkāra* of God consciousness is everywhere found by him.[70]

Here ends your class till next January.

DEVOTEE: Next January?

SWAMIJI: Yes (laughs).

LJA TA05F (32:00)

Para Tattva Antaḥ Praveśa
Entry in God Consciousness

अर्थक्रियार्थितादैन्यं त्यक्त्वा बाह्यान्तरात्मनि।
स्वरूपे निर्वृतिं प्राप्य फुल्लां नाददशां श्रयेत् ॥ ७५ ॥

arthakriyārthitādainyaṁ tyaktvā bāhyāntarātmani /
kharūpe nirvṛtiṁ prāpya phullāṁ nādadaśāṁ śrayet //75//

When you are about to get entry in your own nature,...*

Because the last chapter was regarding *cidātma uccāra*, the vibration of *cidātma*. When *cidātmā*, the reality of consciousness vibrates

70. Swamiji has translated *camatkāra* as "uncommon charm, ecstacy, taste, blissful taste."

within a yogi, within a yogi's heart, then there is possibility of getting entry in the supreme state of God consciousness. That is *para tattva antaḥ praveśaḥ*, and this is the subject we have to deal with now–to get entry in the supreme state of God consciousness. It is only possible when inside your heart *cidātma* vibrates first, then you can get entry in it. Because by the vibration of *cidātma*, when this gets throbbing vibrations within your own nature, then the mouth of *cidātma* is opened and you can enter easily.

JOHN: This is a real vibration?

SWAMIJI: This is real vibration.

JOHN: It's felt as vibration also?

SWAMIJI: It is a feeling.

JOHN: It's felt as vibration.

SWAMIJI: Yes.

JOHN: As something throbbing.

SWAMIJI: Yes.

*...*arthakriyārthitādainyaṁ tyaktvā bāhyāntarātmani*, there a yogi has to do one thing: *artha kriyārthitā dainyaṁ tyaktvā*, just you have to leave aside all pitiable conditions of cravings after objective senses. When you crave for objective senses, this is a pitiable condition. This you have to leave aside altogether, inside and outside. *Bāhyāntarātmani*, within and without you have to leave aside all these pitiable conditions regarding cravings after worldly objects (worldly objects: seeing, touching, smelling, tasting, etcetera). Then *kharūpe nirvṛtiṁ prāpya*, then you will get full rest, you are rested in your own nature of voidness–*kharūpe* (*kha*). *Kharūpe nirvṛtiṁ prāpya*, you rest in the nature of your voidness, when you become void, absolutely away from everything.

JOHN: Is it *pralayākala*?

SWAMIJI: It is not *pralayākala*. It is the real nature of God consciousness.

JOHN: But why do they call it "void"? Void of differentiation?

SWAMIJI: Void of differentiated perceptions, not void of your nature. This is the indication of the letter *kha* in *piṇḍanātha*, the mantra, *piṇḍanātha*. *Phullāṁ nāda daśāṁ śrayet*, after that, you should rest in that state of un-utterable sound, un-utterable super sound of I-consciousness. That is *phullāṁ*, and it is *phullāṁ* (*phullāṁ* means, all-round bloomed, blossomed).

JOHN: Blossomed forth, completely full of...

SWAMIJI: Yes. And this *nāda daśā* indicates the letter *kṣa* in *piṇḍanātha*. This voidness indicates the letter *kha* in *piṇḍanātha*, and this *nāda daśā*, un-utterable sound, the state of this un-utterable sound, indicates the letter *kṣa* in *piṇḍanātha*.

JOHN: '*Rkṣkheṁ*'?

SWAMIJI: '*Rkṣkheṁ*' is the mantra. Next:

LJA TA05F (36:15)

वक्रमन्तस्तया सम्यक् संविदः प्रविकासयेत्।
संविदक्षमरुच्चक्रं ज्ञेयाभिन्नं ततो भवेत्॥ ७६ ॥

vaktramantastayā samyak saṁvidaḥ pravikāsayet /
saṁvidakṣamaruccakraṁ jñeyābhinnaṁ tato bhavet //76//

Antaḥ vaktraṁ, then by that state of *nāda* (*tayā*; *tayā* means, *nāda rūpayā śaktyā*), then by that state of *nāda*, completely you should get bloomed, you should open, you should vibrate outside, vibrate outside the introverted mouth of consciousness, and when that introverted mouth of consciousness is vibrated extremely, then all the wheels of *saṁvit* (*saṁvit* means cognitions, *akṣa* means all organs, and *marut* means all breaths), all the wheels of breaths, all the wheels of cognitions, and all the wheels of the organic field of cognitions…

DEVOTEE: *Marut cakraṁ*?

SWAMIJI: *Prāṇa cakraṁ*.

…*jñeyābhinnaṁ tato bhavet*, it becomes one with that God consciousness. Whatever he feels, whatever he tastes, whatever he smells, it becomes one with God consciousness. Whatever he breathes in and out, it becomes one with God consciousness. And whatever he knows in knowledge, it becomes one with God consciousness. So all these wheels get full oneness with that God consciousness.

Next:

LJA TA05F (38:17)

तज्ज्ञेयं संविदाख्येन वह्निना प्रविलीयते।
विलीनं तत् त्रिकोणेऽस्मिञ्शक्तिवह्नौ विलीयते॥७७॥

tajjñeyaṁ saṁvidākhyena vahninā pravilīyate /[71]
vilīnaṁ tat trikoṇe'smiñśaktivahnau vilīyate //77//

So, when you get entry in your nature first,...*

You have to enter in your nature first and become void of all differentiated perceptions. This is the first state of entry in God consciousness. And then you have to vibrate in such a way that you get your *nāda daśā* (your *nāda daśā* means, un-uttered sound of *ahaṁ*, I-consciousness), it becomes bloomed, highly bloomed, and then you get entry in the outside world also. And in the outside world, you feel that this whole outside world filled with all the wheels of the cognitive world, the world of organs, the world of breaths, are one with that–you feel that.

*...and *tat jñeyaṁ saṁvidākhyena vahninā pravilīyate*, and that *jñeya*, the oneness that they have got with that state of God consciousness (it means, this organic world and breath and all, they have become one with that God consciousness–that is *jñeya*[72]), and that God consciousness also melts away. *Tat jñeyaṁ saṁvit ākhyena vahninā pravilīyate*, and that also melts by the fire of *para para pramātṛ bhāva*, the state of *para pramātṛ bhāva* (super-supreme subjective state). That supreme *pramātṛ bhāva* melts in the fire of *para pramātṛ bhāva* in the end. And this is the indication of letter 'r', the letter *ra* in *piṇḍanātha*. *Vilīnaṁ tat trikoṇe'smin śakti vahnau pravilīyate*, when that melts in the supreme fire of *para pramātṛ bhāva*, and that *para pramātṛ bhāva* remains all-round shining, and that *para pramātṛ bhāva* also melts by-and-by in external God consciousness, external *para pramātṛ* state, and that is the state of will, knowledge and action. So, he can move

71. Swamiji recites "*pravilāpayet*" in place of the published "*pravilīyate*", both of which confer the same meaning: to melt or dissolve.

72. Lit., that which is to be known.

around in this world with that supreme *para pramātṛ bhāva*. That is trikoṇa (*e*).

JOHN: What was the difference here…?

SWAMIJI: Because you have to rise, you have to get entry first.

JOHN: First is entry.

SWAMIJI: First is entry. Then…

JOHN: Establishment in your own nature in *ahaṁ*.

SWAMIJI:…establishment in your own nature, that is *nāda daśā*. Then you have to vibrate with that *nāda daśā* all these wheels of cognitions, organs, and breaths,…

JOHN: So this is still subjective.

SWAMIJI:…when they become one with that, and there is only left aside only that state of supreme-I, God consciousness. And that supreme-I God consciousness is to be melted, is to be melted in supreme *para pramātṛ bhāva*, super God consciousness. And that super God consciousness, when it is established, you get vibrated out in the external world also.

JOHN: So this one isn't vibrating in the external world, when you vibrate the wheels, the *cakra*s of cognition, organs and breath.

SWAMIJI:…organs…no, no. It is just to give them life from that…

JOHN: This is in *samādhi*, this is a yogic state in *samādhi*.

SWAMIJI: Yes, *samādhi*.

JOHN: This last state is not in *samādhi*.

SWAMIJI: No, it is…

JOHN: *Vyutthāna*.

SWAMIJI: It is in *vyutthāna* (external world). It is why he has called this *trikoṇa* (*e*), the state of *trikoṇa*, where there is triangle, triangle state of God consciousness. The triangle state of [God consciousness is] where there is will, functioning of will, functioning of knowledge, and functioning of action. There is not only will, there is knowledge also; and there is not only knowledge, there is action also.

JOHN: In everything.

SWAMIJI: So, this is God consciousness in action, activity.

JOHN: So this *ahaṁ*, this is supreme *ahaṁ*, this un-utterable sound,…

SWAMIJI: Yes.

JOHN:…but because it is transcendental *ahaṁ*,…

SWAMIJI: Yes, it is transcendental.

JOHN:…in this state, it is not transcendental…

SWAMIJI: It is not transcendental, it is universal.
JOHN:…it is universal, in everything.
SWAMIJI: Yes.

LJA TA05F (43:06)

तत्र संवेदनोदारबिन्दुसत्तासुनिर्वृतः।
संहारबीजविश्रान्तो योगी परमयो भवेत्॥ ७८॥

tatra saṁvedanodārabindusattāsunirvṛtaḥ /
saṁhārabījaviśrānto yogī paramayo bhavet //78//

The seventy-eighth *ślokā*.

And there, in that supreme state of *para pramātṛ bhāva* where *para pramātṛ bhāva* is not found within, it is found everywhere in the whole universal activity, *tatra saṁvedana udāra bindu sattā sunir vṛtaḥ*, when that supreme state of *para pramātṛ bhāva* is forcibly made rested in that *bindu sattā* (*aṁ*),…*

DENISE: What is *bindu sattā*?

SWAMIJI: *Bindu sattā* is that state of God consciousness where in this universal activity also you find that nothing is acting, it is only one point where you are resting. If you are doing all these activities of worldly activities, you are doing nothing, you are only rested, you have rested in that one point, nothing has happened.

ERNIE: Is this like that rest within?

SWAMIJI: Yes. *Tatra saṁvedana udāra bindu sattā*, so it is *udāra*, great, great state of *bindu*. This is the great state of *bindu* (*aṁ*) where all this universal state of supreme *para pramātṛ bhāva* rests.

*…*saṁhāra bīja viśrānto*, then the yogi, when he rests in *saṁhāra bīja* (*saṁhāra bīja* means, *ra*, *agni bīja*), *saṁhāra bīja viśrānta yogī paramayo bhavet*, the yogi becomes *paramaya*, one with that supreme state. So this is the end of the explanation of *piṇḍanātha*.

LJA TA05F (45:02)

अन्तर्बाह्ये द्वये वापि सामान्येतरसुन्दरः ।
संवित्स्पन्दस्त्रिशक्त्यात्मा सङ्कोचप्रविकासवान् ॥ ७९ ॥

antarbāhye dvaye vāpi sāmānyetarasundaraḥ /
saṁvitspandastriśaktyātmā saṅkocapravikāsavān //79//

And then he finds, the yogi finds in the internal state and in the external state, in the internal state he finds supreme-I, in the external state he perceives this-ness. I-ness and this-ness. I-ness in the internal state, this-ness in the external state. Not only this, because he finds, he experiences three states: one state of *mantra maheśvara bhāva*, the next state of *mantreśvara bhāva*, and the third state of *mantra pramātṛ bhāva*. *Mantra pramātṛ bhāva* is concerned with Śuddhavidyā, *mantreśvara pramātṛ bhāva* is concerned with Īśvara, and *mantra maheśvara pramātṛ bhāva* is concerned with Sadāśiva. And these three states he experiences, the yogi experiences. In Sadāśiva, he experiences *ahaṁ-idam*, "I am this whole universe." In *mantreśvara bhāva* (Īśvara), he experiences, "This is myself, this universe is one with myself" (*idam-ahaṁ*). There is a difference, there is a difference in [these] two. "I am this universe" and "This universe is I." First "this", predominance goes to "this" first, in the next state of God consciousness–*idam-ahaṁ*.

JOHN: In Īśvara.

SWAMIJI: In Īśvara. In Sadāśiva, predominance goes to "I" first: "I am this." [In Íśvara], "this is I." And *dvaye vāpi*: "I am both. I am, from one point of view, I am the universe, from another point of view, this [universe] is my God consciousness." This is the state of Śuddhavidyā. And *sāmānya itara sundaraḥ saṁvit spanda*, this throbbing of God consciousness, this throbbing state of God consciousness takes place in three ways: one in the supreme way, one in the medium way, one in the inferior way. And this inferior way is also not away from God consciousness. The supreme way is already in God consciousness, the medium way is already in God consciousness, and this inferior way is already in God consciousness.

JOHN: Is the inferior way Śuddhavidyā?

SWAMIJI: Śuddhavidyā, yes. And this is *triśaktyātmā*, this throbbing of *saṁvit*, this throbbing of God consciousness, is threefold, it has got three energies, three energies are functioning this. The energy of will (*icchā śakti*) is functioning God consciousness of Sadāśiva, and the energy of knowledge (*jñāna śakti*) is functioning the God consciousness of Īśvara, and the energy of action (*kriyā śakti*) is functioning the God consciousness of Śuddhavidyā.

JOHN: So the yogi experiences these all at the same time or…?

SWAMIJI: Huh?

JOHN: In universal consciousness, he can experience all these simultaneously?

SWAMIJI: Simultaneously, yes, he experiences…

JOHN: "I am this," "this am I," "this is this/I am I."

SWAMIJI: Yes.

BRUCE H: And it's his choice?

SWAMIJI: Not his choice. It happens. And it is *saṅkoca pravikāsavān*, it vibrates in and vibrates outside, vibrates in and vibrates outside, constantly! This is just like *krama mudrā*.

DENISE: He doesn't get confused (laughs)?

JOHN: But this is not *krama mudrā*, though.

SWAMIJI: It is his nature, he finds that "It is my own nature." How can he get confused?

JOHN: This is not *krama mudrā*, though, in the sense of a yogi in *samādhi*. This is not the same thing, it is like *krama mudrā* but it is not…

SWAMIJI: No. It is the center of *krama mudrā*, it is supreme *krama mudrā*.

JOHN: After *krama mudrā* has been established.

SWAMIJI: Yes.

LJA TA05F (49:19)

असङ्कोचविकासोऽपि तदाभासनतस्तथा।

asaṅkocavikāso'pi tadābhāsanatastathā /

When it is vibrated inside and vibrated outside, it means it has got two states. So, a doubt is possible to readers that it must not be the real state of God consciousness, where there are two ways of happening. He says, *asaṅkoca vikāso'pi tadābhāsana tastathā*, although nothing is vibrated outside and nothing is vibrated inside, it is only the glory of God consciousness that you feel that it is vibrated outside, and the next moment it is vibrated inside, the next moment, the third moment it is vibrated outside, and again inside, again outside, again outside. This outside and inside functioning of God consciousness does not take place at all. It says, *asaṅkoca vikāso'pi*, nothing vibrates outside, nothing vibrates inside. *Tada ābhāsana tastathā*, but this is the glory of his *svātantrya śakti*, the energy of *svātantrya* (freedom), that it seems so. So this creation of the universe, it seems that it is created, but in fact it is not created at all, it is resting in that state of God consciousness. This is what he means here.

It is why yogis do this kind of *sādhanā* (practice), in the 80th half *śloka*. Next he says:

LJA TA05F (51:00)

अन्तर्लक्ष्यो बहिर्दृष्टिः परमं पदमश्नुते ॥ ८० ॥

antarlakṣyo bahirdṛṣṭiḥ paramaṁ padamaśnute //80//

The yogi who feels in this activity of the universe, who sees, who perceives, who perceives *rasa* (taste), all these organs of senses, he functions his organs of senses in the outside world also, but at the same time he is *antarlakṣya*, he directs his supreme consciousness within. Although warming his hands, he is within, he is not warming his hands at all. That is *antralakṣyo. Bahir dṛṣti*, his sight is directed in the external world, but his consciousness is directed within (*antarlakṣyo, bahir dṛṣṭiḥ*). It is Bhairavī *mudrā*, this is the state of Bhairavī *mudrā* when you perceive, when you go on looking on some object and don't feel any object. Just go on looking wide, with your eyes wide open. You perceive this, you go on looking at this fire pot, but don't see the fire pot; but keep your eyes wide open and don't see it at all. When you don't see this fire pot, you are *antarlakṣya*, your real direction of sight is within, resting inside. *Paramaṁ padam aśnute*, that is the real state of God consciousness, what is practiced by these yogis also in Bhairavī *mudrā*.

LJA TA05F (52:58)

ततः स्वातन्त्र्यनिर्मेये विचित्रार्थक्रियाकृति।
विमर्शनं विशेषाख्यः स्पन्द औन्मुख्यसञ्ज्ञितः ॥८१॥

tataḥ svātantryanirmeye vicitrārthakriyākṛti /
vimarśanaṁ viśeṣākhyaḥ spanda aunmukhyasañjñitaḥ //81//

Because this is created, these universal activities are created by the *svātantrya* of God consciousness. This is his free will that it is created outside. *Vicitra artha kriyākṛti*, and it has various forms, various forms in all the five senses–*śabda*, *sparśa*, *rūpa*, *rasa* and *gandha*. *Vimarśanaṁ viśeṣākhyaḥ*, and this is *viśeṣa vimarśanaṁ*, this is *viśeṣa vimarśanaṁ*, particular *vimarśana* (awareness). Particular *vimarśana* takes place in not-particular *vimarśana*.

There are two folds of *vimarśana*: one is particular *vimarśana*, one is not particular *vimarśana*. That [not] particular *vimarśana* is the same in specks and in *kongri* (fire pot)–not particular *vimarśana*. Particular *vimarśana* is different in this and different in this. When there is particular *vimarśana*, particular observation, you find this is a *kongri*. When there is particular *vimarśana*, you find these are specks. When there is not particular *vimarśana*, then there is no difference between specks and *kongri*, it is only the shining of your own God consciousness–when you see it without any formation.

JOHN: Is that the same as that viewing from the top of the mountain the city where you don't see…?

SWAMIJI: Yes, yes, that is it. *Śikharastha jñāna*, just like *śikharastha jñāna*.[73] And this is the *spanda*, this is the *spanda* when you are diverted towards one-pointedness of objectivity. *Viśeṣa vimarśana* is *spanda*, not *sāmānya vimarśana*. *Sāmānya vimarśana* is God consciousness, *viśeṣa vimarśanam* is *spanda*.

JOHN: Because there is differentiation?

SWAMIJI: It is differentiated.

73. Knowledge (*jñana*) from the top or summit (*śikhara*).

JOHN: And in *sāmānya* there is…?

SWAMIJI: When differentiated perception arises from inside, this is *spanda*, this is that throb of differentiated perception, but internally it is not throbbing at all (that is *sāmānya spanda*). *Sāmānya spanda* is one in each and every object, there is no difference between any object in *sāmānya spanda*. In *viśeṣa spanda*, there is difference. And this is nominated, in other words, as *aunmukhya*, it is *aunmukhya*, diversion towards the external world. When your God consciousness is diverted towards the external world, that is *spanda*. When your God consciousness is again [wrapped] inside, folded within, that is not… that is *sāmānya spanda*. And *sāmānya spanda* is within, *viśeṣa spanda* is without.

JOHN: So *sāmānya spanda* is that non-particularized *vimarśa*.

SWAMIJI: Non-particular *vimarśa*.

LJA TA05F (56:17)

तत्र विश्रान्तिमागच्छेद्यद्वीर्यं मन्त्रमण्डले।
शान्त्यादिसिद्धयस्तत्तद्रूपतादात्म्यतो यतः ॥८२॥

tatra viśrāntimāgacchedyadvīryaṁ mantramaṇḍale /
śāntyādisiddhayastattadrūpatādātmyato yataḥ //82//
(not recited)

Tatra viśrāntim āgacchet, there in *sāmānya spanda* (*sāmānya parāmarśa*), the yogi must rest, the yogi must take rest. This is the only abode of peace, *sāmānya spanda*. And this is the *vīrya*, this is the power that vibrates in each and every mantra of the world of mantras. Each and every mantra get power from this *sāmānya spanda*.

JOHN: Not from this *viśeṣa spanda*.

SWAMIJI: *Viśeṣa spanda*, no. *Śāntyādi siddhayas tatra*, all powers which are connected with yogic processes, those powers also vibrate from that *sāmānya spanda*. *Tat tat rūpa tādātmyato yataḥ*, whatever he feels, if he feels that "I will eat," he eats; if he feels "I will smell," he smells; and this kind of power also is got from that *sāmānya spanda*. Smelling, tasting, it is all *viśeṣa spanda*, and *sāmānya spanda* is from within.

LJA TA05F (57:40)

दिव्यो यश्चाक्षसङ्घोऽयं बोधस्वातन्त्र्यसञ्ज्ञकः ।
सोऽनिमीलित एवैतत् कुर्यात्स्वात्ममयं जगत् ॥ ८३ ॥

divyo yaścākṣasaṅgho'yaṁ bodhasvātantryasañjñakaḥ /
so'nimīlita evaitat kuryātsvātmamayaṁ jagat //83//
(not recited)

Divyo yat ca akṣa saṅgho'yaṁ, so he gets the gathering of *divya*. *Divya* means…one is *divya*, one is *adivya*. *Divya* means, that is above everything–*divya*, *divya saṅgha*. What is *divya*?

JOHN: Light or…?

SWAMIJI: No, not light. *Alaukika*, beyond the worldly state.

JOHN: Is it transcendental, not…?

SWAMIJI: Transcendental, transcendental state. So he owns the transcendental state of all his organs, all his breaths and all his actions.

LJA TA05F (58:29) end
LJA TA05G (00:00) start

Divyo yat cākṣasaṅgho'yaṁ, this gathering of all these, gathering and being adjusted with this organic field is divine–divine! *Divya* means, divine, it is not…

DEVOTEE: Divine! Oh!

SWAMIJI: It is not…yes, divine. I couldn't gather this word. It is divine. For him, it is divine, everything is divine. His organic field is divine, his everything is divine, his breath is divine, his talking is divine, he becomes all-divine. So, it is not senses of cognitions, it is not just like senses of cognitions and senses of action. He has not senses of cognition. He does not hold, he does not own the senses of cognition. Although he has eyes, ear, nose, throat, everything, he has all these organs, but these organs are for him divine, they are not just like organs of senses. *Bodhasvātantryasañjñakaḥ*, this is *bodha* and *svātantrya*. For organs of senses, he has got *bodha*, not *buddhi*, not intellect, it is not intellectual. His organs do not reside in the intellectual field of consciousness, they reside in *bodha*, in knowledge, supreme knowledge of God consciousness. And it is *svātantrya*. His actions, his organs of actions do not reside in the state of activity, they reside in *svātantrya*. So *bodha* and *svātantrya* he has nominated in other words, other way. His organs of senses are *bodha* and his organs of actions are *svātantrya*. *So'nimīlita evaitat kuryāt svātmamayaṁ jagat*, and that kind of yogi who has reached that state, *animīlita evaitat*, he does not wind up this activity of God consciousness...worldly activities, he does not wind up worldly activities. *Animīlita eva etat jagat svātmamayaṁ kuryāt*, *animīlita*, he does not wind up this worldly activity. *Animīlita eva etat*, *svātmamayaṁ jagat kuryāt*, and he finds that this whole universe is one with that God consciousness, without abandoning it, without abandoning it, without winding it [up].

JOHN: Right. Not a Vedāntic kind of thing where you leave it.

SWAMIJI: No (affirmative). Not *nimīlita*, [it is] *animīlita*.

JOHN: So he expands his God consciousness into the world...

SWAMIJI: Yes, into the world.

JOHN:...rather than extracting it and negating the world.

SWAMIJI: But how he does it, he says in these two *śloka*s:

LJA TA05G (03:05)

महासाहससंयोगविलीनाखिलवृत्तिकः ।
पुञ्जीभूते स्वरश्म्योघे निर्भरीभूय तिष्ठति ॥ ८४ ॥

mahāsāhasasaṁyogavilīnākhilavṛttikaḥ /
puñjībhūte svaraśmyoghe nirbharībhūya tiṣṭhati //84//

By getting adjustment in the *mahāsāhasa*, the pose of *cakita mudrā*, astonishing pose (yes, that is *mahāsāhasa* yoga), by being adjusted with *mahāsāhasa* yoga, and where *vilīna akhila vṛttikaḥ*, all external states of the world of senses and world of actions have melted away, have melted in *bodha* and in *svātantrya*, all his organs of senses have melted in *bodha* and where all his organs of actions have melted in *svātantrya*, *vilīna akhila vṛttikaḥ*, all his *vṛtti*s (functions) have melted in that oneness of *bodha* and *svātantrya*, there is no possibility of existence for his organic field, it may be intellectual or pertaining to actions. All *jñānendriyas* and *karmendriyas* are gone, melted, melted in *bodha* and *svātantrya*. *Jñānendriyas* have melted in *bodha* and his *karmendriyas* have melted in *svātantrya*. *Puñjībhūte svaraśmyoghe nirbharībhūya tiṣṭhati*, and there he gets established, that yogi gets establishment in all the senses of organs, where all the senses of organs have gathered in one-pointedness of God consciousness, and where *puñjībhūte svaraśmyoghe*, it has become *puñjībhūta*; *puñjībhūta* means, it has been gathered from all sides and has entered in that supreme state of *bodha* and *svātantrya*.

LJA TA05G (05:22)

अकिञ्चिच्चिन्तकस्तत्र स्पष्टदृग्याति संविदम्।

akiñciccintakastatra spaṣṭadṛgyāti saṁvidam /85a
(not recited)

Akiñcit cintakas tatra, there the yogi remains at *akiñcit bhāva*, he does not get any vibration of his senses–*akiñcit cintakas tatra*.[74] And *spaṣṭa dṛk*, although he does not get any vibration of senses, but he is not out of his senses, he does not become out of his senses just like Vedāntists.

JOHN: But he controls his senses, his senses don't control him.

SWAMIJI: No, his senses don't control him. He does not control his senses also.

JOHN: I mean, not control in that way, but he has *svātantrya* and *bodha*, they just…

SWAMIJI: Yes, because they have melted in *bodha* and *svātantrya*. And:

LJA TA05G (06:10)

यद्विस्फुलिङ्गाः संसारभस्मदाहैकहेतवः ॥८५॥

yadvisphuliṅgāḥ saṁsārabhasmadāhaikahetavaḥ //85//

---

74. There (*tatra*) he thinks (*cintaka*) about nothing (*akiñcit*).

And the *visphulliṅga*, by that fire of God consciousness that he perceives there, just a few sparks of that fire make this whole differentiated universe burn in…this universe, the differentiated universe is burnt to ashes, and there is no possibility of its rise again in this universe.

DENISE: Never.

SWAMIJI: Never. He is always there then, although he does everything–*śabda*, *sparśa*, *rūpa*, *rasa* and *gandha*, everything, but he is divine.

DENISE: He does that by habit? He just continues doing that by habit?

SWAMIJI: No, he does that by *svātantrya* and *bodha*. It is not by the pressure of organs, of intellectual organs or organs of actions.

JOHN: He is not acted, he is the actor.

SWAMIJI: No (affirmative), he is divine, his everything is divine then.

JOHN: Why does he take this *mudrā* of astonishment? Why is that *mudrā*…?

SWAMIJI: Huh?

JOHN: This *mudrā* of astonishment, why is that *mudrā* adopted? What does that mean?

SWAMIJI: It means, he has not experienced it beforehand. So when he experiences it, he becomes astonished, all-round astonished: "What has happened? It is something divine that I am experiencing."

LJA TA05G (7:43)

तदुक्तं परमेशेन त्रिशिरोभैरवागमे।

taduktaṁ parameśena triśirobhairavāgame /
(not recited)

It is already told, explained by Lord Śiva himself in the *Triśirobhairava Āgama*:

श्रृणु देवि प्रवक्ष्यामि मन्त्रभूम्यां प्रवेशनम्॥ ८६॥

śṛṇu devi pravakṣyāmi mantrabhūmyāṁ praveśanam //86//

O my dear *devī*, Pārvatī, I will teach you how you should get entry in that supreme state of God consciousness.

मध्यनाड्योर्ध्वगमनं तद्धर्मप्राप्तिलक्षणम् ।
विसर्गान्तपदातीतं प्रान्तकोटिनिरूपितम् ॥ ८७ ॥

madhyanāḍyordhvagamanaṁ taddharmaprāptilakṣaṇam /
visargāntapadātītaṁ prāntakoṭinirūpitam //87//

This is what I am going to explain to you: it is to rise high, high up to that supreme uppermost limit through *madhyanāḍī*, through the central vein of *suṣumnā* (*madhya nāḍya ūrdhvagamanaṁ*), and *tat dharma prāptilakāṇam*, it is not only rising from *madhyanāḍī*, it is to become one with that *madhyanāḍī*. *Tat dharma prāpti lakṣaṇam*, aspects of *madhyanāḍī* become aspects of your nature. *Visargāntapadātītaṁ*, and this is that state which has subsided, which has crossed the state of *visarga*, the state of supreme *visarga*. And *prāntakoṭi nirūpitam*, and he finds that state of God consciousness in each and every top of actions.

JOHN: You mean end-point.

SWAMIJI: For instance, I experience that, I experience that. This is also the top, this is also the top, this is also the top, this is also the top. So he is always residing there.

JOHN: "Top" means?

SWAMIJI: The first force…

JOHN: Moment.

SWAMIJI:…first *spanda*, moment, yes.

JOHN: Like in *śāmbhavopāya*, that first…

SWAMIJI: Yes, yes. So he resides there. *Bas*, we will do this much today.

ERNIE: (laughs)

SWAMIJI: (laughs) It is so tough, because it is only experience. The first sensation, the next sensation, the next sensation, in each and every act he finds that he resides there.

DENISE: And so he feels bliss in each and every act.

SWAMIJI: Yes.

DENISE: The same.

SWAMIJI: The same, same.

DENISE: Not more, not less–the same!

SWAMIJI: Same.

JOHN: Why do you say it is not exactly like *sāmānya spanda*?

SWAMIJI: Huh?

JOHN: Because *sāmānya spanda* is an introverted state?

SWAMIJI: No, *sāmānya spanda* is practicable. It is not practicable, it happens, this is the difference. *Sāmānya spanda* is to be practiced, and this is there, this is there.

JOHN: This is the result of that practice.

SWAMIJI: Yes.

DEVOTEE: *Sāmānya spanda*...(Kashmiri)

SWAMIJI: (Kashmiri) There is no difference between John and Denise there. When Denise is Denise, John is John, this is *viśeṣa spanda*–this kind of perception.

JOHN: So then a yogi should experience the relationship between himself and his master on the level of *sāmānya spanda*, not on *viśeṣa spanda*.

SWAMIJI: *Viśeṣa spanda*, no. Yes.

JOHN: This is wrong thinking to think that the differences in *viśeṣa spanda*, that he is...

SWAMIJI: *Viśeṣa spanda* is in ignorance.

JOHN: The incorrect way of understanding things.

SWAMIJI: Yes. [Now he explains how] the yogi gets entry in that state of supreme God consciousness (*para tattva praveśa*).

LJA TA05G (11:19)

अधःप्रवाहसंरोधादूर्ध्वक्षेपविवर्जनात्।
महाप्रकाशमुदयज्ञानव्यक्तिप्रदायकम्॥ ८८॥
अनुभूय परे धाम्नि मात्रावृत्त्या पुरं विशेत्।

adhaḥpravāhasaṁrodhādūrdhvakṣepavivarjanāt /
mahāprakāśamudayajñānavyaktipradāyakam //88//
anubhūya pare dhāmni mātrāvṛttyā puraṁ viśet /

When the ingoing breath–that is *adhaḥ pravāha*–the ingoing breath has stopped, there is no ingoing breath, activity of ingoing breath is over, and *ūrdhva kṣepa vivarjanāt*, activity of out-coming breath is also stopped (so egress and ingress have stopped), *mahā prakāśam udaya jñāna vyakti pradāyakam*, then the yogi experiences, in that supreme state of God consciousness, *mahā prakāśa* (the great light) that reveals to him the rising state of knowledge (*udaya jñāna*; *udaya pradhāna jñāna vyakti pradāyakam*). And when he realizes that state of God consciousness, which is filled with light on all sides ("light" means the light of consciousness, not this physical light),...*

JOHN: Why do they call *prakāśa*, "light"?

SWAMIJI: Huh?

JOHN: Why do they call it "light"? Because it's like light? It lights everything? It gives rise to everything? That idea? *Prakāśa* means light in a...

SWAMIJI: Light, yes.

JOHN: Why do they call consciousness "light"?

SWAMIJI: Consciousness is, in the real sense, consciousness is light. When, in a dead body, there is that eye, but it won't work because there is no consciousness. Consciousness works. It is only consciousness that infuses the strength of experience realizing in each and every channel of his organs. It is consciousness that hears, it is consciousness that sees, it is consciousness that smells, not the nose, it only the means. A water jug, but it is drunk by consciousness. So it is *mahāprakāśa*. And that supreme [light] of God consciousness is revealed there, which is found there in the rising state of knowledge. It is a rise, it is not descending. Although it is descending, it is a rise. It descends from the supreme state to the lowest state and from the lowest state to the supreme state again. And this whole process is rising, this is not descending and ascending.

*...and *mātrā vṛttyā puraṁ viśet*, and you should get entry in that supreme state of God consciousness, *mātrā vṛttyā*, by *mātrā vṛtti*. *Mātrā vṛtti* means, by repetition, repeating it again and again. But it is done only when the breath has stopped, both the breaths have stopped altogether.

JOHN: So what are you repeating here then?

SWAMIJI: Repeating entry in that God consciousness in the form of rising, that is...

JOHN: In other words, sitting in meditation and again stopping the breath and then…

SWAMIJI: No, you have not to stop it.

JOHN: No, it stops itself.

SWAMIJI: It stops, it stops itself.

JOHN: But you have to do that again and again, and again, and again.

DENISE: You have to experience that again and again?

SWAMIJI: You have not to stop again and again. Breath stops once for all, finished. When breath is finished, then you get entry. When there is breath, there is no possibility of entry. You can't enter in God consciousness when there is breathing. Breathing stops first and then you get entry in that God consciousness, and when you enter in that God consciousness, you have to rise, you have to realize that in the rising state. It is not descending and ascending.

JOHN: It is rising from individuality to universality?

SWAMIJI: No, it is rising from the universal state of God consciousness to the individual state, and from the individual state to the universal state again. And this process should be repeated again and again so that it is firm.

JOHN: Is that like *krama mudrā*? Is that the same as *krama mudrā*?

SWAMIJI: It is automatic *krama mudrā*. It is not that *krama mudrā* which is found, which is experienced by yogis just after coming out from *samādhi*. It is not that. It is internal *krama mudrā*.

JOHN: In *samādhi*, this is in *samādhi*.

SWAMIJI: It is internal.

JOHN: So this is internal movement.

SWAMIJI: Internal movement.

JOHN: The yogi experiences coming to this and back in his mind.

SWAMIJI: Yes. And this is *antaḥ praveśa* (internal entry), this is *para tattva praveśa* (entry into the highest element). Now he explains in the next *śloka*s how it is felt, and how the yogi should experience it. He should not experience it that the universal state of God consciousness is the highest state of God consciousness and the individual state of God consciousness is the lowest state of God consciousness. He should not find, he should not realize that way. He should realize it in divinity, all the states.

JOHN: In sameness.

SWAMIJI: Yes, in sameness.

LJA TA05G (17:04)

निस्तरङ्गावतीर्णा सा वृत्तिरेका शिवात्मिका ॥ ८९ ॥

nistaraṅgāvatīrṇā sā vṛttirekā śivātmikā //89//

This is only one flow, one flow of Lord Śiva, one flow of Lord Śiva, the consciousness of Lord Śiva, that takes place in yogis. But when? When the breath is over, there is no breath. So it is *nistaraṅga*, without tides. There are no tides at all, tides of differentiated perceptions. Differentiated perceptions are not there. *Avatīrṇā sā*, the differentiated perceptions are there. Tides are there, tides are not there. In one way, there are no tides in the ocean of that transcendental God consciousness, and in the other way, there are tides of differentiated perception because differentiated perceptions won't exist without that. So, differentiated perceptions are divine, and undifferentiated perception (knowledge) is divine, too, also.

JOHN: Does this function on…

SWAMIJI: It is internal *krama mudrā*.

JOHN:…in Śuddhavidyā, Īśvara and Sadāśiva? These three are functioning here?

SWAMIJI: Yes, Śuddhavidyā, Īśvara and Sadāśiva–internal.

JOHN: This is the movement.

SWAMIJI: Movement.

JOHN: So then the tides would be on the level of this-ness, and the no-tides would be on the level of *ahaṁ*?

SWAMIJI: *Ahaṁ*, yes. *Ahaṁ* and *idam*, yes. *Nistaraṅga* means, tideless state; *avatīrṇā* means, the state with tides. And these are not two states, *vṛttir ekā śivātmikā*, this is one movement of Lord Śiva–with tides and without tides.

LJA TA05G (18:45)

चतुष्षड्डिर्द्विगुणितचक्रषट्कसमुज्ज्वला ।

catuṣṣaḍdvirdviguṇitacakraṣaṭkasamujjvalā /

Because it is shining in six forms of wheels: fourfold wheels, sixfold wheels, eightfold wheels, twelvefold wheels, sixteenfold wheels and twenty-fourfold wheels. And it starts from fourfold wheels. It is in the *Triśirobhairava Āgama* you will find the exhaustive explanation of these wheels, these six wheels. This is *ṣaṭ cakra*, this is the real *ṣaṭ cakra*. The *ṣaṭ cakra*s found by yogis in *sādhanā* (practice) from *mūlādhāra* to *brahmarandhra*, those are also *ṣaṭ cakra*s but those are inferior *ṣaṭ cakra*s. These are the real *ṣaṭcakra*s: fourfold, sixfold, eightfold, twelvefold, and sixteenfold, and twenty-fourfold.

LJA TA05G (19:58)

तत्स्थं विचारयेत् खं खं खस्थं खस्थेन संविशेत् ॥ ९० ॥
खं खं त्यक्त्वा खमारुह्य खस्थं खं चोच्चरेदिति ।
खमध्यास्याधिकारेण पदस्थाश्चिन्मरीचयः ॥ ९१ ॥

tatsthaṁ vicārayet khaṁ khaṁ khasthaṁ khasthena saṁviśet //90//
khaṁ khaṁ tyaktvā khamāruhya khasthaṁ khaṁ coccarediti /
khamadhyāsyādhikāreṇa padasthāścinmarīcayaḥ //91//
(not recited)

Tat stho, and when he is residing there in those ten movements (they are actually in ten movements in *ṣaṭ cakra bhāva*), *tat stho vicārayet khaṁ khaṁ*, and these ten states are actually ten voidnesses, and when you are established in that void (void means, *śūnya*, where there is nothing, nothing separate from your nature), *tat stho*, when you are established there, *vicārayet khaṁ khaṁ*, so you should concentrate on each and every state, all these ten states [of] voidness repeatedly. *Khaṁ khaṁ* means, repeatedly you should start experiencing that voidness. Then, when you are established in voidness, by the means of voidness, *khasthena saṁviśet*, you should get entry in another voidness. And then, when you enter in that [next] void, and that void you shatter it off and get entry in another void, *khamāruhya*, then you ride on that void. When you are established in that void, you should enlighten the next void. *Kham adhyāsya*, when you are fully established in that voidness, *adhikāreṇa*, when you are holding absolute control on that void, on all these voids, ten voids, *padasthāścin marīcayaḥ*, all your classes of organs (it means the organs of cognition and organs of action), *padasthā*, they will be established in your own divine nature. They are always established in divine nature, so your organs of action and organs of knowledge are divine already for your lifetime, after that also.

JOHN: So these experiencing and moving through these voidnesses, these voidnesses are different levels, different experiences of universality and individuality inside.

SWAMIJI: Yes, yes, yes, yes. That he will explain it. And:

LJA TA05G (22:24)

भावयेद्भावमन्तःस्थं भावस्थो भावनिःस्पृहः।
भावाभावगती रुद्ध्वा भावाभावावरोधदृक्॥९२॥

bhāvayedbhāvamantaḥsthaṁ bhāvastho bhāvaniḥspṛhaḥ /
bhāvābhāvagatī ruddhvā bhāvābhāvāvarodhadṛk //92//

This *bhāva* (state), this actual *bhāva* of God consciousness which resides everywhere, which resides from top to bottom and bottom to top,...*

Because these are two movements in one flash: coming down, going up, coming down, going up. Because it is actual breath, but that breath has stopped. Which breath? External breath, external breath has stopped, so it is internal breath now. He breathes God consciousness within and without. This is the breathing of God consciousness.

JOHN: So this is real breath.

SWAMIJI: This is the real breath.

JOHN: So this breathing is what? Manifestation and dissolution coming in and going out and...?

SWAMIJI: Inside, yes, inside. Because this whole universe, whatever is found outside is actually existing inside–it is there and its reflection has come out and it is manifested, it seems to be manifested outside, but it does not seem...it is not actually manifested outside. Actually this whole universe is residing there, inside.

JOHN: In other words, actually there is only inside, there is no outside.

SWAMIJI: There is no manifestation, no manifestation, not at all.

DENISE: Our senses only tell us that it's outside.

SWAMIJI: Yes, because it is from that lens, lens of that limited lens, we see that it is manifested outside. When you use that internal lens of God consciousness, you will feel that everything is established inside, it is inside, there is no outside. Outside and inside are only one, one move.

*...and this *bhāva*, which is *antaḥsthaṁ*, which is actually residing in your internal nature, you should *bhāvayet*, you should always observe it in continuity. And when you have established in that state, *bhāva niḥspṛha*, then you don't feel any curiosity in this (*bhāva niḥspṛha* means, you don't feel any curiosity in that state of God consciousness). Because when you perceive something new, you are curious, you are so...you are very fond of seeing it again and again. But when you have established in God consciousness in the real sense, then the curiosity is finished, curiosity is over, because it is your own nature. Why to be curious?

DENISE: (laughs)

JOHN: It's always been there.

SWAMIJI: It's always there. *Bhāvā bhāvagatī ruddhvā*, so these two movements, internal, these two movements of breath within (not this outside, external movements is over), *bhāvābhāvagatīruddhvā bhāvābhāva-avarodhadṛk*, then he feels that this movement, these two movements of going down and coming up is no movement at all, it is only there. *Avarodhadṛk*, he experiences it, he experiences the standstill state of breath, inside and outside–within.

Now he says the vocabulary of these ten states:

LJA TA05G (26:11)

आत्माणुकुलमूलानि शक्तिर्भूतिश्चिती रतिः।
शक्तित्रयं द्रष्टृदृश्योपरक्तं तद्विवर्जितम्॥ ९३ ॥
एतत्खं दशधा प्रोक्तमुच्चारोच्चारलक्षणम्।

ātmāṇukulamūlāni śaktirbhūtiścitī ratiḥ /
śaktitrayaṁ draṣṭṛdṛśyoparaktaṁ tadvivarjitam //93//
etatkhaṁ daśadhā proktamuccāroccāralakṣaṇam /

This is tenfold void (*daśadhā*, tenfold), this is void explained. The first void is *ātma*, supreme state of God consciousness, that is the supreme state of God consciousness, because the supreme state of God consciousness takes place just when your breath has stopped and you get entry in that *madhyanāḍī* (central vein) and it is shining–God consciousness (that is *paramātmā*). *Ātma*, this is the first void. The first void is the supreme state of God consciousness. *Aṇu*, the next state is just to go down in individuality from that in a divine way. It is not a fall. What is it? It is a rise. On the contrary, it is a rise. He is rising from God consciousness to individual consciousness. Because God consciousness he feels it is a void, individual consciousness he feels it is a void. *Ātma*, *aṇu*, *kula mūlāni*, then you go to sex (*janmādhāra*). *Janmādhāra* means, *mūlādhāra*, where all sexual excitement vibrates. Because…it does not mean only sex, because sex he has put here because sexual pleasure is the only highest pleasure in the world of pleasures. So he has put for an example, sex. What is that? That is *mūlādhāra*. *Mūlādhāra* is the rectum, this place of the rectum. So he has to rise from God consciousness to individual consciousness, from individual consciousness he has to rise to the sexual state…

ERNIE: That ecstasy.

SWAMIJI: Not that ecstasy. It is not ecstasy. It is only that place, the sexual organ.

JOHN: In his body he moves.

SWAMIJI: Yes, he has to move up in the body, it is not moving down.

BRUCE H: Is there a different experience in each of these movements?

SWAMIJI: No, he feels voidness, he feels all-divinity everywhere. That is the great thing in it. He doesn't feel any difference between…

DENISE:…between universal and individual, they are all the same.

SWAMIJI: Yes.

JOHN: But he experiences some difference, otherwise he wouldn't know that he was passing through these different voidnesses. There must be some differentiating factor.

ERNIE: How does he know when he goes from one to the other?

SWAMIJI: Because it is all stored there, it is all stored there in that supreme transcendental state of God consciousness. Everything is stored there. Because I told you first that this manifestation of the universe is not outside as you see. It is stored inside. Inside first and then you feel that it is outside by mistake–it is a mistake.

ERNIE: (laughs)

SWAMIJI: (laughs)

JOHN: So there is some experience then.

SWAMIJI: There is some experience, yes, some experience there is.

JOHN: Of these voids.

SWAMIJI: There are ten voids. This is the third void. The first void is *parā pramātṛ bhāva*, the second void is *mita pramātṛ bhāva* (individual *pramātṛ*), the third void is *janmādhāra*. *Janmādhāra* is where the birth of the whole universe takes place–that is *janmādhāra*.

JOHN: That is the real sexual organ.

SWAMIJI: Real sexual organ. That is *kulamūla*. *Śaktir*, then there is *madhyanāḍī* (*śaktir* means, *madhyanāḍī*, the central vein, *suṣumnā*). *Śuṣumnā* is connected with that, so that is the fourth void. *Ātma* is the first void, *aṇu* is the second void, *kulamūla* is the third void, *śaktir* (*madhyanāḍī*, the central vein, *suṣumnā*) is the fourth void. *Bhūti*, then *svātantrya*, having control, you have to hold control on it! You have not to degrade yourself as everybody does in this way.

JOHN: With sex.

SWAMIJI: With sex, yes. You have not to be excited physically. You have to be, you have to get excitement spiritually, spiritual excitement, it must be spiritual excitement, it must not be physical external excitement that this is a beautiful woman, and this is this and that. No.

ERNIE: (laughs)

JOHN: Where somebody loses awareness.

SWAMIJI: Huh?

JOHN: Where the ordinary sexual act a person loses awareness, in this other person and…

SWAMIJI: Yes, loses awareness, yes, yes. So there must be *bhūti*. *Bhūti* is the the fifth void, fifth *śūnya*. *Bhūti* means, *svātantrya*. Then *citi*, *citi* is the transcendental state of *turya*, that is *turyātīta*, *turyātīta bhāva*, the state of *turyātīta bhāva*. It must be there, *turyātīta* must be there, otherwise there is no fun in this kind of rise. There must be *turyātīta*.[75] And *rati*, sexual act, real sexual act also must be there. This is another void, there is nothing in it, that is *rati*. How many?

DENISE: Seven.

SWAMIJI: Seven. Now there are three more voids, those are three energies.

DEVOTEE: *Kriyā*, *jñāna*, *icchā*.

SWAMIJI: No, *jñāna śakti*, *kriyā śakti* and *icchā śakti*. It begins from *jñāna śakti*, and it moves to *kriyā śakti*, and it ends in *icchā śakti*. *Śakti trayaṁ*, and this is *draṣṭṛdṛśya uparaktaṁ*, *tat vivarjitam*. *Draṣṭṛ uparaktaṁ* is *jñāna śakti*. That *jñāna śakti*, the energy of knowledge, is attached to the knower, knower-ship, the state of knower-ship. The energy of knowledge is attached to knower-ship, the energy of action is attached to objectivity (the known). The energy of action is attached to the known. The energy of knowledge is attached to the knower.

DEVOTEE: *Dṛśya* is *prameya*?

SWAMIJI: *Dṛśya*, the known, *prameya*. And *tat vivarjitam*, and the energy of will is detached from these two. In the energy of will, in the state of the energy of will, you won't find, you will neither find attachment towards subjectivity nor attachment towards objectivity. So these are three voids: *jñāna śakti*, *kriyā śakti*, and *icchā śakti*. These are three voids. Seven plus three, *etat khaṁ daśadhā proktam*, these are ten voids to be experienced by this great yogi, *uccāroccāra lakṣāṇam*, by successive directing you towards *parā tattva praveśa*, entry in that supreme God consciousness. This is real entry of God consciousness.

JOHN: *Parā tattva sāmaveśa* means?

SWAMIJI: Huh?

JOHN: *Parā tattva* is the highest.

SWAMIJI: Highest *tattva*, highest state.

JOHN: And entry into that.

SWAMIJI: And *samāveśa* means, entry.

JOHN: So, this *rati*...

---

75. Viz., *unmīlana samādhi*. "*Turyātīta* is the state of absolute fullness of the Self with all-consciousness and all-bliss. This is really the last and supreme state of Self. It is not only found in *samādhi*. It is found also in each and every activity of the world." *Kashmir Shaivism–The Secret Supreme*, 83.

SWAMIJI: *Rati*. *Rati* is the sexual act.

JOHN: Now how is that experienced in a void? This is all in *samādhi*, isn't it? This is not in physical…is this in physical act? This is not in…

SWAMIJI: No, no, no, he has to rise outside. He has to rise outside but that outside is not inside.

DENISE: It is not inside?

SWAMIJI: I told you, I told you, I told you nothing is outside.

DENISE: Everything is inside.

SWAMIJI: You have to rise from that spiritual God consciousness to the lowest state, and that is this outside state. And that outside state is not the lowest at all, it is the highest, it is the highest for him.

JOHN: So this is not the beginning state for a yogi. This is for a very great yogi.

SWAMIJI: This is the highest state of a yogi, yes, because it is *parā tattva praveśa*, this is the real entry in that supreme God consciousness.

JOHN: So this also doesn't happen in one second either.

SWAMIJI: Huh?

JOHN: This happens in weeks together, years together?

SWAMIJI: No.

DENISE: These ten voidness take time, lots of time, or they happen…?

SWAMIJI: No, no, no, they happen in a flash.

DENISE: Just '*tcha*', *bas*!

SWAMIJI: Yes, in a flash, yes. When it happens it will happen in a flash, otherwise it won't happen at all. When you lose your self, you must lose it for good, otherwise you won't lose it at all. When you are drowned, you are drowned for good.

ERNIE: You can't hang on a little bit, huh?

SWAMIJI: Huh?

ERNIE: You can't hang on for a little?

SWAMIJI: No, there is not hanging, these are not states in the way of hanging position. It is only one jump, it is one jump in two movements, descending and ascending. You have to descend and ascend. You have to descend from that supreme *tattva* to that, what you call "outside," and from this you have to ascend again.

JOHN: So all these ten voids happen in one flash.

SWAMIJI: In one flash.

JOHN: He moves through all of these.

SWAMIJI: Yes.

JOHN: So what act is this yogi doing, then? This is the sexual act he is doing when he moves through all of these? Because otherwise how would this…?

SWAMIJI: Yes.

JOHN: So this is being accomplished in the sexual act.

SWAMIJI: Yes.

JOHN: So he moves through that also because that's part of this whole process.

SWAMIJI: Yes.

ERNIE: But can he do this without being in the sexual act?

SWAMIJI: But the sexual act will take place by itself if you don't do physical sexual act at all.

ERNIE: In mental.

SWAMIJI: In mental it will take place, you will feel that joy.

DEVOTEE: That excitement, the vibrations (indaudible)…

SWAMIJI: Yes.

JOHN: So there are two sexual acts here. There is *kulamūla.*

SWAMIJI: *Kulamūla* is the place, no, the place, the organ.

JOHN: So this is experiencing of this sipping down and this exciting this *mūlādhāra.*

SWAMIJI: Yes.

JOHN: Then why does this sexual act come after that? Why is that coming as seventh?

SWAMIJI: It comes seventh because he has to experience all these other states to get it strength, otherwise it will lose, he will be lost. He will be lost at *janmādhāra* if it were just after *janmādhāra.* After *janmādhāra* he has to experience other voids also before going in the real act.

JOHN: And so then this real act then has the power to give rise to these other three voids.

SWAMIJI: Other three voids, yes.

JOHN: These three *śakti*s.

SWAMIJI: And this is the highest state.

JOHN: The highest *śakti* is that *icchā*…

SWAMIJI: *Icchā śakti.*

JOHN:…where you experience everything in the beginning of every movement.

SWAMIJI: Yes. Now he explains this in another way, these ten states:

LJA TA05G (38:14)

धामस्थं धाममध्यस्थं धामोदरपुटीकृतम्॥ ९४॥
धाम्ना तु बोधयेद्धाम धाम धामान्तगं कुरु।
तद्धाम धामगत्या तु भेद्यं धामान्तमान्तरम्॥ ९५॥

dhāmasthaṁ dhāmamadhyasthaṁ dhāmodaraputīkṛtam //94//
dhāmnā tu bodhayeddhāma dhāma dhāmāntagaṁ kuru /
taddhāma dhāmagatyā tu bhedyaṁ dhāmāntamāntaram //95//

This is not only void, this is *dhāma*, this is light. These are ten lights, these are not only ten voids. These are ten lights, flashlights, not those poor lights. Those lights which will digest you, your everything, including everything, including everything what you own. *Dhāmasthaṁ*, when he gets entry in that supreme state of *parā tattva*, he resides in that supreme light, and *dhāma madhyastham*, he–what is that?–he drills that *dhāma*, he drills that *dhāma* within. That is *dhāma madhyastham.* After establishing it in that light, he drills that light from within just to see if there is no other foreign matter anywhere. So he drills it.

JOHN: So that's *aṇu*, that's the state of *aṇu*.

SWAMIJI: Huh?

JOHN: That second state, the state of *aṇu*.

SWAMIJI: *Aṇu*, yes. *Dhāmodara puṭīkṛtyam*, then he gets covered by *dhāmodara*, by the entry of that light. In that entrance, he gets covered, he is covered, he is wrapped. *Dhāmnā tu*, and by the state of that light (this is the fourth), *bodhayeddhāma*, you should enlighten the next light. And after enlightening this next light, *dhāma*, that another light must get entry in the next light. *Tat dhāma*, and that light, by means of light, should get entry in the absolute light.

LJA TA05G (40:39)

भेदोपभेदभेदेन भेदः कार्यस्तु मध्यतः।
इति प्रवेशोपायोऽयमाणवः परिकीर्तितः ॥९६॥

bhedopabhedabhedena bhedaḥ kāryastu madhyataḥ /
iti praveśopāyo'yamāṇavaḥ parikīrtitaḥ //96//
(first line not recited)

So, I have explained here the means of *āṇavopāya*. This is the means of *āṇavopāya* that is felt by yogis from above. This is *āṇavopāya*, the supreme, in the supreme way of understanding.

JOHN: So this *āṇavopāya* takes you all the way to *anupāya*.

SWAMIJI: This *āṇavopāya* will take you to *anupāya* and above!

JOHN: And above!

SWAMIJI:

LJA TA05G (41:18)

श्रीमहेश्वरनाथेन यो हृत्स्थेन ममोदितः।

śrīmaheśvaranāthena yo hṛtsthena mamoditaḥ /97a

This *āṇavopāya*, this way of *āṇavopāya*, this means of *āṇavopāya*, is explained to me…is explained to you, I have explained it to you, but it was explained to me by my master, Maheśvaranāthena. And which master? *Yohṛtsthena mamoditaḥ*, he is residing always in my heart, my master is residing always in my heart, and he has made me experience this kind of *āṇavopāya*.

JOHN: So this is Śambhunātha?

SWAMIJI: Śambhunātha, yes. Maheśvaranātha is Śambhunātha there.

LJA TA05G (41:58)

श्रीब्रह्मयामले चोक्तं श्रीमान् रावो दशात्मकः ॥९७॥
स्थूलः सूक्ष्मः परो हृद्यः कण्ठ्यस्तालव्य एव च।
सर्वतश्च विभुर्योऽसौ विभुत्वपददायकः ॥९८॥

śrībrahmayāmale coktaṁ śrīmān rāvo daśātmakaḥ //97//
sthūlaḥ sūkṣmaḥ paro hṛdyaḥ kaṇṭhyastālavya eva ca /
sarvataśca vibhuryo'sau vibhutvapadadāyakaḥ //98//

97th and 98th. Half 97th, half.

The *Brahmayāmala Tantra* also says the same thing. It is not only that my master told me this. *Brahmayāmale Tantra* you will find, in the *Brahmayāmale Tantra*, that *śāstra*, you'll find the same thing. Because he has said in another way, he has said, *rāvo daśātmakaḥ*, there are ten sounds that are experienced by yogis, ten sounds in *samādhi*: *sthūlaḥ sūkṣmaḥ paro hṛdyaḥ kaṇṭhyastālavya eva ca*. First is *sthūla* (gross), *sūkṣma* (subtle), and *parā* means subtlest. Gross, subtle and subtlest, these are three kinds of sounds. And these are successively: *hṛdya*, *kaṇṭhya*, *tālavyaḥ*. *Hṛdya* means rising from the heart, *kaṇṭhya* means rising from the throat, *tālavyaḥ*, rising from palate, you know? *Tālu*. So, that sound which has risen from the heart is called *paśyantī*, and that sound which has risen from the throat is called *madhyamā*, and that sound which has risen from the palate is called *vaikharī*. And these three sounds (*paśyantī*, *madhyamā*, and *vaikharī*)–*paśyantī* is *parā*, *madhyamā* is *sūkṣma*, and *vaikharī* is *sthūla* (gross)–and these three sounds sound every sound. *Paśyantī* sounds in *paśyantī*, *madhyamā*, and *vaikharī*. *Madhyamā* sounds in *paśyantī*, *madhyamā*, and *vaikharī*. And *vaikharī* sounds in *paśyantī*, *madhyamā*, and *vaikharī*. So, there are nine sounds, three in each sound; in *paśyantī* three, in *madhyamā* three, in *vaikharī* three. This is the way these ten ways of experiencing sounds are explained in the *Brahmayāmala Tantra*.

JOHN: Where is the tenth sound? We have nine sounds.

SWAMIJI: *Sarvataśca vibhuryo'sau vibhutva padadāyakaḥ*, and the tenth sound is all-pervading in all the nine sounds. The tenth sound is everywhere!

JOHN: That's called what?
SWAMIJI: Soundless-sound, unuttered-sound.
JOHN: *Anākhya*, is that the same as *anākhya*?
SWAMIJI: *Anākhya*, it is just like *anākhya*.

LJA TA05G (45:01)

जितरावो महायोगी सङ्क्रामेत्परदेहगः।

jitarāvo mahāyogī saṅkrametparadehagaḥ /99a

When a yogi gets entry in the supreme body of God consciousness (*para dehaga*, when you have gone, when you have entered, when you are drilled inside in the supreme state of God consciousness), *jitarāva*, he governs all these sounds, he is the conqueror of all these sounds. Which sounds? How many sounds? Nine sounds.
DENISE: Oh, not ten.
SWAMIJI:

परां च विन्दति व्याप्तिं प्रत्यहं ह्यभ्यसेत तम्॥९९॥
तावद्यावदरावे सा रावाल्लीयेत राविणी।

parāṁ ca vindati vyāptiṁ pratyahaṁ hyabhyaseta tam //99//
tāvadyāvadarāve sā rāvāllīyeta rāviṇī /
(not recited)

Parāṁ ca vinda-…that [tenth] is supreme, that is all-pervading. *Parāṁ ca vindati vyāptiṁ*, because that is *icchā śakti*, that is *icchā śakti*, that is the subtlest unuttered soundless-sound. It is sound, but it is sound without sound. *Parāṁ ca vindati vyāptiṁ*, and this is the supreme pervasion, this is the supreme pervasion of God consciousness which takes place, and for this pervasion, for acquiring this pervasion, *pratyahaṁ hyabhyaseta*, you must be energetically bent on finding it out, leave everything aside and find it out. And you have to do this kind of energetic activity, you have to do only up to that point when *sā rāviṇī*, that energetic state, the producer of all sounds rests in that soundless super-sound, the state of super-sound.

JOHN: That tenth sound, at the end.

SWAMIJI: Tenth, yes. Here ends the *parā tattva praveśa*. This is the end of this chapter. And here in the *Brahmayāmala Tantra*, he has explained these ten sounds in the inferior way. Those will also be explained. *Nadate daśadhā sā tu*, in that…

JOHN: Yes, right here, this quote.

SWAMIJI:

LJA TA05G (47:38)

nadate daśadhā sā tu divyānandapradāyikā /
cinīti prathamaḥ śabdaściñcinīti dvitīyakaḥ //
cīravākī tṛtīyastu śaṅkhaśabdaścaturthakaḥ /
tantrīghoṣaḥ pañcamaśca ṣaṣṭho vaṁśaravastathā //
saptamaḥ kaṁsyatālastu meghaśabdaravastathā /
navamo dāvanirghoṣe daśamo dundubhisvanaḥ //
nava śabdān parityajya daśamo mokṣadāyakaḥ /
anena vidhinā yena vyāhareddaśadhā ravam //
(verses from the *Brahmayāmala Tantra*, quoted in the commentary, not recited)

Nadate daśadhā sā tu divyānandapradāyikā, when a yogi gets entry in that supreme state of God consciousness, at first he feels, he experiences these sounds, ten sounds. First sound is, *cin-cin-cin-cin-cin-cin*, this kind of [sound]. *Ciñcini* is the second sound. *Cin-cini* is just when you close your eye [lids] strongly, close it, that sound, that is *ciñcini*, that is *ciñcini*. The second sound is produced there in *samādhi*. *Cīravākī tṛtīyastu*, *cīravākī* means the same sound but with strong…

JOHN: It becomes louder?

SWAMIJI: Louder, louder, louder. And the fourth sound is *śaṅkha śabda*. You know *śaṅkha*? (In Kashmiri) What do they call that?

DEVOTEE: It's that shell.

DENISE: That conch-shell.

SWAMIJI: By shell, yes. That shell. That is the fourth sound he hears (*śaṅkha śabdastu caturthakaḥ*). *Tantrīghoṣaḥ pañcamaśca*, the fifth sound is *tantrīghoṣaḥ*, of that strings, the sound risen from a string instrument. *Śaṣtho vaṁśaravastathā*, the sixth is *vaṁśarava*. *Vaṁśarava* means when those [bamboo] canes in a forest are burnt by wind, by storm…

ERNIE: They hit each other.

SWAMIJI:…they hit each other and fire is produced there. It is called *vaṁśarava*. And that kind of sound he perceives within.

JOHN: A crackling sound, kind of…?

SWAMIJI: Huh?

JOHN: Burning sound?

SWAMIJI: Burning of these canes.

JOHN: There a crackling sound, popping?

SWAMIJI: Yes. *Saptamaḥ kāṁsyatālastu*, the seventh sound is two plates, two plates of that *kāṁsya* material, *chang-chang-chang*, just as you see in the Khīr Bhavānī shrine. That is the seventh sound.

DEVOTEE: *Megha śabdara*.

SWAMIJI: *Megha śabdara*, the sound of this thunder, thunder sound is next, eighth. He hears that. *Navamo dāvanirghoṣo*, the ninth sound is the sound of burning *with* a storm. The tenth sound is a big drum, the sound of a drum, from drum, from drum. *Nava śabdān parityajya daśamo mokṣa dāyakaḥ*, you should leave aside all the nine sounds and you should reside in hearing this tenth sound of that drum, because this sound of a drum will carry you to that supreme state of God consciousness. It is explained in another way in the *Brahmayāmala Tantra*, but Abhinavagupta has experienced it according to the way he was taught by his master who was residing in his own heart.

JOHN: This tenth sound, this drum sound, how would that be soundless-sound?

SWAMIJI: Huh?

JOHN: If this tenth state is *icchā śakti*…?

SWAMIJI: It carries you to there.

JOHN: So it is not the real tenth sound in the same way that Abhinavagupta has explained these ten.

SWAMIJI: No, no, it is not the same.

JOHN: This is inferior ten sounds.

SWAMIJI: Yes. It is yogis feel like that, ordinary yogis [hear] these ten sounds. I have also felt these sounds in my childhood.

DENISE: (laughs)

SWAMIJI: *Bas*. Now *tatapathalakṣaṇāni*, now, how can you recognize that path of God consciousness? That will be explained in the next lesson.

DENISE: How?

SWAMIJI: How can you recognize? What is the proof of that?

ERNIE: When, Sir?

SWAMIJI: I think Tuesday (laughs). Tuesday or Wednesday, we will see. There are so many days yet.

DEVOTEES: (laughter)

LJA TA05G (52:18)

Discussion:

ERNIE: Do you go through those ten sounds in a flash like you do the lights? No.

SWAMIJI: No, by-and-by.

ERNIE: By-and-by. Weeks, years, months?

SWAMIJI: But this process, which was taught by Abhinavagupta, is in a flash.

BRUCE H: Once that flash begins, can you fall out of that?

SWAMIJI: Huh?

BRUCE H: Once that movement begins, can you fall out of that movement?

SWAMIJI: Never.

ERNIE: Is that right?

SWAMIJI: Yes.

ERNIE: It's like a vacuum (laughs).

SWAMIJI: Keep it there at its place.

JOHN: Are these ten sounds experienced…? They are not really these states, these ten sounds.

SWAMIJI: (Swamiji seems to agree with John).

JOHN: So these are experienced when? In that first state? In the state of *ātma*, in the first void?

SWAMIJI: No, you can't attach them with that.

JOHN: At all?

SWAMIJI: No.

ERNIE: Then how come he followed those right after the ten lights? Why did they follow?

JOHN: No, no, they didn't follow. This is...

SWAMIJI: It is not following, it is another way of experiencing ten ways of God consciousness.

JOHN: But this is very inferior, this is...

SWAMIJI: Most inferior.

JOHN: This is in *kuṇḍalinī* rising or even more inferior than that?

SWAMIJI: When?

JOHN: When *kuṇḍalinī* rises, these sounds are experienced or [are they] even more inferior than that?

SWAMIJI: No, before that.

JOHN: Before that, before sipping down.

SWAMIJI: Yes.

JOHN: In this process of this...

ERNIE: Boy, if I'm lucky, maybe I'll get to experience these first sounds, you know? I'd love to hear that drum!

SWAMIJI: (laughs) To hear drum?

DEVOTEES: (laughter)

LJA TA05G (54:00)

Patha Lakṣaṇam
Recognizing the Path

Para tattva praveśa, the subject of *para tattva* is over. Now he puts signs of that *praveśa* (entry), what are the signs by which you can calculate that he is on the path.[76]

JOHN: Which? Any person on the path? These signs are to calculate for anyone, if you want to know if anyone is on the path. This is for the master to calculate, is it? Or for who?

SWAMIJI: No, he will put signs of the aspirant, what are the signs

76. "Here, the author describes the *patha lakṣāṇam*. *Patha lakṣaṇam* means, whatever you experience on the pathway of supreme God consciousness (pathway, *patha lakṣaṇam*)." *Tantrāloka* 5, additional audio (LJA archive).

of the aspirant by which we can know that he is on the path, he is treading on the path.

LJA TA05G (54:43)

अत्र भावनया देहगतोपायैः परे पथि ॥ १०० ॥
विविक्षोः पूर्णतास्पर्शात्प्रागानन्दः प्रजायते ।

atra bhāvanayā dehagatopāyaiḥ pare pathi //100//
vivikṣoḥ pūrṇatāsparśāt-prāgānandaḥ prajāyate /

Atra, in this state of Bhairavī *mudrā*...because Bhairavī *mudrā* is to be adopted. Bhairavī *mudrā* you know?

JOHN: Seeing but not seeing. With eyes open but not seeing anything?

SWAMIJI: Not only eyes open. Keep your ear wide open for hearing and don't hear anything, hear nothing; keep your skin wide open for touching, don't get any sensation of touch; keep your eyes wide open, see nothing; keep your taste wide open for taste, taste nothing; keep your nose wide open for smelling, smell nothing. This is Bhairavī *mudrā*. When this happens, you must know that you are meditating. This is the sign of a *sādhaka*.[77]

JOHN: Now *sādhaka*s already, in the ordinary course...

SWAMIJI: When one-pointedness comes, then it happens. He keeps

---

77. *yathā nimīlane kāle prapañco naiva dṛiśyate /*
tathaivonmīlane syāccedetaddhyānasya lakṣaṇam //
Kulārṇava Tantra 9.19

"Just as the external differentiated world is not seen at the time of closing one's eyes, so, in the same way, while practicing this meditation, even though his eyes remain wide open, this yogi sees nothing. This is the sign of correct meditation." Verse 2 from *The Wisdom of Kashmir Shaivism*, Swami Lakshmanjoo, 1988. See also *Amriteśvara Pūjā* verses. In an interview with Mother Alice, Swamiji recited this verse and explained that it takes place in the state of Śuddhavidyā.

his eyes wide open and sees nothing; ears wide open, hears nothing; nose wide open, smells nothing; skin wide open for touch, and gets no sensation of touch.

JOHN: *Sādhakas* already do this with all senses except for eyes, in the ordinary course.

SWAMIJI: How?

JOHN: When you are meditating, everything is open, except you close your eyes.

SWAMIJI: But you hear sounds also.

JOHN: But when you are one-pointed, those sounds go away.

SWAMIJI: Sounds also must go away, yes.

JOHN: But in this Bhairavī *mudrā*, you also open your eyes.

SWAMIJI: Yes.

JOHN: So it is more advanced.

SWAMIJI: No, this *sādhanā* (practice) is done with your organs open, wide open. This *sādhanā* is not done [with] organs shut, closed, with closed organs. Just keep your organs wide open and go on meditating. This is *bhāvanā* (contemplation), this is *bhāvanā* of Bhairavī *mudrā*. And this *bhāvanā* will take place by *deha gatopāyaiḥ*, by *āṇavopāya*, by adoption of *āṇavopāya*, various ways of *āṇavopāya*, you know. There are various ways of *āṇavopāya*. By adopting those ways, this *bhāvanā* must come, take place. Which *bhāvanā*? Of Bhairavī *mudrā*. Then, when this *bhāvanā* takes place, then there is hope of getting entry in God consciousness, otherwise there is no hope of getting entry in the God consciousness, he won't enter in God consciousness. That is what he says: *pare pathe vivikṣu*, then he gets, he is ready to enter in the supreme *marga*, supreme path. *Pūrṇataḥ sparśāt prāg ānandaḥ jāyate*, first, this is the first sign when he gets adjusted with the fullness of God consciousness.

LJA TA05G (58:17) end
LJA TA05H (00:00) start

This is not the real *pūrṇatā* (fullness), this is not real attachment in fullness of God consciousness, but there are signs, there is the feeling that the fullness of God consciousness is being attached, will be attached very soon.

JOHN: The *sādhaka* feels this?

SWAMIJI: He feels that, but only when he adopts meditation and gets entry in Bhairavī *mudrā*. You know Bhairavī *mudrā*.

JOHN: Yes.

SWAMIJI: *Prāk ānanda prajāyate*, first he experiences *ānanda* (bliss), and that bliss is felt at the place of the sexual organ. That bliss is felt at the place of the sexual organ. This is the first sign.

DEVOTEE: (Kashmiri) What is it called?

SWAMIJI: (Kashmiri) *Ānanda*.

LJA TA05H (01:13)

ततोऽपि विद्युदापातसदृशे देहवर्जिते ॥ १०१ ॥
धाम्नि क्षणं समावेशादुद्भवः प्रस्फुटं प्लुतिः ।

tato'pi vidyudāpātasadṛśe dehavarjite //101//
dhāmni kṣaṇaṁ samāveśādudbhavaḥ prasphuṭaṁ plutiḥ /

Then there is another sign after that.

Tato'pi vidyutāpāta sadṛśe, then just like the lightening, when there is lightening, flash lightening, each and every particle of the universe is filled with that lightening, nothing else is seen at that second when there is lightening. That is *vidyutā pāta sadṛśe. Deha varjite*, when attachment for the body (attachment for *deha*), attachment for *puryaṣṭaka* and *śūnya*, attachment for the body of wakefulness, the body of the dreaming state, and the body of the dreamless state, when that attachment is lessened (*deha varjite*), and that flash light of God consciousness takes place just like that lightening, only for one second,...

JOHN: Inside.

SWAMIJI: Inside.

...and *dhāmni kṣaṇaṁ samāveśāt*, he gets just one dip in that light. When he gets that dip, he just sinks in that light for only one second, *udbhavaḥ prasphuṭaṁ plutiḥ*, then there is *udbhava. Udbhava* means, he gets afreshed, he gets some rise, he feels that he is rising to some other state. That is *udbhavaḥ*.

DEVOTEE: *Dhāmni*...?

SWAMIJI: *Dāmni* is *teja* (light).
DEVOTEE: *Dhāmni deha varjite dhāmni.*
SWAMIJI: *Dāmni* is light, this is the second sign. Then:

LJA TA05H (03:24)

जलपांसुवदभ्यस्तसंविद्देहैक्यहानितः ॥ १०२ ॥
स्वबलाक्रमणाद्देहशैथिल्यात् कम्पमाप्नुयात्।

jalapāṁsuvadabhyastasaṁviddehaikyahānitaḥ //102//
svabalākramaṇāddehaśaithilyāt kampamāpnuyāt /

Then there is another sign that takes place. Because from times immemorial we are attached to this ego on the body, *saṁvit deha aikya hānitaḥ*, because this body we have understood that this body is myself, this body is my nature, I am not separate from [this body]. *Ānanda*, *udbhava*, *kampa*, *nidrā*, *aur* (and) *ghūrṇi*, these five are the symptoms of that pathway towards God consciousness. First *ānanda* appears, then *udbhava*, then *kampa*, then *nidrā*, and afterwards *ghūrṇi*. *Ānanda* means, absolute state of bliss (this is the first symptom of that pathway). After that, [after] you have experienced that *ānanda*, then afterwards there is *udbhava*. *Udbhava* is, something is growing inside, so you get, so you get…

DENISE: Encouraged?
SWAMIJI: Not encouraged. It is just encouragement towards rising, rising, rising. That is called *udbhava*.
JAGDISH: Rising something (inaudible)?
SWAMIJI: Rising towards higher states.
JOHN: You feel that growing in you?
SWAMIJI: Yes, growing.
JOHN: Some rising is…
SWAMIJI: Then the third state is *kampa* (trembling). *Kampa* is… because we have been, from times immemorial, we have been attached to body consciousness, and it is being shattered, shattered down. This body consciousness is being shattered down and that is not held properly, God consciousness is not held properly, so you get shivering. This

is the third sign of that pathway. That is *kampa*. Then, in the end, you get *ghūrṇi*. *Ghūrṇi* means, intoxicative state. You are nowhere, *bas*, you are just moving from here and there (laughs) and knowing nothing. That is *ghūrṇi*. These are the states which he describes in these *śloka*s. *Dhāmni kṣaṇaṁ samāveśāt udbhavaḥ prasphuṭaṁ plutiḥ* (verse 101), *dhāmni*, in that state, *kṣaṇaṁ samāveśāt*, he gets, he realizes trance, but that trance is not a stationary trance, [it is] just a touch of trance. That is *kṣaṇaṁ samāveśāt*.

JAGDISH: It's momentary.

SWAMIJI: Momentary. Not momentary, but it is just for a short period, just for a short period and it vanishes away. By that, the reaction is *udbhava*, he gets *udbhava*. He gets *udbhava* (rise) and it is gone. Then third is the state of *kampa*. *Ānanda*, *udbhava*, *kampa*. *Kampa* means, shivering. Shivering happens only because he is attached to body consciousness. He is forced to detach body consciousness and attach himself with God consciousness. *Jalapāṁsuvat*; *jalapāṁsuvat* means, when there is a jug full of water and dust is thrown over it. Will dust remain or will water remain? The dust on water.

DENISE: It will go inside, won't it?

SWAMIJI: It goes inside, but it goes inside, it goes down, it goes down in the bottom. But in the long run, the water will remain pure. At first, the water will be agitated by this dust (that is *jalapāṁsuvat*, in water; *pāṁsu* means dust). Just like that, *saṁvid dehaikyahānitaḥ*, God consciousness is in place of water, God consciousness is in place of water and body consciousness is in place of dust. Dust is also mixed in God consciousness. So *svabalākramaṇāt*, but he has to strive to catch hold of God consciousness; by the instructions of his masters, he has to strive for that (*svabalākramaṇāt*). That way, *dehaikyahānitaḥ*, body consciousness will vanish, will begin to vanish. *Dehaikyahānitaḥ*, *kampamāpnuyāt*, so he gets shivering because it is a kind of death. It is not physical death, it is mental death.

JOHN: Spiritual death, I mean, not spiritual death.

SWAMIJI: No, mental death. Spiritual death cannot rise (laughs).

JOHN: Spiritual birth it is.

SWAMIJI: Yes (laughs).

JAGDISH: *Svabalākramaṇāt* means, by his master's…?

SWAMIJI: By his master's instructions he has to strive for that *svabala*, your own *bala*, your own power of God consciousness.

Dehaikyahānitaḥ, and the oneness with body consciousness is being shattered, is being vanished altogether. But it has not vanished completely, it is being, it is in process towards its vanishing away. So, that makes his body shiver, because when a person dies, throws this body on one side and leaves that body…Didn't you see how Bhagavan Das had experienced?[78]

DEVOTEES: Yes.

SWAMIJI: That is *kampamāpnuyāt*. So this is which state?

JAGDISH: The third state, *kampa*.

SWAMIJI: Third state.

LJA TA05H (10:45)

गलिते देहतादात्म्यनिश्चयेऽन्तर्मुखत्वतः ॥ १०३ ॥
निद्रायते पुरा यावन्न रूढः संविदात्मनि ।

galite dehatādātmyaniścaye'ntarmukhatvataḥ //103//
nidrāyate purā yāvanna rūḍhaḥ saṁvidātmani /

Galite deha tādātmya, when this body consciousness is altogether finished, *galite deha tādātmya niścaye*, *deha tādātmya niścaye galite sati*, *antar mukhatvataḥ*, when he goes introverted, introverted, introverted by-and-by, *antarmukhatvataḥ nidrāyate purā yāvat na rūḍhaḥ saṁvidātmani*, unless, until he is sentenced and dissolved in God consciousness…

DENISE: He'll fall asleep?

SWAMIJI:…he falls asleep, he falls asleep. He cannot stand, he cannot stand in this physical world.

JOHN: You mean afterwards, when he comes out?

SWAMIJI: No, [not] when he comes out. When he is in the process of going in, entering in God consciousness. God consciousness he has not entered, he is going to enter God consciousness. Because *galite*

78. Swamiji is referring to when his brother, Bhagavan Das, collapsed and almost died.

deha tādātmya niścaye, deha tādātmya niścaye is vanished, it is over.

JOHN: Body consciousness.

SWAMIJI: Body consciousness he has shattered. *Antarmukhatvataḥ*, so he is introverted, his consciousness is introverted towards God consciousness. *Nidrāyate purā yāvat na rūḍhaḥ, yāvat na saṁvidātmani rūḍhaḥ*, until he is established in the God consciousness, till then he falls asleep and sleep, sleep and sleep.

JOHN: Every time.

SWAMIJI: Every time, every time, every time. He cannot control. This is the fourth sign of that pathway.

JOHN: What is that called, that falling to sleep?

SWAMIJI: *Nidrā, nidrā. Nidrayāte purā*, it is not actual *nidrā* (sleep), so he has put *āya-pratyaya* in it.

JAGDISH: *Nidrā vat ācarati...*

SWAMIJI: *Nidrā vat ācarati*, it is *drāyate*, it is not actual sleep, [it is] just like actual sleep. That is *nidrāyate. Āya-pratyaya*, according to grammarian rules is *āya-pratyaya* there: it is just like that, it is not that. It is not actual sleep, it is just like that.

DENISE: It's because he doesn't have body consciousness and also he can't enter God consciousness yet.

SWAMIJI: Yes, he wants to enter.

DENISE: But he can't.

SWAMIJI: He is towards that process.

JOHN: Is it the *pralayākala* state?

SWAMIJI: No, it is not the *pralayākala* state. It is just, no, it is just nearing the state of God consciousness, *turya*.

GEORGE: Do they sometimes call that *tandrā*?

SWAMIJI: No, not *tandrā*. *Tandrā* is sleep. Now next:

LJA TA05H (13:45)

ततः सत्यपदे रूढो विश्वात्मत्वेन संविदम्॥ १०४॥
संविदन् घूर्णते घूर्णिर्महाव्याप्तिर्यतः स्मृता।

tataḥ satyapade rūḍho viśvātmatvena saṁvidam //104//
saṁvidan ghūrṇate ghūrṇirmahāvyāptiryataḥ smṛtā /

It is after *nidrā*, after *nidrā* he describes this fifth state. *Tataḥ satya-pade rūḍha*, after that, when he is established on the real pathway, the real state of God consciousness, then *saṁvidam viśvātmatvena saṁvidan*...this is another.

JAGDISH: Yes, next.

SWAMIJI: *Saṁvidam viśvātmamatvena saṁvidan*, that *sādhaka*, *saṁvidan*, he knows that his *saṁvidam*, his consciousness, is *viśvātmat-vena*, his individual consciousness has become universal consciousness. *Viśvātmatvena saṁvidam*; *saṁvidam* means body consciousness, *viśvātmatvena*, just like universal consciousness he realizes (*saṁvidan*). After realizing it, then he *ghūrṇate*, he *ghūrṇate*, he gets–you cannot record it–*ghūrṇate*: (Swamiji demonstrates) *ahaaaa*, *ahaaa*, like this.

DENISE: What is that?

SWAMIJI: This is *ghūrṇate*.

JOHN: Just like a drunk person.

SWAMIJI: When you drink at least fifty thousand bottles of [liquor].

DENISE: And you are stumbling.

SWAMIJI: Yes, that is *ghūrṇate*. In the same way, that *ghūrṇate*, that [drunkenness] is unreal, that is an imitation of *ghūrṇi*, [whereas this] is real *ghūrṇi*.

JOHN: So this is the intoxication of God consciousness, then.

SWAMIJI: Yes, that is the fifth state, when you enter in the fifth state.

JOHN: So you actually are just like you are drunk. If somebody was to see you from outside...

SWAMIJI:...outside, he will think that he is drunk. He is absolutely drunk, he is finished!

DENISE: He stays like that for how long?

SWAMIJI: Huh?

DENISE: He stays like that for life?

SWAMIJI: Yes, no, for hours, always.

GEORGE: So these states are for that aspirant who actually rises and still falls. Is that because those *mala*s...? You said it has nothing to do with those *mala*s.

SWAMIJI: No, *mala*s have no approach here.

JOHN: So is this state when he is in that, when he comes to the state of *vyāpinī*, this great pervasion, is he in *jagadānanda* then?

SWAMIJI: Yes, *jagadānanda*, it will be adjusted to *jagadānanda*.

JOHN: So he is permanently established, then.

SWAMIJI: Permanently, yes.

JOHN: So then this state of this intoxication, this drunken [state], he's not always like that.

SWAMIJI: He's always like that, internally he is always, but his body does not move like [a drunkard], but he is drunk, internally he is drunk.

JOHN: So he doesn't really stagger. At first he staggers.

SWAMIJI: [If] you will tell him, "your father is dead," [he'll say], "ohhh, father is dead, ohh, ohh. Oh, Śiva, Śiva, Śiva, Śiva" (laughs). This won't affect his mind because he is in *ghūrṇi* (laughs). "Your son is dead." "Ohhh, my son is dead, ohhhh." He feels just *ānanda* (bliss) there (laughs), like that.

JOHN: So but externally he doesn't act, he doesn't act like a drunkard externally. Or only in the beginning?

SWAMIJI: In the beginning and then he remains there. Because *ghūrṇate*; *ghūrṇate* means…this is *ghūrṇi*, this state of *ghūrṇi* is when the body consciousness is absolutely shattered to pieces. Because *ghūrṇir mahāvyāptir yataḥ smṛtā*, *ghūrṇi* is *mahāvyāpti*, *ghūrṇi* is *mahāvyāpti*, great grand pervasion of universal consciousness.

JOHN: So he sees his God consciousness in everything.

SWAMIJI:

LJA TA05H (18:00)

आत्मन्यनात्माभिमतौ सत्यामेव ह्यनात्मनि ॥ १०५ ॥
आत्माभिमानो देहादौ बन्धो मुक्तिस्तु तल्लयः ।

ātmanyanātmābhimatau satyāmeva hyanātmani //105//
ātmābhimāno dehādau bandho muktistu tallayaḥ /

Ātmani anātmābhimatau. Satyāmeva hi anātmani. Ātmani, in *ātma*, *anātmābhimatau*, when you perceive that, "I am not this, I am not *ātma*, I am the body, I am the fourfold body[79], actually I am not that real

79. This is referring to the four bodies of the individual: 1) *deha*, the body of wakefulness, 2) *puryaṣṭaka*, the body of dreaming, 3) *prāṇa*, the body of deep sleep, and

Self," then *anātmani ātma abhimāno dehādau, anātmani dehādau…*

Anātmani will go with *dehādau. Dehādau* is the adjective of…no, *anātmani* is the adjective of *dehādau.*

…*ātmābhimāna*, when you perceive that you are all these bodies, all these fourfold bodies, *bandha*, that is bondage. *Muktistu tat layaḥ*, actual liberation is *tat layaḥ*, when that bondage, fourfold bondage is finished.

And now he proceeds in the 106th *śloka*:

LJA TA05H (19:27)

आदावनात्मन्यात्मत्वे लीने लब्धे निजात्मनि ॥ १०६ ॥
आत्मन्यनात्मतानाशे महाव्याप्तिः प्रवर्तते ।

ādāvanātmanyātmatve līne labdhe nijātmani //106//
ātmanyanātmatānāśe mahāvyāptiḥ pravartate /

Ādāu anātmani ātmatve līne, first he has to do, first he has to see that *anātmani ātmatve līne*, first he has to see that in the body, in this fourfold body, this I-consciousness is removed from this fourfold body, that "I am not this fourfold body." Then, *nijātmani*, then he will be established in his real nature. After being established in his real nature, *ātmani anātmatānāśe*, then this happens. What?

JAGDISH: In his real Self…

SWAMIJI: In his real Self, *anātmatānāśe*, "I am not this real Self," this does not rise. There is no question of rising this perception.

JAGDISH: That "This is my real Self" or "This is not"?

SWAMIJI: No. *Ātmani anātmatānāśo*, that "This real Self is not me, I am not this real Self," this does not rise at all, this kind of perception. Do you understand what I mean?

DENISE: That would be false, that "I am not the Self"?

SWAMIJI: It is absolutely wrong, wrong perception, untrue perception.

JOHN: So first he says, "He is not his body."

---

4) *śūnya*, the body of the void state.

SWAMIJI: Yes.

JOHN: Then he says he is completely his real Self.

SWAMIJI: Yes. First he has to leave the attachment for all these fourfold bodies. Then *ātmani anātmatānāśe*, then *anātmatānāśa*, that "I am not God consciousness,"...

JOHN: Never comes.

SWAMIJI:...it never comes. There he will find, the yogi will perceive *mahāvyāpti*, great pervasion. Just after great pervasion, *ghūrṇi* will happen, *ghūrṇi*, that real intoxication of God consciousness. Then there [is no] good, bad, wrong, right–nothing. He is always shining in his own way.

JOHN: So this great pervasion means that he automatically, then, his God consciousness is universal in everything. Is that right, Sir?

SWAMIJI: "My mother is dead. Oh, this is the reality of God's grace." "My mother is not dead. This is the reality of God's grace." "I have lost great treasure. This is the reality of God's grace." "I have achieved this treasure. This is the reality of God's grace." The reality of God's grace is everywhere shining for him, so he has nothing to do with this right and wrong and left/right. Left/right is finished.

ādāvanātmanyātmatve līne labdhe nijātmani //106//
ātmanyanātmatānāśe mahāvyāptiḥ pravartate /
(verse repeated)

Then becomes *mahāvyāptiḥ*, supreme pervasion, supreme universal pervasion. *Ādāu*, first [this] happens: *Ātmani ātmatve līne*, when this perception that "I am *ātmani anātmatā*, I am not God, I am not God, I am body," this perception, when this perception ends altogether, *ādāu* (first), *anātmani*, in body consciousness, *ātmatve*, when you are, when you think that "I am body," you are attached to body consciousness, when it is vanished...

JAGDISH: Which state is this?

SWAMIJI: This is the entry of the fifth state. This is the entry of the fifth state on the pathway.

JAGDISH: After *nidrā*?

SWAMIJI: After *nidrā*. *Ādāu* (first), *anātmani* (*anātmani* means *śarīrādau*, in body/in wakefulness, in the dreaming state, in dreamless state, and in *pralayākala*), there, *anātmani ātmatve*, that "I am this, I am this, I am this, and I am this; I am the body in *jāgrat*, I am the body in the dreaming state, I am the body in the dreamless state, I am the body in *śūnya* (or *pralayākala*)," this vanishes first, this is removed first, automatically. This is the course happening automatically inside without your effort.

JOHN: This is the vanishing of *āṇavamala*? This "I am the body," I mean, the feeling that…this is *āṇavamala* or is this something else?

SWAMIJI: No, this is the course…no, we have nothing to do with *kārmamala*, *āṇavamala* and *māyīyamala* here. It is something else, sir. It is just trance, it is just trance, because these are the symptoms on the pathway of God consciousness, that they appear. First you have to get rid of body consciousness.

JAGDISH: Body consciousness.

SWAMIJI: Body consciousness. *Anātmani* means body, *anātmani*, these fourfold bodies. Which are the fourfold bodies?

JEREMY: Gross, breath, *puryaṣṭaka*, void.

SWAMIJI: Yes, good. *Līne*, *labdhe nijātmani*; *nijātmani labdhesati*, then afterwards, *nijātmani*, your God consciousness is under your control, it comes under your control, your God consciousness that, "I am God, I am not the body, I am not this body, I am not this body, I am not this body, I am God myself." That is *labdhe nijātmani*. *Ātmanyanātmatānāśe*; *ātmani anātmatānāśe*, when absolutely vanished is…

JAGDISH: Body consciousness?

SWAMIJI:…body consciousness, fourfold body consciousness, *mahāvyāpti pravartate*, he gets universal pervasion, universal pervasion, *mahāvyāpti*, that is *mahāvyāpti*. That will go to the fifth state of…

JAGDISH: After *nidrā*.

SWAMIJI: After *nidrā*. That is what he says. He refers the *śloka* of the *Mālinīvijaya Tantra*:

LJA TA05H (26:37)

आनन्द उद्भवः कम्पो निद्रा घूर्णिश्च पञ्चकम् ॥ १०७ ॥
इत्युक्तमत एव श्रीमालिनीविजयोत्तरे ।

ānanda udbhavaḥ kampo nidrā ghūrṇiśca pañcakam //107//
ityuktamata eva śrīmālinīvijayottare /

Ata eva, this is why *śrīmālinīvijayottare*, in the *Śrī Mālinīvijaya Tantra*, these five states are prescribed by Lord Śiva. *Ānanda*, first is the state of *ānanda*. *Udbhava*, then *udbhava*, rising.

DENISE: Something is growing.

SWAMIJI: I will give you the example of rising, what kind of rise it is: It is when you go in a [rocket] and you will fly, you will fly high, high, high, high and you will cross the sphere of the moon also, then you have no fear, you don't experience fear of falling down. You rise, you rise there with your own way. You cannot fall! You become so light that you rise, you rise, you are just growing upstairs. This is *udbhava*, this is the second state, like that. *Ānanda* is the first state, *udbhava* is that…

JEREMY: Rising.

SWAMIJI:…the perception of rising. There is no fear of falling down. The fear of falling down is only up to some portion of this cosmical ether. Afterwards you won't fall down, you will rise, you will go. I have heard, I have seen in those newspapers when they were going on the moon. They had to strive to go down, they couldn't put their feet on the ground.

DENISE: There was no gravity.

SWAMIJI: There was no gravity. So they were just…

DENISE: Rising.

SWAMIJI:…rising. That is, in the same way it is rise (*udbhava*). *Ānanda*, *udbhava*, *kampa*, *nidrā* is the fourth state, and *ghūrṇi* is the fifth state.

JOHN: *Ghūrṇi* is *vyāpinī*? Same?

JAGDISH: This is *mahāvyāpti*.

SWAMIJI: *Ghūrṇi* is *mahāvyāpti* (great pervasion).

JOHN: *Ghūrṇi* means literally?

SWAMIJI: Intoxicated, you are nowhere, *bas* (laughs). Just [like] when you take *vīrapāṇ* (liquor), utmost quantity, at least twelve dozens bottles, then you will find.

JOHN: With awareness, though.

SWAMIJI: With awareness. There won't be awareness [with liquor], but [this is] with awareness.

JOHN: But for this person there's awareness.

SWAMIJI: With awareness, yes. In this way, it is said in the *Śrī Mālinīvijayottare*, these five symptoms on the pathway of God consciousness. *Bas*?

JOHN: So this fifth one, this fifth symptom, this *ghūrṇi*, which is this *mahāvyāpti*, then he sees his God consciousness in everything? Everything becomes…?

SWAMIJI: (laughs) Everything becomes…

JOHN: So even his fourfold body becomes filled with God consciousness.

SWAMIJI: Absolutely.

JEREMY: He is God consciousness.

SWAMIJI: Yes, he is God consciousness. Because body is not separate from that, not *jāgrat* (wakefulness), not *svapna* (dreaming), not *suṣupti* (deep sleep), nor *turya*.

JEREMY: Once you've risen.

SWAMIJI: Yes.

GEORGE: Is there any relationship between this and the seven states of *ānanda*, those seven: *nijānanda*, *nirānanda*…?

SWAMIJI: No, no, no, this is just entry to *jagadānanda*. It is just preparation to enter in the state of *jagadānanda*, *bas*.

GEORGE: And this is the highest yogi who is experiencing this.

SWAMIJI: Yes.

GEORGE: Even the highest yogi still shakes.

SWAMIJI: Yes.

JAGDISH: Is there still liberation and bondage in this state, Sir?

SWAMIJI: Liberation?

JAGDISH: Because he talks about *bandha* and *mukti*.

SWAMIJI: Yes.

GEORGE: Yes, bondage to the body.

SWAMIJI: *Bandha* is body consciousness, *mukti* is when you come out from body consciousness. *Mukti* is *tat layaḥ*.[80]

JAGDISH: So he is completely free after this stage.

SWAMIJI: Yes. Absolutely. Stay in *ghūrṇi*.

LJA TA05H (30:58)

---

80. Absorption (*layaḥ*) in God consciousness (*tat*).

You are after joy, after gaining joy again and again. So, the first sign is *ānanda. Udbhava* is the second sign–rise. After joy takes place that rise. He thinks that he is above humanity. Then, when he is above humanity and there is no way to step in [God consciousness] because of his impurity, so he gets shivering, he shivers, that is *kampa*, this is the third sign. Then after that *kampa*, as long as he does not get entry in that *mahāvyāpti*, supreme pervasion of God consciousness (*ghurṇi*), he gets drowsiness. And *ghūrṇi*, afterwards he gets *ghūrṇi*, true intoxication, the true state of intoxication. *Ityuktam ata eva śrīmālinīvijayottare*, this is why it is said, it is explained fully in the *Mālinīvijaya Tantra*, these five states.

Now these five states take place simultaneously: first *ānanda*, then *udbhava*, then *kampa*, then *nidrā*, then *ghūrṇi* in a flash, for that yogi who is fully advanced, really advanced. For an advanced yogi, these five signs take place in a flash, simultaneously.

ERNIE: He shivers, gets drowsy, all this at once.

SWAMIJI: Yes.

ERNIE: He is a mess (laughs).

SWAMIJI: Yes.

JOHN: But this happens every time when that yogi goes into *samādhi*, or it comes quickly, more quickly, more quickly?

SWAMIJI: Not every time. As long as supreme pervasion does not take place, it is not firm. When supreme pervasion is firm, it gets established, then he rises straight from *ānanda* to supreme pervasion without *kampa*, without drowsiness, without anything, because there is a way, there is an avenue, avenue is open, open entry. As long as in the state of when you are beginning in this practice, the avenue is not open, it is…

DEVOTEE: Shrunk.

SWAMIJI:…it is shrunk.

LJA TA05H (33:36)

प्रदर्शितेऽस्मिन्नानन्दप्रभृतौ पञ्चके यदा ॥ १०८ ॥
योगी विशेत्तदा तत्तच्चक्रेशत्वं हठाद्व्रजेत् ।

pradarśite'sminnānandaprabhṛtau pañcake yadā //108//
yogī viśettadā tattaccakreśatvaṁ haṭhādvrajet /

In these already explained fivefold states, when a yogi enters one-by-one, a *manda* yogi, a yogi who is not advanced, he enters in the first state first and he gets the sovereignty on that state. He gets entry in the next state and gets sovereignty on that state, but remains a slave for the other states. He is a slave for the other states, he cannot rule those states, he cannot govern those states. He governs only that state in which he enters with God consciousness. So if he has got entry in *ānanda*, the first state, he becomes the ruler of *ānanda* and a slave of *udbhava*, *kampa*, *nidrā* and *ghūrṇi*. When he enters in *udbhava*, he becomes the ruler of *udbhava* and *ānanda*, two states, and a slave of the other three states, and so on. And when he enters in *kampa*, he governs all these three states, the first three states, and becomes a slave of *nidrā* and *ghūrṇi*. He can't avoid this. And he enters in *nidrā* and then *ghūrṇi* in the end. When he enters in *ghūrṇi*, the state of *ghūrṇi*, then he is an all-powerful king. The whole kingdom is under his control, the whole kingdom of God consciousness. He becomes *cakreśvara* (the lord of the *cakra*s); *cakra*s, these five *cakra*s: *ānanda cakra*, *udbhava cakra*, *kampa cakra*, *nidrā cakra* and *ghūrṇi cakra*.

JOHN: Why do they call, in Shaivism, everything *cakra*s (wheels) in the field of *śakti*?

SWAMIJI: Because those internal states which are felt in *samādhi*, they are in movement, they are not in a standstill form.

ERNIE: Stationary.

SWAMIJI: They are not stationary as Vedāntists find. They perceive that it is stationary,...

JOHN: *Śānta*.

SWAMIJI:...it is *śānta* (appeased). [But] it is always *udita* (rising), it is always in movement.

JOHN: So is this *cakra* the same as this *spanda*, this...?

SWAMIJI: *Spanda*, this is real *spanda*, yes, because this whole universe is established in *spanda*.

LJA TA05H (36:22)

यथा सर्वेशिना बोधेनाक्रान्तापि तनुः क्वचित्॥ १०९॥
किञ्चित्कर्तुं प्रभवति चक्षुषा रूपसंविदम्।
तथैव चक्रे कुत्रापि प्रवेशात्कोऽपि सम्भवेत्॥ ११०॥

yathā sarveśinā bodhenākrāntāpi tanuḥ kvacit //109//
kiñcitkartuṁ prabhavati cakṣuṣā rūpasaṁvidam /
tathaiva cakre kutrāpi praveśātko'pi sambhavet //110//

Yathā sarveśinā bodhena, when [he] who is *bodha*, always filled with God consciousness (that is, Lord Śiva), he has *ākrāntāpi tanuḥ*, when he has entered in a body,...*

For instance, in Denise he has entered in body, in John he has entered in body. Who has entered in body?

DENISE: Lord Śiva.

SWAMIJI: Lord Śiva has entered in body and he has become limited, he has taken the formation of limitation.

*...when he has taken the formation of limitation, *kiñcit kartuṁ prabhavati*, he does only a limited thing. He cannot act unlimitedly as he was doing before in his previous state of Śiva. *Cakṣuṣā rūpa saṁvidam*, it is just like that when by eyes you can see only form, you cannot taste, you cannot feel the sensation of taste, you cannot feel the sensation of hearing though eyes. Through eyes you can feel only form. If you put cheese there, you can't taste it. If you put sound there, you can't hear it. If you put touch, some beautiful figure there, you can't feel that. You can feel only form, only in limitedness. In the same way, in these *cakra*s also, in these five *cakra*s (in *ānanda cakra*, *udbhava cakra*, *kampa cakra*, *nidrā cakra* and *ghūrṇi cakra*), when you get entry in one *cakra*, you govern only one *cakra*, you are absolutely powerless before those other four *cakra*s. But for those yogis who are advanced yogis, they get entry in all these five *cakra*s simultaneously.

DEVOTEE: (Kashmiri)

SWAMIJI: (Kashmiri): Those who do not possess all the five *cakra*s, they remain incomplete.

DEVOTEE: (Kashmiri) *Rojan* means?

SWAMIJI: You have to experience it simultaneously in a flash–(Kashmiri).

DEVOTEE: *Ānanda*, *udbhava* and *kampa…*

SWAMIJI:…*nidrā* and *ghūrṇi*, both. And now he places, explains where *ānanda* is felt, where *udbhava* is felt, where *kampa* is felt, where *nidrā* is felt, where *ghūrṇi* is felt.

LJA TA05H (39:25)

आनन्दचक्रं वह्न्यश्रि कन्द उद्भव उच्यते।
कम्पो हृत्तालु निद्रा च घूर्णिः स्यादूर्ध्वकुण्डली॥ १११ ॥

ānandacakraṁ vahnyaśri kanda udbhava ucyate /
kampo hṛttālu nidrā ca ghūrṇiḥ syādūrdhvakuṇḍalī //111//

Ānanda cakra is felt at the place of the generative organ.

JOHN: *Sparśa dhāma*?

SWAMIJI: It won't be called *sparśa dhāma*. It is the generative organ, at the place of the generative…*Sparśa dhāma* can be here also, you can feel *sparśa* (touch). *Sparśa dhāma* is exactly in consciousness.

JOHN: But joy is *sparśa dhāma*. This is *mūlādhāra*, then. Is it *mūlādhāra*?

SWAMIJI: It is not *mūlādhāra*. It is *vahnyaśri*, *trikoṇa*, it is *trikoṇa*. *Trikoṇa* is the generative organ. You know the generative organ?

ERNIE: (laughs)

SWAMIJI: You already know (laughs). Everybody knows that. *Ānanda cakraṁ vahnyaśri*, at the place of the generative organ, that *ānanda* is felt by a yogi–this first state. That rises from there. *Kanda udbhava ucyate*, when he feels the sensation of rise, rising, and that sensation of rising takes place near the rectum (that is *kanda*[81], *kande udbhava ucyate*, *kanda udbhava ucyate*). And the third sign, he gets shivering (*kampa*). That shivering, the sensation of shivering he feels from the heart, at the place of the heart. And the sensation of *nidrā*

81. Lit., a bulb.

(drowsiness) he feels from the palate, just like (Swamiji demonstrates). On *tālu*, on *tālu* he feels the sensation, so he is drowsy afterwards. And *ghūrṇi syāt ūrdhva kuṇḍalī*, the sensation of intoxication, complete intoxication is felt at the state of *ūrdhva kuṇḍalinī*, the rise of *ūrdhva kuṇḍalinī* inside.

DEVOTEE: *Brahmārandra*?

SWAMIJI: Not *brahmārandara*. *Ūrdhva kuṇḍalinī*. *Ūrdhva kuṇḍalinī*, the rise of *cit kuṇḍalinī* right from the rectum to *brahmārandhara*, skull.

JOHN: The whole, the whole section.

SWAMIJI: The whole section, that is *ūrdhva kuṇḍalinī*.

BRUCE P: It's automatic?

SWAMIJI: It is automatic, everything is automatic! *Ānanda cakra* is automatic, *kanda* is, *udbhava* is automatic, *kampa* is automatic, and *nidrā* is automatic, and *ghūrṇi* is automatic. These take place…

ERNIE: God's grace.

SWAMIJI: Huh?

ERNIE: Through the grace of…

SWAMIJI:…through the grace of the master, yes.

ERNIE: I mean, there is nothing you do.

SWAMIJI: No, you have to do nothing, you have to just witness what is going on.

JOHN: Maintain this Bhairavī *mudrā*.

SWAMIJI: You have to maintain Bhairavī *mudrā* only. *Ānandacakraṁ vahnyaśri*, *ānanda cakra* is called triangle, the organ of triangle. The organ of triangle is the generative organ. *Kanda udbhava ucyate*, *udbhava* is felt [at] *kanda* (*kanda*, the rectum). *Kampo hṛta*, the shivering takes place in the heart. *Tālu nidrā ca*, this drowsiness takes place in the palate. And *ghūrṇi syāt ūrdhva kuṇḍalī*, the *ūrdhva kuṇḍalinī* state is *ghūrṇi*, that is the real state.

LJA TA05H (43:34)

एतच्च स्फुटमेवोक्तं श्रीमत्त्रैशिरसे मते।

etacca sphuṭamevoktaṁ śrīmattraiśirase mate /112a

This is clearly and vividly, exhaustively explained in the *Triśirobhairava Tantra*, this subject is touched in the *Triśirobhairava Tantra*.

The Threefold Liṅgas

एवं प्रदर्शितोच्चारविश्रान्तिहृदयं परम्॥ ११२॥
यत्तदव्यक्तलिङ्गं नृशिवशक्त्यविभागवत्।

evaṁ pradarśitoccāraviśrāntihṛdayaṁ param //112//
yattadavyaktaliṅgaṁ nṛśivaśaktyavibhāgavat /

Evaṁ pradarśita uccāra viśrānti hṛdayaṁ, this is *uccāra*, this is *cidātma uccāra*, this is not *prāṇa uccāra*, this takes place by the *uccāra*, by the throb of consciousness, and the throb of consciousness takes place through Bhairavī *mudrā*; Bhairavī *mudrā* not only in perceiving *rūpa*, form, [but] all the five senses, all the five senses. That is *cidātma uccāra*. *Cidātma uccāra viśrānti hṛdayam*, and when *cidātma uccāra* is resulted, the process of *cidātma uccāra* results–in what?–results in *tat avyakta liṅgaṁ*, it is *avayakta liṅga*. *Avayakta liṅga* is indistinct *liṅga*. There are three *liṅga*s, three *liṅga*s, generative symbols. "Symbols" is correct?

JOHN: Yes.

SWAMIJI: Generative symbols. One generative symbol is the *avyakta* symbol, the next is the *vyaktāvyakta* symbol, and the third is the *vyakta* symbol. The *vyakta* symbol is, truly speaking, the *vyakta* symbol is the Śiva *liṅga* you find in a temple. That is *vyakta liṅga*, that idol of generative symbol, what you adore, what you worship in a temple. That is *vyakta liṅga*. And *vyaktāvyakta liṅga* is the symbol existing in the body, man and woman. That is *vyaktāvyakta liṅga*. And *avyakta liṅga* is the state of the all-pervading state of universal God consciousness. That is *ūrdhva kuṇḍalinī dhāma*. *Ūrdhva kuṇḍalinī*, that is also a *liṅga*, that is the real *liṅga*. And *tat avyakta liṅgam*, that *avyakta liṅga* is an indistinct *liṅga*. One is an indistinct *liṅga*, one is partly indistinct, partly distinct. Is it correct?

JOHN: Yes.

ERNIE: Why? Why is it indistinct? This is the second one.

SWAMIJI: Second one. The second one is partly indistinct, partly distinct. The third one is distinct. The third *liṅga* is distinct. Which third one?

JOHN: This *liṅga* in a temple.

SWAMIJI: *Liṅga* in a temple.

JOHN: Why is this…?

SWAMIJI: Because that distinct *liṅga* is felt by everybody, while [a partly] indistinct [and partly distinct] *liṅga* is felt by only two, two partners, it is not felt by everybody. It is not done, this kind of act is not done on the market, on the roadside.

DEVOTEES: (laughs)

SWAMIJI: (laughs) So it is partly indistinct, partly distinct. And this is known to two partners, and this is known to only one, this *avyakta liṅga*. The rise of *avyakta liṅga* in the state, in the formation of *ūrdhva kuṇḍalinī dhāma*, is known to one person, and that is Lord Śiva. So it is *avyakta liṅga*, it is indistinct, absolutely indistinct *liṅga*. What? The first. The second is partly indistinct and partly [distinct]. I think you have understood now.

JOHN: Yes.

SWAMIJI: And the *liṅga* in a temple is distinct. And this indistinct *liṅga*, which is *avyakta liṅga*, which has taken the formation of the all-pervasive state of *ūrdhva kuṇḍalinī*, is *śiva śakti avibhāgavat*, *nṛ śiva śakti avibhāgavat*, there is individuality (Nara), the union of individuality (Śakti), and universality (Śiva). Individual consciousness unites in the consciousness of energy and universal consciousness. Consciousness of energy and consciousness of individuality and consciousness of Lord Śiva are all the three ways of consciousness. Three states of consciousness melt in one.

JOHN: What is this consciousness of energy?

SWAMIJI: Śakti.

JOHN: Consciousness of Lord Śiva, isn't that the transcendental state–the consciousness of Lord Śiva? And the consciousness of energy is the universal state?

SWAMIJI: Consciousness of energy is not the universal state, consciousness of energy is partly universal, partly individual. This is the universal state, that distinct *liṅga*, this is the universal state that you find in a temple. But this state of *avyakta liṅga* is the union of three. In *avyakta liṅga* you will find not only *avyakta liṅga*, you will find *vyaktāvyakta liṅga* also and *vyakta liṅga* also. So, the powers that you achieve from *vyakta liṅga* and the powers that you achieve from *vyaktāvyakta liṅga* and the powers that you achieve from *avyakta liṅga* are achieved by this *liṅga* only. Which *liṅga*?

DEVOTEE: *Avyakta liṅga.*

SWAMIJI: *Avyakta liṅga*. Because Śiva, Śakti and Nara is *avibhāgavat*, it is one there, it is not distinct. *Nanu evaṁ vyapadeśasya kiṁ nimittam* (comm.)? Why is it so? For that he says why is this united there, why all *liṅga*s are united in that one *avyakta liṅga*:

LJA TA05H (50:49)

अत्र विश्वमिदं लीनमत्रान्तःस्थं च गम्यते ॥ ११३ ॥
इदं तल्लक्षणं पूर्णशक्तिभैरवसंविदः ।

atra viśvamidaṁ līnamatrāntaḥsthaṁ ca gamyate //113//
idaṁ tallakṣaṇaṁ pūrṇaśaktibhairavasaṁvidaḥ /

In this *avyakta liṅga*, *viśvamidaṁ līnaṁ*, in this *avyakta liṅga*, this whole universe is melted, is digested. *Atra antaḥsthaṁ ca gamyate*– this transcendental state of God consciousness is called *liṅga*, *avyakta liṅga*–the whole universe merges in that and the whole universe comes out from this. And the whole universe gets rise from this *avyakta liṅga* and the whole universe rests in this *avyakta liṅga*, and the whole universe gets exit from this *avyakta liṅga*, outside. *Idaṁ tat lakṣaṇam*, this kind of qualification is found only in that Bhairava who is *śakti*-Bhairava, who is one with *śakti*, who is one with universal energy, *svātantrya*.

JOHN: This yogi.

SWAMIJI: Yes.

LJA TA05H (52:05)

देहगाध्वसमुन्मेषे समावेशस्तु यः स्फुटः ॥ ११४ ॥
अहन्ताच्छादितोन्मेषिभावेदम्भावयुक् स च ।
व्यक्ताव्यक्तमिदं लिङ्गं मन्त्रवीर्यं परापरम् ॥ ११५ ॥
नरशक्तिसमुन्मेषि शिवरूपाद्विभेदितम् ।

dehagādhvasamunmeṣe samāveśastu yaḥ sphuṭaḥ //114//
ahantācchāditonmeṣibhāvedambhāvayuk sa ca /
vyaktāvyaktamidaṁ liṅgaṁ mantravīryaṁ parāparam //115//
naraśaktisamunmeṣi śivarūpādvibheditam /

Dehagādhvasamunmeṣe samāveśastu yaḥ sphuṭaḥ.

Here, the second *vyaktāvyakta liṅga* is explained now. *Avyakta liṅga* is already explained. *Avyakta liṅga* means Śiva *liṅga*, *vyaktāvyakta liṅga* is Śakti *liṅga*, and *vyakta liṅga* is Nara *liṅga*. *Avyakta liṅga* is called universal, *vyaktāvyakta liṅga* is called partly universal, partly individual, and *vyakta liṅga* is called individual *liṅga*.

Dehagādhvasamunmeṣe samāveśastu yaḥ sphuṭaḥ, when, in this body, you get entry in this *liṅga*, that is the individuality in that, that is the part of individuality, the state of being an individual, *ahantācchāditaḥ unmeṣa bhāva*, but there is I-ness, I-ness of God consciousness is also pervading there in *vyaktāvyakta liṅga*. I-ness of God consciousness is pervading there and this-ness of individuality is also there. When this-ness of individuality is also there…

Why this-ness of individuality is there in *vyaktāvyakta liṅga*? Have you marked it?

…this-ness of individuality [is there] because there are two partners there. They perceive each other. When there is perceiving, that is this-ness. When they perceive each other, it is this-ness. So this is *vyaktāvyakta liṅga*, this is not *avyakta liṅga*. When there is *avyakta liṅga*, there is no perceiving anything. So *vyaktāvyaktam idaṁ liṅgam*, this is *vyaktāvyakta liṅgam*, this is partly indistinct, partly distinct. And this is *mantra vīrya*, this is the reality of *mantra vīrya*, this is the source of *mantra vīrya.*[82] *Mantra vīrya* flows out from that state. *Mantra vīrya* does not take place from *avyakta liṅga. Avyakta liṅga* is the result of *mantra vīrya*. In the state of *avyakta liṅga*, you have to do nothing. *Mantra vīrya* rises from *vyaktāvyakta liṅga*, *mantra vīrya* does not rise from *avyakta liṅga*, and *mantra vīrya* does not rise from *vyakta liṅga.* It rises from the central *liṅga*.

JOHN: Union.

SWAMIJI: Yes.

JOHN: So then this is practice of union of two…

SWAMIJI: Union of two is practice, yes.

JOHN: *Yoginī* and this…

SWAMIJI: *Siddha* and *yoginī*, *siddha* and *yoginī. Vyaktāvyaktam idaṁ liṅgaṁ mantra vīryaṁ*, and this is the state of *parāpara*, this is supreme and not supreme; supreme because God consciousness is there, not supreme because individuality is there. *Naraśaktisamunmeṣi śivarūpāt vibheditam*, there are only Nara and Śakti functioning. The functioning of two states takes place there: Nara (individual) and Śakti (energy). The individual and energy is working there, whereas in *avyakta liṅga* all the three are functioning.

JOHN: Where is Śakti in this? Śakti is the…

SWAMIJI: Huh?

JOHN: In this *liṅga*, *vyaktāvyakta liṅga...*

SWAMIJI: *Vyaktāvyakta*, there is only Śakti in predominance,

---

82. Lit., the power (*vīrya*) of all mantras. "The state of *mantra vīrya* is the power of all the letters of the Sanskrit alphabet beginning from the letter *a* and ending with the letter *kṣa*. Why? Because all sounds rise from those letters. That sound is called *śabdarāśi*, the collective appearance of all letters. And the power and the essence of all those sounds is one sound, the soundless-sound, the sound of I-being, *ahaṁ*, the supreme I, and that is *mantra vīrya...*The yogic powers which are attained at the perfection of initiation of a great master, when a great master initiates you and you attain those yogic powers, all those yogic powers when compared with this supreme Universal consciousness are not equal to its sixteenth part. So they are nothing! They are to be thrown away, all those yogic powers. Only you have to own and maintain this universal-I mantra, *mantra vīrya*." Swami Lakshmanjoo, *Śiva Sūtras–The Supreme Awakening*, ed. John Hughes (Universal Shaiva Fellowship, Los Angeles, 2002). See also *Tantrāloka* 4, verses 180-193.

because without Śakti you can't, you can't…this won't function.

JOHN: This generative function won't function.

SWAMIJI: Yes. So, *nara śakti samunmeṣi*, this is the fountain of Nara and Śakti only there. *Śiva rūpāt vibheditam*, it is separated from Śiva, it is away from Śiva. It will reach Śiva, it will reach the state of Śiva, but it is away from Śiva. But Śiva is present in that *avyakta liṅga*, *avyakta liṅga* where there is the state of *ūrdhva kuṇḍalinī dhāma*.

JOHN: This is why in Shaivism they say that you always enter Lord Śiva through Śakti.

SWAMIJI: Through Śakti, yes, yes, yes, correct, quite correct, cent-per-cent correct.

DEVOTEES: (laughter)

SWAMIJI: *Yat nyakkṛta-*…yes, he is well-informed now.

LJA TA05H (57:09)

यन्न्यक्कृतशिवाहन्तासमावेशं विभेदवत्॥ ११६ ॥
विशेषस्पन्दरूपं तद् व्यक्तं लिङ्गं चिदात्मकम्।

yannyakkṛtaśivāhantāsamāveśaṁ vibhedavat //116//
viśeṣaspandarūpaṁ tadvyaktaṁ liṅgaṁ cidātmakam /

Where *nyakkṛta śivāhantā*, the I-ness on Śiva is absent (*yat nyakkṛta śivāhantā*), and that trance is *vibhedavat*, absolutely away from Śiva *bhāva*, the state of Śiva, *viśeṣa spanda rūpaṁ*, and it is *viśeṣa spanda rūpa*,[83] when you adore as I will adore after Śiva Rātri and the *jag* (fire ceremony), "*svāhā, svāhā, svāhā, svāhā.*" This is *vyakta liṅga*, this is the state of *vyakta liṅga*.

JOHN: That is individuality only. There is no Śakti in that also.

SWAMIJI: There is no Śakti, there is only individuality. And *cidātmakam*, but it will drive you to *cid bhāva*, it will drive you to God consciousness, this also, if it is done properly with awareness.

DEVOTEE: *Viśeṣa spandarūpaṁ*…?

---

83. Particular (*viśeṣa*) formation (*rūpa*) of the vibration of consciousness (*spanda*).

SWAMIJI: *Viśeṣa*, it is not *sāmānya spanda*, it is *viśeṣa spanda–viśeṣa spanda*, particular *spanda*, *vyakta liṅga*.
JOHN: So this *avyaktam* is *sāmānya spanda*.
SWAMIJI: *Sāmānya sp-*...huh?
JOHN: *Avyaktam*.
SWAMIJI: *Avyaktam* is...no, *vyaktāvyakta* is *sāmānya spanda*.
JOHN: *Vyaktāvyakta*.
SWAMIJI: *Vyaktāvyakta* is *sāmānya spanda*.
JOHN: And this *avyakta* is no *spanda* at all.
SWAMIJI: Above that, above that. This is the energy of *spanda*.

yannyakkṛtaśivāhantāsamāveśaṁ vibhedavat //116//
viśeṣaspandarūpaṁ tadvyaktaṁ liṅgaṁ cidātmakam /
(verse repeated)

JOHN: *Cidātmakam* means?
SWAMIJI: It will drive you to *cid bhāva*, yes.

LJA TA05H (59:02)

व्यक्तात्सिद्धिप्रसवो व्यक्ताव्यक्ताद्द्वयं विमोक्षश्च।
अव्यक्ताद्बलमाद्यं परस्य नानुत्तरे त्वियं चर्चा॥ ११७॥

vyaktātsiddhiprasavo vyaktāvyaktāddvayaṁ vimokṣaśca /
avyaktādbalamādyaṁ parasya nānuttare tviyaṁ carcā //117//

Now he says what kind of powers you get from these *liṅga*s, the threefold *liṅga*s.

Vyaktāt siddhi prasavaḥ, all powers you derive from *vyakta liṅga*. *Vyakta liṅga* is that *liṅga* which is found in a temple. *Vyaktāvyaktāt dvayaṁ vimokṣaśca*, by concentrating and meditating upon *vyaktāvyakta liṅga–vyaktāvyakta liṅga* you know? The central [*liṅga*]–*dvayaṁ vimokṣaśca*, you get all powers, worldly powers, and liberation also.
JOHN: You say *vyaktāvyakta liṅga* is the center.
SWAMIJI: Center, yes.
JOHN: Between those, in that act. In other words, awareness in that act.

SWAMIJI: Yes. *Avyaktāt balaṁ ādyaṁ*, and by the adoption of *avyakta liṅga*, you are sentenced to that power of *bala*, the power of that power, the power of that power.

JOHN: The source of all power.

SWAMIJI: The source of all power.

JOHN: So what powers come in this *vyakta liṅga*? Or just all these worldly *siddhi*s (powers)?

SWAMIJI: Worldly *siddhis*, worldly enjoyments.

DEVOTEE: *Dvayam* means?

SWAMIJI: *Dvayam*, both *siddhi* (power) and *mokṣa* (liberation)– *vyaktāvyaktāt dvayaṁ. Vimokṣaśca avyaktāt balaṁ ādyaṁ*, by the adoption of *avyakta liṅga*, you get liberation and you hold that source of all power.

DEVOTEE: *Vyakta liṅga.*

SWAMIJI: No, *avyakta. Avyaktādbalaṁ ādyam vimokṣaśca.*

DEVOTEE: *Vimokṣaśca…*?

SWAMIJI: (Kashmiri)

DEVOTEE: *Vyaktāvyaktāt dvayaṁ.*

SWAMIJI: *Vyaktāt siddhi prasavaḥ. Vyaktāvyaktāt dvayam, siddhi* and *mokṣa* both by *vyaktāvyakta liṅga*. And *vimokṣaḥ* (liberation) and *ādya bala* (source of power) is derived from *avyakta liṅga. Parasya nānuttare tviyaṁ carcā*, but that supreme God consciousness, where there is the question of supreme God consciousness, these things do not happen at all, that is above that.

JOHN: That's *anupāya*?

SWAMIJI: That is *anupāya*, yes.

DEVOTEE: *Na anuttare tviyaṁ carcā…*

SWAMIJI: *Na anuttare tviyaṁ carcā*, this story is not applied to that supreme state of God consciousness.

JOHN: These stages, successions, *krama*s.

SWAMIJI: These three successions. But we will do only this much. And the day after tomorrow we will do in the morning. Tomorrow there is no hope.

ERNIE: (laughs)

SWAMIJI: I may have to go to Srinagar and they will prepare meals so they would miss this lecture tomorrow if I do. Now, the day after tomorrow this subject will be finished. Then there is *karaṇa, karaṇa upāsana. Karaṇa upāsana*, it will take only one day.

LJA TA05H (1:02:44) end
LJA TA05I (00:00) start

[He says] here, that in the real sense, this whole universe is the kingdom of *avyakta liṅga*, not *vyaktāvyakta* or *vyakta liṅga*. Everywhere you will find the kingdom of *avyakta liṅga*, indistinct *liṅga*, not partly distinct and partly indistinct, and not distinct *liṅga*. It is the kingdom of that *liṅga* which is always indistinct, *avyakta*. So you should find out the glory of the indistinct *liṅga* in the field of *vyaktāvyakta liṅga* and in the field of *vyakta liṅga* also. You must find out that state in the other two states. So:

आत्माख्यं यद्व्यक्तं नरलिङ्गं तत्र विश्वमर्पयतः ।
व्यक्ताव्यक्तं तस्माद्गलिते तस्मिंस्तदव्यक्तम् ॥ ११८ ॥

ātmākhyaṁ yadvyaktaṁ naraliṅgaṁ tatra viśvamarpayataḥ /
vyaktāvyaktaṁ tasmādgalite tasmiṁstadavyaktam //118//

First take the distinct *liṅga*, that is *ātma*/*nara*/individual. And that *liṅga* is the outward *liṅga* that you worship in a temple. And that is *bheda liṅga*, dualistic *liṅga*. It is not the non-dualistic *liṅga*. It is the dualistic *liṅga*, so it is *vyakta liṅga*. *Tatra viśvaṁ arpayataḥ*, you must worship in such a way, you must worship that *liṅga*, *vyakta liṅga*, distinct *liṅga*, in such a way that this whole universe, as it is in mantras said, it is said already in mantras, "O Lord, when a worshipper sits before that *liṅga* in a temple, O Lord, although you are universal, you are everywhere, let you [insert] your universality in this *liṅga* so that I could worship you wholeheartedly." So, this *liṅga* also is universal in the true sense. So you must carry this individual *liṅga* to universality. *Ātmākhyaṁ yat vyaktaṁ*, that *vyakta liṅga*, *tatra viśvam arpayataḥ*, when you will sentence it and carry it to the universality, to the state of universality, then this *ātma liṅga*, this distinct *liṅga* will become *vyaktāvyakta liṅga*, *śakti liṅga*. *Tasmāt galite*, when this distinction, the state of being distinct and the state of being indistinct will vanish by universal meditation, *tasmin tad avyaktam*, then *avyakta liṅga* becomes, remains there.

JOHN: So this converting this *liṅga*, *vyakta liṅga* to *vyaktāvyakta liṅga*…

SWAMIJI: And then to *avyakta liṅga.*

JOHN:…that's not done just through words.

SWAMIJI: No.

JOHN: That's done through awareness.

SWAMIJI: Yes, through awareness.

LJA TA05I (3:35)

तेनात्मलिङ्गमेतत् परमे शिवशक्त्यणुस्वभावमये।
अव्यक्ते विश्राम्यति नानुत्तरधामगा त्वियं चर्चा॥ ११९॥

tenātmaliṅgametat parame śivaśaktyaṇusvabhāvamaye /
avyakte viśrāmyati nānuttaradhāmagā tviyaṁ carcā //119//
(not recited in full)

So, this *ātma liṅga*, this Nara *liṅga*, this distinct *liṅga*, *bheda liṅga*, individual *liṅga*, when *parame śiva śakti aṇusvabhāva maye*, *avyakte*, *avyakta liṅga* is not [just] Śiva *liṅga*. In true sense, *avyakta liṅga* is Śiva *liṅga*, Śakti *liṅga* and Nara *liṅga* also. You will find the state of Nara there, the state of Śakti there, and the state of Śiva there, whereas in Śakti *liṅga* you will find the state of Śakti and the state of individual and the state of Śiva is absent there, and in Nara *liṅga* you will find only the state of individuality, and the other two *liṅga*s are absent there. So, *avyakta liṅga* is, in fact, Śiva, where Śiva is residing, Śakti is residing, and individual is residing. *Śivaśaktyaṇusvabhāvamaye*, *avyakte viśrāmyati*, so it rests in that *avyakta liṅga* which is one in three, in all the three *liṅga*s. *Nānuttaradhāmagā tviyaṁ carcā*, but this case is not applied to that state which is above these three *liṅga*s–*anupāya*. *Anupāya* is above this.

JOHN: So the person who has converted this *vyakta liṅga* to *avyakta liṅga*, he himself has entered that *avyakta* state.

SWAMIJI: Yes.

LJA TA05I (05:16)

एकस्य स्पन्दनस्यैषा त्रैधं भेदव्यवस्थितिः ।

ekasya spandanasyaiṣā traidhaṁ bhedavyavasthitiḥ /*120a*

This is only one movement of *spanda*, this is only one throb of that universal consciousness that has taken threefold formations of *liṅgas*. This is only one throb that has spread and pervaded in all these threefold *liṅgas*. *Ekasya spandanasya eṣā traidhaṁ*, *traidhaṁ* (threefold) *bheda vyavasthitiḥ* (distinct position), a distinct position has been held by this first and the supreme throb of consciousness.

JOHN: What is threefold here?

SWAMIJI: *Ātma*...Śakti and Nara, Śiva.

अत्र लिङ्गे सदा तिष्ठेत् पूजाविश्रान्तितत्परः ॥ १२० ॥

atra liṅge sadā tiṣṭhet pūjāviśrāntitatparaḥ //*120*//

So, a yogi should be bent upon worshipping this *liṅga*, not *vyaktāvyakta liṅga* or not *vyakta liṅga*. Leave these two *liṅgas* aside and worship this *liṅga* only, *avyakta liṅga* only with great awareness.

DEVOTEE: (Kashmiri) *Atra* means here?

SWAMIJI: In this state of God consciousness.

DEVOTEE: (Kashmiri) Meaning *avyakta*?

SWAMIJI: Yes.

LJA TA05I (06:41)

mṛcchailadhāturatnādi-bhavaṁ liṅgaṁ na pūjayat /
yajedādhyātmikaṁ liṅgaṁ yatra līnaṁ carācaram //
bahirliṅgasya liṅgatvamanenādhiṣṭhitaṁ yataḥ /
(*Mālinīvijaya Tantra* 18.2-3, quoted in the commentary, not recited in full)

You must not worship that *liṅga* which is made of mud (*mṛt*), [or] which is made of stone (*śaila*), or which is made of some jewels (*ratna*) or gold or silver or whatever it is–you must not worship that *liṅga*. *Yajet ādhyātmikaṁ*, you must worship that internal, who is situated in your own heart, that *liṅga*, *yatra līnam carācaram*, where this whole universe is existing. You must worship that *liṅga*, that is *avyakta liṅga*.

JOHN: This came from *Mālinīvijaya*–this?

SWAMIJI: Yes, this is *Mālinīvijaya Tantra*.

LJA TA05I (07:25)

योगिनीहृदयं लिङ्गमिदमानन्दसुन्दरम्।
बीजयोनिसमापत्त्या सूते कामपि संविदम्॥ १२१ ॥

yoginīhṛdayaṁ liṅgamidamānandasundaram /
bījayonisamāpattyā sūte kāmapi saṁvidam //121//

This state of *avyakta liṅga* is, in fact, *yoginī hṛdaya*, it is called *yoginī hṛdaya*, the heart of *yoginīs*. The heart of *yoginīs*…why he has not put the heart of *siddhas*? But it is the *yoginī* that creates excitement in *siddhas*, it is the *yoginī* that conceives. So this supreme place of this *vyaktāvyakta liṅga* is *yoginībhūḥ*, not *siddhabhūh*.[84]

JOHN: *Vyaktāvyakta liṅga*.

SWAMIJI: *Vyaktāvyakta liṅga*. And that *vyaktāvyakta liṅga* is, in fact, *avyakta liṅga* in the end.

JOHN: Is that why you said at one point that it's the *yoginī* that helps the *siddha* rise?

SWAMIJI: Yes. *Yoginī hṛdayaṁ, liṅgam idam ānanda sundaram*, and it is glorified with that greatest and supreme joy of super-spiritual excitement. Because whenever you get joy in the ordinary sexual act, that is ordinary excitement, there is no hope of rising of *kuṇḍalinī* in your body. But when that state comes, that excitement is transformed in that spirituality, the *kuṇḍalinī* also rises at the same moment. *Bīja yoni*

84. The offspring (*bhuḥ*) of a *yoginī* (female yogi), not a *siddha* (male yogi).

samāpattyā, by the union of these two, *siddha* and *yoginī*, *sūte kāmapi saṁvidam*, that supreme God consciousness rises in your own self.

LJA TA05I (09:36)

अत्र प्रयासविरहात्सर्वोऽसौ देवतागणः ।
आनन्दपूर्णे धाम्न्यास्ते नित्योदितचिदात्मकः ॥ १२२ ॥

atra prayāsavirahātsarvo'sau devatāgaṇaḥ /
ānandapūrṇe dhāmnyāste nityoditacidātmakaḥ //122//
(not recited)

Atra prayāsa virahāt–next–*atra prayāsa virahāt*, you have nothing to do there, no effort to be done there (*atra prayāsa virahāt*). *Sarvo'sau devatāgaṇaḥ*, all gods are shining there, they are all gods and deities and great souls and priests and incarnations, Lord Kṛṣṇa, Śiva, Christ, every/all elevated beings are present there (*sarvo'sau devatāgaṇaḥ*), *ānanda pūrṇe dhāmnyāste*, and they are witnessing this act, this spiritual act of *yoginī hṛdaya*.

JOHN: This *vyaktāvyakta liṅga*.

SWAMIJI: *Vyaktāvyakta liṅga. Nityodita cidātmakam*, where the state of God consciousness is in continuity, shining in continuity.

DENISE: (unknown gesture)

SWAMIJI: Why?

DENISE: It's really beautiful.

SWAMIJI:

LJA TA05I (10:36)

अत्र भैरवनाथस्य ससङ्कोचविकासिका ।
भासते दुर्घटा शक्तिरसङ्कोचविकासिनः ॥ १२३ ॥

atra bhairavanāthasya sasaṅkocavikāsikā /
bhāsate durghaṭā śaktirasaṅkocavikāsinaḥ //123//
(not recited)

Atra bhairavanāthasya, it is not only this that only gods and priests and incarnates are shining there, [that] they are present. No! Even Lord Śiva is present there. *Atra bhairavanāthasya*, not only Lord Śiva, *sa saṅkoca vikāsikā bhāsate durghaṭā śakti*, his great energy, *svātantrya śakti*, is also present there, *asaṅkoca vikāsinaḥ*, which is produced from that which is not shrunk or expanded.

DEVOTEE: (Kashmiri) That *saṅkoca vikāsa* is *vyaktāvyakta*?

SWAMIJI: The first movement, the first exit from the state of Lord Śiva of *svātantrya śakti* is the exit from that state which is not shrunk, not expanded. When it exists outside, then it is shrunk and expanded also, it is *saṅkoca vikāsa*, shrunk and expanded, shrunk and expanded.

JOHN: So this will be before that *visarga*.

SWAMIJI: Yes, before *visarga*, yes.

JOHN: Is this that state of *aṁ*?

SWAMIJI: No, it is the state of *aḥ*, *visarga*.

JOHN: Is he celebrating, is he saying that this state here, then, this act, in this spiritualized highest…?

SWAMIJI: Because he has united all these *liṅga*s in one, so *vyaktāvyakta liṅga* is also functioning there, *vyakta liṅga* is also functioning there. *Vyakta liṅga* is functioning there because *vyakta liṅga* is also dissolved in that universality.

ERNIE: He says, though, that you do nothing, right? There's nothing to tr-…there's a part there where you just…

SWAMIJI: There is no effort to be done, no effort to be done.

ERNIE: No effort. So there is no physical [exertion].

SWAMIJI: No, nothing, no, no, no, nothing, nothing, no *abhyāsa* (practice), no *abhyāsa*, only awareness.

JOHN: But it's an act, it's the highest act in this universe.

SWAMIJI: It is the highest act, yes. It is *śāmbhavopāya* although the subject is in *āṇavopāya*.

LJA TA05I (12:55)

एतल्लिङ्गसमापत्तिविसर्गानन्दधारया।
सिक्तं तदेव सद्विश्वं शश्वन्नवनवायते॥ १२४॥

etalliṅgasamāpattivisargānandadhārayā /
siktaṁ tadeva sadviśvaṁ śaśvannavanavāyate //124//

Etat liṅga samāpatti, when this *liṅga* is present–which *liṅga*? This *avyakta liṅga*–and this *avyakta liṅga* is watered, is nectarified,...*

JOHN: Nectarized.

SWAMIJI: Nectarized, nectarized...

DEVOTEES: (laughter)

SWAMIJI: (laughs) I can't, I have to...

ERNIE: There is no such word, he made it up! (laughs)

SWAMIJI: Nectarized? Nectarized is...?

JOHN: No, no, that's a word.

SWAMIJI: Nectarized he says. It is not watered, it is nectarized, put nectar, sprinkle nectar on it, over it.

*...*visarga ānanda dhārayā*, *siktaṁ*, when it is *siktaṁ*, when it is soaked by that nectar, and this whole universe becomes soaked with this nectar, and this universe becomes always new to him.

You see, when I was young, I mean, when I was not young, when I was before [in] my youth, say at the age of my tenth year, I was so joyous in this universe to go here and there in houseboats and in motor cars, in motor launch. I was so excited! In the same way, for me, this whole universe was always new, always fresh, always filled with glory.

DENISE: Child-like innocence, everything.

SWAMIJI: Yes. And now, in this old age, everything seems dark to me (laughs). Yes, in this universe, nothing is so tasty for old people, [but it is] for young people, for those who are children, boys. For Shanna, it is everything, everything is delightful!

DENISE: She is constantly excited.

SWAMIJI: In the same way, for that old yogi also, this whole universe takes the same position, the universe becomes shining for him!

ERNIE: And what is the nectarizing?

SWAMIJI: Nectarizing by that *ānanda*, the bliss of God consciousness.

DEVOTEE: (Kashmiri)

SWAMIJI: (Kashmiri)

JOHN: So everything is covered, I mean, his whole perception is filled with *ānanda*.

SWAMIJI: *Ānanda*, yes, yes, he's all-blissful, yes, always fresh. But why have you…? The question can arise here, why this subject he has touched, this author, in this *āṇavopāya*, the inferior way of understanding, the inferior way of means? This was not the place for this subject here in *āṇavopāya*. For that he replies now in the next *śloka*.

LJA TA05I (16:10)

अनुत्तरेऽभ्युपायोऽत्र ताद्रूप्यादेव वर्णितः।

anuttare'bhyupāyo'tra tadrūpyādeva varṇitaḥ /125a

This *upāya*, this means of supreme God consciousness in the *śāmbhava* state, I have explained here. There is no doubt about it. I have explained *śāmbhavopāya* here because of this–what is this? *Para tattvāntaḥ praveśa* (*para tattvāntaḥ praveśa* is *śāmbhavopāya*)–and I have explained it because *tādrūpyāt eva*, because everything is consumed there. In *śāmbhavopāya*, *śāktopāya* is consumed, *āṇavopāya* is also consumed. So I have explained this *śāmbhavopāya* while explaining this *āṇavopāya*. This is one way, so there is no harm if I explained *śāmbhavopāya* here.

The next example he gives: For instance, there are so many candles, many candles are lighted, lit. Lit or lighted?

DENISE: Lit.

SWAMIJI: Lit. Many candles are lit. If there is also sunshine also, there is no harm. If many candles are lit (that is *āṇavopāya* and *śāktopāya*, they are lit), at the same time there is sunshine also, there is no harm in sunshine also. Sunshine will also spread its lustre and effulgence of its light.

LJA TA05I (17:54)

ज्वलितेष्वपि दीपेषु घर्मांशुः किं न भासते॥ १२५॥

jvaliteṣvapi dīpeṣu gharmaṁśuḥ kiṁ na bhāsate //125//

Is there no way of, no room for *gharmāṁśuḥ*? *Gharmāṁśuḥ* means, the sun. The sun can also shine there. So the sun is also shining in *āṇavopāya* and *śāktopāya*.

JOHN: So he is saying that then this *āṇavo-*, I mean, he's saying *āṇavopāya* automatically takes you to *śāmbhavopāya* in the end.

SWAMIJI: Yes. *Artheṣ-*…now the conclusion:

LJA TA05I (18:22)

अर्थेषु तद्भोगविधौ तदुत्थे दुःखे सुखे वा गलिताभिशङ्कम्।
अनाविशन्तोऽपि निमग्नचित्ता जानन्ति
वृत्तिक्षयसौख्यमन्तः ॥ १२६ ॥

artheṣu tadbhogavidhau tadutthe duḥkhe sukhe vā galitābhiśaṅkam /
anāviśanto'pi nimagnacittā jānanti vṛttikṣayasaukhyamantaḥ //126//

I think the commentator of this *śloka* has commentated on this *śloka* wrongly. So, the real commentary for this *śloka* would be as I tell you, explain.

Those yogis, *anāviśanta to'pi*, although they have not entered in God consciousness, they have not entered in God consciousness, they don't enter in God consciousness (for instance, being in *samādhi*, or meditating in a meditative mood, remaining in a meditative mood for hours and hours, they don't do like that)…

JOHN: They don't enter.

SWAMIJI: No, they don't *do* like that.

DENISE: The yogis that don't do like that.

SWAMIJI: Such yogis don't sit for meditation. What do they do then?

DENISE: I don't know (laughs). I was wondering.

SWAMIJI: *Artheṣu* (laughs), he says *artheṣu*, in the objective field, *tad bhoga vidhau*, in the enjoyment of objective pleasures, *tadutthe*, and in experiencing the pain and pleasure thereon (in the enjoyment of the objective world, there is pain, there is pleasure, there are both), *galitābhi śaṅkam*, they have no doubt in that also. They don't remain doubtful in the objective world, in the enjoyment of the objective world, and in experiencing by the enjoyment of the objective world, in experiencing pain and pleasure–they have no doubt about it.

JOHN: Doubt means?

SWAMIJI: Doubt means, they don't get shrunk, they don't get worried, they don't say, "Haaah, I am lost, I am away from God consciousness." *Galitā*, that doubt they have…

JOHN: Put aside.

SWAMIJI: Yes, removed.

JOHN: So this objective world doesn't…these perceptions of pain and pleasure doesn't carry them away from their own nature.

SWAMIJI: No (affirmative). Because *nimagnacittā*, their mind is absolutely introverted in that transcendental God consciousness while doing this external act of universality. They see the objective world, they enjoy the objective world, they experience pain and pleasure thereon, and still their mind is/has sunk in that supreme state of God consciousness without doing *abhyāsa*, without meditating. *Jānanti vṛttikṣaya*, those yogis only experience the *real* state of joyous God consciousness, joyful God consciousness, blissful God consciousness. Blissful God consciousness is experienced by those yogis only, not by those yogis who meditate on it. Because meditation is a fraud. When you meditate, it means you were not meditating, before that you were not meditating, so you were a fraud. You were away from God consciousness when you were not meditating. So what is meditation and what is not meditation? You are always in that, you must remain in that because everywhere it is present whether you meditate on it or not. He is there. So, meditation, doing meditation, particular meditation, it is a fraud. It means you are thief.

ERNIE: I feel like a thief.

SWAMIJI: (laughs)

JOHN: Is this in *anupāya* or *śāmbhavopāya*–this?

SWAMIJI: This is *śāmbhavopāya*, it ends in *śāmbhavopāya*.

ERNIE: What was the other commentator's…?

SWAMIJI: Huh?

ERNIE: The other commentator, what did he say that meant?

SWAMIJI: He says: *Artheṣu tadbhogavidhau tadutthe duḥkhe sukhe vā galitābhiśaṅkam, anāviśanta*, they don't get entry in external worldly pleasures.

JOHN: Oh, a Vedāntin.

ERNIE: He missed it.

SWAMIJI: Yes. *Artheṣu tadbhogavidhau tadutthe duḥkhe sukhe vā galitābhiśaṅkam, anāviśanta*, they do not touch it! On the contrary, they merge in that supreme God consciousness where they enjoy the supreme nectar and supreme blissful state of their being. This is what [Jayaratha] has commentated. This is not my commentary on this *śloka*, because Abhinavagupta would never say like that.

DEVOTEES: (laughter)

SWAMIJI: And, at the same time, the commentator is from another order, it is not from Abhinavagupta's order. He was not a disciple of Abhinavagupta, [he] who has commentated on the *Tantrāloka*. He was very fond of commentating upon the *Tantrāloka*, but he didn't understand it well, so he commentated wrongly at many places.

Now the final conclusion of this chapter he explains in two more *śloka*s, and there ends our lesson.

LJA TA05I (24:31)

सत्येवात्मनि चित्स्वभावमहसि स्वान्ते तथोपक्रियां
तस्मै कुर्वति तत्प्रचारविवशे सत्यक्षवर्गेऽपि च।

satyevātmani citsvabhāvamahasi svānte tathopakriyāṁ
tasmai kurvati tatpracāravivaśe satyakṣavarge'pi ca /127a
(not recited)

Satyevātmani citsvabhāvamahasi, this light of *cit svabhāva*, this light of consciousness which is your own nature and which is your true nature, *svānte tathopakriyāṁ*, and in the mind it elevates one, through the mind, the mind is elevated to these such yogis by this God consciousness. *Tasmai kurvati tat pracāra vivaśe satyakṣavarge'pi ca*, when that *pracāra*, when that movement of that throb gets/travels in the external world also, *satyakṣavarge'pi ca*, all his organs, all the organs of yogis, and all the activities of yogis become divine, become one with God consciousness, they are glorified with that God consciousness. Their perceiving *śabda*, *sparśa*, *rūpa*, *rasa* and *gandha* is not ordinary, it is something divine. He does not see just as we see, he does not touch just as we touch, he does not do excitement with his wife as we do. His acting is something divine, because that God consciousness is inserted in each and every particle of his awareness.

LJA TA05I (26:04)

सत्स्वर्थेषु सुखादिषु स्फुटतरं यद्भेदवन्ध्योदयं
योगी तिष्ठति पूर्णरश्मिविभवस्तत्तत्त्वमाचीयताम्॥ १२७॥

satsvartheṣu sukhādiṣu sphuṭataraṁ yadbhedavandhyodayaṁ
yogī tiṣṭhati pūrṇaraśmivibhavastattattvamācīyatām //127//
(not recited in full)

When such a yogi resides, is established in the objective world, in the world of pleasure and pain, is established in the objective world and its pleasures and pains–but how he is established?–*bheda vandha udayaṁ*, without the least differentiated perception that this is pain, this is pleasure, this is sadness, this is joy, this is right, this is wrong, without that, and he becomes *pūrṇa raśmi vibhāva*, glorified with complete and full energies, rays of God consciousness. *Tat tattvam ācīyatām*, that state of God consciousness is worth searching; *tat tattvam ācīyatām*, you must search for that, you must search for that state, there is nothing else to be done in this world except this. *Bas*.

JOHN: This…

SWAMIJI: *Tat tattvam ācīyatām*, this is to be sought, not by going in cars for search,…

ERNIE: (laughs)

SWAMIJI:…*ācīyatām*, through the mind, through awareness you have to find out. *Ci-cayane*, the '*ci*' verbal root is for *cayane*, just feeling. This is the path of feeling you have to search. You have to search in the world of feeling. You have to feel it! It is there, you have to feel it (laughs), it has gone nowhere. *Bas*, here ends this *para tattvanta praveśa*. Now, tomorrow we will touch and end *karaṇa upāsana*.

JOHN: Is that the end of this fifth *āhnika*, then?

SWAMIJI: No, there is another subject, that is *varṇa tattva*. The *varṇa tattva* subject will be touched after the *jag* (fire ceremony), please (laughs).

JOHN: This *bheda* (duality), he perceives pleasure and pain, but he doesn't perc-...what does this mean that he doesn't...?

SWAMIJI: He is not worried, he is not worried for pain, he does not get joy from pleasure.

JOHN: In the real sense of joy, he is already full of joy. He experiences pleasure.

SWAMIJI: Pleasure and pain is nothing. Pleasure and pain, for instance, there is the greatest joy, universal joy, and there is one point of pleasure. What will it affect to you? When there is the greatest joy [and] there is one point of pain, what will that [pain] affect? So this is nothing. For instance, one's head is burning with fire, there is a big fire on your head, it is burning. When you get a prick, at the same time you get a prick of a needle on the legs, will you feel it? You won't feel it, you won't mind that at all. You are minding for this fire, this greater thing. So this is the case with that state of God consciousness. This was enough.

[*Para tattvanta*] *praveśa* is over, entry in the supreme state of God consciousness, that is over.

LJA TA05I (29:59)

Karaṇa Upāsana
Meditation on the Senses

इत्युच्चारविधिः प्रोक्तः करणं प्रविविच्यते।

ityuccāravidhiḥ proktaḥ karaṇaṁ pravivicyate /128a

So we have explained the way of *uccāra*, not *prāṇa uccāra*. *Uccāra*s are defined in two ways: one is *prāṇa uccāra* and one is, the other is, *cidātma uccāra*. *Prāṇa uccāra* is that connected with breath and *cidātma uccāra* is connected with awareness, not breath.

JOHN: And each of these is connected, one with *prāṇa kuṇḍalinī* and one with *cit kuṇḍalinī*.

SWAMIJI: But that is the offshoot of all these...

JOHN: Yes, it's not the center of that.

SWAMIJI: That is the result. *Prāṇa kuṇḍalinī* and *cit kuṇḍalinī* is the result, it is not the process. We are concerned with the process. *Prāṇa kuṇḍalinī, cit kuṇḍalinī, parā kuṇḍalinī*, all these *kuṇḍalinī*s are the result of processes. You have not to meditate on *kuṇḍalinī*, you can't. This is the result.

JOHN: But this result comes one from one, and one from the other, they don't mix.

SWAMIJI: No, they don't mix. *Karaṇaṁ pravivicyate*, now, I will explain the ways of *karaṇa*. *Karaṇa* means, instrumental process, the process connected with some means, instrumental process.

LJA TA05I (31:39)

तच्चेत्थं त्रिशिरःशास्त्रे परमेशेन भाषितम्॥ १२८॥

taccetthaṁ triśiraḥśāstre parameśena bhāṣitam //128//

This is explained by Parameśvara in the *Triśirobhairava Tantra*–this way of *karaṇa*. And this *karaṇa* is sevenfold.

ग्राह्यग्राहकचिद्व्याप्तित्यागाक्षेपनिवेशनैः।
करणं सप्तधा प्राहुरभ्यासं बोधपूर्वकम्॥ १२९॥

grāhyagrāhakacidvyāptityāgākṣepaniveśanaiḥ /
karaṇaṁ saptadhā prāhurabhyāsaṁ bodhapūrvakam //129//
(not recited in full)

This process of *karaṇa* is sevenfold. First is *karaṇa* regarding *grāhya* (*grāhya* means, object), second is concerned with *grāhaka* (subject), third is concerned with *cit* (consciousness), fourth is concerned with *vyāpti* (pervasion), fifth is–*grāhya*, *grāhaka*, *cit*, pervasion (*vyāpti*)–*tyāga*, *tyāga* is the exclusive process, just to exclude everything.

JOHN: Like *neti-neti*? Not like…[85]

SWAMIJI: Not *neti.* Just exclude and keep yourself absolutely excluded, don't get included with anything.

JOHN: Separate yourself as awareness from all the things.

SWAMIJI: Yes. That is *tyāga.* And [the sixth is] *ākṣepa. Ākṣepa* is, include yourself with each and every object of the world. The process concerned with inclusion, including, that is *ākṣepa.* And the seventh is *niveśanaiḥ*, the postures. If you remain without shaking in one position, that is all, don't think anything, but remain just like a rock. That is *niveśan*, that is just like *mudrā.* So this is the way *karaṇa upāsana* is done–sevenfold. *Grāhya* (objective) is the first, *grāhaka* (subjective) is the second, *cit* is third (*cit*, consciousness), *vyāpti* (pervasion) is fourth, *tyāga* (excluding) is fifth, *ākṣepa* (including) is sixth, and the process of postures, maintaining postures (*niveśana*). For instance, don't meditate, just sit like a rock.

JOHN: You don't do anything with your mind.

SWAMIJI: No, no, nothing. This will un-mind your mind [by staying in this] position, just after two hours. Just after two hours you will get entry in your Self.

JOHN: If you don't move. You can't even move a finger, nothing.

SWAMIJI: No, no, no, not at all!

JOHN: (laughs) Nothing.

ERNIE: Breath?

SWAMIJI: Breath also should be exhaled and inhaled very slowly so that it is not observed. This is the sevenfold way of *karaṇa upāsana.* And this *abhyāsa* (practice) is *bodhapūrvakam*, with awareness.

LJA TA05I (35:15)

तद्व्याप्तिपूर्वमाक्षेपे करणं स्वप्रतिष्ठता ।

tadvyāptirpūrvamākṣepe karaṇaṁ svapratiṣṭhatā /130a

---

85. Vedāntins are instructed to contemplate on Brahman (God) as *neti-neti*, not this, not that.

So *vyāpti pūrvam*, when you pervade and you get sovereignty on these sevenfold *karaṇas*, *karaṇam svapratiṣṭhatā*, then *karaṇa upāsana* gets its fruit. He does not get fruit at the time when it is in process. Just after awhile you will get its fruit. Now he says:

गुरुवक्त्राच्च बोद्धव्यं करणं यद्यपि स्फुटम् ॥ १३० ॥
तथाप्यागमरक्षार्थं तदग्रे वर्णयिष्यते ।

guruvaktrācca boddhavyaṁ karaṇaṁ yadyapi sphuṭam //130//
tathāpyāgamarakṣārthaṁ tadagre varṇayiṣyate /
(not recited in full)

Although this way of *karaṇas*, this sevenfold way of *karaṇas* must be learned through the mouth of a master, *guru vaktrāt ca boddhavyaṁ karaṇaṁ yadyapi sphuṭam*, this is what we have been taught by our masters that this *karaṇa upāsana* must not be explained [publicly], it must be learned through the lips of your master privately, but even then, just with this apprehension that this *karaṇa upāsana* may be lost altogether, I will explain this *karaṇa upāsana* in the body of the *Tantrāloka*. I won't tell you where I will explain what, but I will explain in the *Tantrāloka* scatteredly so that nobody knows where is *karaṇa upāsana*. Because the…just to protect the *āgama*, just to protect this tradition of *karaṇa*, I will explain it in the *Tantrāloka*, not here. Because [Jayaratha] says: *Nāti rahasyam ekatra khyāpyaṁ* (comm. vs. 131a), this secret way of process should not be kept altogether at one place, *na ca sarvathā gopyam*, but it should not be kept secret altogether. You must explain it in such a way that it is not known where it is explained, but the commentator will refer to us where [Abhinavagupta] has explained what in the *Tantrāloka*.

The first way of the process is *grāhya upāya*, *grāhya karaṇa*. *Grāhya karaṇa* means *karaṇa* (process) regarding objectivity. Where are my specks? In the sixteenth *āhnika*, he will explain the process of the object and the process of subjective, the subjective instrumental process–in the sixteenth *āhnika*, in the sixteenth chapter of the *Tantrāloka*.

LJA TA05I (38:21)

arthasya pratipattiryā grāhyagrāhakarūpiṇī /
tā eva mantraśaktistu vitatā mantrasantatau //
(*Tantrāloka* 16.253, quoted in the commentary)[86]

For instance, you observe any object. When you observe any object–this is the objective field, you observe an object in the objective field–there is an observer also, that is subjective (the observer is subjective and that which is observed is the object), but at that moment you have not to think that it is observed, you have not to think that it is observed by the observer. When you perceive that the observer is observing, nothing is observed. When you perceive that the observed, it is observed, nothing is observed. So, you must be absent, at the time of observation you must be absent there. You must not…for instance, this is a fire pot. When I see this is a fire pot, you must not become the fire pot. If you see that, "I am observing a fire pot," that *upāsana* is finished, there is no such meditation. Meditation of objectivity is to be done in such a way that objective perception must not prevail.

DENISE: You mean you must not see it at all?

SWAMIJI: You must see, but you must not see that, "I am seeing." You must not perceive that, "I am seeing."

JOHN: So there mustn't be that subjective-objective, you mustn't have…

SWAMIJI: Not even objective…no, take only the objective process. For instance, this is a *kongri* (fire pot), this is an object, this is an object. Don't think that, "I am perceiving this object."

DENISE: Just perceive it.

SWAMIJI: Just perceive it and see nothing.

JOHN: In other words, don't see the fire pot, see nothing, just like seeing the village, when you see the whole village [from the top of a mountain]?

SWAMIJI: Not like that, it is not that *nirvikalpa* (thought-less) process, this is *savikalpa* (thought) process. This is *karaṇa upāsana*. This is said:

---

86. Swamiji recites "*tā eva*" in place of the published "*sā eva*."

LJA TA05I (40:51)

mūḍho nāpnoti tadbrahma yato bhavitumicchati /
anicchannapi dhīro hi parabrahmasvarūpabhāk //
(*Aṣṭāvakra Gītā*, verse 37, not recited in full)

The Brahma is there, the existence of God consciousness is to be found, is to be realized in the objective world. And that God consciousness in the objective world cannot be realized when you are residing in objectivity. You have not to reside in objectivity and *be* in objectivity.

JOHN: You said, you said don't…

SWAMIJI: It is just like a yogi who is meditating to get entry in *samādhi*. As soon as he is nearing the state of *samādhi*, if he observes that, "This state of *samādhi* is nearing to me now," it will go away. That state of *samādhi* will be no more existing. This is the *karaṇa upāsana* in objectivity.

JOHN: So you have to observe the state as far as…

SWAMIJI: You have to observe as nothing is observed.

JOHN: Without thinking…

SWAMIJI: Don't take it seriously, don't observe it seriously that, "I am observing," that, "I am meditating." Don't be aware of this object. Go on perceiving the object without the least awareness of objectivity. Go on perceiving that you are the perceiver without the least awareness that you are perceiving. This is *karaṇa upāsana. Karaṇa upāsana* is done, it is very minute, minute and a very subtle *upāsana*, subtle *sādhana* (meditation).

ERNIE: It is not easy.

SWAMIJI: It is not very easy. It is to be learnt by the lips of a master. That is what he has explained here. *Nātirahasyamekatra khyāpyaṁ na ca sarvathā gopyam* (comm.). *Tā eva mantra śaktistu* (TĀ 16.253), because there are the energy of objectivity, energy of its energy, energy of its mantra. For instance, this is a *kongri*, this is a fire pot. This is the energy of objectivity. But there is, at the same time, there is attached another energy which is mantra energy, energy of its mantra. And energy of its mantra is *nirvikalpa*, energy of objectivity is *savikalpa*. You have not to remain in *savikalpa*, you have to remain in the *nirvikalpa* state of this object, and the *nirvikalpa* state of that object is automatic, and the *savikalpa* state of this object is functioned. You have not to function, it is *nirvikalpa*. For instance, you are Denise. As long as you perceive that you are Denise, that is not the right way of perceiving yourself. As long as you don't perceive at all, you are Denise, that is all. You are Denise, you are not curious to observe again and again that, "I am Denise, I am Denise, I am Denise, I am Denise, I am Denise." If you observe in this way that, "I am Denise, I am Denise," you are not observing yourself. How you observe yourself? Then you are not observing at all if you don't say that, "I am Denise, I am Denise, I am Denise." But you *are*, because at the time when you are absolutely asleep, in sound sleep, John will call you, "Denise," and you will say, "Yes?" So it means that this observation was there residing but unconsciously in the *nirvikalpa* state. That *nirvikalpa* state is to be brought into life. You have to give life to that *nirvikalpa* state of the *kongri* (fire pot) for each and every object of the world. That is *karaṇa upāsana* regarding objectivity.

JOHN: So then when you experience this *kongri* or your own self, you are to experience this *kongri* or yourself with awareness without using mind and intellect.

SWAMIJI: Without using the mind, you have not to use the mind and the intellect. As long as you are putting/adjusting the mind and the intellect also there, you are not experiencing anything, you are absolutely away from that objective process.

JOHN: Then you are in your thought only. You are only in thought, then, of something else.

SWAMIJI: That is it.

LJA TA05I (45:37)

arthasya pratipattiryā grāhya grāhana rūpiṇī /
tā eva mantraśaktistu vitatā varṇasantato //
(*Tantrāloka* 16.252, quoted in commentary)[87]

This will become mantra, the energy of mantra. The energy of mantra is to be held, not the energy of the object. The energy of the object is to be removed. Because you are Denise. Are you not Denise?

DENISE: Yes.

87. Swamiji modifies the last line of this verse from TĀ 16.252.

SWAMIJI: But you are not concentrating upon this, that you are Denise. Are you concentrating?

DENISE: No.

SWAMIJI: You are just Denise. This is the *nirvikalpa* state of observing that you are Denise. If you observe in this way that, "I am Denise, I am Denise, I am Denise," you are not observing yourself. It means there is doubt because you are reciting this awareness in continuity that you are Denise, you are Denise, so that this perception of being Denise may be washed off. But it is not washed off at all if you are just in its mantra *śakti*. This is mantra *śakti* that is to be observed in the objective world.

JOHN: Can you explain what mantra *śakti* is, what mantra means in this way? I mean, with a *kongri* (fire pot), you said this mantra energy of this *kongri* is the *nirvikalpa* state. What is that?

SWAMIJI: It is the *nirvikalpa* state when there is no perception of this *kongri*, but there is the *kongri*.

JOHN: In other words, nobody is seeing that *kongri*.

SWAMIJI: Nobody is seeing, and the seer also does not see the *kongri*. The seer also does not perceive the *kongri*, but it is perceived.

JOHN: By Lord Śiva.

SWAMIJI: No, it is perceived by you! But you are not perceiving it again and again.

JOHN: In that *vikalpa* (thought-full) way of intellect and…

SWAMIJI: Yes.

JOHN: So what is this mantra energy? Is it what creates these things?

SWAMIJI: This is *nirvikalpa*, this is the *nirvikalpa* state. So, whenever you eat, or talk, or go, or walk, or drive in a motorcar, just drive, don't be aware of this driving, just drive in the *nirvikalpa* state. That is observing mantra *śakti* in the objective world. This is one way of *karaṇa upāsana*. And the next way of *karaṇa upāsana* is that of subjective consciousness. Subjective consciousness must be also like this. So this twofold *karaṇa* is explained in the sixteenth *āhnika* of the *Tantrāloka*. You must find it out there.

LJA TA05I (48:27)

Now, there is the third way of *karaṇa upāsana*, that is of consciousness.

yattu sarvāvibhāgātma svatantraṁ bodhasundaram //
saptatriṁśaṁ tu tatprāhūs tattvaṁ paraśivābhidham /
(*Tantrāloka* 11.21, quoted in commentary, not recited)

That is of consciousness. For instance, consciousness should not be observed. If it is observed, it comes down, or it goes up. For instance, you observe the highest state of Śiva, that is the thirty-sixth element. When you observe the highest state of Śiva, that is the thirty-sixth element. I think that I have explained it to you.

JOHN: You move to the thirty-seventh.

SWAMIJI: Yes. When you observe that thirty-sixth element, the observer won't remain there, the observer will rise to thirty-seventh [element]. When you observe that thirty-seventh element also, the observer will rise to the thirty-eighth element. You won't find the observer. The observer is not to be found, the observer will never be found. Because when it is found, it becomes the observed, not the observer. So it will rise, it will rise, it will be snatched away from your consciousness. When you observe that this is the thirty-sixth element, Śiva, the state of Śiva, and you perceive that, the thirty-sixth element, and that Śiva will rise to the thirty-seventh element. When you are bent upon finding this thirty-seventh element also, then this thirty-seventh element will rise to the thirty-eighth element. And still you are bent upon finding out this thirty-eighth element, where this supreme state of God consciousness has gone. When you begin to observe this thirty-eighth element, that thirty-eighth element will be snatched from your consciousness to the thirty-seventh element. It won't remain in your conscious observation. This is the state of *saṁvitti*, this is the state of consciousness. The state of consciousness is never observed. For instance, you have fixed that this is the state of consciousness. If you hold it, it will be snatched, it won't remain there, because this state of consciousness will never come in your observation, because it is the observer, not the observed! When you observe it, you mean that you want to make it observed. It will never become the observed, it will be always the observer! So this is another state of consciousness, another state of process in *karaṇa upāsana*, that of consciousness. One is the objective state of *karaṇa upāsana*, the other is the subjective state of *karaṇa upāsana*, the third is the state of consciousness in *karaṇa upāsana*, how to hold consciousness. Consciousness is to be held by remaining away from consciousness. You can't feel consciousness directly. In the direct way you can perceive consciousness that this is the consciousness where consciousness is not observed. The thirty-sixth element is the highest consciousness. When you reach that, hold that thirty-sixth element, it will fly to the thirty-seventh element. When you hold that thirty-seventh element also, it will fly to the thirty-eighth element. When you hold that thirty-eighth element also, it will fly down to the thirty-seventh element. It won't come in your clutches because this is the absolute state of the observer. It will never be observed. So this is to be found out, you have to find out in your awareness that this state of consciousness is above. This is another *karaṇa upāsana*.

JOHN: Is this moving from *prameya* to *pramiti*?

SWAMIJI: Huh?

JOHN: Is this a movement from *prameya* to *pramiti bhāva*?

SWAMIJI: No, you can't reach *pramiti bhāva*. You will never reach *pramiti bhāva*. It is not *pramiti bhāva*, it is absolute *para pramātṛ bhāva*, the state of *para pramātṛ bhāva*. *Pramiti bhāva* is always there. *Pramiti bhāva*, as long as the position of observing is existing, the *pramiti bhāva* is there, but the...for instance, you are an authority on Shaivism, and you have no books, you have no books in your hand, you have nothing, and when you go in your brain, enter in your brain [and search for] what is there, where is the Shaivism, you won't find Shaivism in your brain.

DEVOTEES: (laughter)

SWAMIJI: You won't find the philosophy of Shaivism in your brain, but all Shaivism is there in that consciousness.

DENISE: In everyone's consciousness.

SWAMIJI: No, in the Shaivite. In the Shaivite philosopher, Shaivism is there existing, but not in words, not in explanations, not in book-form. As long as Shaivism is in book-form, it is not real Shaivism. Real Shaivism only exists in a vacuum. That is the absolute state of consciousness where nothing is seen. I don't see anything in Shaivism, I don't see the *Tantrāloka*, I don't see anything, but I am a Shaivite. This is the state of holding consciousness, the supreme state of consciousness. This is the third process of *karaṇa upāsana*. The fourth process of *karaṇa upāsana* is *vyāpti*, pervasion, the process of pervasion.

DENISE: Pervading.

SWAMIJI: Pervading. For instance, whatever you think, loose your organs, keep your organs absolutely loose, don't hold, don't control them, keep them just as they are; all your organs, wherever they go, wherever they go, keep awareness, the torch of awareness there. Don't control those organs, you have not to control, just keep the light of your awareness there. So you can do anything in this world, any nasty thing, but [only] at the same time when there is a torch, put that light of a torch in that, you are aware, and it is *vyāpti*, it is pervading, the process of pervading.

JOHN: But you said don't control. What does that mean? Does that mean to allow them to move?

SWAMIJI: Yes, you have to allow them to move.

DENISE: Wherever they move to.

SWAMIJI: Wherever they move! They want to quarrel, they wan't to cut anybodies throat, let them cut.

DEVOTEES: (laughter)

SWAMIJI: They want to tell lies, they want to speak truth, whatever they like, these organs, let them, but…

JOHN: The torch must be there.

SWAMIJI:…the torch of awareness must be there. This is the process of pervading.[88]

ERNIE: And this third process?

SWAMIJI: Yes. This process of pervading, the process of consciousness will be explained in the eleventh *āhnika*–the process of consciousness. The objective process and subjective process will be explained in the sixteenth *āhnika*. The process of consciousness will be explained in the eleventh *āhnika*. And the process of pervasion will be explained in the fifteenth *āhnika* of the *Tantrāloka*. But I won't say where–this is the way of explanation of Abhinavagupta.

---

88. "*Tiṣṭhet*, you must remain *prabuddhaḥ* (aware, fully aware), *prabuddhaḥ sarvadā*, in continuation, in continuity always. Always you must remain aware of what you are doing, what you are talking. You won't talk rubbish things then if you are aware of what you are talking. If you are aware of what you are speaking, you won't speak lies. If you are aware of what you are doing, you won't do that. This is the greatness of awareness that makes you filled with that great God consciousness." *Śiva Sūtra Vimarśinī* (LJA archive).

LJA TA05I (57:54)

iha kila dṛkkarmecchāḥ śiva uktāstāstu vedyakhaṇḍalake /
(*Tantrāloka* 15.338, quoted in commentary, not recited in full)

All in the objective field you will feel the rise of *cit śakti, icchā śakti, jñāna śakti, kriyā śakti*, every *śakti* you will find in each and every disgusted state of worldly pleasures.

JOHN: As long as you keep awareness there.

SWAMIJI: Yes.

JOHN: If awareness is not there, then everything is wrong.

SWAMIJI: No, then you are doing nothing. No, then…no, if you do supreme worship in the Dakṣiṇeśvara temple in Calcutta (that is supposed to be the highest temple of Lord Śiva–Dakṣiṇeśvara), if you worship that [and] you have not awareness, and if you do this disgusted slaughtering action and you have not awareness, that slaughtering and worshipping of Dakṣiṇeśvara is the same, there is no difference. That is also just like slaughtering yourself, and this is also slaughtering. There is no difference between that worship and this slaughter when…

JOHN: There is no awareness.

SWAMIJI:…there is not this torch. So it is no use to keep yourself attached to *dharma* (virtue) and detached from *adharma* (vice) as long as there is no awareness. If there is awareness, everything is divine.

DEVOTEE: Okay.

SWAMIJI: Everything becomes divine.

DEVOTEES: (laughter)

SWAMIJI: (laughs) Now, *tyāga*, the excluding process and including process, these two processes.

evaṁ trividhavisargāveśa-samāpattidhāmni ya udeti /
saṁvitparimarśātmā dhvanistadeva mantravīryaṁ syāt //
(*Tantrāloka* 29.140, quoted in commentary)

This is *tyāga*. And *ākṣepa*:

yatra sarve layaṁ yānti dahyante tattvasañcayāḥ /
tāṁ citiṁ paśya kāyasthāṁ kālānalasamaprabhām //
(*Tantrāloka* 25.172, quoted in commentary)

LJA TA05I (01:00:23) end
LJA TA05J (00:00) start

Ityādinā caikānnatriṁśāhniketyāgasyākṣepasya ca (comm.), and *tyāga*, the excluding process and the including process (*ākṣepa*). The excluding process is just to see God consciousness above everything. When you reach that above-state of God consciousness, realize that God consciousness is above that state too, just like the thirty-sixth *tattva*, the thirty-seventh *tattva*, the thirty-eighth *tattva*, and then again the thirty-seventh *tattva*. This is *tyāga*, excluding. For instance, you see from a distance that God consciousness is here, you try to catch it, you try to catch it and as long, as soon as you reach this spot, you will find God consciousness just away from this.

JOHN: Like a rainbow.

SWAMIJI: And when you try to hold that too, you will find there, at that point also, God consciousness a bit…

DENISE: Just a little away.

SWAMIJI:…a little away. So it won't come in your clutches. This is the exclusive understanding of process, in process. This is the process [of] *karaṇa upāsana*, how God consciousness is just away from your holding, you can't hold it.

JOHN: Because it is the holder. Is it?

SWAMIJI: He does not hold anything. It is neither the holder nor the held. This is the exclusive process, it is *tyāga*. *Ākṣepa*, *ākṣepa* is the inclusive process. The inclusive process is, wherever you are, the starting point is in fact the ending point. You have not to start. When you start, that is the ending point. You have not to go, there is no journey, there is no way. As soon as you reach that starting point, [when] you begin to start from the starting point, you have reached. This is *ākṣepa*, this is the inclusive process. So, the God consciousness is included, everywhere it is there. For instance, we are in the sixth planet of this universe, this is the sixth planet where we are existing in this universe. Because there are one hundred and eighteen planets. We are existing in the sixth, and there are a hundred and eighteen planets…

DENISE: Planets or worlds?

SWAMIJI: Worlds, worlds, worlds, worlds, worlds. Yes, excuse me, worlds. And that hundred and eighteenth world is in *śāntātīta* where Śiva is residing. And this world is where ordinary outcasts, trodden-down, this individual *jīva* is residing–here. So there is so much span of space to be covered. But this inclusive process teaches you how you can reach that supreme state of God consciousness there where you are already. This is inclusive way of process, *karaṇa upāsana*. This is *ākṣepa*. You can hold God consciousness at any moment, you have not to travel, there is no journey. So, this inclusive process and exclusive process will be explained in the 29th *āhnika*.

LJA TA05J (04:39)

And in the 32nd *āhnika*, the process of *saṁniveśā*, poses, *mudrās*, will be explained.[89]

ERNIE: Thirty-second.

SWAMIJI: Thirty-second. So, you must go through that all, all that *Tantrāloka*, and you will find these sevenfold ways of *karaṇa upāsana*, instrumental ways of process.

ERNIE: Now, these explanations of where they are, these different books,…

SWAMIJI: Yes.

ERNIE:…this, Abhinavagupta did not write that down.

SWAMIJI: There, in the *Tantrāloka*.

ERNIE: No, he wrote it in the *Tantrāloka*, he didn't write "it's in twenty-ninth, it's in thirty," he didn't say that.

SWAMIJI: No, no, no, the commentator says that. The commentator commentates [upon Abhinavagupta's] *śloka*s and says that he will…

ERNIE: Do this here.

SWAMIJI: Yes. Abhinavagupta has not, with his own pen he has not written that.

JOHN: He has hidden these in these places.

SWAMIJI: Yes. Because he says, "My masters have ordered me that this secret of *karaṇa upāsana* must not be written in one place so that it will be dishonored." Because *karaṇa upāsana* won't be successful, won't be successful to each and every aspirant, so they will think that this is only imagination, this is nothing. But this is not imagination,

---

89. As Jayaratha says: *ca tattanmudrāsvarūpanirūpaṇadvāreṇa dvātriṁśāhnike saṁniveśasya svarūpaṁ vakṣyati* (commentary).

this is the subject which you must learn from a master, directly from your master.

Tadasmākamapi evaṁ vyākhyāne śrīmadbhinavaguprapādā (comm.), so, I keep Abhinavagupta–the commentator says, the commentator of this *Tantrāloka* says–I keep Abhinavagupta in front of me, so I also won't explain this *karaṇa upāsana* here, I won't write. Because Abhinavagupta has ordered himself and all his disciples not to write in one place, so I also won't explain this *karaṇa upāsana* here.

Bas. This is the end of our lecture today. Now, this is the *upāsana* of Word now, what is Word. Word will be explained now. This is the last subject in this *āhnika*.

JOHN: Thank you, Sir.

LJA TA05J (07:17)

Varṇa Tattvam
Meditation on Word

There is only one subject now left to be explained then. Then we'll go with the sixth *āhnika*.

Evaṁ karaṇasvarūpamuṭṭāṅkya tadanantaroddiṣṭaṁ varṇa tattvaṁ vaktumupakramate (comm.), so *karaṇa svarūpa*, the formation of *karaṇa*, the essence of *karaṇa*, the process of *karaṇa* is over, and after *karaṇa* we have to explain the reality of Word, *varṇa tattva*, Word, the essence of Word, what is the essence of Word. That is to be explained now.

In fact, words are differentiated in two classes: one is that word which is manifested, and the next is the un-manifested Word, which is not manifested. That word which is manifested, it rises and it ends, and that Word which is not manifested, it never ends, and it is always rising, it is always going on.

LJA TA05J (08:38)

उक्तो य एष उच्चारस्तत्र योऽसौ स्फुरन् स्थितः ॥ १३१ ॥
अव्यक्तानुकृतिप्रायो ध्वनिर्वर्णः स कथ्यते।

ukto ya eṣa uccāṛastatra yo'sau sphuran sthitaḥ //131//
avyaktānukṛtiprāyo dhvanirvarṇaḥ sa kathyate /

The *uccāra* which we have already explained, the vibrating movement of consciousness that is already explained, *tatra yo'sau sphuran sthitaḥ*, there, in that vibrating movement of consciousness, that sound which is shining already there always, and *avyaktānukṛtiprāya*, and that sound is *avyakta anukṛti*, it is un-manifested sound, *sa varṇa kathyate*, that is in the real sense meant by "Word," that is Word.

Words are not those which rise from the connection of lips, tongue, throat, teeth–those are not Words. For instance, I am telling you these words, these are not Words, these are manifested words. These words end also, they rise and end, but this Word which is un-manifested, it goes on, it never ends. It ends only when you are away from it. For instance, you are in *samādhi*, you are enjoying that sound within your nature, it is there, it is going on there. You enter there and you feel that that sound is going on, and that sound only ends when you are away from that. When you get out from that *samādhi*, that sound is over, but that sound is there always. So it is un-manifested sound. It is that sound which does not rise from the connection of lips, tongues, throat, and everything.

JOHN: Is this *parā vāk*?

SWAMIJI: This is not *parā vāk*. This is that sound which is existing between *paśyantī* and *parā*. Because this sound is to be practiced, just to get entry in *parā vāk*. In fact, this is called *anāhata* (un-struck) sound.[90]

LJA TA05J (11:35)

nāsyoccārayitā kaścit-pratihantā na vidyate /
svayamuccarate devaḥ prāṇināmurasi sthitaḥ //
(*Svacchanda Tantra* 7.57, quoted in commentary)

This is already existing in the heart of each and every being, this Word. And this Word is not uttered, it is un-uttered Word, and it is

90. For an explanation of The Theory of Speech, See *Kashmir Shaivism–The Secret Supreme*, Chapter 6.

un-destroyed, it is not destroyed, it does not take its end. *Svayamuccarate devaḥ*, it rises, it vibrates by its own nature. And this *nāda*, this Word is one word, it is not only, these are not...because it is the un-manifested Word.

eko nādātmako varṇaḥ sarvavarṇāvibhāgavān /
so'nastamitarūpatvād-anāhataḥ ihoditaḥ //
(*Tantrāloka* 6.216, quoted in commentary, not recited)

This Word is *sarva varṇa avibhāga*, this Word can be found in each and every letter, in each and every word of worldly words. Whatever is ever uttered, you will find that Word in the background of that. For instance, "This is a spectacle," this word, in the background of "This is a spectacle," that Word exists. And "This is a pillow," in this word "pillow," in the background of this word "pillow," that Word exists because that is the life of all words, and these words (pillow, spectacles) are manifested words, whereas that is un-manifested.

JOHN: Does a yogi experience that this contains all words? When he experiences this Word, he experiences...?

SWAMIJI: He experiences that Word only in each and every word.

JOHN: In each and every word.

SWAMIJI: Yes. It is why he is always divine, he is always filled with that divinity of that Word. He finds, he feels the existence of that supreme un-manifested Word in each and every word.

ERNIE: How about sounds?

SWAMIJI: Huh?

ERNIE: Like music or the sound of a bus or a car engine.

SWAMIJI: That Word is existing in the background in those sounds also. Because those are also sounds, but they are manifested. For instance, music, instrumental music, that sound you cannot utter by mouth because it is "*kin kin kin kin*", you cannot utter it. It seems to be un-manifested, but in fact it is not un-manifested because it has come out from strings.

DENISE: And it has an end also.

SWAMIJI: It has an end also. When it is not in the agitation of strings, it ends, so it is manifested. He means the un-manifested Word, that is to be found, that is to be practiced. But what is the place of this Word where it throbs out–this Word? He says:

LJA TA05J (14:48)

सृष्टिसंहारबीजं च तस्य मुख्यं वपुर्विदुः ॥ १३२ ॥

sṛṣṭisaṁhārabījaṁ ca tasya mukhyaṁ vapurviduḥ //132//

This Word is found in the creative and destructive element of internal consciousness–creative and destructive element. You know creative and destructive element? Creative element is *ahaṁ*, destructive element is *ma-ha-a*. So it is creative element and destructive element. At the state of creative element and in the state of destructive element, this Word is found. Creative element is *ahaṁ* and destructive element is *ma-ha-a*. In the distinctive way, creative element is *sauḥ*, *sauḥ bīja*, and destructive element is *piṇḍanātha*.

JOHN: *'Rkṣkheṁ'?*

SWAMIJI: *'Rkṣkheṁ'*, yes. *Sṛṣṭisaṁhārabījaṁ ca tasya mukhyaṁ vapurviduḥ*, this is the predominant formation of this Word. It is existing in the *bījākṣara* of *sṛṣṭi* (creation) and in the *bījākṣara* of destruction–*ahaṁ* and *ma-ha-a*. *Ahaṁ* is the creative way of consciousness and *ma-ha-a* is the destructive way of consciousness. "Destructive" means taking in. Inside and outside.[91]

91. "In fact, this *parā bīja* and *piṇḍanātha* mantra is the commentary of *ahaṁ*. *Parā bīja* is also the expansion of *ahaṁ* and *piṇḍanātha* is also the expansion of *ahaṁ*, but the difference is only *parā bīja* is the creative movement of consciousness whereas the *piṇḍanātha* is the destructive movement, withdrawal movement. It is not a "destructive" movement, it is the withdrawing way of consciousness, how you withdraw from outside to inner consciousness. It is only two aspects of *krama mudrā*. Because as soon as *krama mudrā* takes place, you find in *samādhi*, when you are established in *samādhi*, just after two seconds of experiencing this *samādhi*, you come out, your breath comes out. Till then, in *samādhi* there is no breathing movement. Then breath comes out for one second, and coming out, the process of coming out in *samādhi* is *sauḥ*, is *parā bīja*, and the process of going again inside is *piṇḍanātha*. So the process of going out is *ahaṁ*, is the essence of *ahaṁ*, and going back again is *ma-ha-a*." *Tantrāloka* 4.187 (LJA archive).

LJA TA05J (16:36)

तदभ्यासवशाद्याति क्रमाद्योगी चिदात्मताम्।

tadabhyāsavaśādyāti kramādyogī cidātmatām /133a

By practising on these words, on these states, *sṛṣṭi* and *saṁhāra*, this creative and destructive state of consciousness, when a yogi practices on this Word, successfully he is sentenced to *cidātmatā*, the state of *cidātma* (*cidātma bhāva*), the state of God consciousness, and he gets entry in that consciousness.

He wants to clear it again.

LJA TA05J (17:23)

तथा ह्यनच्के साच्के वा कादौ सान्ते पुनःपुनः ॥ १३३ ॥
स्मृते प्रोच्चारिते वापि सा सा संवित्प्रसूयते।

tathā hyanacke sācke vā kādau sānte punaḥpunaḥ //133//
smṛte proccārite vāpi sā sā saṁvitprasūyate /

He wants to clear it again.

For instance, take any word, any manifested word, which is existing with a vowel or without a vowel. For instance, the word which is existing with a vowel, that is *ahaṁ*, and the word which is not existing with a vowel, that is *rkṣkheṁ*. There is no vowel, there are only the collection of consonants: *r* is without a vowel, *kṣ* is without a vowel, *kh* is without a vowel, and *e* is…like that–*rkṣkheṁ*. *Anacke sācke vā*, *anacke* means without a vowel, that mantra which is without a vowel, and that mantra which is with a vowel. *Kādau sānte*, and those mantras come from *ka* to *sa*, from all these letters from *ka* to *sa*. *Smṛte proccārite vāpi sā sā saṁvitprasūyate*, when it is remembered, when you memorize your consciousness again and again on that…for instance, you utter '*ahaṁ*' internally in your own brain, in your own mind, in your own thought–you utter '*ahaṁ*' (it is not to be uttered by the lips, just think of that). *Smṛte proccārite vāpi*, no matter if it is uttered also, if it is uttered once and then you establish your memory on that utterance which is in the past now, and see the source of that utterance, where that word is uttered, wherefrom that word is uttered, that is the real Word, that is the un-manifested Word. And by practicing on that, this way…because at present that Word is not found, that Word is not in our brain. This Word only shines when it is seen, when it is perceived. This will be perceived only when it is practiced again and again, again and again, and then you enter in that real un-manifested state of Word.

LJA TA05J (20:30)

बाह्यार्थसमयापेक्षा घटाद्या ध्वनयोऽपि ये ॥ १३४ ॥
तेऽप्यर्थभावनां कुर्युर्मनोराज्यवदात्मनि ।

bāhyārthasamayāpekṣā ghaṭādyā dhvanayo'pi ye //134//
te'pyarthabhāvanāṁ kuryur-manorājyavadātmani /

Bāhyārthasamayāpekṣā, it is not only in mantras that you find that Word–by practicing on these mantras. Which mantras?

DENISE: *Ahaṁ.*

SWAMIJI: *Ahaṁ* and *ma-ha-a*, and *sauḥ* and *rkṣkheṁ*, all these mantras, and other mantras also. '*Hrkṣmlvyṇūṁ*', there are so many mantras which are without vowels, and there are so many mantras which are existing with vowels. In those vowels also, when you recite those mantras also, by the mere recitation of those mantras nothing will happen. You have to recite those mantras internally and find out the real Word, un-manifested Word in them.

JOHN: That finding out is through awareness? Through awareness? This is movement from *āṇavopāya* to *śāmbhavopāya*, is it not?

SWAMIJI: Yes, yes.

ERNIE: How do you find out?

DEVOTEES: (laughter)

SWAMIJI: (laughs) You have to find it by meditating on the source of that mantra. For instance, *ahaṁ*. You have not to practice, you have not to be aware on *a* or *ha* or *ma*. You have to be aware on that state wherefrom this *ahaṁ* rises, the source of *ahaṁ*, the source of *ahaṁ*, this word. Because *ahaṁ* is a manifested word. You have to find out the un-manifested Word.

ERNIE: In here.

SWAMIJI: Yes, in the mind.

JOHN: So this un-manifested Word, does it exist on the level of *icchā śakti*?

SWAMIJI: Yes, it is *icchā śakti.*

JOHN: This Word.

SWAMIJI: Yes, because it is done with the nearness of *śāmbhavopāya.*[92] It cannot be done in *āṇavopāya*, plain *āṇavopāya.*

JOHN: But this is beginning in *āṇavopāya.*

SWAMIJI: Huh?

JOHN: This is beginning with *āṇavopāya* because you have mantra and then you move quickly to…

SWAMIJI:…quickly to that *śāmbhava* state. It is not only in mantras you have to find out the real Word.

bāhyārthasamayāpekṣā ghaṭādyā dhvanayo'pi ye //134//
te'pyarthabhāvanāṁ kuryur-manorājyavadātmani /
(verse repeated)

These other words, other gross words also, gross manifested words, not only these sacred spiritual words…which are spiritual words?

DENISE: *Ahaṁ, ma-ha-a.*

SWAMIJI: *Ahaṁ, ma-ha-a*, all these mantras are spiritual words. These worldly words also, "This is a telephone, this is a mike, this is…" You have not fixed the telephone yet.

DEVOTEES: (laughter)

SWAMIJI: I wanted to talk to you from Jammu (laughs).

bāhyārthasamayāpekṣā ghaṭādyā dhvanayo'pi ye //134//
te'pyarthabhāvanāṁ kuryur-manorājyavadātmani /
(verse repeated)

---

92. Also known as *icchopāya* (the means pertaining to the will).

Bāhyārtha samayā apekṣā, these *ghaṭādyā dhvanayo'pi*, these words also which are existing in the outside world, "This is a pot," "This is spectacles," "This is a pillow"–these words–"Where are you going?", "I am not well," "I had a headache," all these words, in these words also, you have to find out the real un-manifested Word because that un-manifested Word is existing in the background of all these sounds, these external gross sounds. *Bāhyārtha samaya apekṣā* (*bāhyārtha samaya* means all these outward objective objects, outward objects), regarding those outward objects, those words which are connected with those objects (*ghaṭa*, *paṭa*, specks, pillow, these, etcetera), *te'pyartha bhāvanāṁ kuryur manorājya vadātmani*, those also will carry you to that supreme un-manifested Word by *manorājya*, by memory, by sentencing or directing your consciousness towards the un-manifested state of these words. Because it is only memory that will carry you to that God consciousness. These words, these mantras have no charm in them, they have no strength, for instance, "*ahaṁ*", "*oṁ namaḥ śivāya*", "*jai guru deva*."

DENISE: In themselves, they have no strength.

SWAMIJI: No, "*jai guru dev*", "*guru ki jai*", "*jai śaṅkara*", all these mantras which are said to be spiritual mantras, they have no strength in them. They will never do you any help unless you find out the essence of that supreme un-manifested Word in the bottom of that, in the background of that. That un-manifested Word is to be sought in these "*jai guru dev*", "*guru mahārāja ki jai*", all these. "*Guru mahārāja ki jai*" won't do you any good unless you direct your consciousness towards that point of un-manifested Word, that is *dhvani*, that is *varṇa*.

LJA TA05J (26:36)

तदुक्तं परमेशेन भैरवो व्यापकोऽखिले॥ १३५॥
इति भैरवशब्दस्य सन्ततोच्चारणाच्छिवः।

taduktaṁ parameśena bhairavo vyāpako'khile //135//
iti bhairavaśabdasya santatoccāraṇācchivaḥ /

This is also pointed out by Lord Śiva himself in his book, the *Vijñānabhairava Tantra*, where there are one hundred and twelve ways to find out the real essence of consciousness.

The *Vijñānabhairava Tantra*, you know? He was very fond of…Maharishi Mahesh Yogi was very fond of this *Vijñānabhairava Tantra*. He wanted me to explain one-by-one all these techniques.

DENISE: He had never heard it before? That was the first time?

SWAMIJI: For the first time he heard it. It is why he then composed a poetry: "When you find yourself blue, dial on 1-1-2!"

DEVOTEES: (laughter)

SWAMIJI: (laughs) You know 1-1-2? One hundred and twelve ways (laughs).

DEVOTEES: (laughter)

DENISE: One hundred and twelve ways of centering.

SWAMIJI: "Lakshmanjoo will meet you on that telephone, on that number." 1-1-2 is one hundred and twelve ways.

taduktaṁ parameśena bhairavo vyāpako'khile //135//
iti bhairavaśabdasya santatoccāraṇācchivaḥ /
(verse repeated)

This is already pointed out by Lord Śiva himself in the *Vijñānabhairava Tantra* that whenever you recite "Bhairava" ("Bhairava" is a great mantra, the greatest mantra ever, it is the greatest mantra found in our Tantras–"Bhairava"), this "Bhairava" mantra also won't do you any good unless *bhairava śabdasya santatoccāraṇāt*, when you find out the background of this "Bhairava," what is Bhairava himself, the source of that "Bhairava," and the source of that "Bhairava" is that un-manifested Word. When you go to the depth of that un-manifested Word, Śiva, you will be one with Lord Śiva. This is quoted, this is pointed out by Lord Śiva himself in the *Vijñānabhairava Tantra*.

But how can it be possible by memory? By awareness it is possible, but how can…? For instance, "This is specks," I'll put awareness on this cognition, "This is specks," this is awareness, but memory is without the specks, memory is just in thought, just to think of that which is not present. How can memory carry you to that depth of Word, un-manifested Word? He puts that question here.

LJA TA05J (29:55)

श्रीमत्त्रैशिरसेऽप्युक्तं मन्त्रोद्धारस्य पूर्वतः ॥ १३६ ॥

śrīmantraiśirase'pyuktaṁ mantroddhārasya pūrvataḥ //136//

The answer of this question is explained in the *Triśirobhairava Āgama*, in the section of mantras.

स्मृतिश्च स्मरणं पूर्वं सर्वभावेषु वस्तुतः ।
मन्त्रस्वरूपं तद्भाव्यस्वरूपापत्तियोजकम् ॥ १३७ ॥

smṛtiśca smaraṇaṁ pūrvaṁ sarvabhāveṣu vastutaḥ /
mantrasvarūpaṁ tadbhāvya-svarūpāpattiyojakam //137//

This is the memory only, it is not...when you find out, when you see that this is specks, this specks won't do you anything unless there is memory. Memory will carry you to that, memory has the greatest power. *Smṛtiśca smaraṇaṁ pūrvaṁ*, because when you memorize your consciousness and give, insert that strength of memory in your consciousness, *sarva bhāveṣu vastutaḥ mantra svarūpaṁ*, it becomes mantra by itself, this memory, *tadbhāvya svarūpāpattiyojakam*, and it will direct you towards that supreme un-manifested Word, the state of Word. Because *sarve'nubhūtā yadi nāntararthā-*...this is a quotation.

LJA TA05J (31:24)

sarve'nubhūtā yadi nāntararthāstvadātmasātkārasurakṣitāḥ syuḥ /
vijñātavastvapratimoṣarūpā kācit smṛtirnāma na saṁbhavettat //
(verse quoted in commentary)

O Lord, all these–this is a hymn by Abhinavagupta quoted somewhere–*sarve anubhūtā*, when you experience something, you experience so many things, when you experience so many things in your factory, when you return from your factory and are seated in your *pūjā* (worship) room, nothing is in your consciousness, nothing is in your brain, nothing exists, but all those things which you had experienced in your factory, they are stored in your consciousness. Although they are not present, they are *antararthā*, *sarve'nubhūtā yadi na antararthā*, they are stored in your internal consciousness, and they are not seen. *Tadātma sātkāra surakṣitāḥ syuḥ*, and in fact all these experiences are protected by your strength of that internal Word. The internal Word digests them in its nature–that internal Word, that un-manifested Word. It is stored in that un-manifested Word and it manifests again when you reach, again return to your factory, all those scenes come in your consciousness. And they come only from that state of that un-manifested Word. The un-manifested Word is the being, the un-manifested Word is the life of all these words. *Vijñāta vastva pratimoṣarūpā*, when this was not stored, this would not have been stored in that un-manifested Word, all these experiences of your outward daily life, if these experiences would not have been stored in that un-manifested Word, it would never rise, they would never rise. For instance, I hand over ten rupees to you for the time-being.

DEVOTEES: (laughter)

SWAMIJI: Just to keep it (laughs), just to keep it, and you have to return it after two days. And this memory remains stored in your consciousness that, "I owe Swamiji ten rupees," and this is stored in that un-manifested Word. You don't feel afterwards that, "Ten rupees are with me." When, after two days, I ask for that ten rupees, if this memory was not stored in that un-manifested Word, you would answer, "I have no ten rupees"...

DEVOTEES: (laughter)

SWAMIJI:...because you would forget everything. *Vijñāta vastu apratimoṣarūpā*, they give rise, this un-manifested Word gives rise again to this memory. *Kācit smṛtir nāma*, then this memory would not take place again if these experiences would not have been stored in that un-manifested Word. They are stored there actually, they are not dead, they are stored and they rise.

Bas. (Kashmiri) I am tired. I was not feeling well. And I will finish this on Saturday.

LJA TA05J (35:30)

स्मृतिः स्वरूपजनिका सर्वभावेषु रञ्जिका।

smṛtiḥ svarūpajanikā sarvabhāveṣu rañjikā /138a
(not recited)

The weight of *smṛti*, the weight of memory is more than the weight of cognition. Memory is very important. Because *smṛti svarūpajanikā*, *smṛti* is, it creates the union of past with present–memory. Something what has happened in the past, five years before, that past-tense is united in this present-tense by this memory. This is *svarūpajanikā*. And *sarva bhāveṣu rañjikā*, it is *sarva bhāveṣu rañjikā*, memory is the only factor that involves all the perceptions in variations of time, space and form. For instance, that time of the past and this time of the present is united, and that space of the past and this space of the present is united in this *smṛti*, in this memory. When you memorize something, you unite the past with this present. For instance, my father was on the death-bed and this is in my memory, and I think of that event now, so that past is united with this present. So this is the union of variations of time, space and forms. That form is united in this form.

LJA TA05J (37:31)

अनेकाकाररूपेण सर्वत्रावस्थितेन तु॥ १३८॥
स्वस्वभावस्य सम्प्राप्तिः संवित्तिः परमार्थतः।
व्यक्तिनिष्ठा ततो विद्धि सत्ता सा कीर्तिता परा॥ १३९॥

anekākārarūpeṇa sarvatrāvasthitena tu //138//
svasvabhāvasya samprāptiḥ saṁvittiḥ paramārthataḥ /
vyaktiniṣṭhā tato viddhi sattā sā kīrtitā parā //139//

Anekākara rūpeṇa I have already explained. *Anekākara rūpeṇa* means, variations of forms, space and time is united there. And this is the state where the originator is observed; *svasvabhāsya samprāptiḥ*, the originator, the thinker is observed, the *pramātṛ bhāva* is observed, the real state of consciousness is observed.

JOHN: In memory.

SWAMIJI: In memory, yes. And *vyaktiniṣṭhā*, and it is residing in past perception.

JOHN: The real state of *pramātṛ*.

SWAMIJI: No, the *smṛti*, this memory. This memory is residing in that past perception. So, it is universal: it collects the past, present and future, everything. *Tato viddhi sattā sā kīrtitā parā*, so, this state of memory is the supreme state of God consciousness. This is the memory only where you can be diverted or directed towards the realization of God consciousness–by memory only. Not by seeing, you can't see God consciousness, but you have to remember his state in awareness, and this is memory.

DEVOTEE: *Vyaktiniṣṭhā* means?

SWAMIJI: *Vyaktiniṣṭhā* means, residing in past perception, *pūrva anubhava*. Past perception is *pūrva anubhava*. When I was forty years old, I remember that. So, that forty years is united in the seventieth year. This is the union.

JOHN: Why is the real state of *pramātṛ* observed here?

SWAMIJI: Because it is universal, because it collects the past, present and future in one point. *Pramātṛ bhāva* is all-pervading. *Pramātṛ bhāva* is not only residing in one point, not only in past or future.

JOHN: Because you can collect all points, it is almost *nirvikalpa* in some sense.

SWAMIJI: *Nirvikalpa*, this is the *nirvikalpa* state. Next:

LJA TA05J (40:12)

किं पुनः समयापेक्षां विना ये बीजपिण्डकाः।
संविदं स्पन्दयन्त्येते नेयुः संविदुपायताम्॥ १४० ॥

kiṁ punaḥ samayāpekṣāṁ vinā ye bījapiṇḍakāḥ /
saṁvidaṁ spandayantyete neyuḥ saṁvidupāyatām //140//
(not recited)

So, this outward objective world, the perceptions of the outward objective world, where these outward perceptions of the objective world are united, what to speak when you think of God with mantra? What to say then when you are reciting your mantra with awareness of God consciousness? It will definitely get you get entry, get yourself entered in that state of God consciousness, *para pramātṛ bhāva*, supreme.

JOHN: That is what it says here, this [verse].

SWAMIJI: Yes. *Kiṁ punaḥ samayāpekṣāṁ vinā*, where there is not *samaya…samaya* means where there is not…

DEVOTEE: Point.

SWAMIJI: No. *Samaya* means, *saṅketa* (convention). *Saṅketa* means, this is this. And it's *samaya* is "the specks." It is not specks. In the real sense, it is not specks. We call it "specks" just to realize it. Otherwise, it is not specks. What is it? It is that which is observed by Rosy (the dog) also. Rosy won't call it ["specks"].

DENISE: She won't call it "specks," right, right.

SWAMIJI: But she will see it, she will see this, she will…

DENISE: Recognize it as an object.

SWAMIJI: But it is adjusted, this "specks," this word is adjusted to it. But this adjusted word is not the word we have to explain. What have we to explain?

DENISE: The un-manifested Word?

SWAMIJI: Un-manifested Word, and that is this. That is this which Rosy will also understand, bird will also understand, cow will also understand. We will understand only "specks", but that "specks" is incorrect understanding. Correct understanding is this–*nirvikalpa*. You can't explain it, but you can perceive it. So there is not *samaya*, there is not adjustment. When this is perceived without adjustment of other things, *saṁvidaṁ spandayantyete neyuḥ saṁvidupāyatām*, they will definitely carry you to the state of God consciousness, that Word. Which word?

DENISE: The un-manifested.

SWAMIJI: Un-manifested.

JOHN: So is mantra the same thing?

SWAMIJI: Mantra directs you to that state.

JOHN: Takes you to that un-manifested Word.

SWAMIJI: Un-manifested Word.

JOHN: So then that means that you should think your mantra, not in a…

SWAMIJI: Not in gross form.

DEVOTEE: (Kashmiri)

SWAMIJI: *Na-īyuḥ.*

DEVOTEE: *Na-īyuḥ.* It is *vatan.*

SWAMIJI: Not *vatan. Kva-kva.*

JOHN: So what does it mean not to think mantra in gross form?

SWAMIJI: Huh?

JOHN: Mantra is mantra.

SWAMIJI: "*Namaḥ śivāya, namaḥ śivāya, namaḥ śivāya,*" this is gross form, thinking of mantra in gross form. But find out the reality of "*namaḥ śivāya,*" what is "*namaḥ śivāya.*" *Namaḥ śivāya* is, "I surrender in the state of supreme God consciousness." Do that. That is the recitation of mantra in its practical shape, not in those manifested words. These are manifested words! Keep these manifested words aside. Go to that un-manifested Word, which is one.

JOHN: In other words, when Shaivism teaches that the mantra, that when…

SWAMIJI: *So'ham.*

JOHN: The *sādhaka* must think the mantra is the very presence of Lord Śiva there.

SWAMIJI: Yes.

JOHN: It has no meaning like "specks" is pointing at this [object].

SWAMIJI: Yes.

JOHN: That's taking that word beyond that meaning to the un-manifested Word.

SWAMIJI: Yes.

JOHN: Is that what Shaivism says?

SWAMIJI: Yes, that is quite…

DEVOTEE: (Kashmiri) *Samaya apekṣā vinā*?

SWAMIJI: *Samaya apekṣām vinā. Samayāpekṣā* means, these words which are adjusted, that is, "it is specks", "it is *kongri*", "it is *kos*", "it is a sheet." In which *samaya*? *Samayāpekṣā*, but *samaya apekṣā*, where there is not this adjustment, those are mantras. Mantras are without attribution, without adjustments.

DEVOTEE: These are conventional words: specks, table, chair…

SWAMIJI: Yes, these are manifested.

JOHN: So mantra can also be manifested, but that is not real mantra.

SWAMIJI: But that is not correct mantra. *Vācyābhāvad…*next:

LJA TA05J (45:11)

वाच्याभावादुदासीनसंवित्स्पन्दात्स्वधामतः ।
प्राणोल्लासनिरोधाभ्यां बीजपिण्डेषु पूर्णता ॥ १४१ ॥

vācyābhāvādudāsīna-saṁvitspandātsvadhāmataḥ /
prāṇollāsanirodhābhyāṁ bījapiṇḍeṣu pūrṇatā //141//

When they are not adjusted, when the differentiated object is absent absolutely, the differentiated object is absent (that is *vācya abhāvāt*)…*

That should be absent, there should not be a differentiated object in that functioning of, practice of Word. When you practice that supreme Word, un-manifested Word, there should not be a differentiated object adjusted to it. When a differentiated object is adjusted to it, "specks," where remains the Word? The word is not un-manifested there.

*…so, *udāsīna saṁvit spandāt svadhamataḥ*; *udāsīna saṁvit spanda*, this *saṁvit spanda* means, the throb of consciousness is *udāsīna* (*udāsīna* is introverted), it is not expanded to manifestation, the throb of consciousness is introverted there in that Word. In practicing that Word, the throb of consciousness is inside.

JOHN: You mean it takes you inside.

SWAMIJI: Yes…no, it is residing inside.

JOHN: It is residing inside.

SWAMIJI: You can't explain it, what it is. When you explain it that, "It is specks," *bas*, finished.

JOHN: You have been taken outside.

SWAMIJI: Yes, you are taken out, you know nothing. When you only perceive it in its own un-manifested way, that is it. And that is the same to each and every living being: crow, dog, pussy [cat], Rosy, everyone. A cow, she will perceive that in that un-manifested way. When you perceive it in the manifested way, it is incorrect perceiving, perception.

JOHN: So in meditation with mantra, that mantra, if awareness is there in meditation, then automatically you go to that un-manifested…

SWAMIJI: Yes.

JOHN: Because you can't make yourself go to the un-manifested.

SWAMIJI: No (affirmative).

DEVOTEE: Is this the same as *arthābhāvanā*, Sir?

SWAMIJI: No, *arthābhāvanā* is not. It is beyond *arthābhāvanā*.[93] And *svadhāmataḥ*, thus, it is residing not in objects but in Self. It does not reside, this Word or *bīja* or *piṇḍa* of mantra, the state of this mantra does not reside in the objective, in those manifested words. For instance, there is *sauḥ*: *sa*, *au*, and *visarga* (*aḥ*). It does not reside there in that un-manifested way. It resides where?

DENISE: Underlying?

SWAMIJI: It resides in one's own consciousness. As long as you cannot explain it, it is real. When you begin to explain it, it is unreal. No sooner you explain it–finished.

JOHN: This, whatever word that is.

SWAMIJI: You can't explain. Explanation is wrong understanding. When you only perceive in its real way, that is the real perception of that Word.

JOHN: So then wrong perception would be if you were thinking the mantra, "Nārāyaṇa," lets say…

SWAMIJI: Yes.

JOHN:…to think that form [of] Nārāyaṇa and his picture and all, that is the wrong way.

SWAMIJI: Yes, that is the wrong way.

JOHN: And the right way is that the word itself is Nārāyaṇa.

SWAMIJI: Self, Self, consciousness, yes. *Prāṇollāsa nirodhābyāṁ*, and there are two aspects which function in this way of recitation of mantra: *prāṇollāsa* and *nirodha*. *Prāṇollāsa*, the expansion of objectivity, and *nirodha*, and just letting it reside in one's own internal consciousness. For instance, "*so'ham*." This is *prāṇollāsa*. When you recite this "*so'ham*" and perceive that, "I am one with that God," this is *prāṇa ullāsa*. *Nirodha* is when that "God" is cleared in its un-manifested Word, when nothing is to be done.

JOHN: In other words, you don't have to think that, "I am one with him."

SWAMIJI: No.

JOHN: You just are.

SWAMIJI: As long as you say, "I am one with him," it is external, it is

---

93. The deliberation over a subject as mentioned in *Yoga Sūtras* 1.28.

the external way of understanding. When you *are* one with that actually, then you don't say. You are, that is all. That is *nirodha*. So, *bījapiṇḍeṣu pūrṇatā*, so, this is how *pūrṇatā* (fullness) arises in these mantras.

JOHN: By taking them from *prāṇa ullāsa* to...

SWAMIJI: *Nirodha.*

JOHN: *Nirodha*. You must always go to *nirodha*.

SWAMIJI: Yes, *nirodha*. Otherwise, there is no, there is no...it is only a waste of time if it is only done in *prāṇa ullāsa*, the way of *prāṇa ullāsa*. You have to put it in *nirodha*, then fullness of mantras appears. So generally he has explained this state of Word. Now, he explains the state of Word in its *viśeṣa*, the general and common and particular way. And that particular way is...you know, Abhinavagupta, when he gives an example of this particular way, he gives the example always of sex, not of form, not of hearing, not of touching, not of thinking, not of smelling, not of tasting, but of sex, because sex is the predominant [act] where you get God consciousness vividly cleared. God consciousness is vividly cleared there. It is what he says. And the mantras will also be adjusted to it.

LJA TA05J (52:29)

सुखसीत्कारसत्सम्यक्साम्यप्रथमसंविदः ।
संवेदनं हि प्रथमं स्पर्शोऽनुत्तरसंविदः ॥ १४२ ॥

sukhasītkārasatsamyaksāmyaprathamasaṁvidaḥ /
saṁvedanaṁ hi prathamaṁ sparśo'nuttarasaṁvidaḥ //142//

First there is the object. What is the object? Two persons of opposite sex, that is *sukha*, that is joy, you get joy.

JOHN: By having these two people together.

SWAMIJI: Not together, not closely together, just perceiving, just like you are here and I am here, from a distance. That is *sukha*. You create that, the sensation of joy is created in both, the sensation of joy, although they don't do anything yet. That is *sukha*, the sensation of joy comes.

JOHN: Initial joy comes at the first moment.

SWAMIJI: Yes. That is *sukha*. Then is *sītkāra*. *Sītkāra* means, act.

And in these two, *sāmya prathama saṁvidaḥ*, when there is *sāmya* (means oneness), when oneness comes with these two, and oneness, that is…you have to go to next *śloka*.

LJA TA05J (54:02)

हृत्कण्ठ्योष्ठ्यत्रिधामान्तर्नितरां प्रविकासिनि।
चतुर्दशः प्रवेशो य एकीकृततदात्मकः ॥ १४३ ॥

hṛtkaṇṭhyoṣṭhyatridhāmāntar-nitarāṁ pravikāsini /
caturdaśaḥ praveśo ya ekīkṛtatadātmakaḥ //143//
(not recited)

Hṛt kaṇṭhyoṣṭhya tridhāma, it possesses three states: in heart, in throat and in lips.

JOHN: This oneness.

SWAMIJI: This oneness. First, at the first state, it rises in the heart.

ERNIE: This is the joy.

SWAMIJI: This is the joy, yes. You are entering it by-and-by. And *kaṇṭha* (*kaṇṭha* is the throat), in the throat that joy is united, it is on the way of union with each other in the throat, because the sensation rises in the throat afterwards. Then it is united with the lips. And there, in these three states, in these three places, what you have to do is *prathama saṁvidaḥ*, *saṁvedanaṁ*, *prathama saṁvedana*, just hold the first source of that joy, just hold the first source of that throb in the throat. Because when you are coming nearer, nearer to your opposite sex, nearer and nearer, a throb in the throat rises. That is a beautiful throb. It does not mean that it is only in a beautiful [throb], in an ugly throb also it must happen. He has given an instance only.

ERNIE: What must happen?

SWAMIJI: The rise of Word, that Word must appear, that un-manifested Word must appear. So, how that un-manifested Word will appear? It will appear only when you take hold of that first throb. For instance, when your opposite, the person of the opposite sex is before you and you get *sukha* (joy), go to the depth of this perception of joy, where this joy is created. That is the reality of that Word (*varṇa*). Or, when you have created that throb also, the throb sensation, when you are nearing and nearing and just [about] to take the formation of the act, the real act, you get a throb first in the throat, but that throbbing you should do, you should perceive wherefrom this throb has appeared. That is Word, that is the real Word. And when you unite your lips with each other, don't kiss, just see wherefrom this kiss is appearing. That is the Word. And this is the state of *sa* in *sauḥ* mantra. This is indicated by this *sauḥ* mantra, the first [letter, *sa*]. *Sauḥ* mantra has three [letters]: *sa*, *au* and *visarga* (*aḥ*). It is not the sexual act, there is no sexual real act yet, it is only the first throb, just to begin with. It is only residing in the state of *sa*. Have you understood?

DENISE: I think so.

SWAMIJI: Or am I wasting my time? (laughs)

DEVOTEES: (laughter)

SWAMIJI: I think you understand it.

ERNIE: It's difficult.

SWAMIJI: It is difficult, because you have to find out the internal Word in each and every action of the world. And he has put only the example of sex first, just to make you understand fully. Because if he would put the example of formation, seeing some form, or tasting, it wouldn't be so clear, clearly explained. Here, everybody knows this.

ERNIE: Universal.

SWAMIJI: This is universal truth for everybody, this sexual act.

JOHN: So this throb, if you gave yourself just to this throb, that would be *prāṇa ullāsa*, is that?

SWAMIJI: Yes, *prāṇa ullāsa*.

JOHN: And when you find the source of this throb, that's *nirodha*.

SWAMIJI: That is *nirodha*, that is *nirodha*.

BRUCE H: So this is true also when great anger arises or pain?

SWAMIJI: Yes, anger also, pain, pleasure, everything!

ERNIE: That is why you said ugly throb or beautiful throb, both throbs.

SWAMIJI: Both throbs. But first you have to try with this real joyful throb.

ERNIE: Why first that?

DENISE: It's easier.

ERNIE: It's easier.

LJA TA05J (59:36) end

LJA TA05K (00:00) start

SWAMIJI: An ugly throb will be, for instance, you get a cut. You won't to go to the depth of that Word at that pain.

JOHN: So with joy it is easy.

SWAMIJI: So with joy it is easier to understand first, and then when you are established fully in this way, and then you can travel in those opposite things also.

ERNIE: So, no sleeping on a bed of nails to find this.

SWAMIJI: No, no, no (laughs).

DEVOTEES: (laughter)

DEVOTEE: If you focus on the first throb, then that means the act won't follow.

SWAMIJI: The act has not taken place yet at all. This is first point of *sa*.

DEVOTEE: Supposing you want to eat something and you get that first sensation [when] you see a tasty thing, and if you focus on that sensation, then you won't go in the actual act of eating.

SWAMIJI: No, you won't go, and you will get that state of Word.

JOHN: So this is all practice, this isn't…

SWAMIJI: It is practice, yes. It is not only practice done only in this way. He will put you in the real act also, when that will happen, that oozing out of that *vīrya* will happen, semen. He will take you to that point also with this Word, and find out this Word, the state of Word there also. This is the first stage, first step.

JOHN: In this you said that animals experience spectacles in their real way.

SWAMIJI: Yes, yes.

JOHN: Do they also have sexual act and all these perceptions and everything in the real way in *nirodha*?

SWAMIJI: Yes, yes.

JOHN: Only human beings have it in *prāṇa ullāsa*.

SWAMIJI: Yes.

ERNIE: Yes, but a crow is not enlightened.

SWAMIJI: Huh?

ERNIE: A cow is not enlightened.

SWAMIJI: But they are residing, but they are residing there, but they don't know.

ERNIE: You mean, I should be like a crow then.

SWAMIJI: Yes, but with awareness.

DEVOTEES: (laughter)

SWAMIJI: With awareness! You should be just a born child, with awareness. Shanna is just like that, residing in that Word, but without awareness. This is the only defect in Shanna. If there were awareness also…

ERNIE: That is the defect with the crow.

SWAMIJI: Yes, that is the defect with a crow, animals, with cows, everyone.

ERNIE: If there was awareness…

SWAMIJI: If there was awareness, then it would be the exact Word, the exact, that un-manifested Word.

ERNIE: Reality.

SWAMIJI: Reality. But we have not, because there is *prāṇa ullāsa* in us…

ERNIE: In our way.

SWAMIJI: In our way.

JOHN: Which is what differentiates…we see everything in a differentiated way.

SWAMIJI: Yes. And, for instance, when you practice yoga, it will take you so many years to reach that state of God consciousness, whereas Shanna, if there is awareness, she will practice and in two minutes she will get entry in *samādhi*–in two minutes. This is the reality of that *nirodha*. Because there is real *nirodha* in children, in crows, in dogs, in…

ERNIE: So how old are you when you lose that?

SWAMIJI: Huh?

JOHN: When does a child lose that? When does that *prāṇa ullāsa* come so strongly in a child?

SWAMIJI: No, *prāṇa ullāsa* comes along [when] the sexual life starts.

ERNIE: At adolescence.

SWAMIJI: Finished! (laughs)

ERNIE: (laughs) So, what stops me, then, is when that starts, I start having memories…

SWAMIJI: Yes.

ERNIE: Right? With these words of this world and I lose it. Is that…?

SWAMIJI: Yes, quite true.

DEVOTEE: Is this the reason why a saint is called *bālavat*, like a child?

SWAMIJI: *Bālavat*, yes, this is that.

LJA TA05K (04:07)

hṛtkaṇṭhyoṣṭhyatridhāmāntar-nitarāṁ pravikāsini /
caturdaśaḥ praveśo ya ekīkṛtatadātmakaḥ //143//
(verse repeated)

Then you have to, after this is over, after this is completed and got in the state of, residence is got in the state of that supreme Word, in first *sa*, then *hṛtkaṇṭhyoṣṭhyatridhāmāntaḥ*, go deep, dive deep after the entry of these three states (heart, throat and lips), then *pravikāsini caturdaśaḥ praveśaḥ*, then there is the fourteenth way of entry takes place. The fourteenth way of entry, that is *au*, that is *kriyā śakti*, that is the real act. When you are busy with the real act, the sexual act, that is *caturdaśa praveśaḥ*, and it is very difficult to understand Word there.

JOHN: In real act.

SWAMIJI: In real act.

JOHN: Because movement is taking place.

SWAMIJI: Movement and agitation and everything and excitement, everything is happening there.

ERNIE: Attachment to the…

SWAMIJI: Attachment, not attachment. Exciting. Excitement.

DEVOTEE: *Prāṇa ullāsa*, it is intense.

SWAMIJI: *Prāṇa ullāsa* is intense, yes.

JOHN: Shaivism doesn't speak much about attachment.

SWAMIJI: No, not attachment.

JOHN: Just awareness. Attachment is okay. Just awareness.

SWAMIJI: *Caturdaśa praveśo ya ekīkṛtatadātmakaḥ*, it is *ekīkṛtatadātmakaḥ*, when they are one, there is nothing, nothing left differentiated. In the real act, nothing is left differentiated. There is no differentiated perception of both persons. There you have to find Word, there you have to find Word, and in the same way, wherefrom, what is the source of this real act, what is the source of this real act, you have to go to that extent there in your awareness [while] doing that act.

JOHN: This is the fourteenth because it is the fourteenth vowel, *au*?

SWAMIJI: Yes. And this is indicated by the letter *au* in *pārabīja* (*sauḥ*). That was indicted by the letter *sa*, and this is indicated by the letter *au* in *pārabīja*. Then, when there is...what do you call that?

JOHN: Climax?

SWAMIJI: Climax. Climax is next. Next, climax will take [place]. And at the time of climax, you have to find out this Word also. If you don't find the Word, that climax is just like the climax of dogs.

LJA TA05K (07:17)

ततो विसर्गोच्चारांशे द्वादशान्तपथावुभौ।
हृदयेन सहैकध्यं नयते जपतत्परः॥ १४४॥

tato visargoccārāṁśe dvādaśāntapathāvubhau /
hṛdayena sahaikadhyaṁ nayate japatatparaḥ //144//

Then, after that, after that process, *visarga uccāra aṁśe*, when the *visarga* (*aḥ*) will flow out (*visarga*, that flow), and it must flow out, not in the external world, it must flow out in *brahmarandhra*, Śiva-*dvādaśānta*. *Dvādaśānta pathāvubhau*, *ubhau dvādaśānta pathau*, it flows out in both ways.

JOHN: In other words, semen flows out?

SWAMIJI: Semen flows out and the rise of *kuṇḍalinī* also takes place.

JOHN: Same time.

SWAMIJI: The flowing of semen out *is* the rise of *kuṇḍalinī* actually in Word. When while the oozing of that semen you hold deeply with awareness, the source of that, the source of that flow, the rise of *kuṇḍalinī* will take place in no [time], in half a minute.

DEVOTEES: (laughter)

JOHN: So this is attached to this *nirāñjana*, *viṣa tattva*.

SWAMIJI: Yes.[94] *Hṛdayena sahaikadhyaṁ nayate japatatparaḥ*,

94. "First was *kāma tattva*, second was *viṣa tattva*, and *nirañjana tattva* is third. So,

then you get entry and oneness in that supreme heart of God consciousness. This is the real *japa* (recitation) of Word. You have to find out the Word, that is the Word.

JOHN: So this first act, this first section, which is experiencing throbbing, that is *āṇavopāya*. Or are they all…? This act itself is *śāktopāya*, is it not? This *viṣa tattva*, *nirañjana*…

SWAMIJI: No, from the very beginning it is *śāktopāya*.

JOHN: This is all *śāktopāya*.

SWAMIJI: This is the field on the *śāktopāya* field. There is no *āṇavopāya*.

JOHN: But why is this in this chapter on [*āṇavopāya*]? Because this is an example.

SWAMIJI: Yes. He told you that the supreme Word, there is no harm if a candle is also lighted, this is also lighted, sun is also shining. If *śāmbhavopāya* also takes place, what is there bad? So he wants you to get union with *śāmbhavopāya*. Exactly, in fact, this is the whole play of *śāmbhavopāya*. *Śāktopāya* is the play of *śāmbhavopāya*, *āṇavopāya* is the play of *śāmbhavopāya*, and in fact all these *upāya*s, this triple way of *upāya*s, is the play of Lord Śiva himself.

JOHN: So the difference then in these *upāya*s is the starting point.

SWAMIJI: Yes, the starting point, starting point. Starting, when you observe that starting point with less effort…with no effort, when you observe that starting point with no effort, it is *śāmbhavopāya*. When you observe that starting point with less effort, it is *śāktopāya*. When you observe that starting point with great effort, that is *āṇavopāya*. This is the difference between *āṇavopāya*, *śāktopāya* and *śāmbhavopāya*, but the goal is one, the Word is one. That is the Word. Which word? Un-manifested Word.

Now he calculates this, the substance of this in next *śloka*.

LJA TA05K (10:55)

---

kāma tattva is in desire, in will, in the energy of will (*icchā*), *viṣa tattva* is in the energy of knowledge (*jñāna*), and *nirañjana tattva* is in the energy of action (*kriyā*). That *icchā śakti* is *śakti kuṇḍalinī*, *jñāna śakti* is *prāṇa kuṇḍalinī*, and *kriyā śakti* is *parā kuṇḍalinī*." *Kuṇḍalinī-Vijñāna-Rahasyam* (LJA archive).

कन्दहृत्कण्ठताल्वग्रकौण्डिलीप्रक्रियान्ततः।
आनन्दमध्यनाड्यन्तः स्पन्दनं बीजमावहेत्॥ १४५॥

kandahṛtkaṇṭhatālvagra-kauṇḍilīprakriyāntataḥ /
ānandamadhyanāḍyantaḥ spandanaṁ bījamāvahet //145//

This creation of mantras, this perception of mantras, this perception of mantras carries you, this perception of mantras carries you to the depth of the center of *kuṇḍalinī*. This way, when you perceive the recitation of mantras, it will carry you to the depth of that *kuṇḍalinī* which is filled with supreme *ānanda*. Where it is existing? *Kanda*, in the rectum, *hṛt*, in the heart, *kaṇṭha*, in the throat, *tālvagra*, in the tip of *tālu*, in the tip of that…you know *tālu*?[95] Then, after that, when you go to the depth of that entry, then *kuṇḍalinī* takes place. And that is *prakriyāntataḥ*, that is the last state. The last state is *kuṇḍalinī*. *Ānandamadhyanāḍyantaḥ spandanaṁ bījamāvahet*, so, this *bīja* should be in such a way uttered that it will carry you to that point of *kuṇḍalinī*.

LJA TA05K (12:33)

संहारबीजं खं हृत्स्थमोष्ठ्यं फुल्लं स्वमूर्धनि।
तेजस्त्र्यश्रं तालुकण्ठे बिन्दुरूर्ध्वपदे स्थितः॥ १४६॥

saṁhārabījaṁ khaṁ hṛtstham-oṣṭhyaṁ phullaṁ svamūrdhani /
tejastryaśraṁ tālukaṇṭhe bindurūrdhvapade sthitaḥ //146//

This, the theory of Word is now explained in *saṁhāra bīja*s also, in destructive mantras, not only in creative mantras. You know creative mantras?

ERNIE: What we've just talked about.

---

95. The uvula, which is part of the soft palate.

SWAMIJI: *Sauḥ*. *Sauḥ* is a creative mantra.

JOHN: *So'haṁ* is also creative?

SWAMIJI: *So'haṁ* is also creative.

JOHN: *Rkṣkheṁ* is...

SWAMIJI: *Rkṣkheṁ* is destructive.

JOHN: And *ma-ha-a*?

SWAMIJI: *Ma-ha-a* is destructive. Now he puts that [process] to one of the destructive mantras. But destructive mantras will also carry you to that same point. First is *saṁhāra bīja*. *Saṁhāra bīja* means [the letter] *kha* (*saṁhāra bījaṁ khaṁ*, *kha* is *saṁhāra bīja*), and that is *hṛt-stham*, that is residing in the heart. Where is the heart? When you perceive joy–that you have already been told–joy comes in the heart first in this act, and that is *kha*, that is *saṁhāra bīja*. *Saṁhāra bīja* means, *kha*, and that is residing in the heart. *Oṣṭhyaṁ phullaṁ*, and in the lips there is *oṣṭhyaṁ*, *pha*, the letter *pha* is residing in the lips. The letter *pha*, 'f', is residing in the lips. *Svamūrdhani tejaḥ*, *svamūrdhani*, in this forehead, *tejaḥ*, the letter 'r' is existing of this mantra.[96] *Tryaśraṁ tālu-kaṇṭhe*, and the letter *e* (*triśraṁ* means, triangle), the letter of triangle, *e*, is residing in *tālu kaṇṭhe*, in both the palate and the throat. And the last letter, *ṁ*, is residing in *dvādaśānta*. *Dvādaśānta* means, the climax and the rise of *kuṇḍalinī*.

ERNIE: That letter exists there.

SWAMIJI: That letter exists there.

JOHN: So what is the full mantra here then?

SWAMIJI: The full mantra is '*khphreṁ*'. *Khphreṁ*, this is a destructive mantra. This is just like *piṇḍanātha*. So in *khphreṁ* mantra also, you must find out the real Word, that un-manifested Word, and that *khphreṁ* mantra should be put in the same way, should be uttered in the same way of this act, sexual act.

JOHN: In these points as you go along.

SWAMIJI: Yes.

JOHN: Why is that called...? *Saṁhāra bīja* is the whole mantra or only that [letter] *kha*?

---

96. *Tejaḥ* means, bright. The letter *ra* is known as *agni bīja*, the seed or letter signifying fire.

SWAMIJI: No, the whole mantra is *saṁhāra bīja*, because it is destructive.

JOHN: Found in these different points.

SWAMIJI: Yes, because this will carry you only to the *nirodha*, always.

JOHN: It destroys differentiated perception.

SWAMIJI: Yes. But what is the purpose of explaining this sacred Word? The theory of un-manifested Word, what is the purpose of explaining this? This is a question, he puts this question. And for that question he writes this answer in next *śloka*.

LJA TA05K (16:32)

इत्येनया बुधो युक्त्या वर्णजप्यपरायणः ।
अनुत्तरं परं धाम प्रविशेदचिरात् सुधीः ॥ १४७ ॥

ityenayā budho yuktyā varṇajapyaparāyaṇaḥ /
anuttaraṁ paraṁ dhāma praviśedacirāt sudhīḥ //147//

But *sudhīh* is the point. A *sādhaka*, an aspirant, with awareness, he is the hero here. A *sādhaka* without awareness is not the hero, he has no right to practice this practice of Word.

JOHN: These two that we've been explaining on these two pages…

SWAMIJI: Yes.

JOHN:…starting with the…I mean, with the sensation here, the pleasure…

SWAMIJI: Heart.

JOHN:…heart…

SWAMIJI: Throat.

JOHN:…tongue…

SWAMIJI: Not tongue. Palate and lips. *Ityenayā*, *anayā yuktyā*, in this way, *budha* (*budha* means that *sādhaka* who is filled with awareness), *varṇa japya parāyaṇaḥ*, he has not put *varṇa* '*japa*' *parāyaṇaḥ*, he is not reciting the word of mantras, he is reciting the substance of mantras, he is reciting the substance of mantras–*japya*. For instance, "*oṁ namaḥ śivāya*," when you recite "*oṁ namaḥ śivāya*," this *japa*, it is *varṇa 'japa' parāyaṇaḥ*. This way you have not to recite mantra. You have to recite mantra in such a way, when you go deep, when you dive deep in the reality of this Word. That is *japya parāyaṇa*. And that *sādhaka*, that kind of *sādhaka* gets entry in that supreme God consciousness very soon, as soon as possible (*praviśet acirāt sudhīḥ*).

[Abhinavagupta says], I'll explain to you this theory of Word in another way as it is explained in the *Dīkṣottara Tantra*. There is another *tantra*, another *śāstra*, it is nominated as *Dīkṣottara Tantra*.

LJA TA05K (18:50)

वर्णशब्देन नीलादि यद्वा दीक्षोत्तरे यथा।

varṇaśabdena nīlādi yadvā dīkṣottare yathā /148a
(not recited)

Varṇa śabdena nīlādi, while practicing the reality of that supreme un-manifested Word, you have to practice on differentiated colors. It is said in *Dīkṣottara Tantra*s. Differentiated colors, the practice on differentiated colors will also carry you to that un-manifested Word–differentiated colors.

ERNIE: Is there a color for the heart, color for the throat?

SWAMIJI: No, he will say, he will explain it. *Saṁhāranra* (Kashmiri), it is not, it is incorrect. *Samhāranāgnimaruto*.[97]

LJA TA05K (19:34)

संहारनाग्निमरुतो रुद्रबिन्दुयुतान्स्मरेत्॥ १४८॥
हृदये तन्मयो लक्ष्यं पश्येत्सप्तदिनादथ।

saṁhāranāgnimaruto rudrabinduyutānsmaret //148//
hṛdaye tanmayo lakṣyaṁ paśyetsaptadinādatha /

97. Swamiji corrected the published "*saṁhāranrāgnimaruto*" to read "*saṁhāranāgnimaruto*."

For this there is a particular mantra explained in the *Dīkṣottara Tantra*. *Saṁhāra* means *kṣa*, the letter *kṣa* is *saṁhāra*. *Na* is the letter 'm', *ma*. *Agni* is the letter *ra*, 'r'. *Maruta* is the letter *ya*. *Rudra* is the letter *o* or *u*. *Bindu* is the letter *aṁ*. So, collectively they form the mantra, '*kṣmryuṁ*'. *Kṣmryuṁ* is the mantra, it is also a destructive mantra, but it is described in the *Dīkṣottara Tantra*. And this mantra also you have to practice according to the same way as we have already explained how you have to perceive, practice in each and every act. And just to make this clear, he has put the act of sex–just to make it's understanding clear.

JOHN: So these mantras [are] in every perception.

SWAMIJI: Every perception, yes.

JOHN: All these points are there, these different points.

SWAMIJI: When he practices this, when a *sādhaka* (aspirant) practices this mantra, this mantra has charm, this mantra has charm. *Lakṣyaṁ paśyetsaptadinā*, in just after seven days he will perceive the various collection of colors inside his consciousness before getting entry in that un-manifested Word. Before getting entry in that un-manifested Word, he will experience differentiated formations of colors in seven days (*paśyet saptadinādatha*).

LJA TA05K (21:58)

विस्फुलिङ्गाग्निवन्नीलपीतरक्तादिचित्रितम्॥ १४९॥
जाज्वलीति हृदम्भोजे बीजदीपप्रबोधितम्।
दीपवज्ज्वलितो बिन्दुर्भासते विघनार्कवत्॥ १५०॥

visphuliṅgāgnivannīla-pītaraktādicitritam //149//
jājvalīti hṛdambhoje bījadīpaprabodhitam /
dīpavajjvalito bindurbhāsate vighnārkavat //150//
(not recited)

Visphuliṅgāgnivat nīla-pītaraktādicitritam, for instance, when there is a fire lighted, a fire is lighted in full strength, you get so many colors of that flame. In the flame, you perceive so many colors–blue, dark-red, black-red, all these colors are perceived in that lighted flame. *Visphuliṅga agnivat*, like that, *nīla pīta raktādi citritam jājvalīti hṛdambhoje*, in the heart he perceives that, in practice of this Word, he perceives that in the heart first. *Bīja dīpa prabodhitam*, this *bīja*, this mantra will carry you to that state. *Dīpavat jvalito bindurbhāsate vighnārkavat*, and then, after a while, when these are collectively shining, these colors are collectively shining in your heart, then you get entry in that supreme un-manifested Word just like the midday sun–bright!

JOHN: So these colors aren't separate, *alag-alag* (separate).

SWAMIJI: These are *alag-alag* and collective, collectively.

JOHN: They are *alag-alag*?

SWAMIJI: Yes.

JOHN: So then, in each section of this mantra you have one color, attached with one…?

SWAMIJI: No. No, this is a mantra, this is a collective mantra. This is a collective mantra, you have to recite it, just recite it, recite it in the gross way. You have not to recite it…with awareness, yes, but you have to recite it in the gross way, and it will carry you to that…

JOHN: And then those colors will come.

SWAMIJI: Colors will come within seven days. Within seven days, and after seven days, when colors are getting thicker and thicker, thicker and thicker, and you get entry in that final state of un-manifested Word.

ERNIE: But nothing happens without awareness.

SWAMIJI: Nothing happens.

ERNIE: (laughs)

DEVOTEE: So, these colors are not external colors.

SWAMIJI: These are not external. "External," that question does not arise. *Bas*?

DEVOTEE: *Bas*, *mara* (enough, Sir).

SWAMIJI: I think we will do only this much. 151 [is next]. But these *śloka*s we must do before I leave for Jammu. You can't do without it.

ERNIE: This is one of the greatest lectures of all time.

SWAMIJI: I'll finish it today, I have to finish it today.

DEVOTEE: Is it different from *nāda* or the same as *nāda*? The un-manifested Word.

SWAMIJI: Yes, it is just like that. He has explained it in the very beginning, that is *anāhata* (un-struck sound).

DEVOTEE: And it is just one sound or a variety of sounds?

SWAMIJI: No, it is not a variety of sound. It is soundless-sound.

It is not sound, there is not sound at all! It is un-manifested Word.

JOHN: It is like *spanda*.

SWAMIJI: It is *spanda*, it is just throb.

JOHN: Vibration-less vibration.

SWAMIJI: Yes. First try with tasty things.

DENISE: *Achaar* (pickle).

SWAMIJI: Not …*achaar*?

DEVOTEES: (laughter)

SWAMIJI: Have you got that pot?

DENISE: No, I was going to bring it later.

SWAMIJI: *Acha*. By tasting that you have to go to that Word.

JOHN: Sweet things are better at first.

SWAMIJI: Sweet things are *easier* first to understand, to make you understand.

DENISE: *Gulab jamun* (an Indian sweet).

SWAMIJI: *Gulab jamun*? I don't mean that kind of sweetness.

DENISE: Oh!

JOHN: You mean nourishing, like…

SWAMIJI: Like *paneer* (cheese), *paneer* is also sweet. *Dal* (pulses) and *nadru* (lotus root) is also sweet.

JOHN: Coconut.

DEVOTEES: (laughter)

LJA TA05K (26:25)

SWAMIJI: *Nanu evaṁ lakṣyatāmāptenātmanāsya kiṁ syāt* (comm.), when on practicing on this mantra, which is already explained in the 149th and 148th *śloka*, by practicing on that mantra and by experiencing those various colors, different colors (blue, etcetera), what does he get out of that? Out of that, what he experiences in the end? This is the question.

स्वयम्भासात्मनानेन तादात्म्यं यात्यनन्यधीः ।
शिवेन हेमतां यद्वत्ताम्रं सूतेन वेधितम् ॥ १५१ ॥

svayambhāsātmanānena tādātmyaṁ yātyananyadhīḥ /
śivena hematāṁ yadvattāmraṁ sūtena vedhitam //151//

Anena svayambhāsātmanā, this is only a practice meant for *ananyadhīḥ*, the one who is fully aware and one-pointed, and who recites this *śloka*, not through lips, but by awareness just while residing in *svayaṁ prakāśa*, in the state of *svayaṁ prakāśa bhāva*.[98] While experiencing the experiences of these colors, he does not stay in these colors, but these experiences of these colors direct him towards the state of Śiva, Śiva *bhāva*. It is the way just as copper becomes gold (these colors are at the stage of copper), and this process of experiencing, this process of experiencing through the practice of that internal Word is to put that herb on that copper so that it becomes gold.

ERNIE: Herb?

SWAMIJI: There is a special herb which is put on copper and that becomes gold. It is called Śiva, that is Śiva, that is the state of Śiva. And Śiva is gold and these colors are copper. And the state of copper carries them, carries those *sādhaka*s to the state of Śiva, Śiva *bhāva*, but only when the *sādhaka* rests with awareness in that state. Just like *yadvat tāmraṁ sūtena vedhitam*, just like *tāmra* (*tāmra* means, copper), copper is *vedhitam*, purified by this alkaline. You know alkaline?

DEVOTEE: Alchemy.

SWAMIJI: *Pārā, pārā.*

DEVOTEE: *Acha, pārā.*

SWAMIJI: What is *pārā*?

DEVOTEE: Mercury.

SWAMIJI: Mercury?

DEVOTEE: Yes, Sir, mercury.

SWAMIJI: Mercury. Mercury is put in a peculiar way on copper, and that copper becomes gold.

DEVOTEE: Indian alchemy.

SWAMIJI: And this is just like that way, this kind of *sādhanā*.

DEVOTEE: It is found in *Rasāyan Śastra* under alchemy.

SWAMIJI: Yes.

98. The state of Self-luminosity.

LJA TA05K (30:07)

उपलक्षणमेतच्च सर्वमन्त्रेषु लक्षयेत्।

upalakṣaṇametacca sarvamantreṣu lakṣayet /152a

It is not meant only for that mantra, that particular mantra which is explained in the *Dīkṣottara Tantra*.

JOHN: With colors.

SWAMIJI: With colors. It is not only done in that process, it is *sarva mantreṣu lakṣayet*, it is to be done in each and every mantra. Each and every mantra should be practiced in the same way, and get entry in that internal un-manifested Word.

Now he puts the question again: When this is the case of all these mantras…for instance, there are mantras which make you strong, which make your physical body strong (*puṣṭīkārī*), some mantras are which direct you towards death, the death point. When you are angry with somebody and there is some enemy of yours, you put that mantra, you recite that mantra for his death and he dies by that mantra. How can that mantra carry you to that internal Word? That will carry you the point of death, and the other mantra will carry you to the point of strengthening your body. How it happens? I wonder.

This is the question. Now he puts the answer here in next verse.

LJA TA05K (31:49)

यद्यत्सङ्कल्पसम्भूतं वर्णजालं हि भौतिकम्॥ १५२॥
तत् संविदाधिक्यवशादभौतिकमिव स्थितम्।

yadyatsaṅkalpasambhūtaṁ varṇajālaṁ hi bhautikam //152//
tat saṁvidādhikyavaśādabhautikamiva sthitam /

Whatever you think in your mind, any word what you think in your memory, or whatever you utter or recite, any word, and it is, in fact, all those words are *bhautikam*; *bhautikam*, they will carry you to the grossness of the world. For instance, there are some particular mantras, by reciting those mantras you get nourishment in your body. That is *puṣṭīkārī* mantras. Some are *maraṇa* mantras. *Maraṇa* mantras, those which carry you to the point of death, you die by the recitation of those mantras. So all these mantras are *bhautika* mantras, gross. *Tat saṁvit ādhikyavaśāt*, when this awareness is attached, adjusted with all these mantras, when awareness of that internal consciousness is adjusted in all these mantras, all these mantras shine in divinity, they become *abhautikam iva sthitam*, they become *abhautikam*, beyond this grossness. They reside in the spiritual atmosphere and they carry you, they carry you…

DEVOTEE: *Tat saṁvit ādhikyavaśāt.*

SWAMIJI: *Saṁvit ādhikyavaśāt*, when *saṁvit* is adjusted in addition…

DEVOTEE: Does that mean that *saṅkalpa* (intention) will be there when you are reciting a mantra for strengthening your body?

SWAMIJI: Yes.

DEVOTEE: Even when the *saṅkalpa* is there for strengthening the body, still the mantra will carry you inside?

SWAMIJI: It will still carry you inside when there is internal consciousness, when there is internal consciousness, when there is practice of internal un-manifested Word.

JOHN: So then this is the essence of Shaivism, is it not?

SWAMIJI: This is the essence of Shaivism.

JOHN: That with awareness, every wretched act or every good act carries you to that, everything carries you to that.

SWAMIJI:…carries you to that. Everything, everything becomes divine!

JOHN: With awareness.

SWAMIJI: Yes. Because, in fact, what is in this world? What is in this world? It is the outcome of that divinity. It must be divine. In the background, everything is divine, death is divine, life is divine, pain is divine, pleasure is divine, sadness is divine, looting is divine, plundering is divine, marriage is divine, everything is divine in the background, because it has flown out from that divinity. So, that *sādhaka*, that yogi, who concentrates on any mantra, not only those particular mantras explained in the *Dīkṣottara Tantra* and all others, any mantra, any wretched mantra, you can recite any wretched mantra with awareness and take hold of that, the source of its recitation. When you recite it, "*oṁ*" [or] "O bloody fool"…

DEVOTEES: (laughter)

SWAMIJI: "O bloody fool," this is also a mantra, this will become a mantra. "O bloody fool," when you hold, while reciting this "bloody fool," take hold of that source wherefrom it came out from your mouth. It becomes divine. It will carry you to that divinity, to that internal Word.

LJA TA05K (35:39)

अतस्तथाविधे रूपे रूढो रोहति संविदि ॥ १५३ ॥
अनाच्छादितरूपायामनुपाधौ प्रसन्नधीः ।

atastathāvidhe rūpe rūḍho rohati saṁvidi //153//
anācchāditarūpāyām-anupādhau prasannadhīḥ /

So, this person, this yogi, whose intellect has become *prasanna* (*prasanna* means, filled with joy),…*

Whose?

DEVOTEES: This yogi's.

SWAMIJI: Whose yogi's?

ERNIE: With awareness.

SWAMIJI: Yes.

DEVOTEE: Swamiji also.

DENISE: This yogi (indicating Swamiji).

SWAMIJI: *…*tathāvidhe saṁvidi rūḍha*, and who is established already in that consciousness of awareness, *atastathāvidhe saṁvidi rūḍha*, the one who is established in that kind of consciousness, that kind of internal un-manifested Word, who is established in that un-manifested Word, he becomes *prasannadhīḥ*, his intellect becomes joyous, filled with joy, his intellect is always joyous. For instance, if he is dying, he will announce he is dying…

DENISE: Happily.

SWAMIJI:…happily, and he will announce he is dying, and while dying he will be smiling. If he is filled with pain, he will tell you, "Oh, I am filled with, my body is filled with pain!"

DENISE: You've done that before (laughs).
SWAMIJI: And he will be laughing (laughs).
DEVOTEE: *Arohati* means…?
SWAMIJI: No, *rohati. Tathāvidhe rūpe rūḍhaḥ, tathāvidhe rūpe rūḍhaḥ prasannadhīḥ*, the yogi, the yogi who is *prasannadhīḥ*, whose intellect has becomes filled with joy and who has become, who is established in that supreme consciousness, internal supreme consciousness with awareness, he *anācchādita rūpāyām saṁvidi anupādhau rohati*, he *rohati* (*rohati* means, he ascends), ascends in that consciousness, he ascends in that consciousness, he goes up,…

"Ascending" is going up?

…he ascends in that consciousness whose formation is never concealed or covered or absent. That state of consciousness which is never concealed, which is never covered, which is always shining, on that state of consciousness he ascends, that kind of yogi.

DEVOTEE: *Rohati* means?
SWAMIJI: Ascends, (Kashmiri) he moves up.

LJA TA05K (38:44)

नीले पीते सुखे दुःखे संविद्रूपमखण्डितम्॥ १५४॥
गुरुभिर्भाषितं तस्मादुपायेषु विचित्रता।

nīle pīte sukhe duḥkhe saṁvidrūpamakhaṇḍitam //154//
gurubhirbhāṣitaṁ tasmād-upāyeṣu vicitratā /

Our masters have also declared and announced in this whole universe that *saṁvit rūpa*, the state of internal Word, the state of un-manifested Word is perceived in the sameness of its existence in blue, in yellow, in pleasure, in pain. In everything, in everything it is experienced in the same level. *Saṁvit rūpam*, it is *akhaṇḍitam*; *akhaṇḍitam* means, it is never…nowhere less or nowhere more. *Gurubhirbhāṣitam*, it is explained by our masters.

These are Abhinavagupta's words.

It is thus *tasmāt upāyeṣu vicitratā*, it is why we have put forth in public the various ways of entering, various ways of entries in God consciousness: one is *āṇavopāya*, one is *śāktopāya*, one is *śāmbhavopāya*, one is *anupāya*, in this way.

Another *śloka*.

LJA TA05K (40:20)

Evamekasminnevopeye prāptavye paramiyadupāya jātumupadiṣṭam (comm.), so, this, all these classes of means–*āṇavopāya*, *śāktopāya*, *śāmbhavopāya*, *anupāya*–these classes of means are explained here in this body of the *Tantrāloka* just to get entry in that internal Word, supreme consciousness. But one way is the direct way, the other ways are indirect ways, but all are directed towards that point.

JOHN: What is this internal Word called in Sanskrit? *Anāhata*?

SWAMIJI: Huh?

JOHN: This Word, this internal Word, this un-uttered Word, what is it called in Sanskrit? Is there a technical word for this Word in Shaivism?

SWAMIJI: It will be God consciousness, internal God consciousness.

JOHN: For this un-uttered Word.

SWAMIJI: Yes, un-uttered Word. It is *varṇa*.

JOHN: *Varṇa*.

SWAMIJI: *Varṇa tattvaṁ*.

LJA TA05K (41:32)

उच्चारकरणध्यानवर्णैरेभिः प्रदर्शितः ॥ १५५ ॥

अनुत्तरपदप्राप्तावभ्युपायविधिक्रमः ।

uccārakaraṇadhyānavarṇairebhiḥ pradarśitaḥ //155//
anuttarapadaprāptāvabhyupāyavidhikramaḥ /

This is what he says in this *śloka*: This way of *upāya*s is explained just to obtain this state of God consciousness, supreme God consciousness, *anuttara pada prāptau*, just to obtain the supreme state of God consciousness by *uccāra*, first by recitation [of mantra], then by holding organic means (*karaṇa*), the means through the organs (seeing, touching, tasting), and then by doing contemplation (*dhyāna*), then *varṇair*, by going in the depth of that un-manifested Word, by these, *pradarśitaḥ*, it is only explained–what is explained?–it is explained that you have to get entry in that internal Word, un-manifested Word, the state of un-manifested Word.

Now he explains why all these various means are put in this *Tantrāloka*.

LJA TA05K (42:50)

अकिञ्चिच्चिन्तनं वीर्यं भावनायां च सा पुनः ॥ १५६ ॥
ध्याने तदपि चोच्चारे करणे सोऽपि तद्ध्वनौ।
स स्थानकल्पने बाह्यमिति क्रममुपाश्रयेत्॥ १५७ ॥

akiñciccintanaṁ vīryaṁ bhāvanāyāṁ ca sā punaḥ //156//
dhyāne tadapi coccāre karaṇe so'pi taddhvanau /
sa sthānakalpane bāhyamiti kramamupāśrayet //157//

The predominant spiritual semen is *śāmbhavopāya*–the predominant spiritual semen.

DEVOTEE: *Akiñcit cintanaṁ* means *śāmbhavopāya*.

SWAMIJI: *Akiñcit cintanaṁ*, that is *vīryaṁ*, that is the predominant *vīrya*, that is the predominant spiritual semen.

JOHN: Semen is that which gives birth to God consciousness, is it? Is that what they mean by semen?

SWAMIJI: Yes.

JOHN: Semen is that which gives birth…

SWAMIJI:…to God consciousness without flowing out. It flows in. It does not flow out, it flows in, and it does not make you lose energy, it gives energy. The flowing in of this *vīrya* gives you energy. You become more energetic by this. It is why it is called *vīrya*. And that *vīrya* is *nir-vīrya*, because by its flow you become *nirvīrya*, without strength.

JOHN: That other semen that flows out, ordinary semen.

SWAMIJI: Yes. You become just *nirvīrya*. For instance, when that queen bee, virgin queen bee mates with that drone in the air, do you know what happens to that drone after mating? It falls down dead on the ground just after mating. When this is discharged in the organ of that *devī*...

Who is that *devī*?

DEVOTEES: Queen bee.

SWAMIJI:...queen bee (laughs), then he falls down dead. So it is not *vīrya* at all. It is *vīrya*, it flows in and gives you strength. So, this *śāmbhavopāya* is the predominant spiritual *vīrya*, spiritual semen. *Bhāvanāyāṁ ca sā, bhāvanāyāṁ ca*, and *bhāvanāyāṁ*, this *vīrya* becomes stronger and stronger by *śāktopāya*, by adopting *śāktopāya*. This spiritual semen of *śāmbhavopāya* becomes strengthened by the adoption of *śāktopāya*. And *śāktopāya*, the *vīrya* of *śāktopāya* gets strength by *dhyāna*, *dhyāne*. *Tadapi coccāre*, and that *dhyāna* gets predominance by *uccāra*, by the recitation of breath. And the spiritual semen of that *uccāra* gets strength by the means of *karaṇa upāsana*. And the *vīrya* of *karaṇa upāsana*, this spiritual semen of that *karaṇa upāsana*, which you have already been explained, *karaṇa upāsana*, the sevenfold way of *karaṇa upāsana*, that *vīrya* gets predominance by this internal Word, and that internal Word, un-manifested Word, the *vīrya* of that un-manifested Word gets strengthened by *sthāna kalpanā* (*sthāna kalpanā* is putting awareness on some point: the throat, *bhrukuṭi*[99], or the heart, or something, which will be explained in 6th *āhnika*). *Iti kramam upāśrayet*, but this is the way we have put these *upāya*s.

JOHN: So then *sthāna kalpanā* in this order is lowest.

SWAMIJI: Lower, yes.

JOHN: Then *varṇa tattva*.

SWAMIJI: Yes.

JOHN: Then *karaṇa upāsana*.

SWAMIJI: No, then *varṇa tattva*. *Varṇa tattva* is higher. Higher than *varṇa tattva* is *karaṇa upāsana*, higher than *karaṇa upāsana* is *uccāra*, higher than *uccāra* is *dhyāna*, this *dhyāna*!

JOHN: Now which *dhyāna* is that? This *dhyāna* of this heart, this...?

SWAMIJI: No, no, *kadalī sampuṭākāram*, that internal, that supreme *dhyāna* which is already explained in the first part of this book–that, the banana fruit, that *dhyāna*.

---

99. Between the two eyebrows.

JOHN: Self-fertilizing.

SWAMIJI: Yes. And that *dhyāna* gets...then that *dhyāna* is *śāktopāya*, and from *śāktopāya* you have to rise to *akiñcit cintanaṁ.*

JOHN: So the *āṇavopāya sādhaka* travels through these.

SWAMIJI: Yes. *Āṇavopāya*, from *dhyāna*, from *dhyāna* he...no, from *sthāna kalpanā* he travels to that un-manifested Word, from un-manifested Word...*

[The dog] has again come.

DENISE: Oh, Rosie! Get out of here.

SWAMIJI: (laughs) He loves you very much. Love is blind (laughs).

*...and [from] that un-manifested Word, you have to rise to *karaṇa upāsana*, from *karaṇa upāsana* you have to rise to *uccāra*. *Uccāra*, not ordinary recitation as we do.

JOHN: No, no, this divine flow of breath.

SWAMIJI: No, the *uccāra* which is already explained here in this book. And that *uccāra* will carry you to that supreme *dhyāna*, supreme contemplation, and that contemplation will carry you to *bhāvanā* (which is explained in *śāktopāya*),...

JOHN: Fourth *āhnika.*

SWAMIJI:...and from that you will rise to *śāmbhavopāya*, and resting in *śāmbhavopāya* you are one with Śiva.

JOHN: So *cakrodaya*, is that the combination of *sthāna kālpana* and *varṇa tattva*?

SWAMIJI: Yes, these are offshoots of *sthāna kalpanā*, not *varṇa tattva.*

JOHN: Not *varna tattva*. That's higher.

SWAMIJI: No, *cakrodaya* is lower.

JOHN: It exists in *sthāna kalpanā* then.

SWAMIJI: It is in *sthāna kalpanā*, *cakrodaya* is in *sthāna kalpanā*. These are the offshoots of *sthāna kalpanā* that we start. We have to start with the...don't get worried about it.

DEVOTEES: (laughter)

SWAMIJI: You will reach to that point (laughs).

DEVOTEE: When you say *śāmbhavopāya* becomes stronger by *śāktopāya*, does it mean the *vīrya* of *śāmbhavopāya* becomes stronger through *śāktopāya*?

SWAMIJI: Yes. Because when you jump in the field of *śāmbhavopāya* at once, you will lose everything there because there is no hold.

You must have full hold on it first before you practice on *śāmbhavopāya*. *Śāmbhavopāya* is not a joke!

DEVOTEES: (laughter)

SWAMIJI: For getting strength to practice on *śāmbhavopāya*, you have to adopt *śāktopāya*. For getting strength in *śāktopāya*, you have to contemplate on this meditation (*dhyāna*). And for getting the strength of *dhyāna*, you have to contemplate on *uccāra* (that is, *nijānanda*, *nirānanda*, [*parānanda*, *brahmānanda*], *mahānanda*, *cidānanda*, *jagadānanda*, all these *ānanda* states). And for achievement of that, you have to adopt the *upāsana* of *karaṇa upāsana*, sevenfold *karaṇa upāsana*. For sevenfold *karaṇa upāsana*, you have to go to that internal Word, un-manifested Word. And for gaining the state of un-manifested Word, that consciousness, maintenance of consciousness on un-manifested Word, you have to do this *sthāna kalpanā*, *cakrodaya*, and all these what we do already. It is all divine!

JOHN: This *śāmbhava sādhaka*, he has such a strength of awareness he doesn't take anything for support.

SWAMIJI: No, he just *akiñcit cintana*, he just…

JOHN: He is, he just is.

SWAMIJI: Yes. *Dhyāne tadapi coccāre karaṇe so'pi taddhvanau*–it is "*dhvanau*", it is not "*hanau*"–*sa sthānakalpane bāhyamiti kramamupāśrayet*, this *krama* is to be adopted.

JOHN: This order of things, of rising.

SWAMIJI: Rising, this order, yes. So, you must rise, you must not fall. It is the question of degradation, when you are reverted, when you get reversion. So don't jump to the highest job. Don't jump to *śāmbhavopāya*, you will be reverted down. It is a disgrace. You must get a promotion; on the contrary, you must get a promotion. So, try on *cakrodaya* and you will rise by-and-by. This is the way, *iti krama upāśrayet*, this is the reality of how to adopt this *abhyāsa* (practice).

LJA TA05K (52:33)

लङ्घनेन परो योगी मन्दबुद्धिः क्रमेण तु।

laṅghanena paro yogī mandabuddhiḥ krameṇa tu /158a

(not recited)

But there are such yogis, there are some yogis who cross this order, they cross this order. For instance, Vivekānanda. He couldn't maintain that awareness on *cakrodaya*. When he was ordered by his master to remain on the practice of *cakrodaya*, he just in some minutes he passed that sphere of *cakrodaya*, because he was internally great, so he was ordered by his master to go on that internal Word. And doing that practice, he surpassed that also, because he was divine, internally he was divine, in his background. So, it is *laṅghana*, it is the way of *laṅghana*, it is a crossing. There are some great souls who cross, they cross just in an instant, instantaneously they cross these states.

JOHN: They go from the lowest to the highest.

SWAMIJI:...highest at once. *Laṅghano paro yogī*, by that crossing, you must understand that that kind of yogi is a supreme yogi. *Manda buddhi krameṇa tu*, and that yogi who cannot cross easily, and who does the same practice day after day, day after day, going on doing it, go on doing it, and gets more and more joy, that is *manda buddhiḥ*. You should not call him a great yogi, he is not a great yogi.

JOHN: He has an inferior intellect? What is that *manda*...?

SWAMIJI: *Manda buddhi*, with inferior awareness. His awareness is not so dense. For instance, "This is Lakṣmanjoo, this is Lakṣmanjoo, this is Lakṣmanjoo," you know, some people who say, "This is Lakṣmanjoo, this is Lakṣmanjoo," only two times they say, "This is Lakṣmanjoo" and then say, "This is a shovel, this is a garden, this is...," and then they divert their attention again, "This is Lakṣmanjoo, this is Lakṣmanjoo," and then after two or three impulses they again go astray. But there are some yogis who say, "This is Lakṣmanjoo" just for half an hour constantly without interruption of any other...

JOHN: Thought.

SWAMIJI:...foreign matter. But just after half an hour, they go, they sink in that foreign matter again.

DENISE: And they have to go back again.

SWAMIJI: They have to divert again. And the supreme yogi never falls from that awareness. It is why, it is how our great master, grand-master, Swami Rām, practiced yoga for twenty years in one place just to develop that strength of one-pointedness. One-pointedness, to develop one-pointedness, these are not mere words. It is a great work, great job to do. But by the grace of a master, you will succeed–promise.

DEVOTEES: (laughter)
SWAMIJI:

LJA TA05K (56:27)

वीर्यं विना यथा षण्ठस्तस्याप्यस्त्यथ वा बलम्।
मृतदेह इवेयं स्याद्बाह्यान्तःपरिकल्पना॥ १५८॥

vīryaṁ vinā yathā ṣaṇṭhastasyāpyastyatha vā balam /
mṛtadeha iveyaṁ syādbāhyāntaḥ parikalpanā //158//

So he has put three sections of this strength of awareness. Those who maintain the strength of awareness, they are classified in three classes: one is supreme, one is medium, one is inferior. The supreme is that [yogi] who has got perfect spiritual semen, developed perfect spiritual semen. And medium is that [yogi] who has got, who has no semen, no spiritual semen, but still some strength of practicing, but not that spiritual semen. And there are such yogis who have no semen at all. You have to push them, the master has to push them each and every moment: "Go on, go on, go on, yes, yes, go on."

DEVOTEES: (laughter)

SWAMIJI: Without giving you a sitting, you will do nothing.

JOHN: You mean a person wouldn't even try. Is that the idea that this person wouldn't even…?

SWAMIJI: He will do, [but] he will do nothing (laughs), internally he will do nothing, he will only try. So the master has to push him again and again, again and again, just with a whip.

DEVOTEES: (laughter)

SWAMIJI: (laughs)

LJA TA05K (58:13) end
LJA TA05L (00:00) start

A man who is a perfect man with full semen, or a man without semen (that is *ṣaṇṭha*, a eunuch), and the third category is a dead person, a dead person. For instance, *vīryaṁ vinā yathā ṣaṇṭha* (*ṣaṇṭha* means, eunuch), a eunuch has no *vīrya*, he has no semen inside, nothing is stored there in that person. Which person?

DEVOTEES: Eunuch.

SWAMIJI: Eunuch. Just like that, our bull.

DEVOTEES: (laughs)

SWAMIJI: But *tasyāpyastyatha vā balam*, but he has also strength, some other strength by which you were afraid [of the bull].

DENISE: Yes! (laughs)

SWAMIJI: He has also some strength. Who? The eunuch. The eunuch person also has some strength, but not this kind of strength, *vīrya* is not there, semen is not there. There is other quarrelling strength, going here and there, this kind of strength.

ERNIE: Lifting rocks.

SWAMIJI: Yes. And there is another: *mṛta deha*. *Mṛta deha* means, a dead body. A dead body has no *vīrya* and no strength. If he is shot by a bullet…

Which?

DENISE: The dead body.

SWAMIJI:…the dead body, he won't…

DENISE: Respond.

SWAMIJI:…he won't respond anything. He won't say, "why." So this is how *sādhaka*s live in this world. Some are absolutely dead and a master has to give him a push, always a push, pushing him, pushing him, by a mental push, by preaching, by doing all this, and he rises. Because as long as a master has taken the burden of his disciples, he has to do their job. He won't be liberated unless his disciples are liberated. So this is the master's worry to look after his disciples. So don't worry about it.

DEVOTEES: (laughter)

SWAMIJI: So it is *bāhya kalpanā*, *antara kalpanā* and *antaratama kalpanā*. *Antaratama kalpanā* is meant for *śāmbhava sādhaka*s, *antar kalpanā* is meant for *śākta sādhaka*s, and *bāhya kalpanā* is meant for *āṇava sādhaka*s.

JOHN: So *āṇava sādhaka*s are all dead bodies.

SWAMIJI: Just like dead bodies, but they are pushed, they are forced to push.

DEVOTEE: *Bāhya kalpanā…*?

SWAMIJI: *Bāhya kalpanā*, *antar kalpanā* and *antaratama kalpanā*. *Antaratama kalpanā* is meant for *śāmbhava sādhaka*s, *antar kalpanā* is meant for *śākta sādhakas*, and *bāhya kalpanā* is meant for *āṇava sādhakas*.

JOHN: So *bāhya kalpanā* means?

SWAMIJI: External *kalpanā*, those who are residing in the external world.

JOHN: Completely.

SWAMIJI: Completely.

JOHN: And this *antar kalpanā*, he is existing inside and outside both.

SWAMIJI:...and outside both.

JOHN: And that other one?

SWAMIJI: *Antaratama kalpanā*, extreme, to the top of internal state.

ERNIE: Can a dead body become a eunuch?

SWAMIJI: (laughs) A dead body is worse than a eunuch.

ERNIE: No, but can...?

DENISE:...he rise to [be a] eunuch?

SWAMIJI: Yes, yes, yes, yes, he will get...no, he will get rise. It is only an example just to make you understand. You are not actually dead.

ERNIE: No, I know, but...

SWAMIJI: You have life and I will produce that force in you so that you rise, not only to this, but to the *śāmbhavopāya* state in the end.

ERNIE: But that's why the master pushes, is to make him come to the eunuch level.

SWAMIJI: Yes. He has to do, he has to do, he has to do, he is a shepherd. He is a shepherd! "Shepherd" you know?

ERNIE: Chauffeur.

JOHN: Shepherd, shepherd, shepherd.

SWAMIJI: He has got all these sheep and he [directs them], "*sh, sh, sh, sh.*"

DEVOTEES: (laughter)

SWAMIJI: (laughs) A wonderful lecture it was today.

DENISE: *Bhaa, bhaa* (mimicking a sheep).

SWAMIJI: Huh?

DENISE: *Bhaa, bhaa.*

SWAMIJI: Yes (laughs).

DEVOTEES: (laughter)

SWAMIJI: It is why Lord Śiva is called Paśupati.

JOHN: Oh, the Lord of animals.

SWAMIJI: Lord of animals, the animal kingdom.

LJA TA05L (05:10)

इत्याणवेऽनुत्तरताभ्युपायः प्रोक्तो नयः स्पष्टपथेन बाह्यः ॥ १५९ ॥

ityāṇave'nuttaratābhyupāyaḥ prokto nayaḥ spaṣṭapathena bāhyaḥ //159//

The last ending *śloka*.

Ityāṇave, so this way, in *āṇavopāya*, I have put here the supreme means of entering in God consciousness, *spaṣṭapathena bāhyaḥ*, which is actually residing in the external state of God consciousness, it is the external state.

JOHN: External state.

SWAMIJI: *Sthāna kalpanā.*

JOHN: Not in the *jagadānanda.*

SWAMIJI: No.

JOHN: No, in the external state of this *bāhya kalpanā.*

SWAMIJI: Yes. Now *bāhya kalpanā* will be explained in the next chapter.

LJA TA05L (05:51)

Discussion:

DEVOTEE: (Speaking in Kashmiri)

SWAMIJI: Yes…no, no, we will do.

ERNIE: What are they saying?

SWAMIJI: They say to explain that next *āhnika* after the birthday. It will be too late.

JOHN: We have so many years of work.

SWAMIJI: Yes. It must be finished before I die.

JOHN: You said a few days ago you are going to translate all the important texts of Shaivism. What does that mean? What texts are those?

SWAMIJI: Huh?

JOHN: Which texts do you consider to be the important texts of Shaivism? *Tantrāloka*?

SWAMIJI: *Tantrāloka*, *Parātriṁśikā*, *Pratyabhijñā*, and *Mahārthamañjarī*. *Mahārthamañjarī* is also very tasty.

JOHN: Will you translate *Mālinīvijaya* [*Tantra*]?

SWAMIJI: No, *Mālinīvijaya* is not to be translated. *Mālinīvijaya* is this, you know "board"? Signboard. *Mālinīvijaya* is the signboard of all Shaivism.

JOHN: Directing sign.

SWAMIJI: Directing s-...it is not understandable. It is why Abhinavagupta has put only a *vārtika* (commentary) on it, he has not translated the *Mālinīvijaya*.

JOHN: He hasn't. Word-by-word, he hasn't explained word-by-word.

SWAMIJI: No, no, he has translated it in another formation–the *Mālinīvijaya*.

ERNIE: What is that?

SWAMIJI: That is the *Tantrāloka*. The *Tantrāloka* is the expansion, explanation of *Mālinīvijaya*–the whole *Tantrāloka*, thirty-seven *āhnika*s.

ERNIE: So who understands that text?

SWAMIJI: The one who has understood the *Tantrāloka*, he has understood that. If you once understand and go through all these thirty-seven *āhnika*s, you can understand it. The *Tantrāloka* is the chief thing to be understood.

JOHN: So you couldn't read the *Mālinīvijaya* with us.

SWAMIJI: Yes, after the *Tantrāloka* is finished.

JOHN: It is possible to read it, but you couldn't translate it. It is not meant to be translated, but you could...

SWAMIJI: I will only give these signs, [that] this is this *āhnika*, this is that *āhnika*, this is that *āhnika*. In the *Mālinīvijaya*, when you read that, I will just put this memory in your brain that this is this chapter of the *Tantrāloka*, this is that chapter of the *Tantrāloka*. In this way I can explain it. *Mālinīvijaya* is only the key of Shaivism. Nobody has understood it. Only a few yogis: Abhinavagupta, my master, grand-master, and myself.

DEVOTEES: (laughter)

SWAMIJI: (laughs) I am joking. You will also understand it.

DENISE: What?

SWAMIJI: You will also understand it. Everybody will understand, who has come near me. You'll carry it?

JOHN: I'll keep it here, Sir.

LJA TA05L (09:50) end

Jai Guru Dev

Appendix

In a letter concerning the meaning of the Aghora mantra and the description of Svacchandanātha (dated: June 13th 1989), Swamiji gave the following explanation of the *piṇḍanātha* mantra:

Chart of mantra by parts	**Chart of *śloka* by parts**	**Chart of *kuṇḍalinī* by parts**
When a yogi melts the *prameya* (objective world) in the world of *pramāṇa* (cognition), this is indicated in the first *bīja* (seed) mantra of *piṇḍanātha* (*r*).	*śiva nabhasi vigalitākṣaḥ* When all *sādhakā*'s or aspirant's organs are melted and vanished in the vacuum of God consciousness, Lord Śiva.	When a yogi's *prāṇa* and *apāna* enters in *suṣumnā*, the central vein (*madhyadhām* or *madhya nādi*).
pramāṇasya mita-pramatṛ samāveśa This stage of yoga is indicated in *piṇḍanātha*'s *mantra bīja* (*kṣ*).	*kuṇḍalinyunmeṣa vikasitānandaḥ* When *kuṇḍalinī* rises and he experiences highest bliss all-round shining with ecstasy and *ānanda* (bliss).	From *mūlādhāra* to *brahmarandra*, when *kuṇḍalinī* (serpent power) rises straight upwards.
At this stage, limited *pramātṛ* (subject) gets entry in *para pramātṛ* (supreme subject) and this state of *samādhi* is indicated in the *bīja mantra* of *piṇḍanātha* in *kh*.	*prajvalita sakala randhraḥ* When all the nine openings of the organs are in their glamorous state (when *urdhva kuṇḍalinī* is functioning).	When *ūrdhā kuṇḍalinī* is blooming, then right from *mūlādhāra* up to *brahmarandhra* all his organs begin to bloom in God consciousness (*praveśa* and *prasarā*).

[*Kārmini*] is called *kriyā śakti*, and by this you have to notice the *svātantrya śakti* of Lord Śiva which is called the mixing state of triple energies. This state represents *piṇḍanātha* (*e*) or *yoni bīja.*	*kāminyā hṛdaya-kuharam-adhi-rūḍaḥ* (*etat traya samāveśah śivo bhairava uccate*, TĀ 3.172) When the energy of will, knowledge and action are mixed or united with each other. This is the [*nirañjana dhāma*]. You will never come down from this state.	*ūrdhva kuṇḍalinyām saṅkoca-vikāsa-prādurbhāva* When a yogi gets entry in *urdha kuṇḍalinī*, then he experiences *vikāsa* (expansion) and *saṅkoca* (contraction) simultaneously. This is the highest state of limited being united with unlimited Being.
avibhāga-vedanātmaka bindu-sattā This is the state of the point (*ṁ*) which cannot be explained in words, only by feeling; not that also, but by becoming.	*yogi śūnya ivāste* In this state, the yogi remains just absorbed with nothing that is something which can neither be seen nor felt, but just [is].	*samādhi vyutthānato saṁ-rasi-bhāvaḥ* This is that state of *kuṇḍalinī* where remaining in *samādhi* or in external worldly activities are absolutely undifferentiated.
piṇḍanātha-mantrasya *kāla-saṁkarṣiṇi-dhāmatayā varṇam* In conclusion: The *piṇḍanātha* mantra, *r-kṣ-kh-e-ṁ*, is that mantra of *ma-ha-a*, which sentences a yogi to the state of God consciousness where time has no existence.	*tasya svayam eva* *yoginī hṛdayam, hṛdaya-nabho-maṇḍalagaṁ-samuccaratyanala-koṭi-śata-diptam* To that heroic yogi, the real heart of *yoginīs* is experienced without any *sadhanā* (practice); on the contrary, it is experienced as this state which was already there–it was his real nature.	*jagadānanda daśāyāḥ* *prasphuṭi-bhāvaḥ* The state of *jagadānanda* is explained in the 5th *āhnika* of the *Tantrāloka* on page 354. This state of *jagadānanda* is the cream of the *piṇḍanātha* mantra.

In fact, *mantra vīrya* is vividly present in *parā-bīja*, *sauḥ* (*sa-au-aḥ*) in the form of *ahaṁ* mantra. This is the state of *vikāsa*, flowing in the worldly state. Also a yogi can experience the *saṅkoca*, the winding-up state in the mantra of *piṇḍanātha*, in *r-kṣ-kh-e-ṁ*, in the mantra, *ma-ha-a*, rising to God consciousness. Both ways are the nature of Lord Śiva.

Prāṇa Tattva Samuccāra from Tantrāloka 5.43-53

The Seven States of Ānanda

<table>
<tr><th>State</th><th>Experience</th><th>Prāṇa</th><th>Pramātṛ</th></tr>
<tr><td>nijānanda</td><td>“the bliss of your own self”</td><td>prāṇa becomes more refined</td><td>sakala</td></tr>
<tr><td colspan="4">After one-pointed practice, the breath become more and more subtle and a yogi experiences a state of giddiness (śūnyatā) where his awareness is disconnected for a moment. This is entering the ‘gap’ momentarily.</td></tr>
<tr><td>nirānanda</td><td>“devoid of limited bliss”</td><td>prāṇa vṛtti becomes prāṇana state when śūnyatā (voidness) appears in its fullness</td><td>vijñāna
kala
sṛṣṭi</td></tr>
<tr><td colspan="4">The yogi experiences a kind of intoxication where his awareness gets established in that voidness (the gap), which is a state of stable giddiness. Here the yogi experiences hideous sounds and furious forms.</td></tr>
<tr><td>parānanda</td><td>“the bliss of breathing”</td><td>apāna vṛtti becomes apānana state</td><td>Śuddha
vidyā
sthiti</td></tr>
<tr><td colspan="4">Breathing becomes full of bliss and joy; the balling of breath in lambikā sthāna (right side of the throat-pit). Here the yogi feels drowned in the sound of that blissful state. All differentiated perception of the objective and cognitive world (prameya-pramāṇa) is gathered in one ball at the junctions of the four passages of lambikā sthāna (apprehension of death occurs). Here, fearful forms and apparitions subside.</td></tr>
</table>

<table>
<tr><td>brahm-
ānanda</td><td>“the bliss which is all-pervading”</td><td>samāna prāṇa to
samānana vṛtti</td><td>Īśvara
samhāra</td></tr>
<tr><td colspan="4">When everything is completely balled in one point and breathing in and out (prāṇāpāna) is finished completely, then there is no fear and he is absolutely filled with the state of joy and bliss. That is the state of samānana vṛtti.</td></tr>
<tr><td>mahānanda</td><td>“the great bliss”</td><td>udāna prāṇa to
udānana vṛtti</td><td>Sadāśiva
tirodhāna</td></tr>
<tr><td colspan="4">The breath which is balled gets melted in that blissful sound, Ssssssssss, and everything rushes inside and the yogi experiences super-sexual joy, and he gets dissolved in the supreme light (tejas). Here the breath enters the central vein and sips down to mūlādhāra. From this point, everything is automatic–bhramavega, the unknown force penetrates mūlādhāra.</td></tr>
<tr><td>cidānanda</td><td>“the bliss of consciousness”</td><td>urdhva kuṇḍalinī dhama
vyāna vṛtti</td><td>Śiva/Śakti
anugraha</td></tr>
<tr><td colspan="4">This is mahā vyāpti, the great pervasion, where you pervade this whole universe. Not only the existence of universe is pervaded, but also the negation of the universe is also pervaded there. There is no adjustment (upādi) of any foreign element here. This is the rise of cit kuṇḍalinī from mūlādhāra to brahmarandhra. Krama mudrā starts from here. It is the bridge between anugraha and the anākhya state.</td></tr>
<tr><td>jagadānanda</td><td>“universal bliss”</td><td></td><td>Parama
śiva
anākhya</td></tr>
<tr><td colspan="4">When cidānanda expands inside and outside, that is the establishment of krama mudrā. Here God consciousness is not felt, it becomes your nature.</td></tr>
</table>

(1) The state (the gap) is revealed when you are aware between sleeping and waking.

(2) That is the point when your awareness is maintained, it is not disconnected. This the state of *spandana*, where awareness is maintained in voidness (*śūnyatā*).

(3) "Just close your eyes tightly, or close your ear openings tightly, and you will hear that sound from inside. It is that kind of sound of sexual intercourse. That is the sound of *apānana* that gives you joy, happiness, entire bliss." Swamiji, TĀ 5.45 commentary. In the *Secret Supreme* audio, Swamiji says, "*parānanda* is in-between *vijñānākala* and Śuddhavidyā."

(4) In the *Trika Śāstra Rahasya Prakriyā*, in the section on *prāṇa tattva uccāra*, Swamiji has listed *prāṇa* as *sṛṣṭi*, *apāna* as *tirodhāna*, *samāna* as *sthiti*, *udāna* as *saṁhāra*, and *vyāna* as *anugraha*.

(5) In this state, there is no room for any *jaḍa rūpata*, any unconscious formation or unconscious state. In *cidānanda*, nothing is excluded because *cidānanda* includes everything in its Being.

NOTE: One has to become an expert in *anuttara dhyāna*-based worship, then only can he do *prāṇa tattva samuccāra* practice.

Bibliography

Published text of Lakshmanjoo Academy Book Series:

Essence of the Supreme Reality, Abhinavagupta's Paramārthasāra, with the commentary of Yogarāja, original video recording (Lakshmanjoo Academy Book Series, Los Angeles, 2015).

Bhagavad Gita in the Light of Kashmir Shaivism (with original video), ed. John Hughes (Lakshmanjoo Academy Book Series, Los Angeles, 2015).

Festival of Devotion and Praise, Shivastotrāvali, Hymns to Shiva by Utpaladeva, ed. John Hughes (Lakshmanjoo Academy Book Series, Los Angeles, 2015).

Kashmir Shaivism, The Secret Supreme, ed. John Hughes (Lakshmanjoo Academy Book Series, Los Angeles, 2015).

Light on Tantra in Kashmir Shaivism, Abhinavagupta's Tantrāloka, Vol. One, chapter 1, ed. John Hughes (Lakshmanjoo Academy, Los Angeles, 2017).

Light on Tantra in Kashmir Shaivism, Abhinavagupta's Tantrāloka, Vol. Two, chapters 2 & 3, ed. John Hughes (Lakshmanjoo Academy, Los Angeles, 2019).

Light on Tantra in Kashmir Shaivism, Abhinavagupta's Tantrāloka, Vol. Three, Chapter 4, ed. Viresh Hughes (Lakshmanjoo Academy, Damascus OR, 2023).

Self Realization in Kashmir Shaivism, The Oral Teachings of Swami Lakshmanjoo, ed. John Hughes (State University of New York Press, Albany, 1995).

Shiva Sutras, The Supreme Awakening, ed. John Hughes (Lakshmanjoo Academy Book Series, Los Angeles, 2015).

Stava Cintāmaṇi of Bhaṭṭanārāyaṇa, ed. John Hughes (Lakshmanjoo Academy Book Series, Los Angeles, 2018).

The Mystery of Vibrationless Vibration in Kashmir Shaivism, Vasugupta's *Spanda Kārikā* and Kṣemarāja's *Spanda Sandoha*, ed. John Hughes (Lakshmanjoo Academy, Los Angeles, 2016).

Vijñāna Bhairava, The Manual for Self Realization, ed. John Hughes (Lakshmanjoo Academy Book Series, Los Angeles, 2015).
Wisdom of Kashmir Shaivism, ed. Viresh Hughes (Lakshmanjoo Academy Book Series, Los Angeles, 2024

Unpublished Texts From the Lakshmanjoo Academy (LJA) Archive:

Bhagavad Gītārtha Saṁgraha of Abhinavagupta, translation and commentary by Swami Lakshmanjoo (original audio recording, LJA archive, Los Angeles, 1978).
Interview on Kashmir Shaivism, Swami Lakshmanjoo with Scholars and John Hughes (original audio recordings, LJA archive, Los Angeles 1980).
Janmamaraṇavicāragranthaḥ, Janma Maraṇa Vicāra of Bhaṭṭa Vāmadeva, Swami Lakshmanjoo (original audio recording, LJA archive, Los Angeles, 1980).
Parātrīśikā Laghuvṛtti, with the commentary of Abhinavagupta, translation and commentary by Swami Lakshmanjoo (original audio recording, LJA archive, Los Angeles, 1982).
Parātrīśikā Vivaraṇa, with the commentary of Abhinavagupta, translation and commentary by Swami Lakshmanjoo (original audio recording, LJA archive, Los Angeles, 1982-85).
Shri Kramanaya Pradīpikā, Shining Light on the Twelve Kālīs, by Swami Lakshmanjoo (Hindi), 1958. English translation by Pranath Kaul, 2003 (LJA archive).
The Tantrāloka of Abhinavagupta, Chapters 6 to 20, translation and commentary by Swami Lakshmanjoo (original audio recording, LJA archive, Los Angeles, 1972-1981).
Vātūlanātha Sūtras of Anantaśaktipāda, translation and commentary by Swami Lakshmanjoo (original audio recordings, LJA archive, Los Angeles, 1979).

Index

A

Abhinavagupta 1, 8, 41, 44, 52, 53, 56, 98, 112, 122, 163, 164, 203, 208, 215, 218, 219, 228, 236, 247, 255, 266

Abhyāsa 42, 198

Acceptance 67

Accomplished 157

Adharma 216

Aghora 268

Agni 30, 31, 96, 108, 115, 127, 135, 245

Ahaṁ 89, 91, 92, 93, 96, 133, 134, 136, 149, 189, 222, 223, 224, 225, 226, 270

Ahaṁ 34, 149, 222, 224, 225

Ahaṁkāra 8, 9, 40

Ajaḍa 15, 16

Alchemy 251

Amṛta 107, 108, 111

Anākhya 34, 35, 69, 70, 71, 80, 107, 161, 271

Ānanda 57, 58, 60, 62, 64, 66, 68, 69, 70, 73, 75, 123, 127, 128, 168, 169, 174, 177, 178, 179, 180, 181, 182, 183, 184, 196, 197, 199, 200, 244, 260, 268, 271

Anāśritaśiva 116, 117

Āṇavamala 177

Āṇavopāya 1, 4, 7, 13, 14, 20, 21, 26, 27, 30, 45, 48, 55, 66, 159, 167, 198, 200, 201, 224, 225, 243, 256, 259, 265

Anger 238

Animal 264

Antaḥstha 115

Aṇu 7, 153, 154, 158

Anugraha 39, 40, 41, 52, 71, 271, 272

Anupāya 42, 43, 44, 55, 86, 101, 102, 103, 159, 192, 194, 202, 256

Anuttara 36, 37, 42, 55, 56, 89, 92, 108, 113, 114, 256, 272

Anxieties 23

Apāna 25, 26, 30, 32, 33, 56, 60, 61, 62, 63, 64, 73, 74, 79, 90, 270, 272

Apāna 60, 61

Apānana 56, 60, 61, 64, 69, 73, 90, 270, 272

Apavedya 9

Apparitions 62, 270

Arka 33, 35

Aspirant 46, 124, 165, 166, 173, 218, 246, 248, 268

Astonishment 55, 144

Ātma 10, 19, 89, 153, 164, 174, 175, 193, 194

Ātma 153, 154, 195

Attachment 116, 117, 155, 167, 168, 176, 241

Avayakta 185

Avyakta 185, 186, 187, 188, 189, 190, 191, 192, 193, 194, 195, 196, 199, 220

Awareness 2, 3, 4, 15, 16, 17, 18, 23, 29, 30, 39, 41, 42, 50, 51, 57, 58, 59, 60, 61, 62, 64, 67, 68, 69, 70, 71, 72, 74, 75, 76, 85, 91, 92, 94, 96, 123, 124, 128, 139, 154, 178, 190, 191, 194, 195, 198, 204, 205, 207, 210, 211, 212, 214, 215, 216, 224, 227, 231, 232, 234, 240, 241, 242, 246, 249, 251, 253, 254, 255, 258, 260, 261, 262, 270, 272

B

Beautified 82

Bhairava 6, 12, 31, 32, 41, 51, 55, 85, 89, 98, 125, 127, 187, 227, 269

Bhairavī 55, 85, 138, 166, 167, 168, 184, 185

Bhakti 14

Bhāva 8, 9, 21, 33, 34, 57, 58, 59, 60, 61, 80, 84, 85, 86, 93, 96, 97, 98, 100, 104, 105, 106, 107, 109, 112, 120, 121, 122, 133, 134, 135, 136, 143, 150, 151, 152, 154, 188, 190, 191, 214, 223, 231, 232, 251

Bhāvā 152

Bhāvanā 167, 259

Bheda 45, 193, 194, 195, 204, 205

Bhoga 3

Bhrūbindu 81, 82

Bhujaṅgavat 103

Bhūmi 62, 79, 123

Bīja 79, 80, 88, 89, 115, 135, 196, 222, 235, 244, 245, 246, 249, 268, 269, 270

Bindu 81, 135, 248, 269

Bliss 18, 45, 46, 47, 50, 51, 57, 60, 62, 63, 64, 65, 86, 92, 103, 127, 145, 155, 168, 169, 174, 199, 268, 270, 271, 272

Blissful 47, 117, 130, 200, 202, 203, 270, 271

Bodha 107, 108, 141, 142, 143, 144, 182

Bondage 37, 175, 179

Brahma 87, 90, 91, 92, 210

Brahmacārins 126

Brahmānanda 62, 66, 70, 260

Breath 7, 9, 10, 11, 14, 15, 19, 21, 22, 23, 24, 25, 26, 27, 32, 56, 57, 58, 61, 62, 63, 68, 71, 72, 74, 75, 76, 77, 78, 80, 122, 133, 134, 141, 147, 148, 149, 151, 152, 153, 177,

205, 207, 222, 258, 259, 270, 271
Buddhi 7, 8, 9, 10, 14, 19, 22, 23, 24, 27, 35, 40, 41, 42, 53, 93, 141, 261
Buddhist 2
Burden 263
Burning 163, 205
C
Caitanyaṁ 19
Cakita 55, 142
Cakra 20, 33, 35, 36, 37, 45, 47, 48, 51, 52, 71, 78, 79, 80, 106, 107, 118, 150, 181, 182, 183, 184
Cakreśvara 181
Cakrodaya 74, 259, 260, 261
Camatkāra 130
Capacity 45, 72, 95, 98
Centering 17, 227
Christ 197
Cidānanda 49, 65, 66, 69, 71, 90, 260, 271, 272
Cit 12, 18, 27, 48, 50, 92, 93, 94, 130, 184, 203, 205, 206, 207, 216, 271
Citi 154
Climax 242, 245
Cognition 33, 35, 57, 63, 93, 96, 100, 104, 106, 108, 134, 141, 151, 227, 230, 268
Color 247, 249, 289
Concealed 70, 71, 255
Concealer 39
Concealing 39, 52, 69, 71
Concentration 11, 24, 27, 75
Conch 162
Conclusion 12, 19, 23, 45, 48, 52, 87, 201, 203, 269
Condition 131
Conqueror 161
Conscious 13, 15, 16, 17, 213
Consciousness 1, 2, 3, 5, 7, 8, 11, 12, 13, 14, 15, 16, 17, 18, 19, 20, 21, 22, 23, 27, 28, 29, 30, 31, 32, 33, 35, 36, 37, 39, 40, 42, 43, 44, 45, 46, 47, 48, 49, 51, 52, 53, 56, 57, 58, 59, 61, 64, 67, 69, 70, 71, 72, 73, 75, 76, 77, 79, 80, 81, 84, 85, 86, 87, 88, 89, 91, 92, 93, 94, 95, 96, 98, 99, 100, 101, 102, 103, 105, 106, 107, 108, 109, 110, 111, 112, 113, 114, 115, 119, 120, 121, 122, 123, 124, 125, 126, 127, 129, 130, 131, 132, 133, 134, 135, 136, 137, 138, 139, 140, 142, 143, 144, 145, 146, 147, 148, 149, 151, 152, 153, 154, 155, 156, 161, 162, 163, 164, 165, 167, 168, 169, 170, 171, 172, 173, 174, 175, 176, 177, 179, 180, 181, 182, 183, 185, 186, 187, 188, 189, 190, 192, 195, 197, 199, 200, 201, 202, 203, 204, 205, 206, 207, 210, 212, 213, 214, 215, 217, 218, 220, 222, 223, 226, 227, 228, 229, 231, 232, 233, 234, 235, 236, 240, 243, 247, 248, 253, 254, 255, 256, 257, 260, 265, 268, 269, 270, 271, 289
Consonants 223
Contemplation 11, 24, 104, 167, 257, 259
Control 143, 151, 154, 172, 177, 181, 215
Copulation 85
Coverings 115
Cravings 131
Creation 34, 35, 39, 52, 69, 70, 94, 106, 113, 114, 118, 138, 222, 244
Creative 82, 88, 113, 114, 118, 119, 123, 222, 223, 244, 245
Creator 34, 38, 94
Culmination 97
D
Dakṣiṇeśvara 216
Darśana 44
Death 8, 44, 68, 170, 230, 252, 253, 270
Deities 197
Desire 1, 43, 102, 117, 243
Destroyer 34, 39
Destruction 34, 39, 52, 69, 70, 99, 106, 222
Destructive 88, 89, 222, 223, 244, 245, 246, 248
Detached 155, 216
Deva 226
Devī 110, 145, 258
Devotion 14, 15
Dhāraṇas 115, 117
Dharma 145, 216
Dhyāna 4, 24, 27, 29, 31, 41, 42, 43, 45, 48, 52, 53, 257, 258, 259, 260, 272
Differentiation 131, 139
Discharge 82
Divine 18, 49, 76, 77, 141, 144, 149, 151, 153, 203, 204, 216, 221, 253, 254, 259, 260, 261
Divinity 49, 148, 153, 221, 253, 254
Dreaming 8, 9, 52, 122, 168, 174, 176, 177, 179
Dreamless 52, 168, 176, 177
Dualistic 193
Dullness 15
Dvādaśānta 242, 245

E
Eagerness 15
Earth 87, 88, 114
Ego 8, 9, 106, 111, 169
Egress 147
Elements 27, 87, 88, 114, 115, 116, 120
Elevated 29, 113, 116, 129, 197, 203
Elevates 203
Enemy 252
Energies 32, 33, 35, 36, 37, 52, 53, 54, 79, 81, 82, 87, 88, 112, 115, 137, 155, 204, 269
Enjoyment 3, 49, 105, 201, 202
Enlighten 44, 150, 158
Enlightened 31, 32, 44, 239, 289
Enlightening 158
Equilibrium 25
Essence 99, 104, 189, 219, 222, 226, 227, 253
Essential 22
Ether 49, 178
Eunuch 94, 262, 263, 264
Excitement 123, 124, 126, 153, 154, 157, 196, 204, 241
Exhale 26, 74, 76
Existence 6, 65, 142, 210, 221, 255, 269, 271
Expansion 84, 85, 106, 107, 120, 222, 235, 266, 269
F
Fear 37, 61, 62, 63, 110, 125, 126, 178, 271
Flux 2
Food 26, 95, 98, 99, 110, 117
Fool 254
Forbidden 38
Force 3, 4, 15, 17, 19, 26, 39, 47, 48, 49, 52, 61, 76, 77, 78, 113, 118, 123, 145, 264, 271
Fountain 190
Fraud 202
Free 12, 90, 139, 179
Freedom 17, 38, 138
Fullness 3, 59, 89, 101, 106, 155, 167, 236, 270
G
Gap 44, 73, 270, 272
Generative 183, 184, 185, 190
Ghūrṇi 169, 170, 173, 174, 176, 178, 179, 180, 181, 182, 183, 184
Glory 119, 138, 193, 199
Goal 243
God 1, 2, 3, 5, 7, 8, 11, 12, 13, 14, 15, 18, 19, 20, 21, 22, 23, 27, 28, 29, 30, 31, 32, 33, 36, 37, 39, 40, 43, 44, 46, 47, 48, 49, 51, 52, 53, 56, 67, 69, 70, 71, 75, 76, 77, 79, 80, 81, 84, 85, 86, 87, 88, 89, 91, 92, 93, 94, 95, 96, 98, 99, 100, 101, 102, 103, 105, 107, 109, 110, 111, 112, 113, 114, 116, 119, 120, 121, 122, 123, 124, 125, 126, 127, 129, 130, 131, 132, 133, 134, 135, 136, 137, 138, 139, 140, 142, 143, 144, 145, 146, 147, 148, 149, 151, 152, 153, 154, 155, 156, 161, 162, 163, 164, 165, 167, 168, 169, 170, 171, 172, 173, 174, 176, 177, 178, 179, 180, 181, 182, 184, 185, 187, 188, 189, 190, 192, 195, 197, 199, 200, 201, 202, 203, 204, 205, 207, 210, 213, 215, 217, 218, 223, 226, 231, 232, 233, 235, 236, 240, 243, 247, 256, 257, 265, 268, 269, 270, 271
Gods 197, 198
Grace 11, 14, 18, 41, 50, 75, 176, 184, 261
Grāhaka 206, 207
Grāhya 206, 208, 211
Grammarian 172
Grammatical 88
Greatest 196, 205, 227, 228, 249
Greatness 127, 215
Gross 29, 30, 81, 94, 160, 177, 225, 226, 233, 249, 253
Grossness 253
Guru 42, 68, 94, 103, 104, 208, 226, 267
H
Habit 101, 144
Happiness 60, 272
Havan 31, 112
Hero 246
Heroes 101
Hidden 40, 42, 53, 218
Hideous 63, 270
Holiness 1
Householders 126
Hṛdaya 69, 126, 129, 196, 197, 269
Hṛdayaṁ 124, 125, 126, 129, 185, 196
Human 76, 84, 112, 115, 239
Humanity 180, 289
I
Icchā 79, 80, 87, 88, 93, 108, 109, 137, 155, 157, 161, 163, 216, 225, 243
Idam 136, 149, 196
Ignorance 10, 19, 106, 107, 108, 146
Ignorant 9, 38, 43
Illusion 20
Imagination 65, 75, 77, 86, 218
Imitation 173

Imperfection 86
Important 230, 265
Impossible 11
Impression 2, 4, 22, 105, 106, 107
Impressions 1, 2, 3, 4, 6, 8, 9, 23, 62
Impulses 261
Impurity 180
Incarnates 198
Incarnations 197
Incomplete 182
Incorrect 96, 97, 119, 146, 232, 234, 247
Incorrectly 100
Independent 12, 27, 28
Individuality 8, 9, 10, 20, 89, 107, 114, 115, 123, 148, 151, 153, 186, 188, 189, 190, 194
Indrā 115
Inertia 12
Infinite 36
Ingoing 147
Ingress 147
Inhale 26, 74, 76
Initiation 103, 189
Innocence 199
Insane 68
Intellect 7, 8, 9, 11, 12, 14, 19, 20, 22, 24, 35, 93, 104, 105, 121, 141, 211, 212, 254, 255, 261
Intellectual 7, 10, 17, 21, 23, 27, 42, 116, 141, 143, 144
Intense 241
Intensification 5
Intention 253
Interconnected 28, 29
Intercourse 46, 60, 272
Intoxicated 178
Intoxication 18, 173, 174, 176, 180, 184, 270
Introverted 17, 132, 146, 171, 172, 202, 234
Īśvara 10, 94, 101, 116, 136, 137, 149, 271

J

Jaḍa 12, 15, 16, 66, 272
Jagadānanda 18, 49, 50, 67, 68, 70, 71, 81, 86, 90, 91, 92, 93, 94, 95, 96, 97, 100, 101, 102, 104, 173, 179, 260, 265, 269, 271
Jāgrat 177, 179
Japya 246, 247
Jayaratha 6, 17, 37, 38, 52, 53, 56, 63, 75, 203, 208, 218
Jāyate 3, 4, 20, 167
Jīva 218
Jñāna 79, 80, 87, 88, 108, 109, 139, 147, 155, 216, 243
Jñānendriyas 143
Jñeya 133
Journey 3, 4, 42, 217, 218
Joy 22, 47, 60, 62, 64, 65, 78, 123, 157, 180, 183, 196, 204, 205, 236, 237, 239, 245, 254, 255, 261, 270, 271, 272
Joyful 61, 202, 238
Joyous 199, 202, 254
Judging 105
Junction 15, 57, 58, 74, 75, 77, 79, 83
Junctions 57, 270

K

Kalā 107, 108, 109, 110, 115, 116, 117, 120, 122, 123, 127
Kālī 36
Kalpanā 29, 258, 259, 260, 263, 264, 265
Kampa 169, 170, 171, 178, 180, 181, 182, 183, 184
Kaṇṭha 11, 57, 78, 237, 244
Karaṇeśvarī 93
Kārmamala 177
Karmendriyas 143
Kaula 103, 104
Kaulikī 114, 118
Khecarī 77
Knower 155
Knowledge 13, 49, 63, 67, 79, 87, 88, 104, 105, 110, 132, 133, 134, 137, 139, 142, 147, 149, 151, 155, 243, 269
Known 77, 78, 94, 105, 133, 155, 186, 208, 225, 245
Krama 17, 18, 40, 41, 49, 50, 52, 55, 71, 73, 80, 85, 86, 88, 90, 91, 94, 95, 97, 98, 100, 102, 103, 104, 110, 137, 148, 149, 222, 260, 271
Kriyā 46, 79, 80, 87, 88, 108, 109, 137, 155, 216, 241, 243
Kṛṣṇa 10, 197
Kula 103, 153
Kulamūla 154, 157
Kuleśvara 118
Kuleśvarī 118
Kuṇḍa 31
Kuṇḍalī 184
Kuṇḍalinī 18, 50, 75, 77, 78, 79, 81, 82, 84, 85, 165, 184, 185, 186, 190, 196, 205, 206, 242, 243, 244, 245, 268, 269, 271

L

Liberated 3, 18, 38, 50, 263

Liberating 3
Liberation 3, 49, 175, 179, 191, 192
Limitation 44, 82, 102, 182
Limitations 37
Limitedness 21, 182
Liṅga 185, 186, 187, 188, 189, 190, 191, 192, 193, 194, 195, 196, 197, 198, 199
M
Mahāprakāśa 147
Maharishi 65, 227
Mahāvyāpti 174, 176, 177, 178, 179, 180
Mahāyogī 161
Maheśvara 136
Maheśvaranātha 159
Maithuna 122
Mālinīvijaya 41, 177, 178, 180, 195, 196, 266
Māṁsa 122
Māna 32, 63
Maṇḍalam 104, 111
Maṅgala 53, 54
Manifestation 79, 151, 152, 154, 234
Mantra 4, 20, 24, 73, 131, 132, 136, 140, 188, 189, 210, 211, 212, 222, 223, 224, 225, 227, 228, 232, 233, 234, 235, 238, 245, 246, 247, 248, 249, 250, 252, 253, 254, 256, 268, 269, 270
Mantrabhūmyā 109
Mantras 4, 20, 42, 73, 75, 140, 189, 193, 223, 224, 225, 226, 228, 233, 236, 244, 245, 246, 248, 252, 253
Mantravīryaṁ 188, 216
Mantreśvara 136
Marriage 253
Masculine 117
Mastery 74, 77
Mātṛkā 52, 118
Matsyodara 83
Māyā 87, 88, 115, 119, 120
Māyīyamala 177
Meditation 24, 27, 29, 31, 37, 40, 41, 42, 45, 54, 55, 71, 72, 148, 166, 168, 193, 201, 202, 205, 209, 210, 219, 234, 260
Memory 124, 224, 226, 227, 228, 229, 230, 231, 252, 266
Mind 2, 3, 5, 8, 9, 15, 17, 30, 35, 45, 72, 93, 104, 105, 108, 148, 174, 202, 203, 204, 205, 207, 211, 223, 225, 252
Misunderstood 53, 75
Mokṣa 163, 192
Momentary 170
Mūḍha 6
Mudrā 17, 18, 49, 50, 55, 71, 77, 80, 85, 86, 88, 90, 91, 95, 97, 98, 100, 102, 104, 137, 138, 139, 142, 144, 148, 149, 166, 167, 168, 184, 185, 207, 222, 271
Mukti 49, 179
Mūlādhāra 78, 79, 150, 153, 157, 183, 271
Mūrti 24
Music 221
N
Nabhi 11
Nāda 81, 131, 132, 133, 134, 221, 249
Nāḍī 123, 125, 145
Nārāyaṇa 235
Nectar 67, 77, 107, 108, 110, 111, 123, 199, 203
Neuter 94, 117
Nidrā 169, 172, 173, 176, 177, 178, 180, 181, 182, 183, 184
Nijānanda 49, 57, 58, 59, 66, 72, 179, 260, 270
Nimīlana 33, 35, 49, 88, 92, 120
Nirānanda 58, 59, 66, 69, 70, 179, 260, 270
Nirañjana 111, 242
Nirodha 235, 236, 238, 239, 240, 246
Nirvāṇa 10
Nirvikalpa 6, 22, 109, 209, 210, 211, 212, 231, 232
Niścaya 7
O
Objectivity 57, 60, 63, 66, 85, 100, 106, 107, 108, 112, 120, 122, 139, 155, 208, 209, 210, 211, 235
Observer 94, 209, 213, 214
Oṁ 73, 81, 87, 226, 246, 254
Omnipresence 45
Oneness 39, 80, 93, 99, 132, 133, 142, 171, 237, 243
Orgasm 123, 124, 128
Originator 231
Outcasts 217
P
Pain 65, 201, 202, 204, 205, 238, 239, 253, 254, 255
Palate 61, 76, 77, 160, 184, 244, 245, 246
Pāṇini 115, 118
Parabhairava 49
Paramāmṛta 67
Parāmarśa 34, 91, 92, 93, 96, 140
Paramātmā 153
Parameśvara 23, 206
Parānanda 60, 61, 66, 69, 70, 260, 270, 272

Parāparā 33, 35, 104
Parātriṁśikā 114, 115, 266
Pārvatī 12, 114, 145
Paśu 37
Paśupati 264
Paśyantī 160, 220
Pathalakṣaṇam 27
Patient 25, 68
Peace 10, 110, 140
Perceiver 210
Perception 5, 46, 76, 90, 109, 110, 140, 146, 149, 175, 176, 178, 199, 204, 209, 212, 231, 234, 235, 237, 241, 244, 246, 248, 270
Pervasion 64, 65, 161, 173, 174, 176, 177, 178, 180, 206, 207, 214, 215, 271
Phala 90
Philosopher 214
Philosophy 115, 214
Piṇḍanātha 88, 89, 131, 132, 133, 135, 222, 245, 268, 269, 270
Pitiable 131
Play 243
Pleasure 3, 22, 153, 201, 202, 204, 205, 238, 246, 253, 255
Poetry 227
Poison 103
Pose 55, 74, 142
Poses 218
Postures 207
Power 20, 25, 37, 77, 80, 116, 140, 157, 170, 189, 192, 228, 268
Powers 79, 140, 187, 189, 191, 192
Practice 9, 11, 14, 16, 22, 23, 24, 25, 26, 37, 58, 59, 86, 103, 126, 138, 146, 150, 167, 180, 189, 198, 207, 224, 234, 239, 240, 246, 247, 248, 249, 251, 253, 260, 261, 269, 270, 272
Prakāśa 27, 33, 89, 96, 147, 251
Pramāṇa 30, 32, 33, 51, 79, 80, 84, 93, 96, 100, 104, 105, 106, 121, 268, 270
Pramātā 23, 26, 32, 52
Pramātṛ 8, 9, 21, 30, 33, 51, 57, 58, 59, 84, 96, 100, 104, 106, 107, 108, 109, 122, 133, 134, 135, 136, 154, 214, 231, 232, 268, 270
Prameya 30, 32, 33, 51, 60, 79, 80, 84, 96, 100, 105, 106, 122, 155, 214, 268, 270
Pramiti 100, 106, 120, 121, 214
Prāṇa 7, 8, 9, 10, 11, 14, 17, 19, 20, 22, 23, 24, 25, 26, 27, 30, 32, 33, 42, 56, 63, 64, 65, 69, 73, 74, 75, 79, 81, 89, 90, 91, 122, 132, 174, 185, 205, 206, 235, 236, 238, 239, 240, 241, 243, 268, 270, 271, 272
Prāṇana 25, 26, 56, 58, 59, 60, 64, 69, 73, 270
Pratyāhāra 118
Praveśa 27, 130, 146, 148, 155, 156, 162, 165, 200, 204, 205, 268
Preservation 96, 106
Pressure 19, 144
Proof 164
Protection 34, 39, 52, 69, 70, 106
Protector 34, 38
Pṛthvī 114
Pūjā 166, 229
Purification 1, 2, 3, 4, 5, 6, 7
Purified 2, 251
Purify 2
Purity 20
Pūrṇa 89, 204
Pūrṇatā 167, 234, 236
Puryaṣṭaka 8, 9, 40, 122, 168, 174, 177

R

Rāga 115,116, 117
Rahasya 129, 272
Rasa 8, 9, 39, 96, 105, 138, 139, 144, 203
Reality 6, 13, 21, 44, 56, 89, 130, 176, 188, 219, 233, 237, 240, 247, 260
Recitation 4, 24, 27, 224, 233, 235, 243, 244, 253, 254, 256, 258, 259
Recitation 24, 56
Recognize 22, 117, 164, 232
Recognized 22, 37, 72
Recognizing 27, 165
Rectum 25, 71, 77, 79, 80, 153, 183, 184, 244
Reflection 151
Representation 79
Representative 114
Rest 48, 49, 69, 78, 83, 109, 131, 135, 140
Revealed 1, 54, 55, 70, 106, 147, 272
Revealer 39
Revealing 39, 52, 69, 71
Reveals 147
Rituals 42
Rkṣkheṁ 132, 222, 223, 224, 245
Rudra 248
Ruler 181
Rules 172
Rūpa 8, 9, 23, 39, 66, 96, 105, 109, 139, 140, 144, 182, 185, 190, 203, 255

S

Śabda 8, 9, 39, 96, 105, 139, 144, 162, 203

Śabdabrahma 9
Sacred 225, 246
Sacrificial 109, 110
Sadāśiva 88, 103, 104, 116, 120, 136, 137, 149, 271
Sādhaka 45, 46, 47, 51, 55, 92, 97, 103, 111, 124, 166, 167, 173, 233, 246, 247, 248, 251, 253, 259, 260
Sādhanā 103, 127, 138, 150, 167, 251
Sadness 204, 253
Sahasrāra 71, 79, 80
Saint 111, 241
Sakala 72, 268, 270
Śākta 75, 263, 264
Śākte 124, 126
Śakti 32, 33, 73, 79, 81, 87, 88, 89, 108, 109, 112, 116, 118, 119, 120, 133, 137, 138, 155, 157, 161, 163, 181, 186, 187, 188, 189, 190, 193, 194, 195, 198, 212, 216, 225, 241, 243, 269, 271
Śaktimān 119, 120
Śaktipāta 41
Śāktopāya 4, 6, 14, 20, 21, 30, 32, 34, 36, 42, 45, 66, 200, 201, 243, 256, 258, 259, 260
Samādhi 8, 9, 10, 17, 18, 35, 43, 44, 45, 49, 67, 86, 90, 91, 100, 125, 134, 137, 148, 155, 156, 160, 162, 180, 181, 201, 210, 220, 222, 240, 268, 269
Samāna 25, 26, 30, 32, 33, 56, 61, 62, 64, 79, 81, 82, 90, 271, 272
Sāmānya 56, 136, 139, 140, 146, 191
Sāmarasyam 93
Samāveśa 17, 18, 49, 155, 268
Sāmaveśa 155
Śāmbhava 33, 34, 200, 225, 260, 263
Śāmbhava avasthā 34
Śāmbhavopāya 4, 30, 33, 34, 42, 45, 55, 65, 145, 198, 200, 201, 202, 224, 225, 243, 256, 257, 258, 259, 260, 264
Śambhunātha 54, 68, 159
Sameness 148, 255
Saṁhāra 34, 39, 40, 52, 70, 88, 135, 223, 244, 245, 246, 247, 248, 272
Saṁhṛti 35, 70, 106
Saṁskāra 1, 2, 3, 5, 6, 7, 22, 23, 46, 47
Saṁvid 110, 170
Saṁvidaḥ 53, 132, 237
Saṁvit 20, 45, 48, 53, 109, 110, 132, 133, 136, 137, 169, 234, 253, 255
Saṁvitti 40, 67, 213
Śaṅkara 226
Śānta 45, 47, 90, 91, 92, 94, 181
Ṣaṇṭha 262
Śānti 35
Śāntoditā 91
Śarīra 23, 26
Satisfaction 84, 110
Satisfied 54, 55, 111
Sattā 135, 230, 231, 269
Sauḥ 73, 79, 88, 89, 222, 224, 235, 238, 242, 245, 270
Savikalpa 209, 210
Secret 8, 18, 49, 50, 53, 69, 79, 94, 129, 155, 208, 218, 220, 272, 273, 287
Semen 127, 239, 242, 257, 258, 262, 263
Sensation 16, 40, 43, 78, 102, 109, 110, 123, 145, 166, 167, 182, 183, 184, 236, 237, 238, 239, 246
Sense 2, 6, 9, 20, 43, 99, 101, 102, 111, 137, 147, 152, 193, 194, 205, 220, 231, 232
Sensitivity 125
Serpent 77, 268
Seventeenth 107, 108, 109, 110, 120, 122
Sex 117, 122, 125, 126, 128, 153, 154, 236, 237, 238, 248
Sexual 46, 47, 51, 60, 61, 64, 117, 123, 124, 126, 127, 128, 153, 154, 155, 156, 157, 168, 196, 238, 239, 240, 241, 245, 271, 272
Shivering 169, 170, 180, 183, 184
Siddha 189, 196, 197
Siddhi 191, 192
Siddhis 192
Signboard 266
Signs 165, 167, 180, 266
Silence 94
Simultaneous 93
Simultaneously 28, 45, 79, 90, 91, 92, 96, 123, 137, 180, 182, 183, 269
Sin 98
Śiṣya 103
Śiva 6, 12, 13, 23, 29, 32, 35, 41, 42, 45, 51, 52, 53, 54, 88, 89, 94, 103, 104, 113, 115, 116, 117, 118, 119, 120, 144, 149, 174, 178, 182, 185, 186, 187, 188, 189, 190, 194, 195, 197, 198, 212, 213, 215, 216, 217, 227, 233, 242, 243, 251, 259, 264, 268, 269, 270, 271
Śivadṛṣṭi 13
Skull 65, 184
Slave 181

Sleep 8, 9, 10, 17, 23, 71, 72, 122, 172, 174, 179, 211
Smell 9, 128, 140, 166
Smṛti 230, 231
Ṣoḍaśakalā 107
Soma 30, 33, 35, 57, 96, 127
Somānanda 13
Soul 8, 29, 41
Sound 8, 9, 39, 60, 61, 63, 64, 71, 74, 77, 78, 122, 128, 131, 132, 133, 134, 160, 161, 162, 163, 182, 189, 211, 220, 221, 249, 250, 270, 271, 272
Soundless 161, 162, 163, 189, 249
Source 188, 192, 224, 225, 227, 237, 238, 241, 242, 254
Sovereignty 181, 208
Space 17, 75, 218, 230
Spanda 37, 45, 56, 59, 136, 139, 140, 145, 146, 181, 190, 191, 195, 234, 250
Spandana 59, 82, 123, 272
Sparśa 8, 9, 36, 39, 96, 105, 125, 139, 144, 183, 203
Speech 81, 220
Sphuṭaḥ 188
Sphuṭatāma 98
Spiritual 37, 68, 81, 117, 123, 154, 156, 170, 196, 197, 225, 226, 253, 257, 258, 262
Spirituality 196
Splendor 103
Spontaneous 83, 95, 102
Spontaneously 95, 102
Sṛṣṭi 34, 35, 39, 40, 52, 70, 106, 118, 222, 223, 272
Standstill 8, 152, 181
Sthāna 29, 77, 258, 259, 260, 265, 270
Strength 18, 19, 50, 58, 72, 95, 98, 128, 147, 157, 226, 228, 229, 248, 257, 258, 260, 261, 262, 263
Stress 127
String 163
Subjective 26, 30, 32, 33, 42, 49, 52, 57, 59, 70, 80, 84, 85, 96, 106, 108, 114, 133, 134, 207, 208, 209, 212, 213, 215
Subjectivity 57, 85, 100, 106, 107, 111, 122, 155
Subtle 8, 9, 58, 78, 94, 160, 210, 270
Subtler 58, 94
Subtlest 94, 160, 161
Śuddhavidyā 88, 116, 120, 136, 137, 149, 166, 272
Sukha 236, 237
Sūkṣma 94, 108, 109, 110, 160
Śūlabīja 88
Sundaram 196
Śūnya 8, 9, 23, 150, 154, 168, 175, 177, 269
Sūrya 30, 57, 96, 106, 127
Suṣumnā 32, 145, 154, 268
Suṣupti 9, 23, 179
Svabala 170
Svabhāva 5, 27, 203
Svacchandanātha 268
Svapna 179
Svarūpa 13, 29, 47, 219
Svasaṁvidi 50, 51
Svatantra 28
Svātantrya 5, 12, 15, 138, 139, 141, 142, 143, 144, 154, 187, 198, 269
Symbol 185
Symbols 185
Symptom 169, 179
Symptoms 68, 169, 177, 178
T
Tādātmya 171, 172
Tālu 61, 76, 77, 160, 184, 244, 245
Tandrā 172
Tanmātras 8, 9, 105, 108
Tarpaṇa 110
Taste 9, 22, 36, 96, 99, 100, 105, 130, 138, 166, 182
Tattva 27, 56, 69, 89, 90, 91, 114, 119, 120, 130, 131, 146, 148, 155, 156, 158, 162, 165, 204, 217, 219, 242, 243, 258, 259, 270, 272
Technique 26
Thinker 231
Thought 2, 3, 4, 6, 22, 23, 65, 71, 72, 209, 211, 212, 223, 227
Thought 261
Thoughts 1, 2, 6, 30, 53, 70, 71, 72, 76, 77
Throat 4, 11, 29, 57, 76, 78, 125, 141, 160, 215, 220, 237, 238, 241, 244, 245, 246, 247, 258, 270
Throb 82, 83, 123, 140, 185, 195, 203, 234, 237, 238, 239, 250
Throbbing 82, 123, 131, 136, 137, 140, 238, 243
Throbs 221, 238
Tideless 149
Tides 94, 149
Time 2, 8, 22, 33, 49, 58, 67, 68, 78, 83, 85,

86, 99, 117, 125, 137, 138, 156, 166, 172, 180, 200, 203, 205, 208, 209, 210, 211, 215, 227, 229, 230, 236, 238, 242, 249, 269
Tolerate 43, 86
Touch 15, 36, 43, 98, 102, 106, 125, 166, 167, 170, 182, 183, 203, 204
Trace 102
Traces 46, 47
Trance 33, 49, 103, 170, 177, 190
Transcendental 18, 35, 92, 93, 94, 101, 107, 110, 119, 120, 134, 135, 141, 149, 154, 186, 187, 202
Transformation 33
Triangle 134, 184, 245
Trick 15, 16, 26, 75
Trika 85, 272
Trikoṇa 134, 183
Triśirobhairava 27, 28, 144, 150, 185, 206, 228
Triśūla 51, 79, 88
True 11, 20, 22, 180, 193, 194, 203, 238, 241
Truth 13, 31, 119, 215, 238
Turya 18, 35, 49, 52, 154, 172, 179
Turyātīta 35, 155
Tyāga 206, 207, 216, 217
U
Uccāra 24, 25, 27, 42, 56, 69, 73, 89, 90, 91, 92, 95, 97, 98, 100, 102, 104, 110, 119, 120, 121, 130, 185, 205, 220, 242, 256, 258, 259, 260, 272
Udyoga 50, 95, 97, 102, 104, 106
Ugly 237, 238, 239
Ullāsa 15, 235, 236, 238, 239, 240, 241
Ultimate 97, 103
Unauthorized 94, 101
Unconscious 13, 15, 16, 272
Unconsciously 211
Undifferentiated 149, 269
Union 32, 129, 186, 187, 189, 197, 230, 231, 237, 243
Unique 29, 110, 113
Unite 85, 230, 238
Universal 18, 28, 29, 31, 35, 36, 45, 46, 47, 48, 49, 50, 51, 53, 67, 83, 85, 88, 89, 92, 93, 95, 107, 108, 110, 111, 112, 119, 120, 125, 126, 135, 137, 139, 148, 153, 173, 174, 176, 177, 185, 186, 187, 188, 189, 193, 195, 205, 231, 238, 271
Universality 148, 151, 186, 193, 198, 202
Universe 3, 12, 14, 18, 28, 36, 40, 43, 44, 45, 46, 47, 48, 49, 50, 51, 52, 53, 54, 61, 65, 84, 86, 88, 89, 94, 111, 113, 114, 119, 120, 125, 130, 136, 138, 142, 144, 151, 154, 168, 181, 187, 193, 196, 198, 199, 217, 255, 271
Unknown 67, 197, 271
Unlimited 11, 82, 85, 269
Unlimitedly 182
Unmanā 82
Unmeṣa 188
Unreal 173, 235
Unsurpassed 27, 29
Untrue 175
Unuttered 161
Upadeśa 69
Upalakṣaṇam 112
Uparaktaṁ 155
Upāsana 4, 27, 192, 204, 205, 207, 208, 209, 210, 211, 212, 213, 214, 217, 218, 219, 258, 259, 260
Upāya 55, 65, 86, 101, 102, 200, 208
Upāyas 7, 65, 68, 86, 101, 103, 243, 256, 258
Uppermost 145
Useless 55
Utpaladeva 44
V
Vācaka 93, 94
Vacuum 164, 214, 268
Vācya 94, 234
Vaikharī 81, 160
Vāyu 115
Vedānta 3, 73, 91
Vedāntic 86, 142
Vedāntins 9, 207
Vedāntists 143, 181
Vein 25, 32, 71, 80, 145, 153, 154, 268, 271
Veins 123
Vibrate 45, 47, 51, 52, 53, 132, 133, 134, 140
Vibrated 122, 132, 134, 137, 138
Vibrates 45, 46, 47, 48, 50, 51, 121, 130, 131, 137, 138, 140, 153, 221
Vibrating 46, 47, 48, 50, 51, 52, 53, 75, 76, 105, 110, 113, 121, 134, 220
Vibration 37, 45, 46, 47, 50, 52, 113, 130, 131, 143, 190, 250
Vibrations 45, 46, 47, 48, 79, 131, 157
Vidhi 5, 83
Vidyā 115, 117, 270
Vijñānākala 272
Vikalpa 2, 3, 4, 5, 6, 23, 212

Vikāsa 84, 85, 107, 125, 198, 269, 270
Vimarśa 92, 93, 94, 140
Vīrapāṇ 178
Virgin 117, 257
Vīrya 20, 140, 188, 189, 239, 257, 258, 259, 263, 270
Visarga 37, 73, 80, 82, 86, 87, 88, 94, 107, 108, 111, 113, 118, 119, 120, 121, 123, 128, 145, 198, 199, 235, 238, 242
Viṣaya 36, 38
Viśeṣa 56, 139, 140, 146, 190, 191, 236
Viśva 112
Viśvarūpa 20
Viveka 99
Vivekānanda 261
Vivid 31, 98
Vividly 32, 100, 185, 236, 270
Void 49, 71, 72, 131, 133, 150, 151, 153, 154, 155, 156, 158, 164, 175, 177
Voidness 8, 10, 21, 23, 58, 59, 60, 70, 72, 131, 132, 150, 153, 156, 270, 272
Voidnesses 150, 151, 153
Vowel vi, 223, 242
Vrāta 85
Vṛtti 26, 56, 58, 60, 61, 62, 63, 64, 65, 73, 74, 90, 147, 270, 271
Vyakta 185, 187, 188, 189, 190, 191, 192, 193, 194, 195, 198
Vyaktāvyakta 185, 187, 188, 189, 191, 192, 193, 194, 195, 196, 197, 198
Vyāna 25, 26, 56, 64, 66, 68, 90, 271, 272
Vyānana 56, 64, 65, 69, 90
Vyāpinī 81, 173, 178
Vyāpti 64, 65, 73, 128, 206, 207, 208, 214, 215, 271
Vyutthāna 85, 92, 134

W

Wakefulness 8, 52, 122, 168, 174, 176, 179
Waking 17, 70, 272
Woman 101, 118, 124, 127, 128, 154, 185
Worldly 37, 97, 104, 123, 131, 135, 141, 142, 191, 192, 202, 216, 221, 225, 269, 270
Worship 185, 193, 195, 196, 216, 229, 272

Y

Yajña 112, 113
Yāmalam 85
Yoga 60, 142, 235, 240, 261, 268
Yogi 17, 18, 30, 34, 35, 36, 38, 40, 41, 49, 50, 58, 63, 65, 74, 78, 79, 81, 82, 83, 84, 85, 87, 88, 99, 113, 129, 131, 135, 136, 137, 138, 140, 142, 143, 146, 147, 148, 155, 156, 157, 161, 162, 166, 176, 179, 180, 181, 183, 187, 195, 196, 199, 204, 210, 221, 223, 227, 253, 254, 255, 261, 262, 268, 269, 270, 271
Yogic 79, 134, 140, 189
Yoginī 129, 189, 196, 197, 269
Yoginīhṛdayaṁ 128, 196
Yoni 123, 196, 269

Lakshmanjoo ACADEMY

The teachings of Swami Lakshmanjoo are a response to the urgent need of our time: the transformation of consciousness and the evolution of a more enlightened humanity.

The Universal Shaiva Fellowship was established under Swamiji's direct inspiration, for the purpose of realizing Swamiji's vision of making Kashmir Shaivism available to the whole world. It was Swamiji's wish that his teachings be made available without the restriction of caste, creed, color or gender.

The Universal Shaiva Fellowship and the Lakshmanjoo Academy, along with the Kashmir Shaiva Institute (Ishwar Ashram Trust), India, have preserved Swamiji's original teachings and are progressively making these teachings available in book, audio and video formats.

This knowledge is extremely valuable and uplifting for all of humankind. It offers humanity a clear and certain vision in a time of uncertainty. It shows us the way home and gives us the means for the attainment of complete Self-Realization.

For information on Kashmir Shaivism or to support the work of The Universal Shaiva Fellowship and the Lakshmanjoo Academy and Kashmir Shaiva Institute (Ishwar Ashram Trust) visit the Lakshmanjoo Academy website or email us at info@LakshmanjooAcademy.org.

www.UniversalShaivaFellowship.org
www.LakshmanjooAcademy.org
www.IshwarAshramTrust.com

Instructions to download audio files

1. Go to https://www.lakshmanjooacademy.org/tantraloka5-445
   coupon code: Tantra05

2. Fill out the email opt-in form to add your name to the Lakshmanjoo Academy email list.

3. When you click the button in the follow-up email to confirm your email subscription you will be directed to the audio page for your purchase.

   If you have any difficulties please contact us at:
   https://www.lakshmanjooacademy.org/contact

www.ingramcontent.com/pod-product-compliance
Lightning Source LLC
Chambersburg PA
CBHW070129080526
44586CB00015B/1617
* 9 7 8 1 9 4 7 2 4 1 1 8 3 *